MAY 2008

Also by Arianna Huffington

Right Is *Wrong*

Right Is *Wrong*

How the Lunatic Fringe
Hijacked America,
Shredded the Constitution,
and Made Us All Less Safe

(and what you need to know to end the madness)

ARIANNA HUFFINGTON

Alfred A. Knopf   New York 2008

THIS IS A BORZOI BOOK
PUBLISHED BY ALFRED A. KNOPF

ISBN 978-0-307-26966-9

Library of Congress Control Number: 2008922853
Manufactured in the United States of America
First Edition

For Christina and Isabella

Contents

Right Is *Wrong*

1

The Right Goes Wrong

The Radical Takeover

The most sweeping takeover of the new millennium didn't take place among the telecoms or the big oil companies, or in Silicon Valley. It took place in Washington, but we can see and hear and feel its effects nationwide on our televisions, radios, and computer screens. And America is much the worse because of it. I'm talking about the takeover of the Republican Party by its own lunatic fringe, and the Right's hijacking of America.

Ronald Reagan's GOP has been replaced by the dark, moldering, putrefied party of Bush, Cheney, Rove, Limbaugh, O'Reilly, and Coulter. Morning in America has given way to Midnight in America.

Yes, the Republican Party has always had its far-right cowboys, its Jesse Helmses and Spiro Agnews. Yet they were removed from the party's more sober core.

But these days, judging by the opinions and actions of the Republicans in office and the party's candidates for president, it has become impossible to tell where this core stops and the fanatical fringe begins. Just look at what the party is endorsing.

We have a Republican Party that continues to back the White House's delusions about Iraq at the expense of our military, our treasure, our safety, and our standing in the world.

We have a mainstream on the Right that supports torture, that confirmed an attorney general nominee who is officially agnostic on torture, and that rallies behind a president who refuses to define what the very word "torture" means.

We have a mainstream that supports—even applauds—the behavior of thuggish Blackwater mercenaries, that supports the gutting of our civil liberties, that opposes universal health care, and that has views on immigration that wouldn't have been heard outside a John Birch Society meeting ten years ago.

It can no longer be denied: the right-wing lunatics are running the Republican asylum and have infected the entire country and poisoned the world beyond.

And just look at who the GOP settled on as its 2008 standard bearer: the most hawkish candidate in the running, who has said he wants the United States to stay in Iraq somewhere between one hundred years and ten thousand years—John McCain.

Despite an avalanche of evidence showing that McCain the Maverick has long ago been replaced by McCain the Pandering Pawn of the Party's Right Wing, the press refuses to believe its own eyes. *Right Is Wrong* will show how the "Straight Talk Express" and its driver have completely and cravenly run off the road—and how the media steadfastly refuse to notice.

Even those bastions of the so-called liberal media, *The New Yorker* and *The New York Times*, have continued to portray McCain as a moderate who, in the words of *New Yorker* writer Ryan Lizza, has "the rare opportunity to reinvent what it means to be a Republican."

Let's see, over the last few years McCain has bowed to the Right on tax cuts, immigration, the intolerance of religious bigots, and torture. So, how precisely is he reinventing what it means to be a Republican?

During the primary campaign, I waited in vain for one of the leading GOP presidential candidates to step away from the twitchy ideologues who have taken over their party, but instead they all held hands with Kristol, Rove, and Limbaugh and jumped. To a man, every one of the top-tier candidates—Giuliani, Romney, McCain, Thompson, and Huckabee—seemed intent on competing to see who could out-Bush Bush. Not a single one of them tried to put any distance between himself and the president—especially on foreign policy, the area of Bush's most catastrophic errors. Former Arkansas Governor Mike Huckabee made a halfhearted attempt to speak out against an "arrogant bunker mentality" at one point and was called out by Mitt Romney to apologize. Huckabee promptly shut up, putting an end to any further rebellious attempts to amble off the reservation. As conservative pundit George Will put it, "They are, if anything, to the right of [Bush] on foreign policy. There's a bidding war to see who can be more hawkish toward Iran."

The reign of Bush and Cheney and the rise of the neocons and the "nea-cons" (the "neanderthal conservatives") have alienated traditional conservative intellectuals as they had Bill Buckley, the godfather of modern conservatism. In April of 2007, less than a year before his death, Buckley called public opinion on the Iraq war "savagely decisive" and concluded, "There are grounds for wondering whether the Republican Party will survive this dilemma."

And Michael Gerson, once Bush's top speechwriter, offered this gloomy assessment of the state of the GOP: "The party is in a funk—a lack of creativity, very little domestic policy energy. I think it's going to be a problem." Of course, along with being one of the party's brightest thinkers, Gerson is a Bush loyalist, so his calling it "a problem" can be translated as "a disaster."

If the Republican Party in its current form loses the next general election and ends up fading into obscurity and irrelevancy, we can use the words of Don Rumsfeld (trying to sugarcoat a different debacle) for its epitaph: "The dead-enders are still with us, those remnants of the defeated regimes who'll go on fighting long after their cause is lost."

That's why it is vitally important to recognize what has happened, to see how the Right's radical ideas became ordinary, and to know how to spot their remnants and echoes wherever they crop up. Regardless of the outcome of this election, the lingering aftereffects of the nea-conservative shift will be with us for a very long time.

A key to understanding the fanatical Right's takeover of the Republican Party and how their ideas spread to the rest of the country is looking at the role of the media—not the Fox News pseudo-newsmen or the talk radio blowhards, but the respectable, mainstream media. Without the enabling of the traditional media—through their obsession with "balance" and their pathological devotion to the idea that truth is always found in the middle—the radical Right would never have been able to have its ideas taken seriously. If not for the media's appeals to balance, nea-conservatives would have been laughed out of the court of public opinion long ago. And when the media do attempt to dig into the ideological underpinnings of debates about policy and current affairs, they get buried in another form of disorder. Besides seeing two sides to every issue, they insist on seeing most political battles through the lens of right vs. left. By reporting everything that's happening in American politics through this prism the media missed the big story: the hijacking of America by the Right.

The other not-so-innocent bystanders to the Right's takeover are the Democrats who have continued to tread far too lightly when it comes to holding the GOP's fanatical core accountable. Time and time again, the Democratic leadership has allowed itself to get played, run over, or distracted. Republicans wanted to deflect discussion of the war by arguing over newspaper ads and radio comments? Okay, Democratic leaders were game. Republicans wanted to avoid talking about children without health care by whining about Democratic Representative Pete Stark's tough assessment of the president and the Iraq war? ("President Bush's statements about children's health shouldn't be taken any more seriously than his lies about the war in Iraq," Stark said on the House floor. "The truth is that Bush just likes to blow things up.") Sure, Democratic leaders were more than willing to take the GOP bait and reprimand one of their own.

Democrats are in the majority today because the positions they campaigned on are in line with mainstream America. But if the Right is to be stopped in its efforts to radically remake this country, Democrats are going to have to step up and defend the mainstream that swept them into power in 2006. So far, they have shown little stomach for that fight.

The Republican race to replace George W. Bush turned into a competition to see Who Could Be the Biggest Neanderthal. Who would stay in Iraq the longest? Who would cut taxes the deepest? Who would be all right with firing gay Americans from their jobs? Who would jump for joy the highest if *Roe v. Wade* were reversed? Who would build the biggest fence around America? Who would put an end to stem cell research the fastest? Who would reject evolution most passionately?

The problem for the nea-con Right is not that it is at odds with my views but that it is at odds with the views of the American people, the majority of whom believe in the science of evolution, don't want *Roe v. Wade* overturned, don't want to turn back the clock on job discrimination laws, and want to bring our troops home from Iraq. The Right flashing back to the Reagan era is one thing; the Right flashing back to the Dark Ages and trying to take the country with it is quite another.

The Only Thing We Have to Fear

The Right's hijacking of America would not have been possible without its masterly use of fear to sway a nation terrified by the 9/11 attacks. It's a symptom of just how sick the radical Right is that their immediate response to 9/11 was to look for opportunities to push their agenda. Abroad they saw a pretext for an attack on Iraq, a long-cherished objective. At home, they saw a chance to solidify a permanent Republican stranglehold on power if they could recast themselves as the "party that will keep you safe" and then keep fear alive. It worked for them in 2004 and they are trying it again in 2008.

Since 9/11, the Right's fear-mongering has been relentless and revolting. It bottomed out during the 2004 presidential campaign with a sewer-level attack ad against Democratic candidate John Kerry put together by a 527 group largely financed by a pair of longtime Bush-backers. The TV spot showed pictures of Osama bin Laden, 9/11 hijacker Mohamed Atta, the Chechen school murderers, and the Madrid train bombings and asked: "These people want to kill us. Would you trust Kerry up against these fanatic killers?"

Somewhere—and I don't think it's heaven—Karl Rove's mentor Lee Atwater was smiling.

During the 2004 race, there was an endless line of members of the Right's establishment eager to parrot the "al Qaeda wants Kerry to win" talking point—including Senator Orrin Hatch, who made the despicable claim that terrorists "are going to throw everything they can between now and the election to try and elect Kerry."

Even without a photoshopped photo of Abu Musab al-Zarqawi sporting a Kerry-Edwards campaign button, this "terrorists for Democrats" routine was laughable, loathsome, and a new low in American politics. It was also patently untrue. Why in the world would the terrorists have wanted to get rid of George Bush? He is their chief recruiter: a man who has alienated our allies, isolated us, and united the Muslim world against us.

The president's preemptive invasion of Iraq has been such a boon to al Qaeda that in 2004 the British ambassador to Italy, Ivor Roberts, called Bush the terrorist organization's "best recruiting sergeant."

My Name Is Arianna,
and I Am a Former Republican

This is probably a good time to say a little something about the transformation of my political views. It has been almost a dozen years since I left the Grand Old Party—years in which I have made my opinions known in books, in newspaper columns, on TV, and, over the last three years, on *The Huffington Post.* (Although I do still get the occasional Republican e-mail sent my way—always good for a little intel. Former membership also has its privileges.)

I left the GOP just as the Right was tightening its grip on the soul of the party. But, I must admit, even as I left I didn't foresee just how suffocating its hold would become.

People often ask me what caused me to change course so radically. In truth, my "conversion" wasn't as dramatic as it might have appeared. On all the so-called values issues—abortion, gun control, gay rights—I have the exact same progressive positions today that I've always had.

The biggest shift in my thinking has been in how I view the role of government. I used to believe that the private sector would address the problems of those in need. But then I saw firsthand—up close and very personal—that this wasn't going to happen. Newt Gingrich and company talked a good game, but I soon came to see that despite all the lofty talk about dealing with poverty and race, their hearts were never in it.

In fact, that's how I first became involved with Gingrich. He reached out to me after he saw me on C-SPAN giving a speech challenging conservatives to remember the Biblical admonition that we will be judged by how we deal with the least among us—and to bring this admonition to the very heart of public policy.

If you read that speech now—it's called "Can Conservatives Have a Social Conscience?"—you'll see that a progressive could easily have given it. After watching it, Gingrich called me up and said, "This is exactly what we should be doing." And when he later gave his first speech as Speaker of the House, it was full of those sentiments, about how there was a greater "moral urgency" in "coming to grips with what's happening to the poorest Americans" than in balancing the budget.

I admit it: I was seduced, fooled, blinded, bamboozled—call it what you will. But it didn't take long before I recognized that the Gingrich spiel was only empty rhetoric. And I saw how unfounded was my belief that the private sector—especially conservative multibillionaires who wail about wanting less government involvement—would rise to the occasion and provide the funding needed to replicate social programs that work, sustain them and to bring them to market.

One of the changes in my thinking was born of the hard reality I confronted when I tried to raise money for poverty-fighting groups and community activists. I discovered how much easier it was raising money for the opera or a fashionable museum than for a homeless shelter or free clinic. So I came to recognize that the task of overcoming poverty is too monumental to be achieved without the raw power of annual government appropriations.

But I also believe more fervently than ever that government dollars, however many trillions of them, will never mend broken lives without citizen engagement. What I've found, whether in South Central Los Angeles or Anacostia in Washington, D.C., is the truth of what the Reverend Henry Delaney, who took on the task of transforming boarded-up crack houses in Savannah, Georgia, once told me: "I want to get people involved in what we're doing. It's like putting a poker in the fire. After a while, the fire gets in the poker too." It certainly does. So you can blame my evolution on the fire getting in the poker.

At the same time my thinking was changing, so was the GOP, in ways I couldn't have imagined. Indeed, many old friends from my Republican days—many of whom couldn't understand why I'd turned my back on the party—are now just as appalled as I am by the lunatic fringe's takeover of the Right, and the Right's takeover of America.

Even Bush's good buddy Pakistani President Pervez Musharraf (a guy who can't afford to share W's delusions when it comes to matters of security) said in 2004 that the war in Iraq has made the world "more dangerous" and "further complicated" the war on terror.

The spinmeisters in the Bush camp would rather you never hear any of this, which is why they've been so quick to smear as unpatriotic all those who paint a less than rosy picture of Iraq—going so far as to imply that merely questioning the president's policies gives aid and comfort to our enemies.

The Right can't seem to grasp that this country is built on dissent and that we are too strong to be endangered by the truth. Indeed, hiding the truth, the hallmark of the Bush presidency, is what is making us weaker and less secure.

The Fear-Mongering Hall of Shame

When it comes to scaring the American people, the Bush administration is in a league of its own—the equivalent of the 1927 New York Yankees, the Steel Curtain Pittsburgh Steelers, or the Showtime-era Lakers of Magic, Kareem, and James Worthy. Everywhere you turn, there is another Alarmist All-Star.

Bush, Cheney, Rice, Rummy, Rove. Over the last seven years, this Murderers' Row of lethal bat-swingers has already guaranteed a place for itself in the Fear-Mongering Hall of Shame with Ruthian blasts of pulse-quickening, anxiety-inducing red alert rhetoric. Call them the Sultans of Cold Sweat.

Then National Security Adviser Condi Rice made herself an all-star back in 2003 with her ominous prewar warning about Saddam: "There will always be some uncertainty about how quickly he can acquire nuclear weapons. But we don't want the smoking gun to be a mushroom cloud."

Cheney ensured his enshrinement during the 2004 vice presidential debate: "The biggest threat we face today is the possibility of terrorists smuggling a nuclear weapon or a biological agent into one of our cities and threatening the lives of hundreds of thousands of Americans."

And who'll ever forget Bush's classic 2003 State of the Union performance? Pushing every panic button in sight, he reeled off all the ways Saddam could rain death and destruction on us, including: "biological weapons materials sufficient to produce over 25,000 liters of anthrax—enough doses to kill several million people"; "more than 38,000 liters of botulinum toxin—enough to subject millions of people to death by respiratory failure"; "as much as 500 tons of Sarin, mustard and VX nerve agent. In such quantities, these chemical agents could also kill untold thousands."

But despite these legendary fear-inducing feats, Team Terror has never been content to take a breather on the bench.

We are always being reminded just before an election of the terrorists' imminent arrival. The president's chat with Matt Lauer on the fifth anniversary of 9/11, less than two months before the 2006 midterm election, was a shoo-in Hall of Shame performance. Here was his up-close-and-extremely-personal response to Lauer's questions about torture: "Matt, I'm just telling you, what this government has done is to take steps necessary to protect you and your family. . . . We're at war. This is people that want to come and kill your families. . . . This isn't make-believe." Gulp.

As if that weren't portentous enough, the president followed up with this leap into the dread end zone at a press conference later that week: "It's a dangerous world. I wish it wasn't that way. I wish I could tell the American people, don't worry about it, they're not coming again. But they are coming again."

Not to be outdone, the always cheerful Cheney cleared the bases on *Meet the Press*, trotting out one of his patented "what if" scenarios of mass murder: "The real threat is the possibility of a cell of al Qaeda in the midst of one of our own cities with a nuclear weapon, or a biological agent. In that case, you'd be dealing—for example, if on 9/11 they'd had a nuke instead of an airplane, you'd have been looking at a casualty toll that would rival all the deaths in all the wars fought by Americans in 230 years." Why do I get the feeling this is a recurring fantasy for Cheney?

Then, before the 2006 election, with the polls heavily skewing Democratic, the administration's panic-button-pushers brought out the big guns, including an ad featuring Osama bin Laden saying that 9/11 was "nothing compared to what you will see next," the specter of colossal tax raises, and Dick Cheney repeatedly mentioning the possibility of "mass death in the United States."

The despicable Republican National Committee ad featured bin Laden's right-hand man Ayman al-Zawahiri, a ticking clock, a nuclear explosion, and the tagline: "These are the stakes. Vote November 7th." What a contemptible piece of work. This collage of horror prompted MSNBC's Keith Olbermann to deliver an acid-tongued response. Here's a taste:

> The dictionary definition of the word "terrorize" is simple and not open to misinterpretation: "To fill or overpower with terror; terrify. To coerce by intimidation or fear." . . . By this definition, the leading terrorist group in this world right now is al Qaeda. But the leading terrorist group in this country right now is the Republican Party. Eleven presidents ago, a chief executive reassured us that "we have nothing to fear but fear itself." His distant successor has wasted his administration insisting that there is nothing we can have but fear itself.

Not content with scaring the bejesus out of voters with the equivalent of a GOP-financed al Qaeda recruitment video, the RNC also produced an ad that made the unfounded claim "If Democrats take over Congress, they will raise taxes by 2.4 trillion dollars to keep up with their reckless spending." "*Their* reckless spending"? Did I miss something?

Then there was a blast-from-the-Jim-Crow-past use of race-based fear, in the form of a slimy RNC ad that accused Harold Ford, who was threatening to take a Republican Senate seat in Tennessee, of accepting donations from pornographers. The ad featured a scantily clad blonde who claimed to have met Ford at a Playboy party winking and saying, "Harold, call me." It was a mudslinging twofer: at once sleazy and laced with racist overtones.

That's the sort of thing we have to look forward to in this election year. But this time, maybe we'll see it coming.

Big Brothers and Our Lizard Brain

In George Orwell's classic *1984*, Big Brother uses fear and perpetual war to keep the citizens of Oceania under control—and to blot out memory. "His memory," writes Orwell of Winston Smith, *1984*'s rebellious hero, "was not satisfactorily under control." "Memory control" is a perfect description of the mind-set that allowed Bush and Cheney to repeatedly lie to the American people and get away with it. Again and again and again. (Which is why *The Huffington Post*, together with ad exec Rich Silverstein, created three different posters of the events, people, and slogans of the last seven years, so that fear does not blot out memory.)

The Big Brothers in the Bush White House feverishly banged the gong of fear like Wagnerian kettledrums. Remember February 2006, when the administration took some hits on its National Security Agency warrantless wiretapping program? Even Republicans such as Senator Arlen Specter and Representative Heather Wilson publicly voiced their doubts. Before a week had passed, out trotted the president, offering up details of shoe bombs and "young men from Southeast Asia" meeting with Osama bin Laden and preparing to attack L.A. (In *1984*, the unseen enemy keeps shifting from Eurasia to Eastasia and back again.)

The president didn't directly link the disruption of the attack with

ABU GHRAIB
HALLIBURTON
PREEMPTIVE WAR
WALTER REED
BLACKWATER
EXECUTIVE POWER
BODY ARMOR
KATRINA
GUANTANAMO
YELLOWCAKE
WATERBOARDING

Had enough yet? EVENTS

GEORGE W. BUSH
DICK CHENEY
KARL ROVE
ALBERTO GONZALES
SCOOTER LIBBY
JACK ABRAMOFF
CONDOLEEZZA RICE
RUMSFELD
PAUL WOLFOWITZ
HARRIET MIERS
PAUL BREMER GEORGE TENET
JOHN ASHCROFT MIKE BROWN
JOHN BOLTON

Had enough yet? PEOPLE

GATHERING THREAT
AXIS OF EVIL
WEAPONS OF MASS DESTRUCTION
SLAM DUNK
SHOCK AND AWE
MISSION ACCOMPLISHED
FIGHT'EM THERE NOT HERE
BRING'EM ON
STAY THE COURSE
LAST THROES
HECK OF A JOB BROWNIE
GLOBAL WAR ON TERROR
I AM THE DECIDER
STUFF HAPPENS

Had enough yet? SLOGANS

the NSA wiretapping, but Frances Townsend, his counterterrorism adviser, "did not rule out the program as a factor in discovering the plan." How very vague of her. The alleged intelligence coup referred, in fact, to a four-year-old plot that we had already been told about years earlier and that some experts believe never got off the al Qaeda drawing board. But the president sure made it sound really, really frightening.

Listening to Bush's speeches, it's hard not to think of comedian Kevin Nealon's classic Subliminal Message Guy character: "Since [9/11] we've taken decisive action *(no time to worry about protections against surveillance)* to protect our citizens against new dangers *(old ones, too)*. We're hunting down the terrorists *(Osama who?)* using every element of our national power *(even illegal elements)*— military *(mission accomplished)*, intelligence *(warrantless wiretapping)*, law enforcement *(more wiretapping)*. . . . When an American president says something, he better mean what he said *(except for all the times he doesn't)*."

Playing the fear card anytime the going gets tough is simple, crude, and has worked like a charm for the Right.

As Dr. Daniel Siegel, a Harvard-trained psychiatrist whose book *The Mindful Brain* explores the physiological workings of the brain, explained to me, the Right's unrelenting fear-mongering has left voters "shrouded in a fog of fear," reacting not with their linear, logical left brain but with their more emotional, right lizard brain.

Deep in the brain lies the amygdala, an almond-sized region that generates fear. When this fear state is stimulated, the amygdala springs into action. Before you are even consciously aware that you are afraid, your lizard brain responds by clicking into survival mode. No time to assess the situation, no time to look at the facts, just fight, flight, or freeze. Fear paralyzes our reasoning and literally makes it impossible to think straight. Instead, we search for emotional, nonverbal cues from others that will make us feel safe and secure.

This is precisely why the Right wants to paint Democrats as having "a pre-9/11 worldview," which, by implication, makes them unwilling to go the extra—often illegal—mile to keep America safe.

Precisely because we have real enemies, and real terrorists keep rearing their murderous heads, it is deeply offensive to have the Right use illogical, over-the-top, fear-mongering rhetoric around political events.

Chutzpah doesn't even begin to describe the vice president of the United States suggesting that the outcome of the 2006 Connecticut Democratic primary—in which political newcomer Ned Lamont, who was against the war, defeated incumbent Senator Joe Lieberman, a staunch defender of it—might embolden "al Qaeda types."

The Right knows how ludicrous it is to keep tying the war in Iraq to victory against terrorism, but it also knows how effective it has been. So Cheney went there again, claiming that Lieberman was "pushed aside because of his willingness to support an aggressive posture in terms of our national security."

The truth is that, far from making us safer, "an aggressive posture" on Iraq has had the exact opposite effect. In a survey of one hundred top foreign policy experts (both Republicans and Democrats), eighty-four said they believed that we're losing the war on terror and eighty-seven thought Iraq has had a negative impact on our efforts to defeat terrorists.

Does the Right really believe that because the majority of Americans think that Iraq is a disaster, we don't have "the will" to, in Cheney's words, "stay in the fight and complete the task" of taking on the terrorists? That we are blame-America-firsters, encouraging "al Qaeda types"?

Of course not. The Right knows that being against the war in Iraq doesn't mean you are against fighting the war on terror. It means you are against a failed policy that has created more terrorists than it has killed, that has cost America almost thousands of lives and trillions of dollars, and that has crippled our standing abroad.

You want to know what really emboldens our enemies? An impotent United States so overextended and bogged down in Iraq it has let real terrorists in Afghanistan and Pakistan thrive and become much more threatening.

It would help if the media reacted to the Right's drivel by treating it with the contempt it deserves instead of dutifully reporting it as if it contained even an ounce of logic or sanity. And it would definitely help if Democrats were emboldened to go on the offensive against the Right's scare tactics.

Indeed when the terrorist attack was thwarted in London in the summer of 2005, John Kerry perfectly summed up the success as exposing "the misleading myth that we are fighting them over there so we don't have to fight them here. In fact, the war in Iraq has become a dangerous distraction. . . . Nearly five years after the attacks of 9/11, we are not as safe as we can and must be. . . . The 9/11 Commission's recommendations to secure our most vulnerable infrastructure remain virtually ignored. And homeland security funding has been cut for cities like Boston and New York."

It's worth noting that the ranking Democrat on the Homeland Security and Government Affairs Committee was none other than Joe Lieberman, whose belief in bipartisan comity kept him from holding the White House's feet to the fire. No wonder Karl Rove and Dick Cheney helped make sure he was returned to power.

The Right knows that this battle is for all the marbles. If Democrats can't effectively repudiate the GOP's fear-mongering strategy of linking Iraq to national security, they can kiss 2008 goodbye.

We can expect the Right to play the fear card every chance it gets. As Democratic Congressman Rahm Emanuel put it before the 2006 election: "After six years, they've only got fear to sell." And after seven years, that's still the only thing they have to sell. So as election day 2008 rolls ever closer, you can be sure the Right's fear-mongers will try and try again—in speeches, in press releases, in campaign ads, and in direct mail come-ons.

Fear is a frighteningly effective sales pitch. It is a powerful, universal emotion—always there to be exploited. And that's why we need a major counteroffensive—a wide-ranging campaign to help spread fearlessness, to inoculate the country against this shameful campaign strategy.

Things are always less scary when the lights are on—so we need to be on a continuous fear watch, keeping our eyes peeled for the attempts to scare voters into voting their fears.

Otherwise, we're going to once again succumb to our lizard brains even as our logical brains tell us that the fear-mongers in power have made us all less safe.

We've had enough of spineless, fear-driven, walking-on-eggshells would-be leaders. Enough of Beltway versions of the Cowardly Lion of Oz, driven by the fear of saying the wrong thing (wouldn't want to give the other side ammo for the inevitable attack ad), of offending someone (anyone!), of going out on a limb, and, above all, of losing.

In this book, I have chosen to describe how the Right is wrong on mainstream issues. Thanks to cable news, we've all seen and heard more than enough from the gun nuts, anti-gay crusaders, and serial blockaders of abortion clinics. But the Right's takeover of the Republican Party was not accomplished by pushing flag-burning and school prayer to the fore. It was accomplished by infiltrating the central policy debates and then, once it had gained enough seats at the table, introducing highly infectious and plain wrong ideas.

So I will be looking at the big issues in the Right's playbook—the war, the economy, health care, torture, immigration, civil liberties. But to start, I want to explain how our straits became so dire without our noticing. And the answer to that question begins with the media.

2

The Media: Equal Time for Lies

Unbalanced Balance

Ever since the meteoric rise of Fox News—a phenomenon accompanied, no doubt coincidentally, by the collapse of the dollar, the decimation of America's international image, and the development of the 1,420-calorie Monster Thickburger—Americans have become increasingly savvy about "ideological" news. It has become more difficult to ignore the likes of Bill O'Reilly, Sean Hannity, Ann Coulter, and Rush Limbaugh; they're no longer lonely kooks wandering in the wilderness; they've got access to the halls of power, and they're staying for dinner. Their infinite string of distortions, spin, and outright lies has left no doubt about whose side these guys are on. "Fair and Balanced" lasted about six months as an affirmation of principle and then quickly became an ironic punch line.

At the same time that the right wing's propaganda organs have banged away at the talking points of Bush and company, a much more pernicious development has corrupted the free flow of accurate information in the United States. The old-fashioned "mainstream" media have, in many cases, become the best friend of the Right—simply by adhering to the belief that every major issue has two sides, two valid perspectives, and both deserve to be given equal weight.

This is fine and dandy when the issue at hand is something like the death penalty, balancing the budget, or abortion. Rational, logical cases can be made on two (or more) sides of each of those issues—substantive arguments based on facts, studies, and personal convictions.

Ann Coulter: Toxic Curiosity

Ann Coulter would long ago have become a toxic curiosity were it not for the mainstream media enabling her and playing both sides of the street: pretending to be shocked by her outrageous, over-the-top invective while continuing to give her a platform. And not just giving her a platform, but singing her praises. Indeed, after Coulter called Al Gore a "total fag" on *Hardball* on July 27, 2006, Chris Matthews told her "you're great" and gushed that he'd "love to have her back."

Talk about enabling. No wonder she felt free to slime John Edwards at the 2007 Conservative Political Action Conference.

If the mainstream media stopped trying to have their Coulter and beat it too, any one of her noxious, hateful statements would have been her Macaca moment. Here's a small collection:

"Liberals hate America."—*Slander: Liberal Lies About the American Right*, 2002, p. 6

"Democrats actually hate working-class people."—*Slander*, p. 27

"Even Islamic terrorists don't hate America like liberals do." —*Slander*, p. 6

"Liberals can't just come out and say they want to take more of our money, kill babies, and discriminate on the basis of race." —*How to Talk to a Liberal (If You Must): The World According to Ann Coulter*, 2004, p. 20

Bill Clinton "was a very good rapist."— 1/3/05, *The New York Observer*

Islam is "a car-burning cult."—2/8/06, "Calvin and Hobbes . . . and Muhammed," Townhall.com

"I think the government should be spying on all Arabs, engaging in torture as a televised spectator sport, dropping daisy cutters wantonly throughout the Middle East and sending liberals to Guantánamo."—12/21/05, "Live and Let Spy," Townhall.com

"[Democrats like Jack Murtha] long to see U.S. troops shot, humiliated, and driven from the field of battle."—11/24/05, "New Idea for Abortion Party: Aid the Enemy," Townhall.com

"Isn't it great to see Muslims celebrating something other than the slaughter of Americans?"—2/3/05, "Iraq the Vote," Townhall.com

"I think our motto should be post-9/11, 'raghead talks tough, raghead faces consequences.' "—2/10/06, speech at the Conservative Political Action Conference

The Democratic Party "supports killing, lying, adultery, thievery, envy."—02/28/05, *Hannity & Colmes*

"A baseball bat is the most effective way [to talk to liberals] these days."—10/06/04, *DaySide*

On February 20, 2006, I had the dubious pleasure of appearing on *Hannity & Colmes* along with Ann Coulter. Sean Hannity loves to whip out statements made by others, then ask his guests whether they "condemn" or are "proud" of those statements. He does it all the time. But when I tried to ask him if, given the fact that Coulter had appeared on his show more than twenty times over the previous two years, he wanted to distance himself from her extreme statements, he refused to answer, instead launching into a diatribe against Al Gore, Nancy Pelosi, Hillary Clinton, Howard Dean, and what he called "the extreme left": "I think you're weak on terror. I think you have a pre-9/11 mentality. You've undermined the president. You've undermined the troops, and your hate-Bush mentality is not winning you any friends among the American people."

And it's not as if Hannity needed to have me quote Coulter's past outrageous statements. She offered one—a real doozy—during the show, claiming that Democrats "have affection for these terrorists."

But none of this mattered to Hannity, who let Coulter spew her venom unchallenged. Indeed, it seemed as if he couldn't get enough of the stuff. As if he were addicted to her toxic tirades.

That's when it hit me: Coulter is the right-wing punditry's equivalent of crack or crystal meth. She's highly addictive—giving users the delirious, giddy high of outrageousness. But then the buzz wears off and they come crashing down, their spirits shriveled, their souls poisoned. Her brand of way, way over-the-top rhetoric, trading on hatred, demonizing, and caricature, is doing to the American body politic what a three-month meth bender does to crank junkies. It's the only way to explain why we keep seeing her more and more.

You've probably seen those horrifying "Faces of Meth" photos of people before they start doing meth and after. Sean Hannity needs to watch out. Or he could easily be the first subject in the "Faces of Coulter" series. As for me, that was the last time I appeared—or ever will appear—with Ann Coulter. On the grounds that life is too short.

But there are other issues that quite simply do not have two sides. Iraq *wasn't* a material threat to the security of the United States—at least not until it melted down into a chaotic cauldron of extremism and ethnic warfare after we invaded it. The health care system *is* broken, and insurance companies and big pharmaceutical-makers *have* gorged themselves at the public trough. And global warming *is* real, and will have deadly consequences for people and species all over the planet. Consequences that are already being felt.

Historically, there was only one morally legitimate view on slavery, women's suffrage, and witch-burning. When you talk to experts—independent health policy institutes, Middle East diplomats, climate scientists—the facts are clear. There are not two valid sides to issues like global warming or health care. We can argue about what to do, but unless you're crazy or a liar, you can't honestly claim that the drug and insurance companies aren't an obstacle to public health, that Saddam Hussein's Iraq was a serious threat to U.S. security, or that global warming is a fraud and then demand equal time to spout some nonsense that gains an aura of legitimacy from the "let's hear from both sides" approach of the news media.

Jim Hansen, a climate scientist and the director of NASA's Goddard Institute, wrote in *The New York Review of Books* about what happens to highly qualified experts when they try to make their case in the mainstream media. We're not talking about *FOX & Friends* or the *Rush Limbaugh Show*. We are talking about *The New York Times*, National Public Radio, and CNN. Writes Hansen:

> I used to spread the blame uniformly until, when I was about to appear on public television, the producer informed me that the program "must" also include a "contrarian" who would take issue with claims of global warming. Presenting such a view, he told me, was a common practice in commercial television as well as radio and newspapers. Supporters of public TV or advertisers, with their own special interests, require "balance" as a price for their continued financial support. Gore's book reveals that while more than half of the recent newspaper articles on climate change have given equal weight to such contrarian views, virtually none of the scientific articles in peer-reviewed journals have questioned the consensus that emissions from human activities cause global warming. As a

result, even when the scientific evidence is clear, technical nit-picking by contrarians leaves the public with the false impression that there is still great scientific uncertainty about the reality and causes of climate change.

It's the quaint notion that both sides are arguing in good faith with at least some of the facts on their side that has been cynically exploited by the Right. It's the key to a media strategy that has confused the public and strapped this country to the suicide bomb that is the Bush agenda. What was once the hysterical venom of a few right-wing showmen, presented by the likes of Morton Downey Jr. and dear, drug-addicted Rushbo, has became the stock-in-trade of message mavens in the West Wing. The major Republican candidates dutifully followed Bush's winning example (despite very negligible gifts as a communicator, or anything else for that matter, he did, after all, get elected twice), and mainstream news organizations have treaded lightly, respecting everyone's views regardless of whether they've been proved wrong a thousand times over.

The Pontius Pilate Press

Like Pontius Pilate washing his hands of responsibility, the Washington media want to pretend they are leaving the question of "what is truth" to the public—refusing to admit that sometimes there is even such a thing as truth. But there is. Progress in Iraq, for example, is actually something that can be measured. A September 2007 report from the Government Accountability Office analyzed various metrics of success and did so accurately and impartially. That's why the GAO report was immediately attacked by Republicans—because it pointed out that Iraq was failing to meet eleven of eighteen key benchmarks.

But the administration had faith (the magic word) that, because of the way too many in the press operate, all it had to do to discredit the report was to sow doubt. The GAO put out one set of facts, the administration put out an opposing set of "facts"—and counted on reporters to refuse to see the difference between real facts and fake facts.

A signature case was an AP story on September 8, 2007, about how General David Petraeus and U.S. Ambassador to Iraq Ryan Crocker wouldn't be meeting with "Mr. Bush or their immediate bosses" in order to protect the "independence and the integrity of their testimony." This was a claim that was patently ridiculous. It was hard to fathom how a journalistic operation could write something so blatantly untrue when there had been numerous stories elsewhere making it clear that the Petraeus Report that was soon to be delivered to Congress had already been discussed and thoroughly vetted by the White House, and that veteran GOP operative Ed Gillespie had set up a war room borrowing the best, the brightest, and the biggest bull-shitters from the Pentagon, the State Department, and the White House to coordinate the Petraeus PR campaign.

But the public was no longer buying it. According to a *Washington Post*–ABC News poll in September 2007, only 39 percent of Americans expected General Petraeus to give an accurate picture of the situation in Iraq. Fifty-three percent believed he would give an overly optimistic presentation. And a whopping two-thirds said it didn't matter what Petraeus said because Bush would hold to his Iraq policy no matter what.

I guess you really can't fool all of the people all of the time.

The driving force of the White House's approach to this war has been the belief that saying something is so makes it so. And, beyond the war, that truly is the first commandment of the Bush administration.

The media cannot stop acting as if there are two sides to the story of what is happening in Iraq even when there is only one. And, therefore, they've become accessories before and after the fact to the Iraq fraud.

Right vs. Left vs. Right vs. Wrong

The traditional media's relentless depiction of the Iraq war as a left/right issue, even as the facts give the lie to this hoary framing, became a hallmark of their war coverage. Poll after poll showed a majority of the American people wanting to bring the troops home. But you'd never know it from watching the pundits on television who presented opposition to the war as a left-wing position.

Here's *Newsweek*'s Howard Fineman on *Countdown with Keith Olbermann* on January 17, 2007: "That's the tension that people like Hillary Clinton, Barack Obama, and Joe Biden are caught in as they try to move to the left on the war without taking themselves out of the mainstream of the country."

What Fineman means by "left on the war" is being in favor of ending the war, and against Bush's handling of it. Yet no Democrat need worry that taking those positions will take him or her out of the mainstream.

But don't tell that to CNN's Candy Crowley. Here is her January 9, 2007, cobweb-covered analysis of Ted Kennedy's anti-escalation measure then being debated in the Senate: "What Senator Kennedy is going to do is lay down the liberal view of things, which is to say, he will say, look, no additional troops and no additional money for additional troops, unless Congress approves."

The "liberal view of things"? More like the predominant view of things. Almost two-thirds of the nation agreed with the senator.

And there was Judy Woodruff saying on *Meet the Press*, on January 7, 2007, that Iraq is "a huge problem for the Democrats. Their base wants the United States out of Iraq yesterday." So anyone who wants out of Iraq belongs to the Democratic base? Someone should give Democratic National Committee Chairman Howard Dean a raise for doubling the size of the party.

Was Republican Senator Chuck Hagel, co-sponsor (along with Carl Levin and Joe Biden) of the Senate resolution condemning Bush's surge plan, a "liberal"? Was he "left on the war"? Was he "part of the Democratic base"? Was he "out of the mainstream"?

Or how about North Carolina Congressman Walter Jones, like Hagel a staunch Republican? After enthusiastically supporting the war, Jones became a harsh critic of Bush's Iraq policy. According to the media framing, that would make Jones a "liberal," right? But he was actually the proud possessor of a 93 percent rating from the American Conservative Union for his seven-term voting record.

Then there's Senator Sam Brownback, also a Republican who, as a short-lived presidential candidate, positioned himself to the right of a notably conservative field. Upon returning from Iraq in January 2007, Brownback announced, "I do not believe that sending more troops to Iraq is the answer. Iraq requires a political rather than a military solution." This flaming liberal had a 100 percent rating from the American Conservative Union, and was considered one of that group's "Best of the Best." Soon after he returned from Iraq, Brownback spoke at the second annual conference of pro-life bloggers in Washington. Those pro-lifers must have been shocked when someone as "liberal" as Brownback showed up in their midst.

When the macro-framing of the war is so warped, it makes productive discussion of how to deal with Iraq even harder.

On the One Hand, the Truth

The "Two Equal Sides at All Costs" approach to reporting was in full garish display in the fall of 2007. By then it was clear listening to the Democratic candidates' discussion of Iraq that they had gotten the message that, no matter what General Petraeus said during his upcoming testimony, the American people were done with this war. As Hillary Clinton put it at the time, "We need to quit refereeing their civil war and bring our troops home as soon as possible."

The opinion of the American people was clear. A CBS/*New York Times* poll had 63 percent opposed to continuing the war. The Democrats running for president and trying to win their votes were clear as well. But far too many in the media were still in a fog.

In *The New York Times* on September 8, 2007, Michael Gordon, chief military correspondent and Judy Miller's backup singer in the Ahmed Chalabi vaudeville production of "Saddam's Got WMD," served up a fact-challenged piece of administration propaganda in which he asserted, "The most comprehensive and up-to-date military statistics show that American forces have made some headway toward a crucial goal of protecting the Iraqi population."

Nowhere did Gordon point out that the methodology the Pentagon used to arrive at the comprehensive stats he cited had been thoroughly discredited in *The Washington Post*, which reported that the military was "cherry-picking positive indicators." Yet he boldly claimed: "Data on car bombs, suicide attacks, civilian casualties and other measures of the bloodshed in Iraq indicate that violence has been on the decline, though the levels generally remain higher than in 2004 and 2005."

Let's take a closer look at that particular sentence. Apparently, it meant that, even though violence was higher at that point than it had been for two years prior to the surge, there was some period in 2006 in which attacks, as measured in some exotic and mysterious manner, were higher than now. Bravo, Michael Gordon. Your White House thank-you note and ornamental desk calendar are in the mail.

Gordon punctuated his piece by adopting the wearisome pseudo-objective "he said/she said" stance. "The figures that have emerged in recent government reports have seemingly provided something for everyone," he wrote.

I guess we just can't know anything for certain, can we?

The National Intelligence Estimate Exposes the Unintelligent National Media

In April 2006 a National Intelligence Estimate was released that, in a single document, did the media's job for them. The story of the year was served up on a silver platter. And it should have cleared the media's muddled heads like a shot glass of Tabasco. The NIE represented the consensus view of all sixteen U.S. intelligence agencies and was a stark and unambiguous repudiation of the Bush administration's counterterrorism strategy and its contention that the war in Iraq has made us safer.

The report suggested just the opposite—that the war in Iraq has fueled a growing hatred of America, spread Islamic extremism, and spawned an expanding crop of newly inspired jihadists around the globe. And it shattered the Bushies' bedrock notion that we are fighting them over there so we don't have to fight them over here. It turns out that the odds of our having to fight them over here have greatly increased precisely because we are fighting them over there.

The report also highlighted the "regenerated" strength of al Qaeda. Not only have we failed to capture bin Laden and destroy those who attacked us on 9/11—we have, as a result of Bush's tragic actions, actually helped make al Qaeda strong and deadly again. Thanks to the Iraq war, al Qaeda made the most unlikely comeback since the '04 Red Sox. We might as well have plastered the Muslim world with recruiting posters that say "Uncle Sam wants you . . . to join al Qaeda."

If this NIE assessment were a "Keeping Us Safe" report card, Bush would get an F. This is another perfect example of a time when there aren't two sides to an issue—when there is no "other hand." The president vowed to keep us safe and, according to sixteen intelligence agencies, he has failed. Period. End of story. But don't wait for the media to tell you about it.

The Pro-and-Con Con

If you watch the news, you've probably seen its "pro and con" formula a thousand times: offering up two "experts," one arguing from the facts, the other presenting nothing but spin. A perfect illustration of the media's embrace of this fake objectivity came with the release of yet another National Intelligence Estimate report on the threat of terrorist violence against America in the summer of 2007. On CNN, Anderson Cooper reported that "both sides in the Iraq debate are spinning [the report] to support their case." To prove his point, he rolled a video clip of Bush making the case for staying the course in Iraq. Back on camera, he said, "The Democrats, of course, see it differently."

"Of course." Cooper then turned to a trio of experts whose ostensible goal was "Keeping Them Honest."

Up first was the always bracing Michael Ware, CNN's Iraq correspondent, beamed in via satellite from Iraq, where he has spent most of the war. Ware took a cudgel to the White House spin machine, ridiculing the administration's attempt to portray the war as a fight between America and al Qaeda by reporting that "al Qaeda would be lucky to make up 3 percent of the total insurgency." Ware's devastating and spot-on verdict on the White House: "They're trying to play the American public."

Next up was CNN terrorism analyst Peter Bergen, who agreed with Ware that al Qaeda in Iraq is a "relatively small" group but then quickly added a caveat beginning with four ominous words. "On the other hand," Bergen said, "the largest number of suicide attackers in Iraq are all foreigners . . . few Iraqis are involved in the suicide attacks. And it's the suicide attacks, of course, that sparked the civil war, that got the United Nations to withdraw, and that made Iraq a much more dangerous place. So, despite their small number, they have had a disproportionate strategic effect on the ground."

For those keeping score at home, that's one "the administration is not being honest" and one "the administration is partially honest and partially dishonest." Hmm . . . I wonder what could be next?

Enter one of CNN's brigade of handy military analysts, retired U.S. General David Grange, reporting for duty as administration apologist. Like the White House, Grange sees a silver lining in the undisputed fact that the war in Iraq has "multiplied" the number of terrorists: "I kind of like the idea [terrorists] assemble in Iraq, because there's more of them there to take down, instead of hunting them around the world of global operations, which are very difficult. Here, we have a license to kill or capture. Many other places, we do not. And, so, I don't think it's a bad thing that they're assembling in Iraq."

I almost kissed my TV when Ware refused to let the general's fuzzy logic go unchallenged: "The whole notion of better to fight them over there than over here—let's bring them in like a honey pot and draw them to Iraq and kill them—is absolutely ludicrous. In fact, it's so ludicrous, it's downright dangerous, because what they're doing is, they're creating an entire generation of jihadis that did not exist. . . . Iraq has been a total disaster, in terms of limiting the number of jihadis on the planet."

So there you have it—a typical media sampler: three plausible talking heads, one saying "It's A," one saying "It's B!," and one saying "Come on, fellas, settle down. We all know it's a little of each."

It seems fair, balanced, and objective. And it's utterly confusing for the public that just wants to be informed.

There are such things as facts. There is such a thing as reality. And refusing to see those facts and report that reality—undiluted by an "on the other hand" mixer—isn't a sign of objectivity, it's a sign of intellectual laziness and journalistic muddled thinking.

Titillated by Terror

Equally flawed was the coverage of more dramatic terrorist-related stories, like the failed car bomb attacks that shook up London and Glasgow in June 2007.

The press latched on to the attacks with their usual red alert ardor. As former CIA and State Department counterterrorism expert Larry Johnson put it: "My main beef remains that much of the cable news media reacts to this nonsense like a fifty-year-old guy on Viagra or Cialis—they pop major wood. And the same warnings are appropriate—an erection lasting more than four hours may be harmful."

Take Tim Russert, whose July 1, 2007, *Meet the Press* interview with Homeland Security Secretary Michael Chertoff was about as priapic a display as you're ever likely to see outside of a porno film or the monkey cage at the zoo, with Russert desperately trying to get Chertoff to pump up the panic meter.

"Will we increase the number of air marshals on flights to Britain and Scotland?" he asked. "Is there any chatter that you can detect regarding terrorism in the United States during this holiday period?" "Will we raise our threat level?" "Considering the simplicity of putting together a suicide bomb by using an automobile, are you surprised that the United States has not been hit harder by this kind of device?" You could almost hear the blood rushing to his loins—and the palpable sense of deflation when Chertoff refused to stroke his fantasy.

When his heavy breathing subsided, Russert turned his attention to warrantless wiretapping. He opened his interview with Senate Judiciary Committee Chairman Patrick Leahy by asking, "As you well know, you have issued subpoenas on the Bush White House regarding the eavesdropping, wiretapping put in place by the president after September 11th. Critics this morning will say, Senator, that this plan is so essential to monitoring contacts between international terrorists and people here in thc United States that subpoenas now is very, very counterproductive and could affect our anti-terrorism situation."

Russert didn't specify which "critics" these might be. Critics of the rule of law? Critics of the Constitution? Critics of our Founding Fathers? Is it possible for an informed person to honestly misread the standoff between the Senate and the White House over the NSA spying program that badly?

In the same vein as the reaction to the failed London and Glasgow bombings was the media response to a Keystone Cops plot to blow up a fuel pipeline at JFK International Airport in New York City in the summer of 2007.

These are the facts: the plot's ringleader made a living exporting broken air conditioner parts to Guyana. There was no set plan. There was no financing. They didn't have any explosives—and yet government officials got the hysteria ball rolling by calling the amorphous plot "one of the most chilling plots imaginable," almost resulting "in unfathomable damage, deaths, and destruction." And people wonder why the public has become cynical about how the war on terror is being used for political purposes.

What's more, the wave of red alert press coverage turned out to have been based on a misunderstanding of how jet fuel pipelines work. "Such an attack would have crippled America's economy," wailed AP's Adam Goldman, following the government's lead.

We've been down this road before, with the Fort Dix Six—a group of Muslim men who allegedly planned to attack Fort Dix in New Jersey. The men were arrested after they brought a video of themselves firing guns and shouting "Allahu Akbar" into a local Circuit City to get it transferred to a DVD. We are told again and again that if we don't fight "them" over there, we'll have to fight "them" over here—perhaps at Circuit City, where new jihadists apparently take their holy war recruitment tapes to be burned onto a DVD.

And we traveled a similar path with a supposedly terrifying plot to bring down the Sears Tower that was hatched by the "Seas of David" nut jobs down in Liberty City, Florida, egged on by the FBI. These things always seem to follow a pattern: Start with a big media splash: "We got the bad guys! We saved the country!" Then it slowly comes out that the terrorists might not have been so terrifying. Indeed, they're boobs that go to Circuit City to get their jihadist video burned onto a DVD, or they're low-level criminals with delusions of grandeur, goaded into grander fantasies and bigger targets by informants who are getting paid or getting their sentences reduced by the FBI if they deliver some terrorists.

Then we got fear-mongering presidential wannabe Rudy Giuliani wasting no time laying the JFK caper and the Fort Dix plot at the feet of "Islamic terrorists"—raising the specter of Osama bin Laden sticking pushpins into an enormous wall map of the United States.

It was almost comical how Giuliani kept trying to present himself as a national security expert even though this was the guy who strongly backed the scandal-plagued former New York City police chief Bernie Kerik to be in charge of Homeland Security.

Michael Bloomberg, Giuliani's replacement as mayor of New York, took a dismissive approach to the JFK plot hype: "You can't sit there and worry about everything. Get a life. You have a much greater danger of being hit by lightning than being struck by a terrorist."

Especially a terrorist like the ones trying to blow up JFK, Fort Dix, and the Sears Tower.

Broken News

When they're not going after a nonstory like the JFK pipeline "plot," the media are filling their insatiable appetites with breaking news like San Francisco Mayor Gavin Newsom apologizing for having a sexual relationship with the wife of his former campaign manager, Alex Tourk.

"I'm deeply sorry," he said during a brief City Hall news conference on February 1, 2007.

CNN described this as "Breaking News." But by what definition?

I mean, really, why was this anybody's business—except for Mr. Newsom, Mr. Tourk, Mr. Tourk's wife, and Mr. Newsom's ex-wife and perhaps their therapists?

Why was this a public matter?

With Iraq continuing to implode (January 2007 set a deadly record for Iraqi civilian deaths) and all the other problems facing the world, a personal peccadillo was identified as "breaking news."

This media fixation on sexual ethics is a perfect example of what G. K. Chesterton warned about: "If there is one thing worse than the modern weakening of major morals, it is the modern strengthening of minor morals."

Instead of a thick line drawn between public matters and private lives, we get a never-ending cycle of public voyeurism, titillation, admission, contrition, and inevitable prime-time absolution. Wolf Blitzer followed up Newsom's news conference by promising: "We're going to have a lot more on this story." Of course they did.

Can we all agree that unless a politician has broken the law, the only legitimate answer to the illegitimate probing of private lives is "It's none of your business"? ("Go to hell!" might be an acceptable substitute.)

Our politicians need to keep their private lives private, and the media need to keep their focus on what does—and what surely does not—constitute news. "Breaking" or otherwise.

The collection of trivial stories elevated far beyond their actual importance is gargantuan. A perfect example of this came in the spring of 2006, when the late Anna Nicole Smith's legal efforts to claim a share of her deceased husband's billions made it to the U.S. Supreme Court. On a day that saw Iraq moving closer to all-out civil war, with at least 76 Iraqis killed and 179 wounded in sectarian attacks, the *CBS Evening News* devoted one minute and thirty-nine seconds to coverage of Iraq and one minute and fifty-six seconds to coverage of Anna Nicole Smith's appearance in front of the Supreme Court.

That's right, car bombs and mortar blasts were ripping through Shiite holy places and Sunni mosques, the Iraqi foreign minister was urging U.S. officials to take a "less visible" role in the talks aimed at forming a new national government, the U.S. death toll hit 2,292, the U.S. ambassador to Iraq was warning of region-wide chaos . . . and CBS thought Anna Nicole was the bigger story.

What's more, a substantial portion of the paltry ninety-nine seconds the Tiffany Network gave over to Iraq was spent updating the latest developments in the Saddam trial where his lawyers—wait for it—had walked out. Again.

Of course, the Mrs. Smith Goes to Washington story came with all that irresistible B-roll of Anna Nicole jiggling her way through a pack of jostling paparazzi into the High Court, and allowed producers to rehash old file footage of Smith testifying that her marriage to octogenarian billionaire J. Howard Marshall was true love: "It wasn't a sexual, 'Baby, oh baby, I love your body'–type love. It was a deep 'Thank you for taking me out of this hole.' " It also gave then CBS anchor Bob Schieffer the opportunity to intro the segment by saying: "The U.S. Supreme Court is one of the great judicial bodies that the world has known" (nudge, nudge, wink, wink . . . provide your own "great bodies" punch line). Hard for civil war to top that.

So, for those of you keeping track, it was Bombs 1:39, Bombshells 1:56. And that was with the venerable, modeled-on-Murrow Schieffer at the helm.

The Bombs vs. Bombshell balance was even more out of whack over on ABC's *Nightline*, which devoted its show-closing "Sign of the Times" segment to "the stripper and the Supreme Court"—and didn't cover Iraq at all.

With Anna Nicole's Supreme Court victory in early May 2006, Schieffer and company took another bite of the Bombs vs. Bombshells apple. So how'd they do? Well, it depends how you slice it. CBS's update of the Smith story was given another minute and fifty-eight seconds of precious airtime—two seconds more than the previous time—while its coverage of Iraq lasted two minutes and ten seconds. Aha, you may say, that's twelve seconds more than they gave Anna Nicole, and a thirty-one-second increase from the last time the two stories went head-to-head. True, but the stories aired on the third anniversary of Bush's "Mission Accomplished" speech—a fairly significant news peg and an opportunity for some truth-telling about Iraq.

While it might seem hard to make compelling TV out of a written Supreme Court ruling, that didn't stop CBS from putting more effort into illustrating the Anna Nicole news than some footage-poor mass grave story from Anbar province. They rolled out lots of cleavage-heavy file footage of Anna Nicole (in all her many hairstyles and dress sizes) and plenty of droll commentary from Schieffer, whose intro slyly ruminated on the mysterious nature of love, and referenced the songs of Rodgers and Hammerstein and Ira Gershwin: "Who knows what draws two people together, that look across a crowded room on some enchanted evening, or the way you wear your hat and dance till three. And, of course, there's that other little motivator, money. But what was it in the case of Anna Nicole Smith and the old fellow she married? The question went all the way to the Supreme Court. And today love found a way."

Schieffer's eyes all but twinkled when he said "old fellow she married." He also put a button on the story with a Friars Club–worthy zinger. Following up Wyatt Andrews's report that the Marshall family had vowed to spend millions fighting to keep Anna Nicole from getting any money, Schieffer ended the segment by saying, "I'll guarantee you the lawyers love her." Rim shot! Witty and snarky stuff, for sure—but couldn't they have had their fun with the Smith story *and* put their considerable talents to use bringing home to the American people the devastating reality on the ground in Iraq?

As it was, CBS's Iraq coverage focused more on poll numbers than the tragic numbers of the war. Schieffer took a fairly biting look at the "Mission Accomplished" anniversary, recalling "what many thought at the time was one of the cleverest photo-ops ever," with Bush "decked out in a dashing flight suit . . . under a banner that said 'Mission Accomplished.' But it turned out not to be. . . . With the president's approval rating now down to another new low, 33 percent," said Schieffer, "I take it this is one anniversary the White House did not want to talk about today."

He then tossed it to CBS White House correspondent Jim Axelrod, who also focused on the poll numbers, citing the 44 percent drop over the preceding three years in the number of Americans that approved of the way Bush was handling Iraq, falling from 74 percent to just 30 percent. Telling numbers, to be sure. But there were some even more telling numbers that weren't included anywhere in the CBS story—namely, the 2,266 American soldiers killed, the 16,927 American soldiers wounded, and the $241 billion that had been spent on the war in the three years between the time Bush landed on the USS *Abraham Lincoln* and announced "major combat operations have ended" and the landmark Anna Nicole Smith decision. Seems like they could have fit those in somewhere if a producer had just been willing to cut back a bit of the Anna Nicole giggle-fest.

And if the CBS report wanted to focus on polling numbers, it could at least have mentioned the bleak results of a poll of Iraqis

by the International Republican Institute that found that 76 percent rated their security situation as "poor," 62 percent said the country was more divided than in the past, and 68 percent said corruption
was getting worse. And—by the way—just one percent named
U.S. and coalition forces when asked whom they trusted to protect
them.

On the plus side, the CBS segment included a stand-up from Allen
Pizzey in Baghdad that highlighted the disconnect between the president's upbeat assertion that the day marked "a turning point for the
citizens of Iraq" and the facts on the ground, where efforts to form a
national unity government continued to falter and sectarian killings
continued to rise. "People here are very much looking to protect
themselves," reported Pizzey, "they're not thinking in terms of nation
right now. . . . We're finding that people are fleeing neighborhoods
where they're in the minority and, in fact, you're getting people coa-
lescing along ethnic lines. And they're not looking to the state for
protection but to ethnically based militias."

No zinger from Schieffer after that grim update. None was
needed.

The News Cycle's Appeals Court

"News stories have a twenty-four-hour audition on the news stage,
and if they don't catch fire in that twenty-four hours, there's no
second chance," said Josh Marshall of *Talking Points Memo*. Elab-
orating on this, Jay Rosen, professor of journalism at New York University, added that "blogs have become the news cycle's appeals
court."

But, unlike a traditional court, the Blog Circuit Court of Appeals
lacks an enforcement arm. The only way its decisions can be enforced
is by constant repetition in the blogosphere.

The difficulty of this was brought home in full force in June of
2005. After over a month and a half of neglect, the mainstream
media, prodded by blogger-fueled public indignation, was finally
starting to pay attention to the story of the Downing Street Memo,
which revealed that almost a year before the invasion of Iraq, the
British government had become concerned that the Bush administration had "fixed" the intelligence on Iraq and was determined to go
to war.

By mid-June, sparked by a Tony Blair visit to the White House, the story was finally gaining traction. But not on the cable news channels, which were still obsessing over the story of an eighteen-year-old girl named Natalee who had gone missing in Aruba three weeks before.

Every time one of these stories comes up, I feel deeply for the family—but I also feel like it's none of the nation's business. When it's finally over I think, now we can get back to real news. But when one of these big-league nonstories ends, the media just call up a new one from the minors, like the Michael Jackson molestation trial, and off they go with another round of breathless reporting.

As a comparison, here are the number of news segments that mentioned these three stories from May 1, 2005 (when the Downing Street Memo was first reported) to June 20, 2005 (three weeks after Natalee Holloway disappeared):

- ABC News: "Downing Street Memo": 0 segments; "Natalee Holloway": 42 segments; "Michael Jackson": 121 segments.

- CBS News: "Downing Street Memo": 0 segments; "Natalee Holloway": 70 segments; "Michael Jackson": 235 segments.

- NBC News: "Downing Street Memo": 6 segments; "Natalee Holloway": 62 segments; "Michael Jackson": 109 segments.

- CNN: "Downing Street Memo": 30 segments; "Natalee Holloway": 294 segments; "Michael Jackson": 633 segments.

- Fox News: "Downing Street Memo": 10 segments; "Natalee Holloway": 148 segments; "Michael Jackson": 286 segments.

- MSNBC: "Downing Street Memo": 10 segments; "Natalee Holloway": 30 segments; "Michael Jackson": 106 segments.

When defending these choices, news execs inevitably fall back on the old "we're just giving the people what they want." But are they? Fox News averages under two million viewers in prime time; CNN hovers over a million; MSNBC pulls in under half a million. We have 300 million people in the country. That means that tens of millions of people actually don't want what they're being given—and that there are huge slices of audience a real news operation could go after.

One wonders what happens to all those enterprising young broadcast journalists being pumped out by j-schools across the country. I speak to them occasionally, and they all seem to be truly dedicated to reporting the news and ferreting out the truth. So what happens to them between grad school and the moment they do their fiftieth windswept, beachfront update on Natalee Holloway? Surely no one actually aspires to spend his or her life describing the pre–Michael Jackson verdict scene outside the courthouse or filling up airtime with a feature on the party scene in Aruba. This can't be what they wanted to do with their journalism degrees, can it?

Mika Brzezinski set a great example. On June 26, 2007, she was co-anchoring MSNBC's *Morning Joe* with Joe Scarborough. It was a big news day, with Republican Senator Richard Lugar having declared that President Bush's Iraq strategy wasn't working. But when Brzezinski (daughter of Carter national security adviser Zbigniew Brzezinski) turned to her script, she realized that it led with a story about Paris Hilton being released from jail. She used a paper shredder, after failing with a cigarette lighter, to destroy her script on air, a move that created a firestorm of positive buzz.

Now, we're in no position to burn or shred every piece of worthless non-news news. But here's my suggestion: Go cold turkey. Just say no. Every time you see or hear mention of a Britney Spears/Amy Winehouse/vanished attractive college coed flavor-of-the-moment on the screen in the next few weeks, turn off the TV, or change the channel. I've been trying it, and it's not easy (I've found the Cartoon Network is a pretty safe—if nerve-rattling—escape valve).

This is not to minimize the tragic elements of Natalee Holloway's disappearance, or the many similar previous (and, sadly, subsequent) disappearances. It is tragic when a young person goes missing or is murdered—but it's not news in the way the Downing Street Memo is news. Or multiple deaths in Iraq are news. I remember reading in the *Los Angeles Times* about the deaths of Lance Corporal Erik R. Heldt and Captain John W. Maloney when their Humvee hit an Improvised Explosive Device in Ramadi during the Holloway blanket coverage, but you didn't hear their names repeated on Fox or CNN or MSNBC.

Be warned: even if you try really hard to go cold turkey, the Scandalous Non-News Story of the Day still has a way of seeping into your consciousness. It's some kind of tabloid osmosis. Despite my best efforts, and an incredibly quick remote-control technique, I've still found myself starting to offer an opinion on one of them at a dinner party before pulling up short. "Wait a second," my brain starts to shout, "I don't even care about this story—why do I know so much about it!"

But it's worth a try. And until the Blog High Court gets a better enforcement mechanism, we, as viewers, will just have to practice jury nullification.

Libby Scoots, Press Snoozes

The commutation of top Cheney aide Scooter Libby's sentence for perjury and obstruction of justice offered a perfect example of the media's knee-jerk attempts to analyze every issue in terms of right vs. left. Libby had outed undercover CIA operative Valerie Plame, whose husband, Ambassador Joseph Wilson, had blown the whistle on the administration's bogus WMD-"yellowcake"-uranium-in-Africa assertion, one of the pretexts used to sell the invasion of Iraq to the American people.

The commutation of Scooter's sentence in July 2007 dragged the media back from their vacations to bring us the news. But their reporting showed that their brains were still roasting on a beach somewhere. Airwaves and news pages were quickly filled with talk of "outrage from the left," "criticism from the left," and how the commutation "will further drive the left crazy."

The "left-right corollary" to the "two sides rule" is positively Pavlovian. Ring the breaking news bell, and reporters start to drool about right vs. left. Even when the facts show that the story, like the Libby commutation—like the war in Iraq, like the war on drugs, like health care, like global warming—was not an issue that split along right/left lines.

In a Gallup poll taken immediately after the commutation was announced, 66 percent of those asked said they disagreed with the decision, including 35 percent of conservatives. And, in an earlier *Time* Magazine/SRBI poll, 72 percent said they would disapprove of a pardon. So unless "the left" has had another incredible growth spurt, a lot of people on the "right" were feeling pretty peeved about Scooter's special treatment too.

And if Libby's Get Out of Jail Free Card was so clearly a right/left issue, how come only Tom Tancredo and Sam Brownback (remember them?) offered an unequivocal "Yes" during the June 6, 2007, GOP presidential debate in New Hampshire when asked if they would pardon Libby (the other candidates either said "No" or took a wait-and-see stance)? When you consider how quickly the candidates' positions were deteriorating into right-wing boilerplate elsewhere, it becomes clear this was not a right/left issue.

Is it really that hard for the media to address an issue without the left/right crutch? Or, if they had to hobble along using that musty terminology, couldn't they at least have done a little research? Because there were plenty on "the right" who weren't exchanging high-fives over Libby dodging the prison bullet.

All they'd have had to do was read conservative blogger Patterico, who wrote: "You do the crime, you do the time. . . . This wasn't right." (Double entendre intended.) Or they could have checked out Orin Kerr, a conservative law blogger who used to clerk for Justice Anthony Kennedy (and we've all seen how liberal he is). Kerr wrote: "I find Bush's action very troubling because of the obvious special treatment Libby received."

And that's the point. Bush's imperial chutzpah—letting Libby off the hook without even consulting with the Justice Department—wasn't a matter of right vs. left, but a clear case of right vs. wrong.

Anyone who believes in the rule of law, who believes that cronyism is wrong, who believes that all citizens should "stand before the bar of justice as equals," and who believes that juries should be overruled only in the most extraordinary cases, knows that the Libby commutation was flat wrong. In this case "anyone" once included George W. Bush, who, as governor of Texas, said: "I don't believe my role is to replace the verdict of a jury with my own, unless there are new facts or evidence of which a jury was unaware, or evidence that the trial was somehow unfair." None of those exceptions applied in this case but, despite promises to respect the system and let justice take its course, Bush had predetermined that any conviction of a friend was "somehow unfair."

Someone please alert the media: not every issue fits your cherished right/left paradigm. Indeed, that way of looking at the world is becoming less and less relevant—and more and more obsolete. And more and more dangerous.

Antiwar Hero in the Crosshairs

The left/right meme was also wielded as a weapon in the media mauling of Pennsylvania Congressman Jack Murtha. Ever since Murtha first stepped forward in November 2005 and courageously called for the withdrawal of U.S. troops from Iraq, the pro-war rhetorical thugs have been after him. And marginalizing Murtha, a lifelong hawk, by identifying him with the Left, was tactic number one. In February 2007, Brit Hume took the attacks to a new low by challenging Jack Murtha's mental acuity. (This was the same Brit Hume who claimed that the murder rate was higher per capita in the state of California than it is in Baghdad. It isn't.)

During a panel discussion on *Fox News Sunday*, the normally expressionless Hume slapped on his finest sneer and said of Murtha: "It's time a few things be said about him. Even *The Washington Post* noted he didn't seem particularly well-informed about what's going on over there, to say the least. . . . This guy is long past the day when he had anything but the foggiest awareness of what the heck is going on in the world." He went on to call Murtha "dotty" and "an absolute fountain" of "naïveté."

Notice the preamble: "It's time a few things be said about him" with its decisive "enough is enough" tone. Anytime anyone on Fox News makes it clear that he's about to let his hair down and get something off his chest, get ready for a lie so bald-faced that it couldn't be sold as straight reporting.

If we are going to say a few things about Jack Murtha, perhaps we should add that after serving as a Parris Island drill instructor and then in the Marine Corps Reserves, Murtha volunteered for service in Vietnam, where he served as an intelligence officer. He was awarded the Bronze Star for Valor, the Vietnamese Cross of Gallantry, and two Purple Hearts. He left the fleet in 1990, retiring from the Reserves as a full colonel.

But unable to win the fight against Murtha's ideas—and his war record—the Right's hit squad made the desperate play of suggesting that the seventeen-term congressman might not have been playing with a full deck. Call it the Senility Surge. Classy.

As they looked out over the political landscape, ready to heap their scorn on a political leader who might not be "well-informed" about Iraq and who doesn't seem to have the "foggiest awareness of what the heck is going on in the world," did their eyes really settle on Jack Murtha first? Not the guy who said he couldn't judge whether Iraq was in a civil war while "living in this beautiful White House"? Just asking.

And while Hume's portrayal of Murtha as ready for a drool bib and the old-age home was in a malicious league of its own, the mudslinging on Fox News by Sean Hannity was equally repugnant. Knowing Hume had already mined the depths of character assassination, Hannity went right for naked distortion—throwing any vestige of truth out the window and portraying Murtha's Iraq proposal as the exact opposite of what it actually was.

Here was Murtha on the troops: "They must have the equipment and the training and they must be certified by the Chiefs of the various services before they can go back."

And here is how Hannity described Murtha's position in a question to one of his panelists: "Do you support the idea of taking away the equipment of troops in harm's way the way John Murtha just described?"

In Hannity's hands, making sure our troops are properly equipped becomes taking equipment out of the hands of soldiers in harm's way. And, by the way, don't you love the way he made it a question? I mean, who's for taking equipment away from troops in harm's way except maybe Osama bin Laden?

The reason for the increasingly frantic targeting of Murtha was very simple: his proposals were gaining traction among politicians on both sides of the aisle.

There was Republican Senator Chuck Hagel on *Meet the Press*, saying he was "open" to Murtha's plans to attach conditions to warfunding, and that "Congressman Murtha makes some very valid points. . . . This debate, partly, is not about supporting the troops there. Now, of course we're going to support the troops. There isn't anybody in the House or Senate that would vote otherwise. What this debate is about right now is a continuation and an escalation of American military involvement in Iraq, putting young men and women in the middle of a sectarian, an intra-sectarian civil war. That's what this debate is really about."

In the meantime, the White House adopted its standard operating procedure: farm out the really vile stuff to surrogate sleaze-peddlers while dispatching its press secretary to *Meet the Press* to take the high road: "We're not in the business of trying to pick personal fights with members of Congress," said Tony Snow. Did Snow really expect us to buy that "golly gee willikers" routine? Thankfully for him, he made that ludicrous claim on *Meet the Press*. So, instead of challenging himself, Tim Russert didn't blink an eye—proving once again why his show is the administration's "best format," as former Cheney communications director Cathie Martin described *Meet the Press* while testifying during the Libby trial.

One of the small satisfactions of the Libby trial was in fact getting certain things that we already knew about our craven media confirmed by various former White House officials.

Like Cathie Martin, confirming that *Meet the Press* was the administration's top choice for push-back as its lies about Iraq were unraveling because the White House could "control" the message more easily there. And like former press secretary Ari Fleischer, confirming what we already knew regarding the infamous "sixteen words" about the Niger yellowcake in Bush's State of the Union speech in 2003: "I had been told to be careful not to stand by the sixteen words, that the ground might be shifting on that," Fleischer said. "You can't say yes. You can't say no. At that briefing, I basically punted. I said yes and no."

Does anyone in the press corps—not to mention the planet—not know that current White House press secretary Dana Perino is still up there "punting," day in and day out? You see more punts in the average White House press briefing than you do in a Chiefs–49ers game. Why, then, do they still bother? Why don't they call the punting what we all know it is: deliberate deception—even . . . gasp . . . lying?

The media's willingness to let punt after punt whiz by, and allow the administration to "control" its message by answering lobbed questions in preferred "formats," is part of what got us into this disastrous war, and what's still allowing Bush to punt this entire debacle over to the next president or, as he put it, "presidents."

It would be a lot harder for the administration to play games with other people's lives if the media refused to go along.

The Day the Press Fought Back

What is interesting is that the White House press corps finally lost its lazy cool and worked itself up into a state of high dudgeon not over being blatantly lied to for years about WMD, Saddam's links to 9/11, looming mushroom clouds, the whole "greeted as liberators" thing, "last throes," the war being able to pay for itself, torture, NSA wiretaps, Plamegate, and on and on and on. The story that got them shouting "How could you!" was being lied to about the Dick Cheney shooting incident.

It is like being involved with a serial philanderer. You find out that he had sex with your kid's nanny—in your bed—and you live and let live, so as not to rock the boat. Then you find out about the secret love child he had with his secretary, and you swallow your anger and hope that your kids will like their new half-sibling. Then he gambles away your life's savings and puts you in debt, and you let him slide with a promise to never do it again.

Then comes Valentine's Day . . . and he gives you a box of milk chocolates when he knows damn well that you love dark chocolate and can't stand milk chocolate. How dare he! All hell breaks loose: "You don't have to yell." "I will yell!" And you finally kick him and his milk chocolates out of the house.

Bush, Cheney, Ari Fleischer, Scott McClellan, Dana Perino, and the entire Bush media operation have been the political equivalent of a philandering husband and the media have been the compliant and silently suffering spouse, willing to put up with being lied to and cheated on again and again and again and again.

But as NBC's David Gregory demonstrated, they weren't about to accept goddamn milk chocolates on Valentine's Day.

As the Press Room Turns: Scott and David—A Lovers' Quarrel

The simmering tension between David Gregory and the hangdog White House press secretary Scott McClellan reached the boiling point on February 13, 2006. The setting was the morning press "gaggle," an informal briefing in which cameras are not permitted. Although Scott had deceived David about many things for many months, it was the administration's careful handling of the news that

Dick Cheney had shot a friend in the face that proved to be the last straw.

Here's the exchange between Scott McClellan and David Gregory:

Gregory: Don't be a jerk to me personally when I'm asking you a serious question.

McClellan: You don't have to yell.

Gregory: I will yell. If you want to use that podium to try to take shots at me personally, which I don't appreciate, then I will raise my voice, because that's wrong.

McClellan: Calm down, Dave, calm down.

Gregory: I'll calm down when I feel like calming down!

The day after:

Gregory: I'm not getting answers here, Scott, and I'm trying to be forthright with you, but don't tell me that you're giving us complete answers when you're not actually answering the question, because everybody knows what is an answer and what is not an answer.

McClellan: David, now you want to make this about you, and it's not about you, it's about what happened. . . .

Gregory: I'm sorry that you feel that way, but that's not what I'm trying to do.

Yes, there it is: The Day (or Two Days) the Press Fought Back. It was a brief golden moment brought about by a trivial dispute over a silly story but it did offer a glimpse of how different things might have been.

A Mine Collapses, the Media Misses the Story

Like firefighters, police officers, and SWAT teams, reporters often have to scramble to react to tragic breaking news. And while police and firefighters have to act quickly in order to save lives on the scene, it's the media's job to go beyond the immediate drama and figure out the context of a disaster—not just the exciting "color" of who died, and when, and how. Tragedies don't happen in a vacuum. The Crandall Canyon Mine collapse in Huntington, Utah, during the summer of 2007 was an object lesson in how *not* to bring perspective to a tragic event as it unfolds on the national stage. And it shows how the media let the bad guys off the hook over and over. At first, the story seemed like a run-of-the-mill industrial accident: six workers were trapped in the mine on August 6, 2007. On August 16, the story took a turn for the worse when a second collapse killed three rescuers and injured six others. None of the original six miners were ever rescued, and even before the second collapse took place, important questions about the safety of the mine were raised by those close to the operation.

A race against time is manna from heaven for the 24/7 news channels, who love to slap a ticking clock on just about anything (who can forget the nerve-racking countdown to Paris Hilton's release from prison?). The traditional media, with few exceptions, focused on only one aspect of the Crandall Canyon Mine tragedy—the desperate attempt to rescue the trapped miners—while paying scant attention to investigating the reasons these miners were trapped in the first place.

Case in point: an August 13, 2007, *New York Times* piece by Martin Stolz, who had been dispatched to Huntington to cover the story. Stolz's report was filled with details about the progress rescuers had made through the collapsed mine (650 feet), and the capabilities of the hi-res camera being lowered into the mine (it can pick up images from one hundred feet away)—but not one word about what led to the collapse, including the role the dangerous practice of retreat-mining might have played in it, or the 324 safety violations federal inspectors had issued for the mine since 2004.

The *Times* story, like most of the TV coverage, featured Bob Murray, the colorful co-owner of the mine. Stolz painted a picture of Murray emerging from the mine "with a coal-blackened face and in miner's coveralls to discuss the latest finding with the families of the missing miners."

Cue the swelling music and start the casting session. Your mind reflexively begins to wonder who would play Murray in the Crandall Canyon TV movie. Wilford Brimley? Robert Duvall? Paul Newman?

As it turned out, Murray's role in all this was much darker than the media conveyed as they stuck to the Compassionate Boss storyline and continued to quote his Hollywood-ready lines like, "Conditions are the most difficult I have seen in my fifty years of mining" and "There are many reasons to have hope still" (as he was quoted saying in two *Times* stories).

If the media had mined Murray's past a little more extensively, they would have learned that he was a politically connected Big Energy player whose company, Murray Energy Corp., has nineteen mines in five states that had incurred millions of dollars in fines for safety violations over the eighteen months before the collapse. And of the 324 violations, 107 were considered, in the words of a federal mine safety agency spokesman, "significant and substantial."

The media's infatuation with Murray gave him a chance to repeatedly air his theory that the mine collapse was the result of an earthquake—a claim disputed by seismologists at, among other places, the University of Utah and the University of California, Berkeley. Whenever Murray appeared on television the real explanation for what caused the Crandall Canyon Mine disaster was staring the media in the face, but they simply refused to see it.

So why was so much of the coverage focused on folksy Murray, the stalwart and kindly mine owner, instead of mining mogul Murray, who may have been at least partly responsible for decisions that led to the disaster?

It's because, as Jon Stewart has put it, one of the best ways to deal with members of the media is to show them a shiny object over here, which distracts them from investigating the real story over there. And the hopeful, coal-covered Murray was a very shiny object indeed. For the reporters and producers who hit the ground looking for a storyline—and who don't generally socialize in mining circles— Bob Murray fit a Frank Capra plot that was camera-ready. Murray was at the mine directing the rescue efforts himself. You don't usually see corporate kingpins with dirty fingernails. He must be a good guy.

The New York Times was repeatedly scooped by the *Salt Lake Tribune*, which uncovered a memo revealing that there had been serious structural problems at the Crandall Canyon Mine—in an area just nine hundred feet from the section of the mine that collapsed. The Associated Press also did much better than the paper of record. AP reporter Chris Kahn wrote about the role retreat-mining—"a sometimes dangerous mining technique that involves pulling out leftover sections and pillars of coal that hold up the roof of a mine"—might have played in the collapse.

Despite so many questions left unanswered about the mine's safety and the decisions the mine's owners made, the *Times* did story after story on the rescue effort without any reference to the possible causes of the original disaster. Indeed, *New York Times* readers—and shareholders—would have been better (much better) served if *Times* editors had spared the expense of sending reporters to Huntington and had just republished the reports from the *Salt Lake Tribune* and AP.

Not that the *Times* was alone. Most of the traditional media's coverage of the tragedy also tilted toward the shiny objects, causing them to neglect the issues that might help prevent yet another mine disaster, another desperate attempt to rescue another group of trapped miners, and more sloppy journalism.

So we continued to get cloying coverage like the segment on the August 13, 2007, edition of *Anderson Cooper 360°*. This is how Cooper introduced Murray: "He's really been the public face of this ordeal, keeping the families up to date—he meets with them once or twice a day—trying to explain the latest rescue efforts." And Murray got to go all aw shucks: "Mr. Cooper, I appreciate you having me on your program. And I appreciate the interest of all Americans in our tragedy."

But we got precious little on the Murray who had enough political muscle to get a Mine Safety and Health Administration district manager who had cracked down on safety issues at one of Murray's mines reassigned (contributing $213,000 to Republican candidates over the last ten years, as well as another $724,500 to Republican candidates and causes through political action committees connected to Murray's businesses, clearly has its benefits). Or the Murray who railed against the United Mine Workers of America, claiming it wants "to damage Murray Energy, Utah American and the United States coal industry for their own motives." Or the Murray who called Hillary Clinton "anti-American" for saying America needs a president who will fight for workers' rights, and told a Senate committee that Al Gore was bent on "the destruction of American lives and more death as a result of his hysterical global goofiness with no environmental benefit."

After the tragic second collapse at the mine, there was a dramatic shift in the TV coverage of the story. All at once, faux folksy mining boss Bob Murray, who had been everywhere, was nowhere to be found (even sending in a junior executive to handle the post–second collapse morning press conference). In his place, at long last, were actual scientists, and experts on mine safety and the workings of the Mine Safety and Health Administration. Richard Stickler, the head of that agency, was also absent the night of the second collapse.

At last the media were asking some tough questions. But that prompts several more: What took so long? Why did it take a tragic second collapse before the Murray and Stickler PR Show was replaced by actual journalism?

Why did it take until the morning after the second disaster for CNN to finally run a chyron saying "Safety of Rescue Operation Debated"? For twelve days, there was precious little debate about why the mine had collapsed in the first place, or about the safety of the rescue operation—which was, by law, in the hands of Stickler, another "heck of a job" Bush special, a coal industry insider who couldn't even win the approval of a GOP-controlled Senate and had to get his job through a recess appointment. And, by the way, "Debated"? With three rescuers dead, I think it was pretty clear that the rescue operation wasn't very safe. But by making it sound ambiguous, CNN managed to conceal the extent to which it had missed the story.

Coal miners, we are told, operate under a code similar to the Marines: no one gets left behind. So there is little doubt that the rescuers would have done everything in their power to try to save their fellow miners. But might the second tragedy have been avoided if the media watchdogs had been asking tougher questions from the start?

What if, instead of giving endless airtime to Bob Murray, they had brought on some legitimate experts and asked them questions about the chances of another collapse occurring? What if they had given us Professor Larry Grayson, who was interviewed after the second collapse by Dan Abrams on MSNBC and contradicted once and for all Murray's assertion that the company had not been doing retreat mining where the original collapse had occurred? What if they had gotten Stickler on the record on this, and had him definitely say whether or not Murray was lying when he repeatedly denied that the dangerous technique was being used in the Crandall Canyon Mine?

What if they gave as much airtime to the seismologists denying that the collapse was the result of an earthquake?

Might things have turned out differently? We'll never know. But we do know that a number of miners—perhaps as many as a dozen—had asked to be moved to a different part of the rescue operation out of fear for their safety. And that, according to the *Salt Lake Tribune*, Murray had abruptly pulled Bodee Allred, the Crandall Mine's safety director (and a cousin of one of the missing miners), away from the cameras when the questions Allred was being asked veered too close to the bone for Murray's comfort.

Here's a question for the media: since when do the owners of mines—especially owners who have been fined millions of dollars for numerous safety violations—set the news agenda?

Twelve days after the first collapse, with three heroic rescuers dead, six others injured, and the original six trapped miners almost certainly lost forever, Utah Governor Jon Huntsman finally suggested we "focus like never before on workplace safety."

Why wasn't the focus on workplace safety the focus of the media from Day One? With special attention being paid to the consequences of the Right's success at installing foxes to guard the henhouses?

It shouldn't have taken the deaths of three rescuers for those covering the story to have gotten that message.

In the weeks after the initial collapse, Congress launched a series of investigations into the Crandall Canyon disaster. Murray ignored an invitation to appear before a Senate panel in September 2007, and was later subpoenaed. But as of February 2008, Murray had yet to testify before Congress. Meanwhile the Labor Department was dragging its feet in complying with a request from a House committee for documents related to the disaster, and the Bush administration reappointed Stickler acting assistant secretary at the Mine Safety and Health Administration. And anyone wanting to follow the details of the aftermath of the Crandall Canyon disaster would have to dig into the Internet, since only the local press was providing any sort of follow-up reporting.

The national media missed the story, failed to follow up, and, finally, forgot about the whole thing altogether. Apparently, if you want to stay in the news spotlight, you have to disappear after a night of drinking in Aruba, not underground in a Utah coal mine.

Hurricane Katrina Blows Off the Front Page

The media's coverage of Hurricane Katrina demonstrates the same attention deficit disorder. Even though the media did a good job of capturing public outrage at the time, they quickly moved on, with Katrina becoming a news afterthought suitable for occasional anniversary pieces and ribbon-cutting video. And even at the time, the White House was able to use anonymous sources to sell its spin. The administration's strategy was to hang the post-Katrina debacle around the necks of Louisiana state and local officials and, in the process, erase its image of crass incompetence.

Hence the Presidential Visit to the Gulf, Take Two. Bush's flyover visit immediately following the disaster hadn't played so well. And those shots of him peeking out the window of Air Force One at flooded streets thousands of feet below were not helping the ol' approval rating. Indeed the flyover had been the perfect metaphor for his entire presidency: detached, disconnected, and disengaged. Preferring to take in America's suffering—whether caused by the war in Iraq or Hurricane Katrina—from a distance. So it was time for a retake with slightly better production values. You could just see Karl Rove yelling "Cut!," hopping out of his director's chair, pulling Bush aside, and whispering in his ear: "Okay, Mr. President, this isn't *Armageddon Meets Wedding Crashers*. So this time, 86 the stories about how you used to party in New Orleans, and, for heaven's sake, do not focus on the loss of Trent Lott's beachfront home in Mississippi and his blown-away porch. And no more hugging only freshly showered black people who look like Halle Berry—this time you gotta get a little closer to the stuck-in-the-Superdome-for-a-week crowd. All right . . . Action!"

Putting on a clean shirt (don't forget—no tie!) and standing in front of a scenic backdrop and then trying to save face by deflecting blame and sliming your enemies may be ugly, but it's straight out of the Rove playbook and has proven highly effective. Why? Because distracted, the media buy it every time. What didn't make sense was why the media continued to be star players on the Bush damage control team. Take the way that both *The Washington Post* and *Newsweek* obediently passed on—and thus gave credence to—the Bush party line that then Louisiana governor Kathleen Blanco's hesitancy to declare a state of emergency had prevented the feds from responding to the crisis more rapidly.

Anderson Cooper: Getting It Right

There were some dramatic interviews during the early coverage of Katrina that stand out as examples of the passion and moral outrage journalists could demonstrate a lot more of.

One of the most memorable came on September 1, 2005, when the extent of the devastation was beginning to become clear. Anderson Cooper confronted Senator Mary Landrieu, D-La., in a live interview:

Cooper: Joining me from Baton Rouge is Louisiana Senator Mary Landrieu. Senator, appreciate you joining us tonight. Does the federal government bear responsibility for what is happening now? Should they apologize for what is happening now?

Landrieu: Anderson, there will be plenty of time to discuss all of those issues, about why, and how, and what, and if. But, Anderson, as you understand, and all of the producers and directors of CNN, and the news networks, this situation is very serious and it's going to demand all of our full attention through the hours, through the nights, through the days.

Let me just say a few things. I thank President Clinton and former President Bush for their strong statements of support and comfort today. I thank all the leaders that are coming to Louisiana, and Mississippi, and Alabama to our help and rescue.

We are grateful for the military assets that are being brought to bear. I want to thank Senator Frist and Senator Reid for their extraordinary efforts.

Anderson, tonight, I don't know if you've heard—maybe you all have announced it—but Congress is going to an unprecedented session to pass a $10 billion supplemental bill tonight to keep FEMA and the Red Cross up and operating.

Cooper: Excuse me, Senator, I'm sorry for interrupting. I haven't heard that, because, for the last four days, I've been seeing dead bodies in the streets here in Mississippi. And to listen to politicians thanking each other and complimenting each other, you know, I got to tell you, there are a lot of people here who are very upset, and very angry, and very frustrated.

And when they hear politicians slap—you know, thanking one another, it just, you know, it kind of cuts them the wrong way right now, because literally there was a body on the streets of this town yesterday being eaten by rats because this woman had been laying in the street for 48 hours. And there's not enough facilities to take her up.

Do you get the anger that is out here?

Landrieu: Anderson, I have the anger inside of me. Most of the homes in my family have been destroyed. Our homes have been destroyed. I understand what you're saying, and I know all of those details. And the president of the United States knows those details.

Cooper: Well, who are you angry at?

Landrieu: I'm not angry at anyone. I'm just expressing that it is so important for everyone in this nation to pull together, for all military assets and all assets to be brought to bear in this situation.

And I have every confidence that this country is as great and as strong as we can be to do that. And that effort is under way.

Cooper: Well, I mean, there are a lot of people here who are kind of ashamed of what is happening in this country right now, what is—ashamed of what is happening in your state, certainly.

And that's not to blame the people who are there. It's a desperate situation. But I guess, you know, who can—I mean, no one seems to be taking responsibility.

I mean, I know you say there's a time and a place for, kind of, you know, looking back, but this seems to be the time and place. I mean, there are people who want answers, and there are people who want someone to stand up and say, "You know what? We should have done more."

The unquestioning regurgitation of administration spin through the use of anonymous sources is the major fault line of modern American journalism. You'd think that after all we've seen—from the gullible reporting on WMD to Judy Miller and Plamegate (to say nothing of all the endless navel-gazing media panel discussions analyzing the issue)—the media would finally get a clue and stop making the Journalism 101 mistake of granting anonymity to administration sources out to smear their opponents.

After the media caravan moved on, both the struggle to rebuild New Orleans and the quest for accountability went largely ignored. In December 2005, only four months after the storm, the New Orleans *Times-Picayune* reported that documents dating from 1990 showed that the Army Corps of Engineers had questioned the design of the 17th Street Canal floodwall. But as Harry Shearer pointed out in multiple posts on *The Huffington Post*, the media had given up on the search for accountability.

The Right's Horror Double Feature: Conventional Wisdom and Zombie Lies

The mainstream media's tendency to buy into certain myths has shaped the way the 2008 presidential candidates are viewed. Dateline: December 27, 2007, the day of Benazir Bhutto's assassination. Immediately the media, as if they had all been on a conference call, started mouthing the same frothy bromides about the possible benefit that chaos in Pakistan might have for the various candidates. The conventional wisdom about the war in Iraq came back from the ash heap of history, validating the absurd media conceit that the more wrong you were about Iraq, the more credibility your opinion has about anything having to do with terrorism, the Middle East, Islam, and national security.

Accordingly, the media had it that the main "beneficiaries" of the turmoil in Pakistan were Rudy Giuliani, who had yet to utter a critical word about the Bush strategy in the Middle East, and Hillary Clinton, the Democratic candidate who took the longest to separate herself from that strategy. The public, at least, didn't accept the conventional wisdom. Giuliani was out of the race before Super Tuesday, having spent almost $60 million to capture a single delegate. And Hillary Clinton's position on Iraq continued to be an albatross during the campaign.

You might think that the one positive thing to have come out of the Bhutto tragedy would have been the opportunity to question not only our strategy in Iraq, Pakistan, and Afghanistan but the conventional wisdom that gave rise to this strategy and continues to sustain it.

But you would be wrong. Because the prevailing narrative about most of George Bush's foreign policy is composed largely of what the blogger Atrios calls "zombie lies." They cannot be stopped. For a moment or two, it may seem like you've killed them, but back they come over the horizon. Again and again and again.

One of the biggest zombie lies about our national security is that our disastrous invasion of Iraq exists in a bubble and has nothing to do with events in other countries in the region—like Pakistan. Another zombie lie is that the people who supported this catastrophic enterprise are the ones best qualified to decide how to clean up the mess they helped create. Hey, no one ever said zombies are logical— just relentless.

But to even raise this point is an invitation to be attacked by the conventional wisdom zombies. They thrive on linking individual zombie lies to form zombie lie theories, zombie lie explanations, and zombie lie arguments. They can all be easily disproved but not easily defeated. Challenging them is like covering yourself with chum and diving into shark-infested waters.

Just ask Barack Obama's campaign adviser David Axelrod. In response to being asked if the Bhutto assassination would benefit Hillary, he told reporters: "She was a strong supporter of the war in Iraq, which, we would submit, was one of the reasons why we were diverted from Afghanistan, Pakistan and al Qaeda, who may have been players in this event today, so that's a judgment she'll have to defend."

Who could possibly consider this a controversial statement?

The Clinton campaign, for starters. Its spokesman Jay Carson shot back with: "This is a time to be focused on the tragedy of the situation, its implications for the U.S. and the world, and to be concerned for the people of Pakistan and the country's stability. No one should be politicizing this situation with baseless allegations." With all the solemn disappointment at the terrible bad taste of Axelrod's remarks, you'd think he'd accused Hillary Clinton of killing Bhutto herself. In fact all he had done was to tell the truth: that Clinton had been a strong supporter of the Iraq war and that the Iraq war has caused us to take our eye off the ball in a critically important and unstable part of the world.

So how was hazarding the opinion that the Iraq war had diverted us from Pakistan and Afghanistan and suggesting that Hillary Clinton should have to defend her judgment to support that war "politicizing" the situation? She was running for president, wasn't she? Of course questions about what happened in Pakistan, what factors contributed to it, and what we should do about it are politicized—as they should be, since the policy we eventually embark on will be decided politically.

It's no secret why the arbiters of conventional wisdom get so defensive when these kinds of questions are raised: their opinions helped lead to the war in Iraq, so anytime the conventional wisdom is threatened, they rise in its defense. They'd rather keep us all locked in the same paradigm, where the mistakes they made could have been made by any reasonable person.

Exhibit A came during Barack Obama's appearance on *Meet the Press* on December 30, 2007. Tim Russert, one of the temple guards of conventional wisdom, used one of the classic weapons in its defense: the straw man. So in asking Obama about Axelrod's comments, Russert played dumb-dumb and twisted the argument:

> **Russert:** *The Washington Post* has said in an editorial that Mr. Obama committed a foul in some of your comments and some of your staff comments to the situation in Pakistan, specifically—let me ask you a question—do you believe that Senator Clinton's vote for, for the war in Iraq in any way, shape or form led to the events that transpired in Pakistan on Thursday?

Obama knocked the straw man down and gave *The Washington Post* a kick in the ribs while he was at it.

> **Obama:** Of course not, and that's never what any of my aides said . . . my staff said that I think candidates will be judged based on the judgments they have made, and they made then an indisputable, I believe, comment, although *The Washington Post*, I think, may disagree with this. And that is that, by going into Iraq, we got distracted from Afghanistan, we got distracted

from hunting down bin Laden, we got distracted from dealing with the al Qaeda havens that have been created in northwestern Pakistan. . . .

Russert, the conventional wisdom zombie, kept ambling forward.

Russert: But a vote for the war in Iraq, in your mind, distracted us from Pakistan and that could have led to the situation?

Obama took another stab:

Obama: I am not drawing a causal relationship between any single vote and the tragedy there. The tragedy resulted from a suicide bomber. But what I do believe is that, if we are going to take seriously the problem of Islamic terrorism and the stability of Pakistan, then we have to look at it in a wider context. What we do in Iraq matters, what we do with respect to Iran matters, what we do with respect to [President] Musharraf matters and not giving him a blank check and conditioning military aid that's not related to terrorism on him opening up the election so that there's greater legitimacy and less anti-American sentiment in Pakistan. Those are all parts of a broader foreign policy, and I believe that I'm best equipped to chart that new direction in foreign policy that will ultimately make America safer.

The Will Smith character in *I, Robot* couldn't have blown away that zombie any more effectively. But make no mistake, it will be back. The news media are more hooked on sequels than Hollywood. Once they've got a compelling storyline, they stick with it, hoping that it will bring blockbuster returns every time.

And this is how the conventional wisdom is able to come back to life no matter how often it seems to have been mortally wounded by some event.

RussertWatch! Or Russert Interruptus: Tim Russert Can't Follow Through

The reason the conventional wisdom survives no matter how many times its lies are exposed is that shows like *Meet the Press* allow their guests to go unchallenged. Starting on May 22, 2005, soon after launching *The Huffington Post*, we began a regular feature called RussertWatch, in which I did just that: watch Tim Russert. Week after week, I watched as he interviewed members of the Washington establishment—and week after week, I watched the conventional wisdom survive unscathed. Here are a few examples of how the game is played, and why it's not just Fox News that's responsible for the Right hijacking America.

On June 6, 2005, *Meet the Press* featured Ken Mehlman, then chairman of the Republican National Committee. It was another classic example of why host Tim Russert has become journalism's answer to the EZ Pass, those electronic tags that allow drivers to go through toll booths without having to stop. On the show, Mehlman was allowed to distort, twist, manipulate, obfuscate, and disssemble his way through every stop on the disinformation highway.

The key to the EZ Pass method is no follow-ups—or lame follow-ups quickly abandoned. And Mehlman is a master at dealing with those. His technique? Just repeat or slightly rephrase his talking point, and trust that Russert will give up, wave him on, and proceed to the next prepared question.

To see a master in action, let's go to the transcript.

Early in the interview, Russert asked Mehlman whether "the president has hit a wall with his domestic agenda. . . . What's the problem?"

The RNC chair danced around the question so deftly his moves should be taught by Soulja Boy: "Tim, I don't think there's a problem," he responded, and then promptly changed the subject to Ronald Reagan before closing with an RNC commercial: "Before we provided prescription drugs for Medicare, we were told it wasn't going to happen. Before the president was able to move forward with No Child Left Behind, we were told it was stalled. We just passed class-action reform for the first time in six years and that, too, was predicted not to happen."

If Russert had been doing his job, he would have countered with some well-established problems with these three accomplishments: the Medicare prescription drug plan was promised to cost under $400 billion over ten years but now stands at $1.2 trillion (and, in a stunning giveaway to the drug industry, the government gets no bulk purchasing discount); the No Child Left Behind Act has been such a massively underfunded disaster that twenty-one states were at the time considering legislation to get out of it; and the class-action "reform" will just make it harder for injured people to get a fair day in court.

But EZ Pass Russert mentioned none of the above. Instead, he waved Mehlman through and moved on to stem cell research, about which Mehlman said: "This is the first administration ever that has funded with federal dollars embryonic stem cell research."

Did Russert bother to point out that this is not much of a claim since this is the first administration that ever *could* have funded embryonic stem cell research because the science is so new? Of course not. Mehlman was in the GOP Express Lane. No need to slow down for little things like facts. Move right along.

Russert actually allowed Mehlman to get away with saying, "So you have an administration that is unprecedented in our commitment to more scientific research," without offering a spit take, a rim shot, or a "Please, Ken, not even I can let you slide on that one!"

Russert then switched to his pet interrogatory method: asking his guest for a reaction to a pointed quote from someone else—in this case, former Republican Senator John Danforth: "By a series of recent initiatives, Republicans have transformed our party into the political arm of conservative Christians. . . . As a senator, I worried every day about the size of the federal deficit. I did not spend a single minute worrying about the effect of gays on the institution of marriage. Today it seems to be the other way around."

Mehlman bypassed the criticism altogether, leaving Danforth in his rearview mirror with a condescending, "I think he's a good man. I would respectfully disagree with that." And Russert let him get away without even attempting to answer a serious charge from a senior member of his own party.

And on and on Mehlman rolled . . . on issue after issue after issue.

On the deficit, he followed the administration's standard "In An Emergency Break Glass" procedure and sought refuge in 9/11: "Well, Tim, I would say that what we've suffered, unfortunately, was an attack on this country."

When asked about the Downing Street Memo, which showed that Bush was determined to go to war almost a year before the invasion, Mehlman fell back on an out-and-out fabrication: "Tim, that report has been discredited by everyone else who's looked at it since then."

Russert actually managed a follow-up on this whopper: "I don't believe that the authenticity of this report has been discredited."

But Mehlman just flashed his EZ Pass again: "I believe that the findings of the report, the fact that the intelligence was somehow fixed have been totally discredited by everyone who's looked at it."

And so Mehlman cruised on through. And, returning to form, Bulldog Russert just gave up.

The interview eventually turned to football star Pat Tillman, who gave up a lucrative NFL contract to enlist in the army after 9/11, and the fact that Tillman's family was deeply offended by the Pentagon's lies regarding the circumstances of their son's death in Afghanistan and its attempt to make him a poster child to sell the war.

Mehlman responded by saying that he "respectfully disagrees" with Tillman's mother.

In fact, Mehlman said he "respectfully disagrees" a total of seven times over the course of the interview. Sometimes he respectfully disagreed with people, sometimes with a report, sometimes with numbers. Mostly, he respectfully disagreed with the truth.

But there was something about the way Mehlman said it that made him come off like a prissy doorman. You know that when he says "I respectfully disagree" he really means "Fuck off."

"Ken Mehlman," Russert intoned in closing, "we hope you'll come back."

And, given the obliging treatment he got, of course he'll accept the invite.

On January 15, 2006, Russert devoted the program to one of his favorite tasks: promoting someone's self-laudatory memoir.

We all know the drill: an administration official leaves and writes a book promising some "bombshell" revelations that he or she couldn't reveal while still on the inside, a few of these explosive revelations are leaked before publication to prime the PR pump, and then a book tour follows, with the author making the talk show rounds.

Paul Bremer, former U.S. administrator of Iraq and author of *My Year in Iraq: The Struggle to Build a Future of Hope* (which got my vote for least ambitious subtitle of the year), is a perfect example.

The problem was that (a) his revelations turned out to be not all that revelatory, and (b) on his book tour in general, and on *Meet the Press* in particular, he ran away from even these watered-down revelations.

The only utility of such books—since it's clearly not the writing—is to get closer to the truth about history as it's happening. But if you're just going to parrot the spin of the administration you are no longer part of, well, we can get that from the administration for free, thanks very much.

What made Bremer's appearance on *Meet the Press* particularly troubling is that although Russert challenged Bremer on a few points, he refused to acknowledge the big elephant in the room—that Bremer's "memoir" was a complete sham. If he's not prepared to tell the truth, why is our time being wasted with more half-truths, and why did Tim act as though this "insider's perspective" remotely passed the smell test? He might as well have infamous fabricator James Frey on to discuss his "insider's account" of running Iraq. (And, actually, *A Million Little Pieces* would be a far better title for Bremer's book than *My Year in Iraq*.)

Here's how Simon & Schuster sold the book (emphasis mine):

- The only senior **insider's perspective** on the crucial period following the collapse of Saddam Hussein's regime. In vivid, dramatic detail, Bremer reveals the

- **previously hidden** struggles among Iraqi politicians and America's leaders.

- His memoir carries the reader **behind closed doors** in Baghdad.

- He describes his **private meetings with President Bush**.

Turns out that Bremer's "insider's account" was remarkably similar to the account we'd all witnessed from the outside.

For instance: one of Bremer's bombshell revelations was that he knew even before he arrived in Iraq that we needed more troops. Wow. What a bombshell. Thanks, Paul. So did everyone else in the world except Don Rumsfeld.

The other big juicy detail his buzz machine touted was that Rumsfeld ignored a memo Bremer sent him before heading to Iraq in which he drew the defense secretary's attention to a draft RAND report on postwar stability that suggested the need for 500,000 ground troops. But here was Bremer's attempt to back away from even this "revelation":

Bremer: Well, first of all, this was a report, as I said, that I saw before I went to Iraq, before I saw the situation on the ground. And as you—your excerpt just showed what I did basically was send it forward to Secretary Rumsfeld and say "take a look at this." We didn't discuss that report specifically, we had a lot of discussions over the next fourteen months that I was there about my concerns about maintaining combat capability along the lines I already explained.

Russert: But Rumsfeld didn't respond to you.

Bremer: Well, he responded in the sense that we talked often— very often, about this question of maintaining combat capability.

Russert: But you make a point of saying, you're making a point of saying he didn't respond.

Bremer: Well, I'm making a point he didn't respond but I left for Iraq two days later, three days later.

Well, that explains everything. Rumsfeld sent his reply UPS and Bremer had to be in Iraq from twelve to four on the day of the third delivery attempt, so he never got it. Another lesson learned from the war: Mail Boxes Etc. And another bombshell turned out to be a wet firecracker.

But Tim left unasked the big questions like: "What the hell happened to the $9 billion earmarked for Iraqi reconstruction that the Coalition Provisional Authority you headed can't account for?"

And what about that week's true bombshell, the decision by Abdul Aziz al-Hakim, Iraq's most influential Shiite leader, to renege on his pledge to amend the new constitution in a manner acceptable to Sunnis—a decision that brought the country much closer to full-scale civil war?

Here is the delusional answer Tim let Bremer get away with: "They will have to make some modest changes in this constitution coming up and put together a government of national unity, and I think they'll do that."

Great, thanks, Paul. We'll keep an eye out for that. There you have it. An insider bringing all his wisdom to bear on a thorny problem!

But just because Bremer wrote a book full of spin and half-truths, and Simon & Schuster tried to sell it, doesn't mean the mainstream media, like *Meet the Press*, have to so willingly accept their role in the book promotion's dog-and-pony show—especially when matters of war and the country's national security are involved.

On *Meet the Press* on February 26, 2006, it was Meet the Republicans. Russert's well-rounded lineup included Republican Senator John Warner,

Republican Congressman Peter King, and Republican Governor Arnold Schwarzenegger. Perhaps the phone lines were down on the other side of the political divide.

It was not only the partisan imbalance that was troubling. It was the fact that with Iraq heading toward civil war, we were in greater need than usual of a guest—or two—who actually knew something about Iraq and was able to talk about it in something other than RNC clichés. Isn't contempt for real knowledge and expertise what got us into this mess in the first place?

In the first segment, the only civil war Tim's guests seemed concerned with was the one within the Republican Party. The "debate" featured Warner as Chief White House Water-Carrier, and King comically trying to, on the one hand, express opposition to the White House on the Dubai Ports World deal, which would let the United Arab Emirates company run key U.S. seaports and, on the other hand, remind Bush how much he's still in the club. But King found out the hard way what happens when you question Bush—he turns around and questions not your facts but your motives.

> **King:** When the president suggests that people are questioning this because it's an Arab nation or because it's a Muslim nation . . . that was wrong. And nobody has more regard for President Bush. I've supported him down the line, but on this issue it's really wrong. And I thought it was inappropriate to say that a person like myself—who lost over 150 friends, neighbors and constituents on September 11—is questioning the United Arab Emirates because of its past record, and instead implying that I'm doing it because they're Arabs and Muslims. That's wrong. There are real issues here, and the White House should realize it.

It wasn't so much fun having your motives questioned, Mr. King, was it? Where were you when the same was happening to Vietnam veterans Max Cleland and Jack Murtha?

And then there was Warner parading his concern for our standing in the Arab world without ever once being questioned by Russert about a few other incidents that have done a lot more damage to our standing in the Arab world than the cancellation of the UAE port deal would, like the abuse of prisoners at Abu Ghraib and Guantánamo, or the story in that morning's *New York Times* that the United States was expanding a prison in Afghanistan to slowly take the place of Guantánamo—a prison that, according to the *Times*, would hold prisoners in "more primitive conditions, indefinitely and without charges." But, in fairness to Russert, that story was hidden on the front page of the *Times*, above the fold.

Since Tim was apparently unable to reach any Democrats to be on the show, he decided to channel them: "I—gentlemen, the Democrats have—are saying very loudly that they have tried repeatedly to put more money into port security."

King's non-answer isn't even worth going into, but it's notable that Tim's channeling skills were put to use only on the port issue, and not the war, where the lameness of his booking choices became even starker.

Instead of hearing from someone who could actually elucidate what was going on in Iraq, we got this:

Warner: I believe that there is not at this time the civil war that one would envision that meets the traditional definitions.

That kind of expert insight from the head of the Armed Services Committee was no doubt of major comfort to the parents of soldiers in Iraq. But it got worse:

Warner:: We have trained two-hundred-some-odd-thousand of these forces today. There's a hundred battalions of Iraqi military. Over fifty of those battalions are able to take the lead in a fight with minimal U.S. support. So there's in place today, I think, sufficient military under the control of the Iraqis with certain limited support from us.

You might think that Tim immediately countered with the previous day's news that the number of Iraqi battalions fully capable of operating without the Americans had gone from one to zero. But of course he didn't. Instead he went into a prepared question for King. Indeed, if Tim knew anything about this fairly major story, he kept it carefully hidden.

We may have learned exactly nothing about the war on this particular show, but one thing came through: we were making great progress in shifting blame to the Iraqi government. "You've got to get your act together" was Warner's admonition to them.

But that was only half the show. Then came an interview with Arnold Schwarzenegger.

Russert: Do you think the Iraq war was a mistake?

Schwarzenegger: No, I think it's always easy in hindsight to go and say maybe if we wouldn't have gone in, we wouldn't have had all this hassle.

All this "hassle"? I know English is Arnold's and my second language, but couldn't he come up with a better word than "hassle" to describe the carnage going on in Iraq? "Headache," perhaps?

On January 8, 2006, I was almost looking forward to *Meet the Press*. It had been a big week. The party in charge of the White House, the House, and the Senate was in meltdown. Tom DeLay had resigned his position as House majority leader less than twenty-four hours before Tim Russert went on the air. One GOP House member had already been indicted (and wore a wire), and there were reports that another, Bob Ney, would soon join the mug shot gallery.

The guests in the first segment: Senators John Cornyn, a Republican, and Chuck Schumer, a Democrat.

And, sure enough, Tim opened the show with the Jack Abramoff lobbying scandal. So what did he choose to focus on? This: will Nevada Democratic Senator Harry Reid return the contributions he's received—not from Jack Abramoff himself, mind you, but from three Indian tribes and from members of Abramoff's former lobbying firm? Go get 'em, Tim! Some might look at the events of that week and decide that the story lay somewhere in the intersection between the Republican Party and the culture of corruption. But not Tim. He knew the real story was whether Harry Reid would return the loot.

That kind of editorial judgment is no doubt why, according to his bio at MSNBC.com, Tim isn't just the moderator of *Meet the Press* but also its "managing editor," as well as the "senior vice president" and "Washington bureau chief" of NBC News, and a "political analyst" for *NBC Nightly News*.

DeLay? Abramoff? Ney? They barely managed a mention from the managing editor. Even a conservative like David Brooks would have done better in the moderator's seat. "I don't know what's more pathetic," Brooks wrote in his *New York Times* column at the time. "Jack Abramoff's sleaze or Republican paralysis in the face of it. Abramoff walks out of a D.C. courthouse in his pseudo-Hasidic homburg, and all that leading Republicans can do is promise to return his money and remind everyone that some Democrats are involved in the scandal, too."

It may not have cleaned up Washington, but if there's one thing the Abramoff affair did, it separated the shills for business as usual from the super-shills for business as usual.

The classic *MTP* moment came a few minutes later, when Tim played one of his "gotcha" clips for Chuck Schumer. Here is the exchange:

Russert: Senator Schumer, back in 2001 you wrote a letter to President Bush and you said this: "The [American Bar Association] evaluation has been the gold standard by which judicial candidates are judged." Gold standard.

Schumer: Yes.

Russert: And now we have this from the ABA: "Samuel A. Alito Jr. (nominated 11/10/05), to be an associate justice to the U.S. Supreme Court. Rating: 'Well qualified' by unanimous vote of the standing committee" of the ABA. It's the gold standard. He's rated well qualified. Game, set, match.

Game, set, match? A good choice of metaphor, helping, as it does, to clear up any remaining doubt about how the Beltway Blowhards regard even a Supreme Court nomination as just a game. It's all just more grist for their (if I may change game metaphors) fantasy football league Sunday beer brunch.

To the country, this is serious stuff—whether a guy gets to sit on the Supreme Court for life and interpret laws we all have to live under. So we are not quite ready to call "game, set, match" on the direction the country is going to take because of something Chuck Schumer once said about the ABA.

The show's last segment featured James Risen, the *New York Times* reporter who broke the story of Bush's illegal spying, and the author of *State of War: The Secret History of the CIA and the Bush Administration*. I was curious to see whether Russert would ask Risen about the question Andrea Mitchell posed to him regarding the NSA's possible spying on CNN's Christiane Amanpour. Nope. No mention. Thus keeping Russert's nearly perfect record of covering up for himself and his friends intact. Game. Set. Match.

3

The Media: Snoozers, Losers, and the Honor Roll

How Wrong Do You Have to Be to Get Kicked Out of the Media?

Proving the conventional wisdom that those who were the most wrong about Iraq should be listened to most fervently about how to go forward, Bill Kristol was given a weekly column in *The New York Times*—the "paper of record."

William Kristol is neoconservatism's crown prince. The son of one of the movement's founders, Irving Kristol, Bill Kristol is less of a journalist and more of a spokesman. And despite the fact that some of his pronouncements on Iraq have been so laughable that you'd expect to hear them from Billy Crystal, he's still the person the media go to when they want to know what conservatives are thinking.

Kristol is a founder of the Project for the New American Century, which helped spawn the Iraq war. His editorials in *The Weekly Standard* often seem to be inserted directly into the president's speeches, and he once boasted that "Dick Cheney does send over someone to pick up thirty copies [of *The Weekly Standard*] every Monday." He was hired by the *Times* at the end of 2007 after having written earlier in the year the single most deceptive story of the entire war. And that's a pretty high bar.

The charitable view at the time was that he'd lost his mind. The less charitable view was that he'd officially surpassed Dick Cheney as the most intellectually dishonest member of the neocon establishment (the highest of all high bars). Kristol's truth-shattering piece appeared July 15, 2007, on the front page of *The Washington Post*'s Outlook section. It was entitled "Why Bush Will Be a Winner."

I had had a preview of this deluded triumphalist drivel a couple of days earlier—on a Thursday afternoon specifically. Even more specifically on the 4:00 P.M. Amtrak Acela from New York to Washington.

Kristol was sitting a row behind me, talking on his cell phone with someone who apparently shared his optimism. " 'Precipitous withdrawal' really worked," I overheard him say, clearly referring to the president's use of the term in a July 12 press conference. "How many times did he use it? Three? Four?" he asked the person on the other end of his call, and the conversation continued with a round of back-slapping for the clever phrase they had "come up with."

I, of course, have no idea who Kristol was talking to. White House press secretary Tony Snow, perhaps? After all, he and Kristol were colleagues before Snow left Fox for the White House. But whoever it was, the emphasis during their conversation on the significance of the "clever" phrase was emblematic of the White House prepping of the president.

Instead of sending their boss out with the real facts or logical arguments, Bush's aides and their friends (see Kristol) concoct some nonsense phrase in the spin lab centrifuge, hand it to him, and tell him to go out there and repeat it as often as he can. The flavor à la mode that summer was "precipitous withdrawal." It was the new "cut and run." And it was actually not all that new. Back in November 1969, Richard Nixon used it again and again in his famous "Silent Majority" speech: "The precipitate withdrawal of American forces from Vietnam would be a disaster not only for South Vietnam but for the United States and for the cause of peace." Over and over throughout the speech, Nixon used the phrase to paint the nightmarish consequences of a "precipitate withdrawal" from Vietnam. Almost forty years later, George Bush used the slightly tweaked "precipitous withdrawal" to paint his own nightmarish scenario of what would happen if American forces were to leave Iraq. And for that, apparently, we had Bill Kristol to thank. At least partially.

In an interview with *New York Times* writer David Carr in March 2003, Kristol displayed the same puckish glee about the Right's takeover that I would hear in his voice four years later on the Acela. "I'm a little amused but pleased," he said to Carr, "that the bus has become more crowded and that it is headed in the right direction." Well, the bus is a lot less crowded today—and a lot more dilapidated. But Kristol remains as confident as ever that he and Cheney and their other neocon friends are still steering it in the right direction.

It is truly incredible that, at this late date in the Iraq debacle, there are still people who believe that a few well-focus-grouped phrases will change the tragic facts on the ground. And that the media are not only letting them get away with it but rewarding the spinmeisters with a weekly column in the venerable Gray Lady.

My chance encounter on the Amtrak was a glimpse into their thinking. Kristol's famous *Washington Post* piece was the entire Bush-era conservative brain laid bare.

It wasn't a pretty sight. In fact, *The Washington Post* should have put some kind of warning on the piece for pregnant women, heart patients, and anyone with an allergy to bullshit.

I'll take it in order, focusing on national security.

After allowing that the Iraq war had been "difficult," Kristol wrote that "we now seem to be on course to a successful outcome."

Not only did he give no evidence for this, and not only did he ignore all the overwhelmingly contradictory evidence, he also conveniently neglected to even define what a "successful outcome" would be.

Then came an onslaught of lies about Afghanistan:

"The war in Afghanistan has gone reasonably well."

Afghanistan is, in fact, teetering on the precipice of chaos. Indeed, 2007 saw the highest number of coalition deaths there since the war began. The next highest before that? 2006. The Taliban is making a comeback, opium production is booming (up 17 percent in 2007), and unrest among Afghans is growing. Obviously, Kristol's definition of "reasonably well" is very different from most people's.

Then he moved on to Pakistan, where, Kristol admitted, "al-Qaeda may once again have a place where it can plan, organize and train." But, according to the National Intelligence Estimate, there was no "may" about it, and this was not a future possibility, but a current reality. And, in what is unequivocally one of the greatest failures of the Bush administration, a National Counterterrorism report concluded that al Qaeda was "better positioned" to "strike the West" than at any time since 9/11.

But no worries, because, according to Kristol, "These Waziristan havens [in mountainous Pakistan] will have to be dealt with in the near future. I assume Bush will deal with them, using some combination of air strikes and special operations."

Hear that? We were apparently just going to sort of casually start bombing our ally Pakistan. That's the sort of thing that would make me nervous if I thought Kristol had any pull with the White House. Oh, wait . . .

Then on to Iraq. Just imagine what would have happened if we hadn't gone in: "Saddam Hussein would be alive and in power and, I dare say, victorious."

Victorious? What does that mean? This, according to Kristol: "He might well have restarted his nuclear program, and his connections with al-Qaeda and other terrorist groups would be intact or revived and even strengthened."

Ah, yes, that old, completely discredited warhorse, the Saddam–al Qaeda connection, rides again. That'll no doubt be high on the set list if Kristol and Cheney are still touring with BushMania in 2012.

Then, putting aside his future delusions, Kristol treated us to his victory lap: "We are routing al-Qaeda in Iraq, we are beginning to curb the Iranian-backed sectarian Shiite militias and we are increasingly able to protect more of the Iraqi population."

Actually, a growing percentage of the Iraqi population is no longer even in Iraq. According to a Reuters report, since we invaded Iraq, around two million Iraqis have left the country, with another two million still there, but having fled their homes.

But Kristol was just warming up. "Political progress is beginning to follow," he added.

Preposterous. What "political progress" was he talking about? Even President Bush's own "mixed bag" interim report on the benchmarks had found little or no positive movement on political goals.

So how did Kristol propose we keep this great success going?

"It would help if the administration would make its case more effectively and less apologetically."

In other words: they should be repeating more of the clever phrases he was sending over to them.

Also: "It would help if Bush had more aides who believed in his policy, who understood that the war is winnable and who didn't desperately want to get back in (or stay in) the good graces of the foreign policy establishment" (i.e., more people like Kristol).

"If the president," Kristol concluded, "stands with [General] Petraeus and progress continues on the ground, Bush will be able to prevent a sellout in Washington."

What did he mean by "a sellout"? Was he already dusting off the stabbed-in-the-back theory from Vietnam: that, of course, we could have won, if only the soldiers hadn't been stabbed in the back by the media and antiwar liberals?

Kristol had plans for the next president too: "Following through to secure the victory in Iraq and to extend its benefits to neighboring countries will be the task of the next president."

Extend its benefits? Hear that, 2008 GOP presidential candidates? Bill Kristol thinks you should run on a platform of "I pledge to take what we did in Iraq to even more countries around the world."

For Kristol, "What it comes down to is this: If Petraeus succeeds in Iraq, and a Republican wins in 2008, Bush will be viewed as a successful president. I like the odds."

I'll take that bet, Bill, and will continue reading you every week in *The New York Times*. The problem for the *Times* is that Bill Kristol was a prime mover in the war, he lied repeatedly about it, and he's been discredited over and over. He's not a responsible conservative or even a responsible anything. The *Times* might as well have given a column to Jayson Blair.

Trying to Win the War on Words

Kristol shares the Bush White House belief that if you win the war on words, you win the war. So in the fall of 2005 the Bush administration decided to stop using the words "insurgency" and "insurgent" to describe those fighting U.S. forces in Iraq.

Donald Rumsfeld said during a Defense Department news briefing on November 29 that "over the weekend" he'd had "an epiphany" that "this is a group of people who don't merit the word 'insurgency.' "

President Bush apparently had the same epiphany because in his big speech on Iraq the next day, he went to great pains to rebrand the enemy as "a combination of rejectionists, Saddamists, and terrorists." Indeed, he uttered "insurgents" only one time in the entire speech— and even then it was when quoting an American lieutenant colonel (who apparently had been too busy training Iraqi troops in Tikrit to have time for weekend vocabulary epiphanies).

So in the middle of a whole lot of the same tired rhetoric we'd heard before ("September 11," "as Iraqi security forces stand up, coalition forces can stand down," "we will never back down, we will never give in"), here came the president's latest "Plan for Victory in Iraq": win the war on words.

Who says Bush's only strategy was to "stay the course"? Not true. In previous big speeches, the administration had set out to dazzle the media with impressive-sounding numbers (inconsistent with the numbers coming from its own field commanders) about the rapid growth of Iraqi forces. In November 2005, they switched the focus to improved terminology. It was Victory Through Vocabulary!

So "insurgents" were out and "rejectionists, Saddamists, and terrorists" were in. Here's how the president broke down the new lexicon:

Rejectionists were "ordinary Iraqis, mostly Sunni Arabs" who "reject an Iraq in which they're no longer the dominant group." According to Bush, rejectionists made up "by far the largest" portion of "the enemy."

Saddamists were former Saddam loyalists who "still harbor dreams of returning to power." This group was "smaller" than the rejectionists "but more determined."

And the terrorists? Well, they were the ones who "share the same ideology as the terrorists who struck the United States on September 11" . . . the ones "responsible for most of the suicide bombings and the beheadings and the other atrocities we've seen on our television." While Bush called them "the smallest" of the enemy groups, they are still clearly the president's favorite: he mentioned "terrorists" forty-two times in his speech, compared with the five times he mentioned the "rejectionists" and the four times he brought up the "Saddamists."

Following the president's speech, White House communications director Dan Bartlett appeared on MSNBC and addressed the administration's counter-"insurgency" strategy, saying the word had been replaced because "insurgents" implies that they are on the side of the people.

Fine. But, at the end of the day, we were losing the war not because of what we called our enemies in Iraq but because of how the people of Iraq saw our enemies—and us.

And as long as American troops were seen as what a report by an Iraqi National Assembly committee called "occupation forces"; and as long as Shiite, Kurdish, and Sunni leaders agreed, as they did at a U.S.-backed conference in late November 2005, that the insurgency was "legitimate"; and as long as Iraqi leaders like former Prime Minister Iyad Allawi and Shiite leader Abdul Aziz al-Hakim continued to paint a dark picture of what was going on in George Bush's Iraq, the president's victory vocabulary was just another pathetic diversion for the benefit of the compliant media. A diversion ginned up to fight the enemy he was most concerned with: the rejectionists here at home who were finally rejecting his lies.

Not Everyone Was Wrong About the War

"WMD—I got it totally wrong. . . . The analysts, the experts and the journalists who covered them—we were all wrong," Judy Miller said in her *Times* mea culpa in October 2005.

To which a number of journalists rightfully responded: No, we weren't.

We cannot stand by and allow the rewriting of history, or allow those who helped the Bush White House market the war to fall back on the comfort and safety of a collective "we all screwed up." After all, as *Slate*'s Jack Shafer pointed out, even in *The New York Times* there were "at least four non-Miller stories published during the war's run-up that glower with skepticism about the administration's case and methods." So here is a (by no means exhaustive) honor roll of the analysts, experts, and journalists who got it right.

Joe Lauria, a reporter who had covered the United Nations since 1990 for a variety of papers, including *The Daily Mail, The Daily Telegraph*, and *The Boston Globe*. He bridled at Miller's claim. "I didn't get it wrong," he told me. "And a lot of others who covered the lead-up to the war didn't get it wrong. Mostly because we weren't just cozying up to Washington sources but had widened our reporting to what we were hearing from people like Mohamed ElBaradei [head of the International Atomic Energy Agency] and Hans Blix [the U.N. weapons inspector], and from sources in other countries, like Germany, France, and Russia. Miller had access to these voices, too, but ignored them. Our chief job as journalists is to challenge authority. Because an official says something might make it 'official,' but it doesn't necessarily make it true."

Judy Miller: Trading Truth for Access

Signs of trouble and Judy Miller were like Mary and her little lamb. Everywhere that Judy went, a flashing warning sign was sure to follow.

Indeed, in looking back on her career, it's clear that there were more red flags popping up around Miller's work as a journalist than at a May Day parade in Red Square.

We now know that Miller's bosses were being warned about serious credibility problems with her reporting as far back as 2000—including a warning from Craig Pyes, a Pulitzer Prize–winning colleague of Miller who was so disturbed by her journalistic methods he took the extraordinary step of writing a warning memo to his editors and then asked that his byline not appear on an article they had both worked on.

In October 2005, Howard Kurtz quoted in *The Washington Post* from Pyes's December 2000 memo.

"I'm not willing to work further on this project with Judy Miller. . . . I do not trust her work, her judgment, or her conduct. She is an advocate, and her actions threaten the integrity of the enterprise, and of everyone who works with her . . . She has turned in a draft of a story of a collective enterprise that is little more than dictation from government sources over several days, filled with unproven assertions and factual inaccuracies," and "tried to stampede it into the paper."

That's the journalistic equivalent of White House counsel John Dean telling Richard Nixon that Watergate was "a cancer on the presidency." But while the *Times* corrected the specific stories Pyes was concerned about, the paper, like Nixon, ignored the long-term diagnosis. And, of course, the very same issues Pyes raised in 2000—her judgment, her advocacy, her willingness to take dictation from government sources—were the ones that reappeared in Miller's prewar "reporting" on Saddam's WMD.

And Pyes wasn't the only one at the *Times* raising concerns about Miller's reporting. As Roger Cohen, who was foreign editor at the time of Miller's WMD reporting, put it in an October 2005 article: "I told her there was unease, discomfort, unhappiness over some of the coverage." And as has been reported by Franklin Foer in *New York* magazine, Cohen did not express his concerns only to Miller: "During the run-up to the war, investigations editor Doug Franz and foreign editor Roger Cohen went to managing editor Gerald Boyd on several occasions with concerns about Miller's over-reliance on Chalabi and his Pentagon champions. . . . But executive editor Howell Raines and Boyd continually reaffirmed management's faith in her by putting her stories on page 1." (So, as Eric Alterman pointed out, the neocons got their Manchurian Reporter.)

Franz's and Cohen's visits (piled on top of the Pyes memo) are eerily reminiscent of the e-mail then Metro editor Jon Landman sent regarding Jayson Blair, in which he wrote, "We have to stop Jayson from writing for the *Times*. Right now." Here were a number of respected journalists all but pleading: "We have to stop Judy from reporting for the *Times*. Right now."

But, instead, Miller was allowed to keep doing pretty much whatever she pleased. In fact, as a journalist insider told me: "Howell Raines was thrilled with Judy's WMD coverage, however credulous, because it allowed the *Times* to slough off the liberal label and present themselves as born-again tough hawks—perfect for the post-9/11 zeitgeist." That was Raines. What was his successor Bill Keller's excuse?

Because perhaps the most damning admission in the *Times*'s quasi-self-examination was Keller's claim that, despite being removed from her WMD beat, Miller "kept kind of drifting on her own back into the national security realm." "Kept kind of drifting on her own"? When did the *Times* stop being edited?

Miller was very questionable goods. And everyone knew it. Yet this is the person the *Times* chose to rally behind, body and soul. And reputation. It was an utter disgrace, and an integral part of the paper's disastrous WMD coverage, which is without a doubt the blackest mark in the paper's long history.

Joby Warrick. Check out this excerpt from Warrick's January 24, 2003, *Washington Post* article "U.S. Claim on Iraqi Nuclear Program Is Called into Question":

> After weeks of investigation, U.N. weapons inspectors in Iraq are increasingly confident that the aluminum tubes were never meant for enriching uranium, according to officials familiar with the inspection process. . . .
>
> Moreover, there were clues from the beginning that should have raised doubts about claims that the tubes were part of a secret Iraqi nuclear weapons program, according to U.S. and international experts on uranium enrichment.

Warrick's story ran on page one. But not in *The New York Times*.

Colum Lynch. Here's what he wrote in his January 29, 2003, *Washington Post* article "U.N. Finds No Proof of Nuclear Program":

> The head of the International Atomic Energy Agency, Mohamed ElBaradei, said today that two months of inspections in Iraq and interviews with Iraqi officials have yielded no evidence to support Bush administration claims that Iraq is secretly trying to revive its nuclear weapons program.
>
> ElBaradei said in an interview that "systematic" inspections of eight facilities linked by U.S. and British authorities to a possible nuclear weapons program have turned up no proof to support the claims. "I think we have ruled out . . . the buildings," he said. ElBaradei also cast doubts on U.S. claims that Iraq has sought to import uranium and high-strength aluminum tubes destined for a nuclear weapons program.

Bob Simon. Also giving the lie to the "we were all wrong" routine is this exchange from a December 6, 2002, *60 Minutes* segment in which Simon interviewed David Albright, a physicist who was a weapons inspector in Iraq during the 1990s:

> **Simon:** It seems that what you're suggesting is that the administration's leak to *The New York Times*, regarding aluminum tubes, was misleading?
>
> **Albright:** Oh, I think it was. I think—I think it was very misleading.
>
> **Simon:** So basically what you're saying is that whatever nugget of information comes across, the Bush administration puts it in a box labeled "nuclear threat," whereas it could go many other places.
>
> **Albright:** That's how it looked, and that they were selectively picking information to bolster a case that the Iraqi nuclear threat was more imminent than it is, and in essence, scare people.

Ian Williams. On January 30, 2003, Williams wrote a piece in the *LA Weekly* titled "Missing Evidence: Poking Holes in the Case for War":

Demetrius Perricos, chief inspector of the U.N. Monitoring, Verification and Inspection Commission (UNMOVIC), commented, "What we're getting and what President Bush may be getting is very different, to put it mildly."

The events of the last weeks make it seem likely that in the best Texan death-row tradition of first deciding verdict and sentence, and only then looking for clues, the White House does not in fact have any substantive evidence. . . .

One sign of desperation was when both Brits and Americans began to say that instead of looking for the smoking gun or the bubbling vat of botulin, the Security Council should draw conclusions from the "cumulative" buildup of clues that Iraq was in flagrant material breach, and therefore the Security Council should attack.

However, even much of what has been brandished as part of this pattern has not held up under examination. The aluminum tubes for nuclear weapons materials were in fact for artillery rockets. Even people with the U.N. Inspection Commission think that the empty chemical warheads discovered were in fact mislaid rather than concealed.

Walter Pincus. On March 16, 2003, days before Shock and Awe, *The Washington Post*'s Pincus reported on the growing skepticism in the intelligence community:

Despite the Bush administration's claims about Iraq's weapons of mass destruction, U.S. intelligence agencies have been unable to give Congress or the Pentagon specific information about the amounts of banned weapons or where they are hidden, according to administration officials and members of Congress.

Senior intelligence analysts say they feel caught between the demands from White House, Pentagon and other government policymakers for intelligence that would make the administration's case "and what they say is a lack of hard facts," one official said. . . .

The assertions, coming on the eve of a possible decision by President Bush to go to war against Iraq, have raised concerns among some members of the intelligence community about whether administration officials have exaggerated intelligence in a desire to convince the American public and foreign governments that Iraq is violating United Nations prohibitions against chemical, biological, or nuclear weapons and long-range missile systems.

John MacArthur. In June 2003, while Judy Miller was still getting it totally wrong, *Harper's* publisher MacArthur was getting it completely and frighteningly right—about Iraq, Judy, and her cozy relationship with the Bush administration—in the *Globe & Mail*:

Take the case of staff reporter Judith Miller, who covers the atomic bomb/chemical-weapons-fear beat, and hasn't heard a scare story about Iraq that she didn't believe, especially if leaked by her White House friends. On Sept. 8, 2002, Ms. Miller and her colleague Michael Gordon helped co-launch the Bush II sales campaign for Saddam-change with a front page story about unsuccessful Iraqi efforts to purchase 81-mm aluminum tubes, allegedly destined for a revived nuclear weapons program.

Pitched to a 9/11-spooked public and a gullible, cowardly U.S. Congress, the aluminum tubes plant was a big component of the "weapons of mass destruction" canard, which resulted in hasty House and Senate war authorization on Oct. 11. . . .

When officials leak a "fact" to Ms. Miller, they then can cite her subsequent stenography in the *Times* as corroboration of their own propaganda, as though the *Times* had conducted its own independent investigation. On Sept. 8, Dick Cheney cited the *Times*'s aluminum tubes nonsense on *Meet the Press* to buttress his casus belli.

And as late as May 2005 former CIA director and Bush apologist James Woolsey was challenged by CNN International's Daljit Dhaliwal in very un-Timesian fashion about the absence of weapons and the world's resulting skepticism. Mr. Woolsey replied, "Well, I think the key thing on that is the very fine reporting that's been done by Judith Miller of *The New York Times*. The first article on the front page was three or four weeks ago, about this Iraqi scientist who was captured by the Americans, who was in charge of a major share of the nerve gas program, and was apparently ordered just as the war began to destroy a substantial share of what he had and to hide very deeply the rest."

Bob Drogin and Maggie Farley. Here's what they wrote in a January 26, 2003, *Los Angeles Times* article headlined "Hard Claims but Only Soft Proof So Far in Iraq":

> After two months and more than 350 inspections, United Nations weapons teams in Iraq have so far been unable to corroborate Bush administration claims that Saddam Hussein is secretly building chemical, biological or nuclear weapons.
>
> In particular, inspectors have found no proof of prohibited activities at a series of suspect sites—including nuclear facilities, chemical factories and missile production plants—that the CIA publicly identified last fall.

Julian Borger. Writing for *The Guardian* on October 9, 2002, Borger penned a piece titled "Threat of War: US Intelligence Questions Bush Claims on Iraq: President's Televised Address Attacked by CIA":

> President Bush's case against Saddam Hussein, outlined in a televised address to the nation on Monday night, relied on a slanted and sometimes entirely false reading of the available US intelligence, government officials and analysts claimed yesterday.
>
> Officials in the CIA, FBI and energy department are being put under intense pressure to produce reports which back the administration's line, *The Guardian* has learned. In response, some are complying, some are resisting and some are choosing to remain silent.

Dafna Linzer. Check out her September 18, 2003, article for the Associated Press titled "No Evidence Iraq Stockpiled Smallpox":

> Top American scientists assigned to the weapons hunt in Iraq found no evidence Saddam Hussein's regime was making or stockpiling smallpox, the Associated Press has learned from senior military officers involved in the search.

A special place on our honor roll must be reserved for Knight Ridder reporters **Jonathan S. Landay** and **Warren P. Strobel**—and their Washington bureau chief, **John Walcott**. As media critic Michael Massing wrote in *The New York Review of Books*, Knight Ridder "almost alone among national news organizations . . . decided to take a hard look at the administration's justifications for war." On February 5, 2004, Landay and Strobel were awarded the Raymond Clapper Memorial Award from the Washington Press Club Foundation for their coverage. And in August 2004, the *American Journalism Review* singled the two out for praise, calling their stories "compelling," and noting that "on many occasions, it seemed like they were banging the drum alone."

Here are excerpts from two of their articles:

On October 8, 2002, they wrote an article titled "Bush Hawks Accused of Distortions; Experts List Case After Case of Misleading the Public About Iraq":

A growing number of military, intelligence and diplomatic leaders have deep misgivings about the Bush administration's march toward war in Iraq.

These officials say administration hawks have publicly exaggerated evidence of the threat that Iraqi President Saddam Hussein poses, including:

- Distorting his links to the al-Qaida terrorist network.

- Overstating the amount of international support for attacking Iraq.

- Downplaying the potential repercussions of a new war in the Middle East.

They also say intelligence analysts are under intense pressure to produce reports supporting the White House's argument against Saddam.

On October 27, 2002, the two followed up with an article titled "Infighting Among U.S. Intelligence Agencies Fuels Dispute over Iraq":

The Pentagon and the CIA are waging a bitter feud over secret intelligence that is being used to shape U.S. policy toward Iraq, according to current and former U.S. officials. . . . The dispute pits hardliners long distrustful of the U.S. intelligence community against professional military and intelligence officers who fear the hawks are shaping intelligence analyses to support their case for invading Iraq.

It's time for the "everyone was wrong, so no one was wrong" line the media have been repeating to be thoroughly discredited.

An interesting lesson can be learned at journalism schools by contrasting the relentless search for truth undertaken by journalists on our honor roll with the majority of the prewar coverage.

In May 2004, the *Times* in an editorial, acknowledged problems with its prewar reporting: "We consider the story of Iraq's weapons, and of the pattern of misinformation, to be unfinished business. And we fully intend to continue aggressive reporting aimed at setting the record straight."

In the ensuing seventeen months between the article and Keller's memo, they did nothing of the sort. Indeed, the Miller "episode" made the paper of record even less aggressive, something Keller himself admitted when he told staffers in October 2005: "With any luck you can resume your undistracted, full-throttle pursuit of putting out the best news report in the world."

It was a particularly opportune time for the *Times* to engage in "aggressive reporting," with a growing chorus of voices reaffirming that Plamegate was really an opportunity to understand how we went to war.

"What makes [Special Prosecutor] Patrick Fitzgerald's investigation compelling," wrote Frank Rich, "is its illumination of a conspiracy . . . that took us on false premises into a reckless and wasteful war."

This was not the first opportunity we, as a nation, had to delve into the administration's lies that led us to the debacle in Iraq. In fact, the stench of White House deception wafted up many times—both during the run-up to the war and after the flowers that were supposed to be tossed at the feet of our troops were supplanted by Improvised Explosive Devices.

We could have had a sustained national discussion back in May

2002, when *Time* published an article describing Cheney as saying that "the question was no longer if the U.S. would attack Iraq . . . the only question was when," and offering that "Rumsfeld has been so determined to find a rationale for an [Iraq] attack that on 10 separate occasions he asked the CIA to find evidence linking Iraq to the terror attacks of Sept. 11. The intelligence agency repeatedly came back empty-handed."

We could have had a sustained national discussion in July 2003, when, following publication of Joe Wilson's op-ed regarding the deceitful Niger-Saddam uranium connection, a firestorm broke out over the president's bogus claims of such a connection in his State of the Union speech. The administration fanatics so badly wanted it to be true they refused to let it die the death it deserved (still wonder why the White House wanted to discredit Wilson?).

We could have had a sustained national discussion in January 2004, when former Treasury Secretary Paul O'Neill let it be known that invading Iraq had been Bush's goal before he had even learned where the Oval Office supply closet was, just ten days after the president was inaugurated. "It was all about finding a way to do it," O'Neill said. "That was the tone of it. The president saying 'Go find me a way to do this.' "

We could have had a sustained national discussion in March 2004, when Richard Clarke published *Against All Enemies*, painting a devastating portrait of an administration teeming with zealots for whom evidence was little more than an obstacle on the path to greater glory: " 'Look,' " Clarke quoted Bush as saying on the day after 9/11, " 'I know you have a lot to do and all, but I want you, as soon as you can, to go back over everything, everything. See if Saddam did this. See if he's linked in any way.' 'But, Mr. President, Al Qaeda did this.' 'I know, I know—but see if Saddam was involved. Just look . . .' "

We could have had a sustained national discussion in April 2004, when Bob Woodward published *Plan of Attack*, which showed a vice president so obsessed with linking Saddam to 9/11 that no piece of intelligence that supported his hypothesis was deemed too unreliable to be used. Cheney was like an al Qaeda alchemist, converting shards of faulty intel into golden reasons for preemptive war. It also revealed the way out-of-the-war-loop Secretary of State Colin Powell made like a Good Soldier when the president asked him to carry his sample vial of faux anthrax to the United Nations, and set out to hoodwink the world.

And we could have had a sustained national discussion in May 2005 when the Downing Street Memo story hit, and we learned that, in July 2002, Richard Dearlove, the head of British intelligence, had reported that in Washington "the intelligence and facts were being fixed around the policy."

Our go-along media have a grave responsibility for the fact that the sustained national discussion never took place.

The Fool's Gold Standard

If the media had a face—confident, clubby, clinging to half-truths, and, above all, safeguarding their own cherished "access"—it would be Bob Woodward's.

"I've spent my life," Woodward told Larry King in November 2005, "trying to find out what's really hidden, what's in the bottom of the barrel."

Then how did he miss what Frank Rich summed up at the same time as the administration's cover-up of "wrongdoing in the executive branch between 9/11 and Shock and Awe"?

"Each day," wrote Rich, "brings slam-dunk evidence that the doomsday threats marshaled by the administration to sell the war weren't, in Cheney-speak, just dishonest and reprehensible but also corrupt and shameless. . . . The web of half-truths and falsehoods used to sell the war did not happen by accident; it was woven by design and then foisted on the public by a P.R. operation built expressly for that purpose in the White House."

It was during this time that Woodward was writing two books—*Bush at War* and *Plan of Attack*—and enjoying unparalleled access to many of those guiding the aforementioned PR operation, including head shills Dick Cheney, Scooter Libby, and White House chief of staff Andy Card.

So how come Woodward, supposedly the preeminent investigative reporter of our time, missed the biggest story of our time—a story that was taking place right under his nose?

Some would say it was because he was carrying water for the Bushies. I disagree. I think it's because he's the dumb blonde of American journalism, so awed by his proximity to power that he buys whatever he's being sold.

In her scathing 1996 essay in *The New York Review of Books*, Joan Didion criticized Woodward's reporting as marked by "a scrupulous passivity, an agreement to cover the story not as it is occurring but as it is presented, which is to say as it is manufactured." And this assessment applies just as well to many in the rest of the media.

Far from shying away from his reputation as a stenographer to the political stars, Woodward has embraced his inner bimbo and wears his "scrupulous passivity" as a badge of honor, proudly telling Larry King that his "method" means that "everyone in the end . . . pretty much gets their point of view out."

Woodward also told King: "I am strictly in the middle." The problem is, the truth isn't always in the middle; it's not always or even often to be found by splitting the difference between right and left. It's often located on the sidelines, or hiding in the shadows amid the endless rush of detail Woodward so loves to fill his books with.

What Woodward fails to do again and again is connect the dots. He prefers a sort of journalistic pointillism, gathering as many dots as he can, jam-packing his pages with them, and then letting the little buggers hang out by themselves, hoping that they form a picture in the eye of the beholder. Critical thinking that draws conclusions can make a dumb blonde's brain hurt.

For a taste of how the Woodward Method plays itself out, let's look at one of the big headline-grabbing moments from *Plan of Attack*—the scene where CIA Director George Tenet, at a meeting in December 2002, assures the president that the intel on WMD is a "slam dunk."

After Tenet goes Dick Vitale, Woodward writes: "Card was worried that there might be no 'there there,' but Tenet's double reassurance on the slam dunk was both memorable and comforting. Cheney could think of no reason to question Tenet's assertion. He was, after all, the head of the CIA and would know the most."

It's hard to believe that Woodward was able to type this last bit without breaking into hysterics. "Cheney could think of no reason to question Tenet's assertion"? Is this the same Cheney who has been at odds with the CIA for more than a decade, frequently challenged CIA findings in the run-up to the war, and once wrote on an intelligence report prepared by the Defense Department's Doug Feith: "This is very good indeed. . . . Not like the crap we are all so used to getting out of the CIA"?

But does Woodward say any of that? No. He doesn't even present those Cheney–CIA dots here—let alone connect them. He just gives us Cheney's POV. As for the president, in this scene, Woodward paints him as a scrupulous, meticulous, and honest leader who "told Tenet several times, 'Make sure no one stretches to make our case.' "

For those keeping score: Tenet twice said the intel was a slam dunk, while Bush warned against stretching to make the case "several times."

Again, did Woodward have to stifle his outrage when he wrote this? Or just suppress his memory? Remember, this key meeting took place in December 2002, by which time the president and his team had been stretching to make their case for months. And not just a little—their elasticity with the facts would put Mister Fantastic to shame.

Here's just a little of what they'd been saying:

Bush: "The Iraqi regime possesses biological and chemical weapons. . . . And according to the British government, the Iraqi regime could launch a biological or chemical attack in as little as 45 minutes." (9/26/02)

Bush: "You can't distinguish between al-Qaeda and Saddam." (9/25/02)

Cheney: "Simply stated, there is no doubt that Saddam Hussein now has weapons of mass destruction. There is no doubt that he is amassing them to use against our friends, against our allies, and against us." (8/26/02)

Rice: "We do know that [Saddam] is actively pursuing a nuclear weapon." (9/8/02)

Rumsfeld: "[Saddam has] amassed large, clandestine stockpiles of biological weapons, including anthrax, botulism, toxins and possibly smallpox. He's amassed large, clandestine stockpiles of chemical weapons, including VX, Sarin and mustard gas." (9/19/02)

Any reporter worth his salt would have used these publicly available quotes to—yes, connect the dots and show Bush's "make sure no one stretches" comment to be the PR pap it so obviously was. But Woodward just swallowed it.

Nor did he stop at failing to connect the dots in his book. He went on the air and repeatedly presented a presidential portrait belied by endless facts available on LexisNexis without any special access. On *The NewsHour* in the spring of 2004, he gushed about the president's "moral determination, which we've not seen in the White House maybe in 100 years." This in the wake of Abu Ghraib. "Moral determination" indeed.

In a conversation with Carl Bernstein, I mentioned what Woodward had said to Jim Lehrer. Bernstein defended his former partner but did draw my attention to an op-ed he had written for *USA Today* that ran a month after Woodward's appearance on *The NewsHour*. It was filled with diligent dot-connecting and bristled with outrage:

"At a juncture in history," Bernstein wrote, "when the United States needed a president to intelligently and forcefully lead a real international campaign against terrorism and its causes, Bush decided instead to unilaterally declare war on a totalitarian state that never represented a terrorist threat; to claim exemption from international law regarding the treatment of prisoners. . . . Instead of using America's moral authority to lead a great global cause, Bush squandered it."

It is, indeed, a tale of two reporting styles, one that makes you wonder what *All the President's Men* would have been like if Woodward had written it alone.

What makes matters worse is that a whole year before *Plan of Attack* was released, Woodward had helped Walter Pincus, national security correspondent for *The Washington Post*, put together a story challenging the White House's claims on WMD. "I blame myself mightily for not pushing harder," Woodward told Howard Kurtz in August 2004 (four months after his book came out). "We should have warned readers we had information that the basis for this was shakier [than widely believed]."

The question is: why didn't he warn the readers of his book? He repeatedly boasted to Larry King about his "aggressive reporting mode." So why not aggressively report the WMD story and connect those dots in his book?

Woodward is a master of offering readers minute details that give them a sense of being behind-the-scenes observers of history in the making, but which, in fact, mask the real story of what is going on. This can lead to inadvertent comedy. Check out this tidbit from *Plan of Attack* in which he recounts a meeting the Bush team had with outgoing Secretary of Defense William Cohen and the Joint Chiefs of Staff just before taking office:

"The Joint Chiefs of Staff's staff had placed a peppermint at each place. Bush unwrapped his and popped it in his mouth. Later he eyed Cohen's mint and flashed a pantomime query. Do you want that? Cohen signaled no, so Bush reached over and took it. Near the end of the hour-and-a-quarter briefing, the chairman of the Joint Chiefs, Army General Henry 'Hugh' Shelton, noticed Bush eyeing his mint so he passed it over."

Feel like a fly on the wall? Perhaps, but wouldn't you rather hear more about the fact that, according to Woodward, Cheney had told Cohen that "Topic A should be Iraq"? Iraq as Topic A—months before 9/11, indeed even before Bush was inaugurated. But instead of connecting those dots he connects the mints and we get not a vice president ravenous for Saddam's head but a president ravenous for breath fresheners.

Thanks to reporting like this, the sum total of the abundant facts Woodward always gives us is actually less than its parts. Instead of the truth, we get these shiny baubles of information. Shiny baubles that distract us, diminish our understanding of what is really going on, and—as the lies that led us into war are revealed—ultimately delay our discovery of what's really hidden in the bottom of the barrel.

And when Woodward started to dig his way out of this ditch of his own making, the rest of the media had a vested interest in helping him get out. So despite years of fawning coverage of the Bush administration, he got the journalistic hero treatment for *State of Denial,* his self-revising 2006 reassessment of the Bush administration's handling of Iraq—including a cover plug from *Newsweek* (which called him "the best excavator of inside stories in the nation's capital") and a laudatory lead story segment on *60 Minutes.*

Talk about being in a state of denial: praising Woodward for his very-late-to-the-party Iraq pile-on was like a music critic writing a rave of *Let It Be* and getting credit for discovering the Beatles. Or, more fitting, having someone be the 100th—or is it 100,000th?—person to call 911 to report a car crash and then getting kudos for alerting the authorities.

Yet there was Mike Wallace on *60 Minutes,* gushing about how Woodward had "unearthed" a "secret" classified graph revealing that—wait for it—attacks on "U.S., Iraqi, and allied forces . . . have increased dramatically over the last three years." What did Woodward have to do to "unearth" that one? Pick up a newspaper? Or log on to a blog or two—or two hundred?

Then there was the revelation, breathlessly delivered by Wallace in his intro, that after two years and more than two hundred interviews, including "most of the top officials in the administration," Woodward had come to "a damning conclusion: That for the last three years, the White House has not been honest with the American public." Stop the presses, hold the front pages! And burn all the copies of *Fiasco, Cobra II, The One Percent Doctrine, Hubris*—plus 99.9

percent of the blog posts on Iraq that have appeared on *HuffPost* since we launched—that came to exactly the same "damning conclusion." Why fork over $30 for much-older-than-yesterday's news?

In her *New York Times* review of *State of Denial*, Michiko Kakutani said that Woodward paints a portrait of President Bush as "a passive, impatient, sophomoric and intellectually incurious leader, presiding over a grossly dysfunctional war cabinet and given to an almost religious certainty that makes him disinclined to rethink or re-evaluate decisions he has made about the war."

To which I say: "Welcome to 2002, Bob." I can only hold my breath in anticipation of what headline-grabbing insights "the best excavator of inside stories" will "unearth" for his next book: "Paris Hilton: Shallow Party Girl," or, perhaps, "Islamic Fundamentalism: Could Be a Problem in the Future." Or maybe "Bin Laden Determined to Strike in U.S."

Sure, I suppose we should welcome the fact that Woodward finally joined the rest of the sentient world in his appraisal of Bush. But without any expiation for the role his earlier hagiographic renderings played in enabling all the behaviors he belatedly was aghast over, it was hard to take his rude awakening seriously. After all, if there's one thing you can say about Bush, it's that he is who he is.

Bush had that same religious certainty, lack of curiosity, impatience, and disinclination to rethink things back in 2004, when Woodward published *Plan of Attack*, and in 2002, when Woodward published *Bush at War*.

But in those books, Woodward saw things a bit differently—which would explain why *Plan of Attack* was given the top slot on the Bush-Cheney 2004 campaign website's recommended reading list (ranking even higher than Karen Hughes's Bush-worshipping *Ten Minutes from Normal*). But Woodward emerged from his *State of Denial* PR blitz never having to admit how wrong he had been, and indeed getting away with making the laughable claim "I found out new things, as is always the case when you replow old ground."

Without some accounting in his third Bush book about how Woodward himself could have been in a state of denial for the first five years of the Bush presidency, it was hard not to reach the "damning conclusion" that Woodward didn't write *State of Denial* because he suddenly realized Iraq was going to hell: he wrote it because he realized his reputation was going to hell.

Woodward, the classic Washington weather vane, knew, with his unerring weather-vane instinct, that it was finally okay to openly criticize Bush—and that, indeed, anyone who wanted a seat at the grown-ups' table after Bush leaves had to admit Iraq has been a disaster (while making the new conventional-wisdom mistake of calling the surge a success). And Woodward definitely doesn't want to give up his special seat at the grown-ups' table.

Bob Woodward's personal state of denial deepened during his appearance on *Larry King Live*, in October 2006.

How else to explain the total disconnect between the story he was reporting—an administration that repeatedly failed to tell the truth about a war in which, according to Woodward, "the stakes could not be higher"—and his takeaway from that story.

After spending much of his hour-long appearance presenting examples of the administration's dishonesty about the war ("In this period of difficulty and darkness, we have not been getting the straight story unfortunately"), Woodward was asked if the revelations in his latest book had caused him to reconsider what he wrote in his previous two books about Bush.

Woodward's reply? "No, because that's what happened." Even the usually unflappable King was taken aback, asking, "You don't change any opinions?"

"No," said Woodward, "I don't."

To which I say: Why the hell not?

Then came this stunning exchange:

King: One of our key staff members wants to know if you think we can trust George Bush.

Woodward: You know, that's a good, interesting question, but I don't address it . . . it's not my job.

Not his job? He put together a devastating catalogue of the president deceiving the American people—what Woodward describes as "Let's pretend it's another way"—but he still wasn't ready to say that George Bush can't be trusted?

In fact, he repeatedly let Bush off the hook, twice telling King the reason for the president's serial dishonesty about Iraq is his sunny outlook: "Bush is an optimist," he said. So the explanation for Bush BS-ing the American people is his optimism? And new facts are not allowed to change a journalist's opinion? And a long list of presidential mendacity and deception doesn't lead to the inevitable conclusion that the perpetrator can't be trusted?

"What I do is all on the page," said Woodward. "I don't weaponize my words. I don't feel the need to write, 'Guilty, guilty, guilty.' " Well, Bob, you might want to try it sometime—especially if the powerful people you are writing about are "guilty, guilty, guilty." "I don't take a position," he responds to questions about his position on the war. "Paul Wolfowitz said it in *Vanity Fair*: 'You needed a vehicle.' The vehicle was WMD." Exactly, but instead of following up on doubts about the administration's WMD claims, Woodward chose to pen his chronicles of the determined president and his fearless aides.

Woodward's incestuous relationship with his sources tangled him up in Plamegate as well. He was neither suspended from *The Washington Post* nor asked to take a leave after admitting that he had waited two years before telling his editor Len Downie—and his readers and the prosecutor—that he had been a Plamegate player. And that he had commented on the case, including maligning Fitzgerald, without divulging his own role in it. For Woodward, Plamegate was another case of very little truth and absolutely no consequences.

He tried to put a positive face on things by making it sound as if he had decided to come forward and disclose his Plamegate involvement to Downie of his own free will. But a telltale excerpt from his appearance on *Larry King Live* the night before the Libby indictment indicated that he had to be prodded into coming clean. Let's go to the tape:

It's October 27, 2005. Woodward is part of the *Larry King Live* panel discussing the anticipated Plamegate indictments. Coming back from a commercial break, King dramatically announces that *Newsweek*'s Michael Isikoff (also on the panel) had whispered to him during the commercial that he had "a key question" for Woodward. Isikoff then pops the question, triggering an exchange that in hindsight is very revealing.

Isikoff announces that a White House source has told him that Woodward has information about Plamegate that he has not yet revealed. Excited, King prompts Woodward to "come clean," but Woodward denies that he has anything to offer. In fact, he doesn't just deny it, he scoffs at the notion. "I wish I did have a bombshell. I don't even have a firecracker." Come on, Bob, being perhaps the first recipient of the Plame leak isn't even a firecracker? Just a touch misleading, don't you think?

Then Woodward helpfully provides the evidence that indeed he finally came clean only because he had to:

> **Woodward:** I got a call from somebody in the CIA saying he got a call from the best *New York Times* reporter on this saying exactly that I supposedly had a bombshell. Finally, this went around that I was going to do it tonight or in the paper. Finally, Len Downie, who is the editor of *The Washington Post*, called me and said, "I hear you have a bombshell. Would you let me in on it?"

So this wasn't something that Woodward suddenly decided to do. Instead, the cat was already out of the bag and Downie was pressing him for answers. At that point Woodward realized he needed to fess up to Downie. Lying to the public on national TV is one thing, but directly lying to your editor when confronted is apparently quite another in Woodward's ethics book.

On November 17, 2005, *The Washington Post* said of its assistant managing editor: "Woodward has periodically faced criticism for holding back scoops for his Simon & Schuster–published books. . . ." So here's one more question for Mr. Woodward: Was this another scoop you were saving for your next book?

Just think about Woodward's career arc. From exposing a presidential cover-up in Watergate to covering up his role in Plamegate. And being forced to apologize to his own paper. And asking a colleague, Walter Pincus, not to mention Woodward's role in the story. And failing to tell his editor that he had vital information about a major story. And, to bottom it out, doing the TV and radio rounds, minimizing the scandal as "laughable" (*Fresh Air,* July 7, 2005), "an accident," "nothing to it," and denigrating Fitzgerald as "disgraceful" (*Hardball,* July 11, 2005) and "a junkyard dog" (*Larry King Live,* October 27, 2005) without ever once divulging that he was not just an observer of the CIA leak case but a recipient of the leak.

Once again, I called Carl Bernstein to ask what he thought of his old partner's behavior. He was loyal as ever but he did say something very revealing—and unintentionally damning. "This investigation," he told me, "has cast a constant searchlight that the White House can't turn off the way it has succeeded in turning off the press. So their methodology and their dishonesty and their disingenuousness—particularly about how we went to war—as well as their willingness to attack and rough up people who don't agree with them are now there for all to see. They can't turn off this searchlight, which is shining on a White House that runs a media apparatus so sophisticated in discrediting its critics it makes the Haldeman, Ehrlichman, Ziegler press shop look like a small-time operation." And these are the very thugs that Woodward was protecting while attacking the guy operating the searchlight.

"The medium is the message," Marshall McLuhan told us in the sixties. But, as we've seen, during the Right's takeover of America the media became the messenger. As the Right took power, so did its media mouthpieces. And their outrageous views became an accepted part of the national conversation. A regular topic of discussion, pounded home incessantly, was the myth of "the liberal media." It was repeated so often, it became an accepted truth—like Saddam Hussein being behind 9/11.

The fringe dwellers took a seat side by side with the enablers— and the careerists. Boat-rocking has never been considered a great career move, requiring courage and the willingness to be shunned by those with their hands on the wheel. But over the last twenty years the media have gotten especially cozy with those in power. Reporters have forgotten that their mission is to speak truth to power—not to hop in bed with the powers that be. And far too many traded their press passes for an all-access White House pass, and in doing so sacrificed their duty to the public—and to the truth.

Clubbiness has trumped inquisitiveness, and coziness has begotten timidity. Corrupted or just complacent, our media watchdogs have turned into lapdogs, curling up by the fire while our leaders used the freedom from oversight to dismantle our democracy and lead us into an immoral and unnecessary war.

In this way, another memorable sixties slogan—"the revolution will not be televised"—was utterly turned on its ear. In fact, the Right's revolution was beamed into our homes—live and in living color—and published on the front pages of our most important papers.

4

Dim Bulbs: Congress's
Low-Wattage Energy Bill

Coal in the Stocking—
the Christmas Energy Bill of 2007

Last December, with the price of oil insistently poking the underside
of the $100 per barrel milestone in the midst of the busiest travel
period of the year, George Bush finally signed an energy bill (point-
edly entitled the "Energy Independence and *Security* Act of 2007"),
which brought to a close one full term in office and three-quarters of
a second term without an energy policy. And even this bill, which, in
draft form, had seemed a promising piece of legislation, ended up
being watered down into exactly what we should have expected from
the Bush administration: a medicine so diluted that it had lost all its
potency.

Although the bill did include a long overdue increase in fuel efficiency standards and funding for research and development of alternative fuel sources, a funny thing happened on the way to the White
House. It seems that the Edison Electric Institute, which lobbies on
behalf of electric utilities, the National Association of Manufacturers,
the American Petroleum Institute, and the refining and mining
industries were solicited for a little last-minute input. They got out
their red pens, their black pens, their scissors, and their machetes
and, before long, the bill *The New York Times* had hailed as a "breakthrough" had more deletions, redactions, and cross-outs than a CIA
interrogation transcript.

Gone was a tax increase on the oil industry, which would have
channeled a small part of its windfall cash-gusher into federal coffers,
along with a key requirement that utilities generate 15 percent of

their power from renewable sources. Brent Blackwelder, president of Friends of the Earth, blasted the compromise: "When the Republican leadership and polluter lobby have blocked important legislation, Senate Democrats have been all too willing to move in their direction. The result is that the two most positive provisions of the energy bill—a clean energy mandate and a tax package reining in handouts for fossil fuels and promoting clean energy—are being removed."

At the same time the Energy Bill—sorry, the Energy *and Security* Bill—was limping over to the president's desk, another deal was being hammered out that would dull any pain that the energy sector might have suffered. This other deal, part of a huge government spending bill, authorized the Energy Department to provide $18.5 billion in loan guarantees for nuclear power plant construction and another $2 billion loan for a uranium enrichment plant.

Soon after, at the beginning of 2008, oil finally hit triple digits, accelerating the stock market's slide and pushing the economy toward recession. Oil's surge reminded us that we had lost the War for Oil that the Bush administration was never willing to admit we were fighting.

Corporate Welfare Gone Wild

The president may turn to God when it comes to shaping his foreign policy, but his energy policy is strictly courtesy of the Men Upstairs at Big Oil.

Back in 2006, Moe, Curly, and Larry—sorry, I mean Bush, Hastert, and Frist—engaged in a little bit of slapstick that involved getting all blue in the face about skyrocketing gas prices, and calling on the Energy and Justice Departments to look into possible market manipulation by oil companies. It was the least believable call for an investigation since O.J. set out to find the real killer. If it wasn't so despicable it would have been laughable.

There was Frist, at the time the Senate majority leader, offering a little advice for cash-strapped energy consumers on *Good Morning America* in the spring of 2006, putting aside the video diagnostic skills he had shown during the Terri Schiavo death watch to become one of the *Car Talk* guys. Among Frist's many helpful money-saving tips for drivers forced to consider taking out a second mortgage in order to fill up their tanks: get a tune-up, drive slower, carpool, and use mass transit. Thanks, Dr. Goodwrench! But Frist's patent-medicine cure for our energy ailments paled in comparison to the president's highly suspicious display of concern at a meeting of the Renewable Fuels Association, where he claimed that "energy companies don't need unnecessary tax breaks." That was *after* he had signed a GOP-generated boondoggle bill that was stuffed with some $14.5 billion in tax breaks, tax subsidies, and tax deductions for his cash-rich energy industry chums. I guess *those* tax breaks were "necessary."

Bush also scored big with his impression of a guy who cared about fuel efficiency: "And the easiest way to promote fuel efficiency is to encourage drivers to purchase highly efficient hybrid or clean diesel vehicles." Yes, this from the same guy whose administration didn't increase fuel efficiency standards for passenger cars even a single mpg for seven years. I guess the lure of touting vehicles that can run on alternative energy sources to an alternative energy trade association was just too hard to resist. How gullible do they think we are?

All this huffing and puffing about manipulated markets and record gas prices was simply a blatant attempt to inoculate Republicans from consumer rage over massive oil company earnings. ExxonMobil's earnings went from $10.7 billion in the fourth quarter of 2005 to $40.6 billion in the fourth quarter of 2007. With profits like that, former ExMo CEO Lee Raymond's $400 million retirement package might even look a little stingy. Except to those paying through the nose at the pump.

Our oilman president may want us to think that he's shocked, shocked by the "large cash flows" of the oil companies, and the sticker shock drivers are experiencing at the pump, but even before Team Bush was dreaming of toppling Saddam, it was laying the groundwork for the gargantuan windfall the oil industry is seeing—starting with Dick Cheney's secret Energy Task Force. It's not a coincidence that the oil and gas industries donated nearly $26 million to our lawmakers in 2004 (with 80 percent of that money going into Republican coffers), and over $20 million in the 2006 cycle (with 82 percent going to the GOP). They also doled out over $4.5 million to Bush's 2000 and 2004 presidential runs. And what did they get for their largess? According to Public Citizen, the top five oil companies have pocketed just under a half trillion (that's with a "T") in profits from Bush's swearing-in through the first quarter of 2007. *The New York Times* estimated that ExxonMobil "earned more than $1,287 of profit for every second of 2007." Or, to put it another way, "the company's sales, more than $404 billion, exceeded the gross domestic product of 120 countries." Yet John McCain voted twice against a temporary tax on oil companies' windfall profits (*and* against asking the president for a plan to reduce foreign oil consumption). Talk about a return on investment. That's a gusher! So for American consumers, payback is a bitch.

Heads in the Sand of the Middle East

There are problems we face—and about which the Right is wrong— that lack an easy and obvious solution. While we may agree that universal health care is a necessity, reasonable people may differ on the precise plan that should be used to deliver it. Energy independence is not, however, a baffling conundrum that defies human intelligence and creativity. Nor is it the futuristic dream of woolly-headed idealists. We don't need to wait for someone to invent the water-powered car or the eternal lightbulb in order to see it come to pass. There are steps we can take right now that will begin to slow—and eventually reverse—the drain of dollars to the petro-vampires, foreign and domestic.

The result would be a stronger, safer, and cleaner America that would, once again, be leading the rest of the world to a more promising future. (I know that's a controversial goal—call me a dreamer.)

But mobilized by nervous corporate interests, the Right has had a hysterical response to even the most modest proposal for true energy independence, including seriously raising mileage standards (Regulation!) and imposing a dollar-a-gallon "Patriot Tax" (Taxation!). As *Grist* magazine staff writer David Roberts pointed out on *The Huffington Post*: "This isn't supporting markets, it's supporting businesses—a very different approach, one that bears a large share of responsibility for the farce that our energy policy has been for the last many years. Just as with the Republican passion for privatization, it isn't about marshaling market forces—freedom coupled with competition and the real possibility of failure—it's simply about offloading as much of the government's work onto private actors as possible."

Fuel for Thought: Energy by the Numbers

The Bush administration has turned the White House into a full-service filling station for Big Oil. And we're the ones being forced to pick up the tab. How has Bush responded to Big Oil's call to "fill 'er up"? Let me count the ways:

$3.25: the average cost of a gallon of gas in the seventh year of George Bush's presidency, compared to $1.52 in the first year.

325: average motorist heart rate while suffering a bout of "pump panic."

33: the number of oil refinery mergers the Bush administration allowed just during its first term, while refusing to block a single oily takeover. Who needs all that messy free market competition, anyway?

41: the number of top-level Bush administration officials with ties to the oil industry, including Bush, Dick Cheney, Don Evans, Gale Norton, and Condoleezza Rice—the only national security adviser in history to have an oil tanker named after her.

67%: the percent of foreign oil consumed in the United States— up from 57% in 2001. And the increase happened while the president was pledging to reduce our energy dependence in every State of the Union address since taking office.

$25,000: the amount that buyers of gas-guzzling SUVs are able to write off in taxes thanks to a scandalous loophole that survived the passage of the energy bill.

$13 billion: the amount of corporate welfare included in the Bush-backed energy bill. The president was ready to veto his own energy bill if there were cuts to the $13 billion in government subsidies and tax breaks to oil companies.

$3.4 billion: total of bids received by the Bush administration for oil leases in shrinking polar bear habitat.

$31.6 billion: the total figure of taxpayer handouts to oil companies for five years beginning in 2006.

$27.6 billion: Shell Oil Company's record annual earnings in 2007.

$40.61 billion: Exxon's record annual earnings in 2007.

$3.5 million: what oil companies donated to George Bush's 2000 and 2004 presidential runs.

½: President Bush's 2007 budget funded less than half of what the Congress's energy bill had set aside for renewable energy and energy efficiency—the two simplest ways to break our addiction to oil.

2020: the year by which CAFE standards need to be 35 miles per gallon—the first increase in more than thirty years, and the United States will still be way behind where Japan (at 46.3 mpg) and China (at 43 mpg) are *today.*

It should be the first lesson in Political Chemistry 101: oil money and good government don't mix. Not in Saudi Arabia, and not in the United States.

Among the solutions the Right has offered to free us from economic slavery to Arab sheiks is greater exploitation of dirty deadly coal. In "Coal's True Cost," environmental activist Robert F. Kennedy Jr. pointed out on *HuffPost* the folly that coal is a cheap and potentially clean domestic resource:

> In fact, there is no such thing as "clean coal." And coal is only "cheap" if one ignores its calamitous externalized costs. In addition to global warming, these include dead forests and sterilized lakes from acid rain, poisoned fisheries in forty-nine states and children with damaged brains and crippled health from mercury emissions, millions of asthma attacks and lost work days and thousands dead annually from ozone and particulates. Coal's most catastrophic and permanent impacts are from mountaintop removal mining. If the American people could see what I have seen from the air and ground during my many trips to the coalfields of Kentucky and West Virginia—leveled mountains, devastated communities, wrecked economies, and ruined lives—there would be a revolution in this country.

But the coal industry knows how to rile up the Right just as well as its brethren in the oilfields. Just ask Kansas governor Kathleen Sebelius, who opposed yet another dirty coal-fired power plant in her state and found herself pilloried in a coal industry TV ad that made the preposterous assertion that the decision by the Sebelius administration "means Kansas will import more natural gas from countries like Russia, Venezuela, and Iran." The truth is that Kansas is a natural gas *exporter*, and no state in the union imports any gas from Russia, Venezuela, or Iran.

Perhaps my favorite right-wing proposal on energy policy was a short-lived 2006 effort by Senate Republicans to subsidize further consumption, rather than discourage it, by playing Ed McMahon and sending $100 gas rebate checks to most Americans. The mind boggles at how the party of fiscal responsibility—that routinely chastises the other side for its free-spending ways—could seriously ask us to consider spending irresponsibly in order to encourage more responsible spending.

Lining the Pockets of Terrorists and Tyrants

To hear the Right tell it, the administration's dance to Big Oil's tune is just as it should be because the business of America is business and what's good for ExxonMobil, Chevron, Conoco, and Shell is good for you and me.

The funny thing is that oil isn't just the business of America. It's also the business of the feudal Wahhabi autocrats in Saudi Arabia where fifteen of the nineteen 9/11 hijackers were taught to hate the United States. It's the business of the Holocaust-denying, nuke-lusting mullahs in Tehran. And it's the business of the Right's least favorite Latin American nuisance, Venezuela's Marxist dictator Hugo Chávez. That extra money you pay at the pump doesn't grease the wheels of American industry, build value in our pension funds and savings accounts, or sow the seeds of sustainable economic growth here at home. Instead it buys the explosive charges that Iran smuggles into Iraq to kill American troops. And it weakens our country by creating a pipeline of dollars that flow at ever-increasing volume from the Land of the Free to the dictators and terrorists of the Middle East.

High prices at the pump are tribute to terrorists, a tax that's collected not in Washington but in Osama bin Laden's cave and Hamas's bomb factories and spent when Hezbollah goes missile shopping and Mohamed Atta takes flying lessons.

In 2003, the Detroit Project—which I co-founded with Lawrence Bender and Laurie David, producers of *An Inconvenient Truth*, and agent Ari Emanuel—produced a series of TV ads urging American consumers to think about the effect that wasting oil was having on the environment as well as on our national security, and to make the connection between oil and terror.

The ads were a satiric response to the outrageous drug war ads the Bush administration had flooded the airwaves with, linking drug use to financing terrorism.

The drug spots featured earnest, anonymous, ordinary-looking folk addressing the camera and confessing to the most appalling crimes:

Actor #1: I helped murder families in Colombia.

Actor #2: It was just innocent fun.

Actor #3: I helped kidnap people's dads.

Actor #4: Hey, some harmless fun.

Actor #5: I helped kids learn how to kill.

Actor #6: I was just having some fun, you know.

Actor #7: I helped kill a policeman.

Actor #8: I was just having fun.

Actor #9: I helped a bomber get a fake passport.

Actor #10: Other kids do it.

Actor #11: I helped kill a judge.

Actor #12: I helped blow up buildings.

Actor #13: My life, my body.

Actor #14: It's not like I was hurting anybody else.

The idea of asking Americans to think carefully about the ultimate consequences of their actions seemed like a game that two could play.

So, we decided to turn the tables and point out the much more credible link between gas-guzzling SUVs and America's national security. Here's our version (written by filmmaker Scott Burns):

Actor #1: I helped hijack an airplane.

Actor #2: I helped blow up a nightclub.

Actor #3: So what if it gets a lot of miles to the gallon?

Actor #4: I gave money to a terrorist training camp in a foreign country.

Actor #5: It makes me feel safe.

Actor #6: I helped our enemies develop weapons of mass destruction.

Actor #7: What if I need to go off-road?

Actor #8: Everyone has one.

Actor #9: I helped teach kids around the world to hate America.

Actor #10: I like to sit up high.

Actor #11: I sent our soldiers off to war.

Actor #12: Everyone has one.

Actor #13: My life, my SUV.

Actor #14: I don't even know how many miles it gets to the gallon.

WHAT IS YOUR SUV DOING TO OUR NATIONAL SECURITY? DETROIT, AMERICA NEEDS HYBRID CARS NOW.

Even before they were released, the ads caused a sensation—getting a lot of media attention (and free airplay) while being rejected by TV stations in Detroit, New York, and Los Angeles as too controversial. What's more, many of the president's supporters accused us of being unpatriotic, of attacking all that was good about America—which apparently included an insatiable demand for oil and driving a car that makes us feel like Indiana Jones.

We called it the Detroit Project because our primary target was the big three U.S. automakers—GM, Ford, and Chrysler—which had entered into a suicide pact with the American people over SUVs, which, powered by clever marketing that sold safety to women and macho outdoorsiness to men, had become a consumer megatrend. No matter that, on average, SUVs eat up over six miles per gallon more than a family station wagon. The hucksters made buying an SUV an all-American activity, and the government did its part by giving extra tax breaks to the biggest of the gas-guzzlers.

Though I don't consider myself an automotive fashionista, I must admit that as the turn of the twenty-first century neared, I followed the thundering herd of protective parents unable to resist the allure of what is basically a comfy Sherman tank. The SUV I dutifully acquired, a Lincoln Navigator, was, I was told, the safest way to transport my kids. And, as an added bonus, I could haul around my daughters' entire Girl Scout troop and all the cookies they could sell.

But it turned out that despite those TV ads showing them heroically scaling snow-capped mountains in a single bound, SUVs are actually risky to drive: four times more likely than cars to roll over in an accident and three times more likely to kill the occupants in a rollover. Honest advertising would have shown SUVs rolling down those snow-capped mountains after they had driven up.

Soon after 9/11, I swapped my SUV for a Prius, Toyota's category-busting sexy hybrid. (Or, at least, it became sexy after assorted movie stars started pulling up at the red carpet in them.) After waiting in vain for our leaders to lead, I joined thousands of other Americans and simply drove around them.

RIP: GM

There are signs that, at long last, Detroit is getting the message, albeit the hard way. As thousands have made the same move I did and traded down from their Soccer Mom Fighting Vehicles to something more sensible and economical, often with a foreign carmaker's name over the rear fender, the automakers, once the pride of American industry, have endured a series of disasters. They have become corporate Frankenstein monsters, barely surviving by tacking on bits and pieces of other companies, shedding a limb or organ when it stops working, and getting a jolt of government-subsidized electricity when all seems lost.

Just look at the head-on collision at General Motors, which, along

The Short Life of the Electric Car

For a GM tale that is cautionary and also shows how little sacrifice we might really have to make if only the ideologues would get out of the way and our scientists and engineers are given a clear run at the problem, one need look no further than the sad story of the electric car. It was jump-started by the state of California, which in 1990, choking on blankets of smog, passed regulations designed to force car companies to start producing emission-free vehicles (indeed, 2 percent of new cars needed to be exhaustless by 1998). Since a number of companies, including GM, were already working on electric car prototypes, business and environmental concerns seemed in sync.

In 1996, GM introduced the EV1, which you could juice up by plugging it into a wall socket. The cars quickly developed a small but passionate following (small because GM produced fewer than a thousand of them; passionate because they were terrific—and terrifically efficient—cars). But, behind the scenes, numerous forces were hard at work, fighting to undermine the California zero-emission mandate—and the success of the clean car.

The lobbying and lawsuits by oil companies and the Bush administration, cheered on by the Right, caused California to soften its rules and allowed GM, which was making money hand over fist on SUVs, to pull the plug on the EV1. It was never really given a fighting chance. GM had leased only eight hundred of them over a four-year period (none was sold) and never put even the tiniest fraction of the marketing muscle behind them that they'd put behind the giant gas-guzzlers that had become the company's cash cow. The auto giant then claimed that the demand for the electric cars just wasn't there—and, in a bizarre act of industrial infanticide, reclaimed EV1s and flattened almost all of them like pancakes.

For chapter and verse (and some amazing footage) on this depressing tale, check out *Who Killed the Electric Car?*, a powerful and lively documentary that features interviews with Mel Gibson, Ed Begley, Jr., Phyllis Diller (yep, that Phyllis Diller), former CIA head James Woolsey, and Reagan administration official Frank Gaffney, intercut with disturbing doings by GM, Big Oil, the Bush administration, and the smog-fighting California Air Resources board to create a blistering and surprisingly entertaining cinematic *j'accuse*.

The film plays like a cinematic game of Clue. But instead of "Professor Plum, in the library, with a candlestick," we get: "GM, in the boardroom, with a blunt profit motive," "Big Oil Companies (aided and abetted by the Bush administration), in the courtroom, with lawsuits forcing the rollback of California's rules," and "American Consumers, in the showroom, with a poisonous mix of an ad-fueled desire for gas-guzzling SUVs, tax incentives, and zero financing."

with the rest of the industry, has enjoyed fuel economy loopholes and tax rebates. But when demand for SUVs finally tumbled, GM's fortunes plunged along with it. Sales of models including the Hummer H2 dropped by double digits, and General Motors took a record $39 billion loss in the third quarter of 2007. GM's sales dropped 6 percent from 2006 to 2007, continuing a long-running trend. And, at the beginning of 2008, Toyota was poised to dethrone GM as the world's number one carmaker. Other U.S. car companies have struggled alongside GM. Ford's stock slid to a twenty-two-year low at the beginning of 2008, at the end of a long run of cutting jobs and closing plants spurred by a record loss of $12.6 billion in 2006. Chrysler's sales also dipped in 2007, a year for which the company posted a $1.6 billion loss and announced tens of thousands of job cuts.

At the same time, Toyota and Honda, companies that have shown a commitment to higher fuel efficiency and fuel-saving hybrid technology, are running away with Detroit's market share. In blockheaded fashion, GM at first responded to its troubles by redoubling its focus, and its multibillion-dollar advertising budget, on hawking more SUVs—a muscle-headed move to sell more muscle cars. They just didn't get it, and for that obstinate blindness they are paying a heavy price.

Our leaders in Washington—their pockets overflowing with oil, gas, and auto industry donations—have been willing accomplices in this financial fiasco. Bush and company call themselves free marketeers, but by indulging Detroit they've discouraged innovation and made it much easier for companies like GM to slowly destroy themselves. It's assisted suicide, Beltway-style.

Think of that: at a time when our leaders are touting the importance of reducing our dependence on foreign oil, the people being given a financial incentive to purchase a new vehicle are those buying fuel-chugging SUVs.

"I was surprised," said Karl Wizinsky, a health care consultant from Michigan who bought a giant Ford Excursion even though he admitted he didn't really need it, "that a $32,000 credit on a $47,000 purchase was available in the first year. I mean, it is a substantial credit." Yes, it is. And it created a substantial—and artificial—demand. By contrast, tax credits for hybrid cars topped out in the $3,000 range, and many were phased out in 2007.

This is the kind of deranged public policy, sadly typical of the energy sector, that makes you want to slam on your brakes and scream out your car window: How can this kind of thing happen? If your steering wheel suddenly starts to pull to the Right, you have your answer.

Bush's Dangerous Addiction to Dishonesty

While the Bush administration has continued to do the bidding of the Midland Mafia that repeatedly gave Bush a helping hand when he had trouble making a go of it as a businessman, the president has, on occasion, paid lip service to the notion that there may be other ways to slake our thirst for energy besides downing another round of pricey petrol. With the interests of the oil companies and, until recently, the automakers, so clearly divergent from that of ordinary gas-pumping Americans, some token gesture was clearly needed—so long as it didn't upset the applecarts of any big donors.

There is nothing more infuriating than hearing something you passionately believe in—and indeed have been advocating for years—cynically co-opted by someone who clearly doesn't mean it. There's that sinking sensation in the pit of your stomach when you realize that a false friend is more dangerous than an honest enemy. That's why the smoke started pouring out of my ears January 31, 2006, when, during his State of the Union address, President Bush announced: "America is addicted to oil, which is often imported from unstable parts of the world."

The utter insincerity of the president's statement became crystal-clear the day after the State of the Union, when his own energy secretary, Samuel Bodman, said that the president's call "to make our dependence on Middle Eastern oil a thing of the past" should not be taken literally. Trust me, Sam, I didn't take it literally.

His words may have said break the oil addiction, but his policies have kept mainlining the stuff into the body politic. If the president had been serious about helping us break the habit, his headline-grabbing rhetoric would have been accompanied by concrete proposals that would have an immediate effect on reducing our reliance on foreign oil.

The forum for the president's ritual embrace of renewable energy is the State of the Union address, one of the few times a year when a president, by tradition, is supposed to at least *appear* reasonable.

The retrograde Right is prepared to tolerate a little pie-in-the-sky talk about hydrogen cars—which I fully expect to be driving at about the time you're able to read this book in pill form—as long as it's understood that none of the money used to subsidize corporate lollipops for the energy industry is actually diverted and, of course, that no new taxes are levied for the same purpose. Or any purpose. Read their lips: "No new taxes!" Maybe if we let the market work, energy independence will just happen. In 2006, despite his ringing call at the State of the Union, Bush authorized only $1.1 billion to fund the Office of Energy Efficiency and Renewable Energy while handing out $2 billion worth of tax breaks to the oil and gas industry. The day after the president called for an end to our foreign oil dependence through renewable energy initiatives, the Department of Energy's National Renewable Energy Laboratory had to lay off forty researchers due to a $28 million budget cut. And in 2008 the laboratory's budget was cut again.

If he'd really wanted to put his policies where his mouth is, he could have gotten behind the ten-year, ten-point plan for achieving energy independence developed by the Apollo Alliance, a remarkable coalition of business, labor, environmental, and community leaders working together to bring about a clean energy revolution, founded in 2004, its name inspired by President Kennedy's call to meet the challenge of the Sputnik launch and put a man on the moon. Here's the plan:

1. Promote advanced technology and hybrid cars.
2. Invest in more efficient factories.
3. Encourage high-performance building.
4. Increase use of energy-efficient appliances.
5. Modernize electrical infrastructure.
6. Expand renewable energy development.
7. Improve transportation options.

8. Reinvest in smart urban growth.
9. Plan for a hydrogen future.
10. Preserve regulatory protections.

Oil's Fair in Love and ANWR

The use of the term "addiction" back in 2006 was, perhaps, an unfortunate blunder by the president's speechwriting team. These days, most people recognize that addictions are serviced by a team of enablers: drug dealers, fellow addicts, and friends and relatives in denial. Once the president declared that we were all addicts, the question was obvious: "And what does that make you, Mr. President?" Are you the dealer, the pal who's got a problem of his own, or a parent in deep denial? Or all three? He certainly wasn't serious about getting the country into rehab. Instead of twelve steps, we got just two or three, and none was taking us in a new direction.

In the quick-fix category, there was the president's bizarre and long-standing obsession with drilling for oil in the Arctic National Wildlife Refuge. I mean, how retro can you get? Instead of pushing to seriously increase fuel efficiency standards and calling for a national commitment to investing in renewable sources of energy, he proposed one more hit of dinosaur by-products from one of the world's last pristine places. Which might be understandable if making an ExxonMobil theme park out of the refuge would actually reduce our dependence on foreign oil. But there's only enough oil there to satisfy U.S. demand for about six months. And it won't be available for at least a decade—which is the only forward-looking aspect to Bush's ANWR dream.

Drilling in ANWR is one of those "Don't get me started" topics that can really flush out the crazies on the Right. There's Alaska ecocidal madman (and senior senator) Ted Stevens, who has said: "I think the American people are asking: 'Why don't we have enough energy?' And they're not susceptible anymore to misrepresentations that [the Arctic National Wildlife Refuge] is some kind of pristine wilderness. It's empty. It's ugly." Stevens, as astute followers of politics may remember, is also the guy who described the Internet as "a series of tubes" and fought vigorously to preserve the $320 million Ketchikan bridge—immortalized in public discourse as "The Bridge to Nowhere."

And the ever-reliable Rush Limbaugh gave voice to a right-wing trope when he declared, "If you put together a video of ANWR, you would see nothing but snow and rock. It is no place anybody's ever going to go. The wildlife that lives there wishes it didn't, but it's too stupid to figure out how to move anywhere. They don't have moving vans sent to their places like people in Philadelphia do when they want to get out of someplace. This is absolutely absurd."

As much as we might hope that Rush would move to ANWR, the fact that he's more comfortable in Florida doesn't prove anything about the refuge's value as an irreplaceable pristine habitat for wildlife. Notwithstanding any Oxycontin-addled aesthetic judgments and whether or not humans might care to move there, ANWR is worth preserving for its own sake.

Of course, if we leave conservation up to individual opinion and hidden agendas, everything's fair game. For instance: "If you look at this place on video, you'd see nothing but desert and rock. It's 120 degrees in the shade, if you can find any. It's got so many cliffs that even mountain goats don't want to live there but they're just too stupid to move somewhere flatter. But for some crazy reason, no one wants to drill there for natural gas." I'm talking, you may have guessed, about the Grand Canyon.

Why the Right Is Wrong on Energy Policy

There is a broad spectrum of agreement across political lines that, at least in theory, it would be a good idea to reduce America's dependence on foreign oil. But the problem is that it isn't possible to reduce foreign oil consumption without reducing *all* oil consumption. Oil is a commodity that is traded on an open market. There's no "foreign" or "domestic" button at the gas pump.

The simple, obvious, and immediate solution to our foreign oil problem—and the collateral damage it does by propping up repressive regimes, funding terrorism, and draining our national bank account—is to keep raising the fuel economy standards for all cars and trucks. Increasing these standards would buy us the time we need to develop true alternative energy solutions and bring them to market. These, by the way, are true "market solutions."

To the Right, this is crazy talk. The energy policy of the Bush years consists of nothing but speed bumps and roadblocks to delay or prevent all efforts to cure our addiction to oil. The Right's hysterical response to anything that carries a whiff of regulation, no matter how responsible, or taxation, no matter how slight or how necessary, has effectively shut down progress on a central issue of our time. And unless you're an oil company CEO, you're the worse for it. Oh, and while Bush has been in the White House, our dependence on foreign oil has actually gone up from 57 percent in 2001 to 67 percent in 2008.

5

The Right's War on Science

Requiem for an Atoll

In 1995, two small islands in the middle of the South Pacific lost most of their shoreline to rising seawater. Another island was cut in two. It was the beginning of a process of flooding that over the next decade would lead to the destruction of the local agricultural economy (the soil ruined by saltwater), less and less room to live as the beachfront moved inward, and, eventually, the evacuation of the entire population as it became clear that the islands would be entirely and permanently under water by 2015.

The waters that will soon drown the islands of the Carteret Atoll have been swollen by the rapid melting of the polar ice caps as a result of the phenomenon variously called global warming or global climate change, which is, in turn, the direct consequence of human activity, primarily the production of greenhouse gases.

If those same waters had flooded Washington, D.C. (imagine the Potomac bursting its banks and Lincoln sitting waist-deep in a murky swamp), or Crawford, Texas, then the whole ridiculous "debate" over global warming would have ended long ago, and the long-overdue debate over what to do about it would have already reached the implementation phase. We'd be attacking the problem across the broadest front that human ingenuity could claim. If, instead of the president's backyard, it was the Hamptons and Malibu that had been inundated, the response might have been a little slower, but a consensus would still have been reached, because the financial-turned-political pressure would simply be too great.

But because it was in the impoverished South Pacific islands—and the less remote but still impoverished Ninth Ward of New Orleans—where these dramatic and tangible effects of this growing environmental catastrophe occurred, the Right has tried to keep firmly shut the increasingly small window of time for effective action to save the planet.

In responding to global warming, the Bush administration has lived according to its own perverse variant of the eco-mantra "Think Globally, Act Locally." Because climate change effects are not immediately apparent locally, the United States carries on in a manner that is having enormous consequences globally. The Right is acting like the dopey local weatherman who reports on an unseasonably cold day by announcing, "So much for global warming!"

By willfully delaying action on climate change, the administration keeps faith with the Right, which has decided for the time being to adopt an obstinate flat-earth policy on the issue. The specific "arguments" (to dignify them with an intellectual coherence they lack) range from "it isn't happening" to "it might be happening and, gosh, I wonder why" to "it's probably happening but any cure will be worse than the disease." Perhaps the biggest mystery about global climate change is not whether it's happening but exactly why the Right doesn't want to acknowledge it, since, as many have pointed out, it seems only natural for self-professed "conservatives" to want to conserve things. Reactionaries, on the other hand, resist change of any sort on principle.

The Right's allies in the oil industry have a lot to fear from sustained action on global warming—starting with a drop in the obscene profits they've been making. There's also the possibility that the Right opposes environmental action of all sorts simply because it's usually been associated with liberals. And if Ted Kennedy is for it, well, you know it has to be bad, right? And there is the religious factor: by inventing conflicts between "science" and "religion"—and coming down firmly against science—the Right rallies the fundamentalist and evangelical sectors of its base. But, ultimately, the explanation for the Right's do-nothing response to global warming that makes the most sense—and is also the most disturbing—is that in the faith-based world of the Right, facts themselves have become the enemy, and nothing produces more cold, hard, indisputable facts—more inconvenient truths, to co-opt a phrase—than science.

The Scientific Definition of "Lunatic"

To drag us all back to the pre-factual, pre-science Stone Age where divinely inspired shamans who commune directly with God lead unquestioning masses, the War on Science, didn't have to be won outright, just fought to a stalemate. Because science requires questions about how the universe works to be decided through the scientific method, persuading the public that matters of science are really just matters of opinion, even if you don't persuade them to accept a particular opinion, is to achieve a victory of sorts. The thin edge of the wedge is once again the faux reasonable position that there are two sides to every question and that it's always useful to hear from multiple points of view before making up one's mind. Once you can get equal time for the insane positions that the principle of evolution is debatable and global climate change is unverified alarmism, then you've begun the process of turning back the clock of history and human progress. They're not asking for you to be certain in your agreement with their position, just that you doubt not only the truth of the scientific position but *the very idea that there can be truth*. And all in the name of being reasonable—just trying to get a hearing for all sides.

As is the case elsewhere, with respect to science, the Right's agenda might be irrational, but their method of pursuing it has been coldly rational, like a comic book supervillain who harnesses cutting-edge technology for insane ends. In fact, the Right's attack on science has been almost, well, scientific in its use of trial-and-error experimentation to discover effective methods to sow doubt, confusion, fear, and ambiguity. Chief among these successful methods is the now ubiquitous "on the other hand" format of "debate." Scientists, who can be a little dry, rarely have media training or publicists and are professionally predisposed to be modest in the conclusions they extrapolate from their research, are no match for a rabble-rousing showman who is getting constant assists from a "fair and balanced" Fox News host. The Fox News hack's definitions of "known" and "unknown" are very different from those of an actual scientist and have spread way beyond Fox News. By getting scientists to acknowledge that some things are unknown or that scientists have been wrong in the past—which no scientist disputes—the anti-science con artist can try to push the audience into making the leap of faith that,

QED, everything is unknown and that scientists are often wrong and always in disagreement. Scientists pursue the truth—they know that any claims they make not borne out by evidence would be corrected through peer review or attempts at replication of their results. No such thing exists in cable news. Glenn Beck is not much of a corrective to Bill O'Reilly.

But it is in flogging the false choice between science and religion that the Right truly bares its cynical soul. Science is not a religion. It's a matter of fact, not faith. Many scientists are also deeply religious without any cognitive dissonance whatsoever. And there are plenty of churchgoers who are able to accept evolution, stem cell research, and climate change without touching off a theological crisis. But by preaching the gospel that science is anti-religion, the Right recruits Christian soldiers for its voting rolls. Once the army is mobilized you can deploy it wherever it's needed: to battle environmental protection on behalf of corporate interests or as conscripts to defeat the teaching of evolution in the classroom.

Evolution Devolves into Evil–ution

I won't fall into the Right's trap by arguing the facts of evolution. The Right uses the scientific term "theory" to suggest that the "theory of evolution" is sort of a trial balloon—a very different way than the word is used in science. In this way, Creationism is offered as just another competing theory that—in the name of fairness and balance—deserves equal time.

Dr. Lawrence Krauss, chairman of the physics department at Case Western Reserve University, elegantly debunks the "theoretical" attack on evolution:

> Theologians as ancient as St. Augustine and Moses Maimonides recognized that science, not religion, was the appropriate and reliable method to try to understand the physical world. Yet it is precisely this ancient wisdom that is now under attack. Foes of evolution and the Big Bang in this country do not operate with the direct and brutal actions of the Taliban. They have marketing skills. Openly condemning evolution as blasphemous might play well to the fundamentalist true believers, but it wouldn't play well in the heartland, which is the real

target. Thus the spurious argument is created that evolution isn't good science. This "fact" is established by fiat. The Discovery Institute in Seattle supports the work of several Ph.D.s who then write books (and op-ed articles) decrying the fallacy of evolution. They don't write scientific articles, however, because the claims they make—either that cellular structures are too complex to have evolved or that evolution itself is improbable—have either failed to stand up to detailed scrutiny or involve no falsifiable predictions.

By the way, since the predictive quality of the proven fact of evolution underlies so much of modern biological science, it would be fun to ask the Right some hard questions on how willing they are to put their money where their mouths are in unraveling some of the practical applications of this supposedly shaky "theory." The Right likes to attend to the two parts of their base—anti-science evangelicals on the one hand, and corporate America on the other—separately. Having them both to dinner at the same time, however, would make for awkward conversation. How would the agri-giants like Archer Daniels Midland and Cargill feel about giving up their blasphemous hybridization of grain and corn? Do the ordinary folks down on the family farm agree that animal husbandry is just a random process subject only to God's will? Oh, and what about the avian flu and other emerging diseases? Try to persuade the big pharmaceutical companies to develop their next big moneymaking drugs using creation science. The Right knows that the premises that underlie their two constituencies are fundamentally incompatible.

Despite their Elmer Gantry pretensions, is there any doubt that, privately, the college-educated elite who dominate the Right don't really question the fundamental truth of evolution? If they were, say, to get a letter from Sidwell Friends or Princeton saying that evolution had been dropped from their children's curriculum and replaced with creation science, or even that their children's biology courses would be taught by a professor who saw the two "theories" as equally valid, you can imagine the consternation in the offices of the Heritage Foundation, *National Review*, and *The Weekly Standard* (similar to the consternation expressed at the mere possibility of a true evangelical who does not believe in evolution as the party's nominee). Paying lip service to creationism is no different than putting on a cowboy hat and throwing horseshoes when you're campaigning in Texas: a calculated act to suck up to people you'd never in a million years socialize with or, God forbid, let your son or daughter marry. Education is supposed to be the solution to ignorance, not the pathway. But by catering to the small minority who regard the Bible the way Islamic true believers regard the Koran and who can be goaded into lifting their torches and pitchforks to demand that their children not hear otherwise in a public school, the Right has taken the idea of egalitarianism to a ridiculous extreme: ignorance for all!

Not Even Warm on Global Warming

In the yearly contest for the coveted title of "Dumbest Senator," James Inhofe, Republican of Oklahoma, is always in the running. Even in years when it seems like Kentucky's Jim Bunning may edge him out, Inhofe will perform a thrilling last-minute come-from-behind act of utter stupidity that wins him the tarnished cup for yet another year.

And, to top it off, Inhofe is usually a contender for "Craziest Elected Official," as well. His stiffest competition for that title is Georgia's former Representative Ben Bridges, whose office sent out a memo containing the startling news that "indisputable evidence—long hidden but now available to everyone—demonstrates conclusively that so-called 'secular evolution science' is the Big-Bang 15-billion-year alternate 'creation scenario' of the Pharisee Religion. . . . This scenario is derived concept-for-concept from Rabbinic writings in the mystic 'holy book' Kabbala dating back at least two millennia." Yikes! I guess this is what has replaced "congressional oversight" on the Right.

Inhofe, the ranking member of the Senate Committee on Environment and Public Works, has described global warming as "the second greatest hoax ever perpetrated on the American people after the separation of church and state." Inhofe has compared environmentalists to Nazis and the EPA to the Gestapo. He has also suggested that the global warming hoax might be perpetrated by the Weather Channel: "We all know the Weather Channel would like to have people afraid all the time." Inhofe may actually believe these things, or he may simply be overdoing it a bit trying to please his patrons in the oil and gas industries, which contributed more to his campaign in 2002 than to any other senator's except for Texas's John Cornyn.

In the state competition, Alaska's congressional delegation has

consistently been a pacesetter in anti-environmental ravings. Reacting to the Arctic Climate Impact Assessment, a study by three hundred climate scientists around the globe that concluded that the
Arctic is heating up twice as fast as the rest of the world, Republican
Representative Don Young waxed sarcastic: "My biggest concern," he
said, "is that people are going to use this *so-called* [italics mine] study
to try to influence the standard of living that occurs within the United
States. . . . I don't believe it is our fault. That's an opinion. It's as
sound as any scientist's."

Over in the Senate, Ted Stevens, the senator most in favor of rendering his own state uninhabitable, told the *Anchorage Daily News*,
"I'm just not sure [these scientists] are the only people we should listen to with regard to that subject." I agree. Stevens should check with
his state's Inuit villagers, park rangers, and Board of Tourism, as well.
They'll tell him that native villages are disappearing, wildlife is under
severe stress, and ancient glaciers are melting away to nothing in a
single decade.

Al Gore deserves much of the credit for getting the word out—and
for connecting the assault on science with the assault on our democracy.

When I interviewed Gore in May of 2007, it was clear that he is
obsessed with two kinds of pollution—the pollution of our planet,
and the pollution of our politics and culture. In other words, the toxicity of the atmosphere and the toxicity of the public sphere:

> It's a problem that George Bush invaded Iraq. It's a problem
> that he authorized warrantless mass eavesdropping on Ameri-
> can citizens. It's a problem that he lifted the prohibition against
> torture. It's a problem that he censored hundreds of scientific
> reports on the climate crisis—but it's a bigger problem that
> we've been so vulnerable to such crass manipulation and that
> there has been so little outcry or protest as American values
> have been discarded, one after another. And if we pretend that
> the magic solution for all these problems is simply to put a dif-
> ferent person in the office of the president without attending
> to the cracks in the foundation of our democracy, then the
> same weaknesses that have been exploited by this White House
> will be exploited by others in the future.

On the media side, scoffing at global warming has been, you
will not be astonished to learn, a staple of Rush Limbaugh's show,

where it fits comfortably into Rush's long-running nonsense about the pernicious influence of "crybaby" liberals who are "feminizing" our politics. Global warming isn't happening and, if it is, so what? We can just suck it up and take it like a man. Provided we've got enough Hillbilly Heroin to ride out a few storms. Rush's "big lie" approach to environmental science hinges upon ignorance compounded by malice and makes allegations that NASA faked the moon landing seem reasonable by comparison: "Despite the hysterics of a few pseudo-scientists," he insists, "there is no reason to believe in global warming."

You might expect more from Michael Crichton, the Harvard-educated doctor, *E.R.* co-creator, and author of many entertaining science fiction novels. But then you would be disappointed. He makes a good salesman for anti-intellectual nonsense, because he attacks global warming from the persuasive position of the proselyte. You see this a lot on cable news. Some rational-looking person will be introduced to present the "on the other hand" side of some argument and will preface his or her remarks with a stimulating account of their own personal journey along the Road to Damascus. It usually goes something like this:

"I used to believe in global warming/abortion rights/being a homosexual. In fact, no one was more of an ardent believer in global warming/abortion rights/being a homosexual. I even participated in rallies and marches and went on television to declare my commitment to global warming/abortion rights/being a homosexual. But then, one day, I took a closer look at the facts . . ."

There is, of course, nothing wrong with changing your mind— God knows I did. But Crichton likes to indulge in this little charade by claiming that he used to be just another global warming dupe, before he saw the light and came to believe what is literally pure science fiction. In his 2004 best-seller *State of Fear*, Crichton adds a flourish to the usual "global warming is a hoax and, if it isn't a hoax, it's too complicated to do anything about" routine. He is providing a motive for the massive deception being practiced upon the gullible public by science: money. Yes, that's right, greedy scientists have ginned up the idea of global warming in order to squeeze the government, universities, and corporations for grant money. Apparently they've run out of other scientific problems to solve and are reduced to digging holes so that someone will hire them to fill them.

Crichton's science fiction has been invented—like some of the best science fiction—with an audience of adolescent boys in mind: people are phonies, and whenever they pretend they are doing something noble, it turns out they're just in it for the money! Holden Caulfield couldn't have put it better. Except he's not on cable news demanding we change our public policy to conform with his adolescent angst.

Bush Takes the Public's Temperature

Faced with the always tricky balancing act of keeping the base out in force pressed against the barricades while at the same time not ruffling the well-groomed feathers of educated country club Republicans, President Bush has once again shown a rare talent for weaseling. Environmental concerns can be a dangerous crossover issue that will sometimes strike a chord among the political donor class, especially if they happen to, say, own waterfront property. Bush has publicly given the minimum necessary lip service to the issue to avoid being dismissed as a loony, which means he says he believes global climate change is taking place and that it has been caused or accelerated by human activity. "I recognize the surface of the earth is warmer and that an increase in greenhouse gases caused by humans is contributing to the problem," he grudgingly admitted during a 2005 trip to Scotland. Of course, this statement—which merely served to preface yet another criticism of the Kyoto agreement on climate change—came after years of the usual "more study needed" procrastination (not that he isn't still punting the issue down the road by claiming more study is still needed before we can decide on a course of action).

Writing in *The New Yorker*, Elizabeth Kolbert beautifully articulated the administration's policy of malign neglect, a signature tactic of the Right, ostentatiously playing "hands off" when "hands on" are desperately needed:

> When the Bush Administration's policy on climate change was first articulated by the President, in early 2002, critics described it as a "total charade," a characterization that, if anything, has come to seem too generous. Stripped down to its essentials, the Administration's position is that global warming is a problem that either will solve itself or won't. The White

The Right Rewrites Science:
The Blogosphere Reacts

You see a scandal on the front page of *The New York Times* and you assume that steps will be taken. Wrongs will be righted. Villains will be brought to justice. You can scratch it off your mental checklist: done.

But time and time again that turns out not to be the case.

Take the revelation in *The New York Times* on June 8, 2005, about Philip Cooney, an oil-industry lobbyist–turned–White House official, doing extensive rewrite work on government reports to make it sound as if global warming weren't really that big a problem—indeed, that it might not be a problem at all. I guess Michael Crichton was too busy—or too pricey.

Haven't we seen this story before? On the front page of *The New York Times*? In June 2003, the paper of record reported on how the White House had made so many changes to a section of an EPA report on climate change that Christie Todd Whitman finally threw up her hands and pulled the section on global warming altogether.

It was outrageous and soon forgotten. Another front-page casualty.

And it's not like we're talking about some minor behind-the-scenes scandal, either. There are stories with potentially cataclysmic consequences. I mean, I can understand people suffering scandal-fatigue over yet another revelation of yet another congressman's golf trip being paid for by yet another sleazy lobbyist. But we're talking about politicians routinely ignoring scientific evidence, acting like a PR arm of Exxon-Mobil and playing fast and loose with grim realities getting grimmer. Seems like a story worth pursuing, doesn't it?

But then, so was the story of how Kenny Boy Lay and his Enron gang played such a big part in Dick Cheney's secret Energy Task Force. And so was the revelation that large chunks of the Bush administration's new rules on mercury emissions had been taken—word for word—from memos prepared by power and energy company lobbyists. And so was the disclosure that ExxonMobil had played a big role in bringing about the White House's cavalier kiss-off of the Kyoto treaty.

Despite all the front-page ink, the Right's oiligarchs are repeatedly allowed to skate on their criminal treatment of the environment. But not this time. On June 10, 2005, Philip Cooney was forced to resign.

The blogosphere definitely helped. It was immediately all over the "White House Rewrites Science" story. Here's a quick roundup of some of what was said:

"Editing Out Inconvenient Facts"
Steve Benen, The Carpetbaggerreport.com

A report from the Environmental Protection Agency was going to provide the first comprehensive review of what is known about various environmental problems, where gaps in understanding exist, and how to fill them. Naturally, there was a large section on global warming—right up until the White House stepped in to delete it because it was inconsistent with Bush's political agenda. As it turns out, the Bush gang was so fond of editing out information about global warming they don't like, they've done it again.

Let's put this in context. Qualified scientists prepared reliable reports based on real information. Before the reports could be shared, however, the White House turned them over to a former lobbyist for the American Petroleum Institute, the largest trade group representing the interests of the oil industry, to edit to his heart's content. This is the Bush administration's approach to quality science. In one instance, a report noted the need for research into how warming might change water availability and flooding. The Petroleum Institute's Philip Cooney saw a section on projected reduction of mountain glaciers and snowpack, didn't like it, and deleted it. Cooney has no background in science—he's a lawyer by trade—but the Bush gang has now made him the chief of staff for the White House Council on Environmental Quality.

"Hating on the Lab"
Ezra Klein, Prospect.org

One thing that's worth remembering is that the war on science isn't a Bush administration innovation. Not at all, in fact. Newt Gingrich's 1994 revolution had its own set of ideas for recasting the role of science in regulatory law, and they, if possible, were even more sophisticated about it than the Bush administration. Rather than going for simple Stalinist tactics like changing language and erasing information, they tried to discredit the science itself. Under their plan, all new regulations would have to come with a risk report, explaining how bad the problem to be regulated was and how certain we were that it would get to that point, thus codifying scientific uncertainty so it could be used in political fights. Next up, all science had to be objectively verifiable and reproducible by outside scientists, meaning industry experts. After that, any large-scale regulation needed to face a panel composed of industry reps and private scientists, and any and all questions they raised had to be answered and put to rest. Lastly, courts would be empowered to hold hearings on the science underlying the regulations and throw out the law if they deemed the science inadequate. This meant that industry could get the best lawyers and pseudo-scientists into a courtroom, hoodwink a judge not trained in the subject, and get him to throw out the offending regulation.

House has consistently opposed taxes or regulations or mandatory caps to reduce, or even just stabilize, greenhouse-gas emissions, advocating instead a purely voluntary approach, under which companies and individuals can choose to cut their CO_2 production—that is, if they feel like it.

As with the war in Iraq, climate change will be just another disaster Bush leaves behind for the next White House occupant to deal with.

Pro-Life Becomes Pro-Cell

Part of the thesis of this book is that the otherwise harmless axiom "reasonable people may differ" has become a dangerous one because of the way it has been cynically abused by the Right to cast doubt on matters not of opinion but of fact. Yes, there will always be a cutting edge of policy and science where matters are in legitimate flux. And, of course, the idea of what's "reasonable" may vary and evolve over time. There are those who, out of strong religious convictions (or even compelling agnostic beliefs), are against embryonic stem cell research.

But if you take this position, in order to be consistent you'd also have to oppose not just abortion, but also in vitro fertilization and the death penalty. And some people, to be fair, do take such a consistent stand. If you believe that embryonic stem cell research is no different from Dr. Mengele vivisecting twins, then you would have to be strongly opposed to it.

Most Americans, however, disagree—54 percent back research on both embryonic and adult stem cell research, according to a December 2007 study undertaken by Virginia Commonwealth University. They do so on the grounds not only of the potential for stem cell research to save the lives and ease the suffering of millions, but also because the so-called victims are tiny clusters of cells that are doomed to eventual decay and can serve no other purpose. The blastocysts from which embryonic stem cells have been harvested for research purposes are no more a "human" than a hard-boiled egg is a chicken. Less, really.

But with the infallible sixth sense that allows him to cynically detect a mother lode of valuable voters where others see only a featureless landscape, George Bush has made hay from the stem cell issue by linking it with abortion and the reliable pro-life voting bloc. Although he vetoes bills about as often as most other modern presidents give inauguration speeches, two of Bush's rare vetoes have been for bills providing federal funding for stem cell research. In 2001, he said, "The ethics of medicine are not infinitely adaptable. There is at least one bright line: We do not end some lives for the medical benefit of others."

Which is, of course, a complete distortion of stem cell research. But Bush didn't behave as though there actually was a bright line by banning stem cell research altogether. If it's really so wrong, and wrong on principle, then the courageous and right thing for the president to do would have been to outlaw it altogether. But, instead, he tried to please the cake-havers and the cake-eaters by acting as though he was taking decisive action to impress one group while telling the other that, not to worry, nothing had really changed.

The president is clearly on the record in support of in vitro fertilization, the process that enables millions of infertile couples to have children—even though it usually results in the eventual destruction of unused embryos, ending, according to Bush's own interpretation, "some lives for the medical benefit of others" to a much greater extent than any form of stem cell research.

Late in 2007, two teams of scientists announced the sort of breakthrough that Michael Crichton would probably say was all part of some shady moneymaking scheme: they were able to give ordinary human skin cells, which each of us—even "bright line" Bush—sloughs off by the thousands every day without feeling like a mass

The Connection Between Global Warming and Our Children's Health

America's children are at risk not just from the kidnappers, pedophile priests, and horny teens trolling MySpace that fill our headlines and sweeps weeks news broadcasts but from the air they breathe, the water they drink, the food they eat, and the chemicals that fill their homes and schools. And from our own government.

In June 2006, a battle was taking place within the Environmental Protection Agency, where a group of EPA workers charged the agency with endangering our children by kowtowing to the demands of chemical companies.

According to a letter sent in May 2006 to EPA administrator Stephen Johnson, EPA staffers in the agency's Pesticide Program were "besieged by political pressure exerted by Agency officials perceived to be too closely aligned with the pesticide industry" as well as former EPA officials now lobbying for pesticide manufacturers. The workers claimed that EPA higher-ups were essentially doing the bidding of the chemical companies, and in the process were in danger of undermining the Food Quality Protection Act, a law designed to protect children from the harmful effects of pesticides—many of which have been linked to childhood cancers.

And this wasn't the only time EPA workers, including scientists, had blasted Johnson for failing to protect America's children. In December 2005, a letter to Johnson pointed out that a rule designed to protect the privacy of subjects of human research was, in fact, so laden with loopholes that it would allow data from third-party studies conducted in an unethical manner. And in March 2006, a letter from twenty-six scientists blasted the EPA for its new standard for perchlorate, an ingredient of solid rocket fuel. The goal was "not supported by the underlying science and can result in exposures that pose neurodevelopmental risks in early life," wrote Melanie Marty of California's Office of Environmental Health Hazard Assessment, who chaired the EPA's Children's Health Protection Advisory Committee.

I started becoming aware of how particularly vulnerable our kids are to environmental contaminants as soon as I became a mother. For starters, children's immune systems aren't fully developed. Plus, they take in more air, water, and food than adults relative to their size. And kids tend to come into closer contact with toxins because they spend more time on the ground, play outdoors, and put their hands and other objects in their mouths. No small concern since the National Cancer Institute says that two-thirds of all cancers have an environmental cause.

This is where global warming and our children's health come together. All the factors that create the CO_2 emissions that cause global warming—car fumes, coal-burning power plants, pollution from factories and farms—are also putting our children's lives at risk.

Nine million kids in America have been diagnosed with asthma—with the percentages particularly high among minorities (who more often live in high-pollution urban areas).

So, at a time when these kids should be growing and discovering and playing with abandon, far too many of them are sent to school supplied with pencils, rulers, and inhalers. In some urban areas, like West Oakland (which is located near a busy port), children are seven times more likely to be hospitalized for asthma than kids in the rest of the state. Many are afraid to run and play because they can't tell the difference between being out of breath and having a life-threatening asthma attack.

For many people the signature image of global warming—brought home so vividly in *An Inconvenient Truth*—is the disappearing snowcap atop Mount Kilimanjaro. But for me, it's the image of those kids on the playground, having to stop playing so they can suck on their inhalers.

murderer, the unusual properties of embryonic stem cells, which is that they can develop into any sort of cell in the body. It would seem like a heaven-sent (if you believe in that sort of thing) resolution to the stem cell conflict, since it opened up the prospect of continuing—and greatly expanding—stem cell research without having to "sacrifice" any more embryos. A triumph for science, for research, for reason, and for human ingenuity, none of which has been exactly nurtured under George Bush. The discovery would seem to be a major win-win, but Michael Kinsley, who has Parkinson's disease, cautioned in *Time* that the breakthrough was not necessarily the nick-of-time rescue from an untenable position the Right may have hoped it was:

> But any Republicans who think the stem-cell breakthrough gets them off the hook are going to end up very unhappy. This issue will not go away. First, even the scientists who achieved the latest success believe strongly that embryonic-stem-cell research should continue. No one knows for sure whether the

new method of producing pluripotent cells will pan out or where the next big developments will come from. . . . Second, even if this were a true turning point in stem-cell research, people like me are not going to quickly forget those six lost years.

Why the Right Is Wrong About Science

The Right's War on Science rages these days over global warming, over evolution, and over stem cell research. But, in the future as we enter an Age of Dis-Enlightenment, who knows what the Right might try to call into question? Once you've gotten rid of facts and the experimental method, the sky, aka heaven, is the limit. If astrophysics leads some to question the biblical account of creation, well, let's start teaching kids that the Earth is the center of the universe and undo the work of those notorious secular humanists Galileo, Kepler, and Copernicus. If the shifting of plate tectonics winds up costing us too much in tsunami relief, let's go back to the theory that volcanoes are God's wrath and there's just no point in trying to figure them out (of course, other than by denying rights to homosexuals, who are probably the source of all that wrath). DNA research letting too many death row inmates off the hook and making the citizens of death-penalty-loving states think twice? Well, maybe it's time to rethink this whole double helix business. We may yet reach a point where the only sector of scientific inquiry that is safe from the anti-science mobs on the Right is weapons research.

Elsewhere in this book, when the shoe seems to fit, I've called the Right Neanderthals. With respect to the War on Science, this seems less like name-calling and more like an empirical statement of fact. If they continue on their present course of know-nothingism, they may yet return to the comforting pre-intellectual world of the distant past. Trouble is, they want to drag the rest of us back along with them. Here's NASA's top climate scientist, Jim Hansen, on what may happen if we don't take swift action on climate change:

If human beings follow a business-as-usual course, continuing to exploit fossil fuel resources without reducing carbon emissions or capturing and sequestering them before they warm the atmosphere, the eventual effects on climate and life may be comparable to those at the time of mass extinctions. Life will survive, but it will do so on a transformed planet. For all foreseeable human generations, it will be a far more desolate world than the one in which civilization developed and flourished during the past several thousand years.

But at least we won't have to worry about flag-burning, gays getting married, and *Roe v. Wade* anymore.

6

Iraq: The Beginning of a War Without End

American Waterloo

It happens in every great tragedy, Greek or Shakespearean. The fatal deed from which there is no return. For Macbeth, it was, of course, killing King Duncan ("Had I but died an hour before this chance, I had lived a blessed time").

George W. Bush's fatal deed was invading Iraq. It led to a toxic brew of lies and deceptions—and cover-ups to hide previous lies and deceptions—all concocted to sell an unnecessary war to the American people. The Iraq invasion derailed the war on terror, fueled anti-American feeling around the world, contributed to the soaring budget deficit, aggravated an economic recession, and made us less safe here at home.

Indeed, in late January 2008, on the very same day that America's top commander in Iraq, General David Petraeus, said he needed *yet another* six months to determine if there was any light at the end of the Iraqi tunnel, a study by two nonprofit journalism organizations concluded that President Bush and his closest advisers had ladled out hundreds of false statements about the national security threat from Iraq in the time between the 9/11 terrorist attacks and the invasion of Iraq—935 to be precise.

The study said that the official lies "were part of an orchestrated campaign that effectively galvanized public opinion and, in the process, led the nation to war under decidedly false pretenses." Shortly after the study was released by the nonpartisan Center for Public Integrity, partnered with the Fund for Independence in Journalism, White House spokesman Scott Stanzel engaged in what was undoubtedly one more deception: saying no one around him had bothered to read the report.

And yet, Stanzel went on unblinkingly to reiterate the official line, just knocked down by the study, saying the invasion was fully justified by the threat posed by Saddam Hussein. We can now add Stanzel's statement to the pile. The study found that in speeches, briefings, interviews, and other venues, in the run-up to the war, Bush and administration officials stated unequivocally on at least 532 occasions that Iraq had weapons of mass destruction or was trying to produce or obtain them or had links to al Qaeda.

"It is now beyond dispute that Iraq did not possess any weapons of mass destruction or have meaningful ties to al Qaeda," according to the authors of the study. "In short, the Bush administration led the nation to war on the basis of erroneous information that it methodically propagated and that culminated in military action against Iraq on March 19, 2003."

Of course, it wasn't just George Bush who was engaged in the serial lying. The report details the stiff competition for most prolific dissembler waged among big-hitters Dick Cheney, Condi Rice, Don Rumsfeld, Colin Powell, Paul Wolfowitz, as well as by White House press secretaries Ari Fleischer and Scott McClellan.

But President Bush, perhaps owing to his experience as a former owner of the Texas Rangers, easily walked away with the MVP award in this World Series of mendacity.

Bush topped the field with 259 false statements, 231 about weapons of mass destruction in Iraq and 28 about Iraq's links to al Qaeda. Powell finished a close second with 244 lies about weapons of mass destruction in Iraq and about 10 linking Iraq and al Qaeda.

It's worth repeating that none of this would have mattered nearly as much if the national media hadn't served as such a loyal home team crowd. I mean, if you play a rigged baseball game in an empty stadium, does it really matter? Instead, from the crowded press bleachers and peanut galleries, the national media played right along, cheering on each dazzling falsehood by the White House, often punctuated with a synchronized, celebratory wave. Says the study: "Some journalists—indeed, even some entire news organizations— have since acknowledged that their coverage during those prewar months was far too deferential and uncritical. These mea culpas notwithstanding, much of the wall-to-wall media coverage provided additional, 'independent' validation of the Bush administration's false statements about Iraq."

Even before this study was published, bookstore shelves were sagging with canonical works whose titles tell the sorry tale all by themselves: *State of Denial, Hubris, Losing Iraq, The End of Iraq, The Five Biggest Lies Bush Told Us About Iraq, Blood Money, The Torture Papers: The Road to Abu Ghraib, Thinking Beyond War: Civil-Military Relations and Why America Fails to Win the Peace*, and Tom Ricks's heartbreaking *Fiasco*.

My purpose is not to retrace the timeline of this tragic disaster or to rehash what went wrong or why. What is important to understand is how the war was, from the very start, a cherished project of the Right, a scheme hatched by the most fanatical of the fanatics long before 9/11 provided a handy pretext—and how, after the Twin Towers fell and the Pentagon burned, each misstep that was taken on a road that included Abu Ghraib, the Haditha massacre, and four thousand unnecessary American deaths was a direct result of the pernicious ideology of the Right. The fact that our troops were forced to execute a reckless, faith-based foreign policy in spite of informed military advice and those niggling little inconvenient truths, the facts on the ground, is the Right's greatest disgrace.

And yet there are signs that, through mindless flag-waving, cynical charges of abandoning the troops, and the energetic efforts of their media enablers, the Right may still be able to wring some political mileage out of Iraq. From the beginning, the Right's strategy has been to ignore the facts and believe that, if you throw up enough flak, the public might ignore the facts too.

That's why it's essential we hold fast to the truth about Iraq—and the belief that truth isn't relative. And that we pin the Iraq Bad Conduct Medal right where it belongs: on the uniform of the neoconservative true believers.

The war in Iraq has become a right-wing suicide-bombing. It kills and maims innocent bystanders and is being waged for ideological purposes to satisfy a dangerous belief system that's as far removed from coherent political thought and rational foreign policy as radical Islamic fundamentalism is from mainstream Islam. And, in both radical faiths, nonbelievers and apostates face the terrible uncompromising wrath reserved for heretics and infidels.

Still, we'll take our chances.

The Iraq Obsession

You don't have to be a conspiracy theorist to believe that flying the Stars and Stripes over Iraq had been a recurring dream of a small but very powerful cabal of right-wing thinkers ever since Bush 41 stopped Norman Schwarzkopf from stormin' Baghdad back in 1991. The exact reason for this dream is subject to debate, ranging from Freudian theories (finish the job Daddy couldn't) to vast geopolitical master plots (the American Empire and global hegemony) to more prosaic economic interests (the War for Oil) to domestic political scheming (rally the public around our brave warrior-president). But in a multiple choice test, the correct answer would undoubtedly be "all of the above." The War for Oil motive, for one, is no longer subject to dispute, having been conceded by, among others, former Chairman of the Federal Reserve Alan Greenspan. Greenspan explained to Charlie Rose in September 2007, "People do not realize in this country, for example, how tenuous our ties to international energy are. That is, we on a daily basis require continuous flow. If that flow is shut off, it causes catastrophic effects in the industrial world. And it's that which made [Saddam] far more important to get out than bin Laden." That we have lost the War for Oil is similarly indisputable, as anyone who's been to the gas station lately will attest. Iraq has similarly been a disaster for America's role in the world and the president's legacy. As for finishing the job Daddy couldn't, Daddy has never looked better or wiser.

Although Paul Wolfowitz, Richard Perle, Doug Feith, and their fellow armchair warriors on the Defense Policy Board had lusted for an Iraq adventure for many years, political calculation suggested that the public at large was not going to support regime change without a stronger case than the wishful thinking of a bunch of defense intellectuals.

Then September 11 happened.

Before long "good soldier" Colin Powell was lecturing the United Nations about those aluminum tubes, George Tenet was tailoring the CIA's reports to suit the current fashion, and the president himself was mesmerizing the nation with fairy tales about WMD. In parallel with the carefully stage-managed attempt to make the case for war, the Right was honing their tactic of shouting down the skeptics by questioning their patriotism and invoking 9/11.

The Iraq invasion was an irrational response to 9/11, striking at a convenient scapegoat rather than the real villains. But after the Right's psychological terror campaign to frighten the public with the specter of American cities vaporized into radioactive dust by the fantasy tag team of Osama and Saddam, it's no wonder they got their way.

The Imperial Delusion: Crazy Talk from the Right

The Right is wrong about Iraq in every respect. But it was really, really wrong—about its reverse domino theory that our invasion and the toppling of Saddam would result in a flowering of democracy in the Middle East. Doug Feith, the former undersecretary of defense policy and a key figure among the administration's hawks (and, according to the Iraq war's commanding general, Tommy Franks, "the stupidest fucking guy on the face of the planet"), explained the Right's grand vision to Nick Lemann in a 2003 *New Yorker* profile:

> Then, you have the phenomenon that this greater freedom that came to Latin America, that came to various parts of Asia, largely missed the Middle East. And there is all kinds of writing on the subject, on whether there is anything inherently incompatible between either Muslim culture, or Arab culture, and this kind of freer government. This Administration does not believe there is an inherent incompatibility. And if Iraq had a government like that, and if that government could create some of those institutions of democracy, that might be inspirational for people throughout the Middle East to try to increase the amount of freedom that they have, and they would benefit both politically and economically by doing so.

In particular, as one of the chief architects of the Iraq war, Richard Perle, explained on PBS's *Frontline*, one of the anticipated regional benefits would be a newly docile Iran:

> First it will inspire the opponents of the regime in Iran. I have no doubt about that. And the opponents are many because life is miserable under the mullahs. If a tyrant like Saddam Hussein can be brought down, others are going to begin to think— they're already thinking—they may begin to act to bring down

the tyrants who are afflicting them in pretty much the same way. So I would think the results would be beneficial in Iran.

Five years later, instead of standing tall with our arm around the shoulder of our democratic little buddy Iran, we are developing contingency plans to invade.

And in the Arab countries the United States supposedly has the most influence over—Saudi Arabia and Egypt—human rights have taken one beating after another. In 2007 alone, Egypt dissolved one of the country's leading human rights organizations, jailed editors and reporters critical of the government, repressed religious minorities, and engaged in a crackdown on dissident groups. In Saudi Arabia, one of the most notable events last year was the flogging of a gang-rape victim for "adultery." After her lawyer appealed her initial sentence of ninety lashes, his law license was suspended and her punishment was upped to two hundred lashes. These are our allies.

And though Israel and Palestine returned to the bargaining table in January 2008, the Palestinians are accusing the Israelis of trying to sabotage the talks through their continued military activity in the West Bank, while hard-line Israeli politicians are threatening to abandon the Jewish state's fragile coalition government merely for talking to the other side.

In countries where U.S. influence is more precarious, such as Lebanon and Syria, post-Iraq events have fueled the rise of the terrorist-political organization Hezbollah. And parallel to Hezbollah's rise has been a booming increase in the power of the fundamentalist Hamas in the Occupied Territories.

How did this happen? As the United States became known as the underwriting sponsor of Abu Ghraib and Guantánamo, it became harder for Arab moderates to fight for human rights and U.S.–friendly policies. And as "democracy" became linked with market bombings and massacres in Iraq and Afghanistan, the concept lost its appeal in many corners of the Middle East. Clearly, things haven't precisely worked out as war promoters such as Doug Feith said they would.

"One of the principal reasons that we are focused on Iraq as a threat to us and to our interests," Feith said the month before the United States invaded Iraq, "is because we are focused on this connection between three things: terrorist organizations, state sponsors, and weapons of mass destruction. If we were to take military action and vindicate our principles, in the war on terrorism, against Iraq, I think it would . . . *register* with other countries around the world that are sponsoring terrorism, and would perhaps change their own cost-benefit calculations about their role in connection with terrorist networks."

Lieutenant Colonel Karen Kwiatkowski, who worked in the Office of Special Planning and was one of the few people involved with the planning of the war who had the decency to resign after it turned into a debacle, said that anyone looking for answers to "why the post-Hussein occupation has been distinguished by confusion and false steps . . . need look no further than the process inside the Office of the Secretary of Defense." She also had this to say about Feith: "He was very arrogant. . . . He doesn't utilize a wide variety of inputs. He seeks information that confirms what he already thinks."

Colonel Kwiatkowski's intellectual honesty and willingness to take responsibility stand in stark opposition to one of the key players in the Iraq disaster. CIA Director George Tenet will go down in history as "Mr. Slam Dunk." He played a central role in selling the Iraq war to the American public, resigned a few years later, and then tried to distance himself from Bush and the war by talking to Bob Woodward and writing a book portraying himself as a poor, hapless victim who knew the truth at the time and really, really wanted to tell it, but, somehow, just had no choice but to go along. What more could you possibly expect from a mere CIA director?

Each version of this contemptible tale shares the same fatal flaw. It requires that the remedy that was readily available—public dissent followed by resignation—did not exist.

Poor George Tenet. Flogging his book, *At the Center of the Storm: My Years at the CIA*, on *60 Minutes* in April 2007, he told Scott Pelley about how his phrase "slam dunk" was misused by the Bush administration. Tenet, you see, didn't mean it was a "slam dunk" that Hussein actually had WMD, he only meant it was a "slam dunk" that a public case could be made that Hussein had WMD.

I can't really see that the distinction matters, but Tenet apparently does. "I became campaign talk," Tenet told Pelley. "I was a talking point. 'Look at what the idiot told us, and we decided to go to war.'

Well, let's not be so disingenuous. Let's stand up. This is why we did it. This is why, this is how we did it. And let's tell, let's everybody tell the truth."

Great—except he was about four years too late in coming clean. Tenet seemed to believe there was a major distinction between lying and standing by silently while others lie (and then proudly receiving a Medal of Freedom from the liars).

He could have simply resigned back in 2003 and freed himself to "tell the truth." And the passion and anger he displayed in 2007 in the service of book sales could have been used in earlier times in the service of his country.

"It's the most despicable thing I've ever heard in my life," Tenet told Pelley, referring to the way he was treated at the White House. "You don't do this. . . . You're gonna throw somebody overboard . . . Is that honorable? It's not honorable to me."

The problem is, the Honor Train had left the station a long time ago, and Tenet wasn't on board.

But others were. Others like Karen Kwiatkowski. Or like John Brady Kiesling, a career U.S. diplomat who resigned from the State Department. As he wrote in his resignation letter to Colin Powell:

> I am resigning because I have tried and failed to reconcile my conscience with my ability to represent the current U.S. administration. I have confidence that our democratic process is ultimately self-correcting, and hope that in a small way I can contribute from outside to shaping policies that better serve the security and prosperity of the American people and the world we share.

That, Mr. Tenet, is how it's done.

How long do you think it's going to be after the end of the Bush administration before we are treated to General Petraeus's memoir explaining how the surge would have worked "if only I had been given the troops I needed to implement it properly"?

As Tenet said on *60 Minutes*: "At the end of the day, the only thing you have is trust and honor in this world. It's all you have. All you have is your reputation built on trust and your personal honor. And when you don't have that anymore, well, there you go."

George Tenet and I are both Greek, and there is a great word for what he is talking about: *filotimo*. It's difficult to translate, but basically it means honor, conscience, and integrity—three traits sadly lacking among Tenet and his war-making cronies on the Right.

Kristol Unclear

For William Kristol, the Right's in-house scribe, the stakes in Iraq were high indeed.

> I do think Bush also went beyond the particular case of Iraq in his thinking after Sept. 11. The way I would reconstruct his thought process might be something like this: "Look, we live in the 21st century in a world in which . . . the big picture story in the Middle East has been increased extremism, increased anti-Americanism, increased support for terrorism, dictators developing weapons of mass destruction. And you can't just sit back and let that go on." We made good faith efforts in all kinds of ways to help the Middle Eastern countries in the 90s. But, we weren't serious about fighting terrorism, didn't crack down at all on the export of extremist Islam. We've seen the dictators developing weapons of mass destruction and getting away with it. And the effect of that was really disastrous. That has to be reversed.
>
> Obviously, there are exercises of American power that could be unwise, and where we could be too hasty, and we could be hubristic. We're against that. . . . But on the biggest question, is the great danger too little an exercise, too mean an exercise of American power, or too great, too forward-leaning an exercise of American power? I think that's an easy question to answer. The danger is American withdrawal, American timidity, American slowness. . . . The danger is not that we're going to do too much. The danger is that we're going to do too little.

Actually, the danger lay not in *how much* or *how little* we did, but in *what* we did. The Right's restless and arrogant abuse of power was inspired by a schoolyard bully mentality. But the Middle East's naughty boys—autocrats, mad mullahs, and spoiled princes—were not, shall we say, receptive to the lesson America chose to teach.

Sweets and Flowers

There's no adequate penance for the monstrous folly of the Right in getting us involved in Iraq. But, if I had to pick, I'd suggest that each of the war's promoters have the phrase "sweets and flowers" tattooed across their foreheads. "Sweets and flowers," of course, are what Kanan Makiya, the Right's second favorite pet Iraqi (after Ahmed Chalabi), told President Bush we'd be greeted with upon arrival in Baghdad. As Al Franken points out, he left out the key word "exploding."

The selling of the war, like all good marketing, stimulated more than one of the public's erogenous zones. On the one hand, it was *necessary*. On the other hand, it was going to be *easy*. Wolfowitz told *The Philadelphia Inquirer,* "It is entirely possible that in Iraq you have the most pro-American population that can be found anywhere in the Arab world. If you are looking for historical analogy, it's probably closer to post-liberation France after World War II." (For the record, the American occupation forces in France did not lose a single soldier to enemy action after the German surrender. As a matter of fact, we didn't even lose one in Germany. Not one.)

Cheney reported to the credulous Tim Russert that he had been told—probably over sweets and flowers—just what a feel-good excursion the war was going to be by unnamed White House visitors. I'm going to guess he's talking about Makiya and Chalabi. "I really do believe that we will be greeted as liberators. I've talked with a lot of Iraqis in the last several months myself, had them to the White House. . . . The read we get on the people of Iraq is there is no question but that they want to get rid of Saddam Hussein and they will welcome as liberators the United States when we come to do that."

When Russert broke the news to Cheney a few months after the invasion that we had not been greeted as liberators but, rather, as occupiers and invaders—and infidels, to boot—Cheney responded once again by asserting something as the truth, even if it didn't jibe with the facts. "Well, I think we *have* by most Iraqis. I think the majority of Iraqis are thankful for the fact that the United States is there, that we came and we took down the Saddam Hussein government."

Richard Perle was excited about the experimental nature of the enterprise: "I think there is a potential civic culture in Arab countries that can lead to democratic institutions and I think Iraq is probably the best place to put that proposition to the test." He also made this famous prediction: "And a year from now, I'll be very surprised if there is not some grand square in Baghdad that is named after President Bush. There is no doubt that, with the exception of a very small number of people close to a vicious regime, the people of Iraq have been liberated and they understand that they've been liberated. And it is getting easier every day for Iraqis to express that sense of liberation." Now, I don't know if there's a square named for President Bush in Baghdad. Perhaps there is. But if there is, I'll bet just about anything that it's surrounded by concrete blast walls and guarded by American tanks and helicopter gunships—unless that job has been outsourced to Blackwater.

"Necessary." "Easy." And did we mention "cheap"? The war would pay for itself. Wolfowitz explained to Congress how it would all work: "There's a lot of money to pay for this. It doesn't have to be U.S. taxpayer money. We are dealing with a country that can really finance its own reconstruction, and relatively soon."

The Right was so cocksure about its project—or so willing to lie about it in order to sell it to the public—that it sent United States Agency for International Development chief Andrew Natsios on *Nightline* in April of 2003 to tout the amazing deal we were getting on a rebuilt Iraq.

> **Ted Koppel:** I mean, when you talk about 1.7, you're not suggesting that the rebuilding of Iraq is going to be done for $1.7 billion?
>
> **Natsios:** Well, in terms of the American taxpayer's contribution, I do, this is it for the U.S.
>
> . . .
>
> **Koppel:** You're saying the, the top cost for the U.S. taxpayer will be $1.7 billion. No more than that?
>
> **Natsios:** For the reconstruction. And then there's $700 million in the supplemental budget for humanitarian relief, which we don't competitively bid 'cause it's charities that get that money.
>
> **Koppel:** I understand. But as far as reconstruction goes, the American taxpayer will not be hit for more than $1.7 billion no matter how long the process takes?

Natsios: That is our plan and that is our intention. And these figures, outlandish figures I've seen, I have to say, there's a little bit of hoopla involved in this.

Andrew Natsios's calculus was off, conservatively, by over two *trillion* dollars.

Cakewalk: Days of Shock and Awe

With the actual start of the war, the Right breathed a sigh of relief. No last-minute reprieve for Saddam courtesy of Hans Blix, Mohamed ElBaradei, or the United Nations. Now that Saddam's departed this life for that great spider hole in the sky, we'll always be left to wonder why the hell he didn't just let the weapons inspectors back in. Since Saddam had proven himself both wily and crazy, it's hard to know which part of his brain was doing the thinking during the endgame. But it's possible that Wily Saddam preferred to take his chances with a U.S. invasion rather than risk the opportunistic takeover by his southern neighbor Iran—with whom Crazy Saddam had fought a devastating and inconclusive eight-year war—which might follow if he were seen to back down. Based on what eventually happened—an emboldened Iran moving aggressively into a regional power vacuum—it appears that, wily or crazy, Saddam was not being paranoid when he was worrying about Iran.

The rapid and overwhelming success of the American military surprised no one except possibly Saddam, Uday, and Qusay. These were heady times on the Right. American technical superiority, utter dominance in airpower, and the skill and bravery of our troops brought success after success as the Iraqi military simply evaporated without even bothering to surrender. And the best news of all was that Saddam was not able to deploy his weapons of mass destruction against our troops, his neighbors, or Israel. This was not, as we would later learn, a rare instance of prudence or restraint on Saddam's part. It was because he didn't have any, a thought that bears repeating at least 935 times.

Baghdad fell on April 9, 2003, and the American military shifted into occupation mode. With the notable exception of the Oil Ministry, the military did little to secure the property of either the government or private citizens, resulting in the first drops of rain on the

Right's parade: widespread looting and violent score-settling. Television news reports showing the looting yielded one of the war's most enduring sound bites. "Stuff happens" was Donald Rumsfeld's summation, followed by his cantankerous definition of freedom: "Freedom's untidy, and free people are free to make mistakes and commit crimes and do bad things. They're also free to live their lives and do wonderful things. And that's what's going to happen here."

Another immediate mistake, which would lead to the collapse of any semblance of order in Iraq, was the disbanding (but not, crucially, disarming) of the Iraqi military, the one institution in Iraq that had the potential to hold the country together after its leaders had been removed. These were not just mistakes of the generals or of Bush and Rumsfeld, these were mistakes made by the invasion cheerleaders on the Right, stemming from their "never is heard a discouraging word" preparations for battle. By ignoring the planning done by the State Department and not allowing any worst-case scenarios about what might happen after the invasion, the Right managed to sustain momentum for the attack itself but at the enormous cost of all that has happened since.

Mission Accomplished!

On May 1, 2003, 1st Lieutenant George Bush (ret.), whose spotty service record remains a matter of dispute more than thirty years after he partied his way through a brief stint with the Air National Guard, landed on the deck of the aircraft carrier *Abraham Lincoln* and was immediately clapped in irons, thrown in the brig, and charged with gross dereliction of duty.

Actually, that's not what happened.

Wearing a crotch-hugging flight suit, Bush strutted around the deck high-fiving sailors and pilots underneath a banner reading, "Mission Accomplished." While the RNC's cameras rolled and Karl Rove sat drooling in a corner, Bush announced the end of major combat operations. The war was over, just a few small details to take care of to get Iraq back on its feet, and that's all she wrote.

Public derision of "Mission Accomplished" ripened to the point where it became a punch line for Bush's opponents during his run for reelection. But thanks to the relentless Swift Boating of Democratic candidate John Kerry—an actual combat veteran—Ohio tipped into

McCain the Cheerleader

John McCain, because of his military bona fides and stature as an independent thinker, was called upon to provide cover fire for the president:

"But I believe, Katie, that the Iraqi people will greet us as liberators." —to Katie Couric, NBC, 3/20/03

"It's clear that the end is very much in sight." —ABC, 4/9/03

"There's not a history of clashes that are violent between Sunnis and Shias. So I think they can probably get along."—MSNBC, 4/23/03

"This is a mission accomplished. They know how much influence Saddam Hussein had on the Iraqi people, how much more difficult it made [it] to get their cooperation." —*This Week*, ABC, 12/14/03

"I'm confident we're on the right course." —*ABC News*, 3/7/04

"The initial phases of [the war] were so spectacularly successful that it took us all by surprise." —CBS, 10/31/04

"I do think that progress is being made in a lot of Iraq. Overall, I think a year from now, we will have made a fair amount of progress if we stay the course. If I thought we weren't making progress, I'd be despondent." —*The Hill*, 12/8/05

"We are succeeding. We are succeeding. And I unequivocally put my career and my political fortunes on the line and unequivocally said we're going to support this surge. We're not going to talk about timetables or anything else; we're going to talk about winning and what's necessary to win." —GOP debate, Reagan Library, 1/30/08

Dear Lord.

And despite his record as a pork-buster and a champion of the need for Congress to have strict oversight of military acquisitions and spending, McCain failed to join the calls for the creation of a modern-day Truman Committee to investigate the Bush administration's massive mismanagement of funds earmarked for the rebuilding of Iraq. In 1941, as the United States was on the verge of entering World War II, Senator

Harry S. Truman had launched an investigation into reports of wide-spread waste, corruption, and mismanagement in the nascent war effort. Over the next three years, the Truman Committee held hundreds of public hearings, visited military bases across the country, and ended up saving taxpayers $15 billion. His efforts also saved countless lives by rooting out contractors using inferior materials and producing shoddy equipment. We sure could have used "Maverick" McCain as a modern day "Give 'em Hell, Harry," but he was AWOL in the battle to bring accountability to the war in Iraq.

the GOP column on election day, guaranteeing another four years of government deception about the war.

Meanwhile, back in Iraq, young sergeants who had been trained to be warriors were finding it increasingly difficult to perform the tasks of policing, mediating, and community-building that Bush, Rumsfeld, and Wolfowitz had so casually assigned to them. And the initial round of score-settling devolved into vicious sectarian warfare between Shiite and Sunni, a prospect dismissed out of hand at the war's outset by Kristol on NPR's *Fresh Air*: "There's been a certain amount of pop sociology in America . . . that the Shia can't get along with the Sunni and the Shia in Iraq just want to establish some kind of Islamic fundamentalist regime," Kristol said. "There's almost no evidence of that at all. Iraq's always been very secular."

The country's violent implosion had never been imagined by Bush, who was unaware of the very existence of different Islamic sects in Iraq even as the war began. And although the Iraqi army had collapsed with startling rapidity, there were troubling signs that American forces were becoming a target for a shadowy new enemy who was never going to stand and fight. Instead, the insurgents planted roadside bombs, lobbed mortar shells into U.S. bases from beyond the wire, and intimidated and killed anyone who dared to work with the Americans.

The viceroy from central casting, General Jay Garner, first head administrator of the Coalition Provisional Authority, the transitional government set up by the United States, was quickly replaced in May 2003 with the technocratic Paul Bremer, whose lasting monument in Iraq will be the so-called Bremer Walls, the enormous concrete barriers that began sprouting up to separate American forces from the Iraqi people. Back in Washington, the Bushies struggled to explain what the new mission was and how, if at all, it was going to be accomplished.

Facts? We Don't Need No Stinkin' Facts

Throughout 2005, the president sounded like a man willing to sacrifice everything—including Republican control of Congress—for what he believed would allow him to go down in history as a great president, the one who dragged the Middle East kicking and screaming into the bosom of democracy.

The president's fanaticism was—and remains—a scary prospect for the country. Nothing seemed to penetrate the Bush bubble—not the rising death toll, not his depressed poll numbers, not the continuing revelations about the deceptions his administration used to lead us to war. Not even the growing skepticism about the war being expressed within his own party appeared to faze him. In a speech he gave in December 2005 to the World Affairs Council in Philadelphia, it was clear that the situation might be even worse than we thought. Bush came across as a zealot who had utterly convinced himself that fighting on (and on and on) in Iraq is the right thing for America and the world.

This man-on-a-mission mien was particularly evident during the brief Q&A session the president engaged in after his speech.

The most revealing moment came when a questioner asked why the president continues to "invoke 9/11 as justification for the invasion of Iraq" when no such link existed. After saying he appreciated the question, the president proceeded to once again link 9/11 to Saddam and said of the decision to remove him: "And knowing what I know today, I'd make the decision again."

So knowing what we know today about WMD, and knowing what we know today about how poorly the occupation has gone, how surprisingly resilient the insurgency has been, how failed our efforts at reconstruction . . . knowing all that, he'd "make the decision again"? Just call him a cockeyed optimist. A deluded cockeyed optimist.

The president made the task of building "a lasting democracy in the heart of the Middle East" the central focus of his speech—mentioning "democracy" and variations on the word fifty-nine times.

Er, Mission Accomplished?

At a news conference on May 19, 2005, Condoleezza Rice was asked about a *New York Times* story depicting U.S. military commanders as increasingly pessimistic about the outcome of the war in Iraq. Her answer was a model of that Bush administration specialty—complete and unrelenting deception. As an important historical exercise—and a service to those who prefer their leadership straightforward and candid—I've taken the liberty of translating her response from Modern Bush-speak to plain English.

Rice: I believe the president has always said that his strategy is a strategy for success. He doesn't have an exit strategy; he has a success strategy.

Translation: What we say is true by virtue of our having said it. We do not reside in the "reality-based community." In fact, not only do we not have an exit strategy, we don't have any strategy at all. We're screwed.

Rice: As I said when I was recently in Iraq, the United States is there, along with other coalition members, to support the Iraqis, to help them with their security until their forces are capable of doing that on their own.

Translation: I'm now answering a question that wasn't asked with a complete non sequitur. And even that's a lie. Because the other "coalition members" do have a success strategy: they're getting the hell out.

Rice: The Iraqi security forces are making progress.

Translation: The Iraqi security forces are not making progress.

Rice: I think no one believes that [the Iraqis] are currently capable of carrying out those missions on their own, but if you look at the way that they performed at the time of the elections, for instance, they performed really very, very well.

Translation: At least the ones that didn't run away or get killed.

Rice: The foreign minister and I did have discussions about the importance of an Iraqi political process that is inclusive of all Iraqis.

Translation: . . . though we steered clear of the rebuilding process, which is inclusive of all American companies with ties to Dick Cheney.

Rice: So it's a difficult proposition that the Iraqis are engaged in.

Translation: So it's a difficult proposition that we imposed on the Iraqis.

Rice: They are just emerging from a very long national nightmare with tyranny. Saddam Hussein was a terrible threat not just to his own people but to his neighbors.

Translation: Unlike that other guy who is still at large and a threat to the United States but whose name my boss and I can't, for the life us, seem to remember.

Rice: And so it is not as if the situation that we found ourselves in was somehow preferable to the situation that we're in now, but it's going to be a difficult road to help the Iraqis to have a sustainable democracy. That's our goal.

Translation: Or at least that is the "fallback goal" we landed on after all our original reasons for going to war were exposed as lies.

He ended his appearance by saying, "My job as the president is to see the world the way it is, not the way we hope it is." Well, then, he has utterly failed at the assignment. In fact the hallmark of his position on Iraq has been turning a blind eye to reality and operating entirely on wishful thinking.

From the moment the Bush War Room started the clock on Operation Desert Disaster, it found itself confronting various time-honored processes for which it would show little patience since, in every case, inconvenient facts were brought up and had to be steam-rolled by ideology. Why bother with the kind of deliberation and consideration of options and worst-case outcomes the public (and the troops) have a right to expect from any responsible leadership? For the Right, "what ifs" are a sort of heresy that pragmatists have been using for years to frustrate their grand schemes. So the State Department's Future of Iraq Project—which anticipated a startling number of the subsequent problems, from the looting to the Shiite and Sunni tensions to the difficulties of forming an effective Iraqi government post-Saddam, was completely ignored. The State Department has always been high on the neocons' list of suspect institutions, filled, as they see it, with tweedy Ivy League party-poopers.

General Eric Shinseki, a heroic combat-tested officer who had risen to become the army's chief of staff, was also ignored—and shoved to the sidelines—when he dared to tell a congressional committee that a successful occupation required far more boots on the ground than the Defense Department was prepared to commit. The general clearly had not gotten the memo that the war had to be sold as quick, cheap, and painless. Secretary of Defense Rumsfeld did not even bother to attend the ceremony marking Shinseki's hasty retirement—just to make sure all his other generals got the message and stayed on the reservation.

And efforts at diplomacy, both to engage the international community and force Saddam to comply with United Nations weapons inspectors, were met with much eye-rolling from the gang at the Department of Defense. Even more contemptible to the Right was the notion of world opinion and, horrors, international law. Here's Richard Perle: "I think in this case international law stood in the way of doing the right thing."

So the administration strong-armed a bunch of micro-countries (Tonga, Singapore, Dominican Republic, Iceland, Moldova), former Soviet satellites glad to antagonize Moscow (Poland, Ukraine, Estonia, Latvia, Hungary, Romania), and Great Britain into the Coalition of the Willing. Notably absent was the vast majority of Muslim states. And of the Willing, many sensibly declined a combat role, offering instead to roll bandages or install porta-potties in exchange for generous bribes in American aid and George Bush's undying gratitude. The Willing governments of Spain, Italy, and Ukraine fell in short order and were replaced by Not So Willing successors. Talk about blowback.

You can hear the impatience (and perhaps the presidential toe tapping restlessly on the ground) with diplomatic formalities in this exchange between Bush and the soon-to-be prime minister of Spain, José Aznar (reported in the Spanish paper *El País*, nearly a month before the war began):

President Bush: Saddam Hussein won't change and he'll continue playing games. The time has come to get rid of him.

That's it. As for me, I'll try from now on to use a rhetoric that's as subtle as can be while we're seeking approval of the resolution. If anyone vetoes, we'll go. Saddam Hussein isn't disarming. We have to catch him right now. Until now we've shown an incredible amount of patience. There are two weeks left. In two weeks we'll be militarily ready. . . . We can win without destruction. We're already putting into effect a post–Saddam Iraq, and I believe there's a good basis for a better future. Iraq has a good bureaucracy and a civil society that's relatively strong. It could be organized into a federation. Meanwhile, we're doing all we can to attend to the political needs of our friends and allies.

Prime Minister Aznar: It's very important to count on a resolution. It isn't the same to act with it as without it. It would be very convenient to count on a majority in the Security Council that would support that resolution. In fact, having a majority is more important than anyone casting a veto. We think the content of the resolution should state, among other things, that Saddam Hussein has lost his opportunity.

Bush: The resolution will be tailored to help you as best it can. I don't care much about the content. . . . This is like Chinese water torture. We have to put an end to it.

Aznar: I agree, but it would be good to be able to count on as many people as possible. Have a little patience.

Bush: My patience has run out. I won't go beyond mid-March.

A Factual Quagmire

Faced with mounting American casualties, horrific sectarian slaughter in the streets, a corrupt government hardly worthy of the name, and a glaring absence of weapons of mass destruction, by 2005 the tide of public opinion had begun to turn against the Right's Iraq war and their grand plan to remake the Middle East as a new cradle of Jeffersonian democracy.

So the Right reverted to form and a war they knew they could win: a War on Facts. When the facts are against them, the Right argues the very existence of facts.

And as pretty much every fact turned against the administration in Iraq, the fallback position increasingly became: well, who can really know anything? Everything is so complex. You've got Sunnis, you've got Shiites, you've got Kurds . . . the truth is . . . well, the truth is that we can't know the truth . . . so how can we be held accountable when nothing is really knowable?

Bush, Cheney, Rumsfeld, and their cohorts didn't invent this way of thinking. The funny thing is that these anti-elitist moral absolutists started arguing a variation of postmodernism—an elitist linguistic theory laden with moral relativism.

Here's the short version of postmodernism, via Wikipedia: "In the broadest sense, denial of objectivity is held to be the postmodern position, and a hostility towards claims advanced on the basis of objectivity its defining feature . . . all standards are arbitrary and meaningless."

Sound like any defense secretaries you know?

If you want to know how postmodern poster boy Jacques Derrida would have sounded in a political context, check out Rumsfeld's answer at a DoD press briefing six weeks before he was fired, when asked about the number of Iraqi security forces that were ready to conduct operations on their own:

> **Rumsfeld:** Trying to get a single, simple answer for a complex situation where you have, I'm going to guess, fifteen or twenty different categories of Iraqi security forces that have different purposes, different training, different equipment—so the number is 171,500 currently, last time I looked—last week. But it's made up of apples and oranges. So it isn't useful to try to oversimplify.

Of course not. The whole thing's just way too complex, and it's way too impossible to know how many Iraqi security forces there really are.

Here's another classic Rummy answer Derrida would have been proud of. This one was in response to Tim Russert's question: "Did you make a misjudgment about the cost of the war?"

> **Rumsfeld:** I never estimated the cost of the war. And how can one estimate the cost in lives or the cost in money? I've avoided it consistently. And how can that be a mis-estimate? We've said that there are always going to be unknowns, that the battle was

going to change, depending on what the enemy does and how they adjust and how we adjust.

And, of course, there was this all-time great postmodernist Rummy riff:

Rumsfeld: As we know, there are known knowns. There are things we know we know. We also know there are known unknowns. That is to say we know there are some things we do not know. But there are also unknown unknowns, the ones we don't know we don't know.

While Rumsfeld and his chums claimed that nothing concrete is really knowable, they remained certain that we were winning. It's just that any fact or statistic that might disprove this assertion was dismissed as invalid in a complex, postmodern world. If you set all the facts aside, you could be absolutely certain that we were making progress.

It's fascinating how sure they were back when they were lying about WMD. Then it was all about solid facts, and aluminum tubes, and Tenet saying "slam dunk," and Cheney saying "no doubt."

But now that all that had vanished, so too had our ability to know anything about anything. Yet the Bush administration continued to refuse to even consider the idea of developing an exit strategy beyond the worthless reassurance that it will be just as soon as Iraqi troops are ready to take over the fight, sometime during the administration of Ahmed Chalabi's great-grandson.

Bush has lost touch both with reality and with the sentiments of a growing majority of Americans. But he seems strangely unaffected by the disconnect. Perhaps this was yet another consequence of his belief that God had saved poor, sinning, preppy frat president George Bush from drinking and drugs so that he could be reborn as a God-fearing U.S. President and spread democracy in Iraq. But hubris and incompetence—always a dangerous cocktail—combined to offer a nasty surprise as 2006 approached. Unlike Harry Truman and Lyndon Johnson, George Bush didn't have any more elections to lose—but his party did.

A Soldier's Sacrifice Repackaged as PR

Near the end of 2005, the president's PR push on Iraq hit the Woodrow Wilson Center, stop four on his Grudging (Kinda, Sorta) Admissions on Iraq speaking tour. The halfhearted attempt of the moment was his statement that "much of the intelligence turned out to be wrong." Nothing, mind you, about him and Cheney and Condi and Rummy using every trick in the book to gin up and sell that "wrong intelligence" to the American people. No, just a generic statement of something that's been obvious since "slam dunk" turned into "What WMD?"

During the speech the president told the story of Lieutenant Ryan McGlothlin, a Marine killed the previous month during a firefight near the Syrian border.

It is indeed an amazing story of duty, selflessness, and patriotism. And sacrifice. McGlothlin was a Phi Beta Kappa graduate of William and Mary who had received a full scholarship to pursue his doctorate in chemistry at Stanford—then gave it up to follow his lifelong dream of joining the Marines, where he was the top graduate in his class at Officer Candidate School.

According to his parents, Ryan had been enraged by 9/11 and felt he had a duty to serve and protect America—even if it meant risking his life.

Making the story even more dramatic was the fact that McGlothlin had not voted for Bush in either 2000 or 2004. "Ryan didn't support me in the last election," said Bush in his speech, "but he supported our mission in Iraq." Or, as Ryan's father told the *Los Angeles Times*: "My son told us . . . 'I won't vote for Mr. Bush, but I'll take a bullet for him.' "

Bush wrapped up his telling of McGlothlin's story by explaining that in the fallen soldier's pocket was a poem that, as the president put it, "represented the spirit of this fine Marine. The poem was called 'Don't Quit.' "

Then the topper: "In our fight to keep America free, we'll never quit."

And just like that, the sacrifice of this courageous young American had been co-opted in the service of a disastrous war. Reduced to a zippy one-liner, a heartrending punch line, a camera-ready sound bite used to equate a wise change of course with cowardly quitting.

As if that two-word title justified all the tragic mistakes made in Iraq and all the lives tragically cut short.

Now, I'm glad that the poem—which was written by Edgar Guest, and has absolutely nothing to do with this or any other war—gave Lieutenant McGlothlin comfort. But what in the world do these sentiments in "Don't Quit" have to do with what the right course of action is in Iraq?

Life is queer with its twists and turns,
As every one of us sometimes learns,
And many a failure turns about
When he might have won had he stuck it out.

Sticking it out is one of the most valuable traits a person can have. But isn't it an essential quality of leadership to know when it's folly—not strength, not wisdom—to stick to a disastrous course? If only the president's motto had been "face the facts," Ryan might still be alive.

Why the Right Was Wrong About Iraq— the Beginning

The Right was wrong about Iraq in the beginning because the war was neither cheap nor easy. They were wrong because we were not greeted as liberators. They were wrong because democracy did not spread in the Middle East. They were wrong because Saddam did not have weapons of mass destruction and was not a state sponsor of international terrorism. They were wrong because the war did not have to be fought and 4,000 young Americans and 150,000 Iraqis did not have to die.

7

Iraq: The Long Hard Slog Gets Longer and Sloggier

When in Doubt, Revise Your Talking Points

After months of mounting U.S. losses in Iraq, after polls reporting that six in ten Americans wanted the United States to withdraw some or all of our troops, after lawmakers from both parties introduced resolutions in both houses demanding the president come up with some kind—any kind—of exit strategy, after one deadly day after another, the president finally admitted that some changes were needed.

And that's why he decided to take the bold step of *changing rhetoric.* The self-proclaimed "war president" announced in the summer of 2005 that he would dedicate several speeches to the war.

That's right. The president had come to the tough conclusion that what the public needed was more lies, more spin, more rationalizations of failed policies and dishonest leadership. In short, better PR.

Sure. Just what would help quell the insurgency, bring Sunnis to the political table, train Iraqi troops faster, and convince other countries to take some of the deadly burden off American troops.

Giving bad policy a new coat of paint doesn't change the policy. Only changing policy changes the policy. Seems obvious, right? Not to this White House.

"The president takes seriously his responsibility as commander in chief to continue to educate the American people about the conduct of the war and our strategy for victory," Dan Bartlett, then Counselor to the President, explained, leaving us all to shudder at the thought of what this war would look like if Bush hadn't taken it so seriously.

But the problem wasn't that the public was insufficiently "educated" about Bush's strategy; it was that he had no strategy.

So what was the new "sharper focus" the president brought to the Iraq problem? According to a top administration official at the time, Bush would admit that some Iraqi troops are "more prepared than others."

He was also willing by the time the Iraq Study Group had presented its recommendations, at the end of 2006, to concede that the war might require "difficult choices and additional sacrifices," and that there was "unspeakable sectarian violence" taking place. In the same breath, however, he was happy to say that he "[didn't] believe most Americans want us just to get out now."

The backing away from the Iraq Study Group didn't end there. *The New York Times*, with unintended comic irony, noted: "Administration officials say their preliminary review of the bipartisan Iraq Study Group's recommendations has concluded that many of its key proposals are impractical or unrealistic." Thank God we have George Bush to protect us from doing anything impractical or unrealistic in the Middle East.

But there was one thing we could be sure Bush would take from the report—the slogan. Bush may not be into things like facts, truth, or reality, but he loves a good slogan.

While Bush may not have liked any of the Study Group's seventy-nine proposals (too impractical and unrealistic), he was ready to adopt its slogan, "New Way Forward."

That had been the problem during this entire fiasco: the substitution of rhetoric for policy, the belief that reality can be changed simply by changing the language used to describe it. Bush makes a big show of his religious faith, but what's truly impressive is his incredible faith in the power of PR and, accordingly, his lack of faith in the American people, who he thinks can be deceived over and over.

Nowhere was this rationale laid out more succinctly than in the internal memo Rumsfeld wrote in his last month in office, which included this slippery strategy: "Announce that whatever new approach the U.S. decides on, the U.S. is doing so on a trial basis. This will give us the ability to readjust and move to another course, if necessary, and therefore not 'lose.' "

It's not about losing and winning, but, rather, about "losing" and "winning," which are very, very different things.

The Iraq War Slogan Timeline: Past, Present, and Future

2001:   GATHERING THREAT

2002:   AXIS OF EVIL

2003:   SLAM DUNK

        SHOCK AND AWE

        MISSION ACCOMPLISHED

        POCKETS OF DEAD-ENDERS

2004:   FIGHT 'EM THERE, NOT HERE

2005:   LAST THROES

        ADAPT TO WIN

        STAY THE COURSE

2006:   NEW WAY FORWARD

2007:   SURGE TO VICTORY

2008:   A NEW WAY BACKWARD

        A FASTER NEW WAY BACKWARD

        HOLY SHIT, LET'S GET OUT OF HERE

2009:   A NEW WAY OF FORGETTING IT EVER HAPPENED

2010:   MISSION ACCOMPLISHED

2011:   THE NEW GATHERING THREAT

So we shifted from "Stay the Course" to "New Way Forward." Did that change anything? No. But, in Bush's mind, it bought him some time, at least until the next slogan.

Studying the Iraq Study Group

The Iraq Study Group, also known as the Baker-Hamilton Commission, named for co-chairs James Baker (a former Republican Secretary of State) and Lee Hamilton (a former Democratic member of Congress), consisted of ten members (five from each party). The panel's final report assessing the situation in Iraq was released on December 6, 2006.

In the end, all the Iraq Study Group's recommendations ended up being ignored. But there were at least half a dozen that were doomed from the get-go:

Recommendation 4: "As an instrument of the New Diplomatic Offensive, an Iraq International Support Group should be organized immediately following the launch of the New Diplomatic Offensive."

Reason it was doomed: We would've loved to think that an International Support Group would have worked but, really, it was just going to be a lot of people sitting in a circle on folding chairs wondering when this guy was going to shut up about his wife leaving him for some other guy who blew up the Golden Mosque in Samarra.

Recommendation 23: "The President should restate that the United States does not seek to control Iraq's oil."

Reason it was doomed: Too hard for him to pull off with a straight face.

Recommendation 32: Minorities. "The rights of women and the rights of all minority communities in Iraq, including Turkmen, Chaldeans, Assyrians, Yazidis, Sabeans, and Armenians, must be protected."

Reason it was doomed: Beautiful sentiment, but not exactly our strong suit.

Recommendation 64: "U.S. economic assistance should be increased to a level of $5 billion per year rather than being permitted to decline."

Reason it was doomed: Five billion in economic aid? I can just hear Senator Brownback complaining about welfare insurgents driving Escalades.

Recommendation 73: "The Secretary of State, the Secretary of Defense, and the Director of National Intelligence should accord the highest possible priority to professional language proficiency and cultural training, in general and specifically for U.S. officers and personnel about to be assigned to Iraq."

Reason it was doomed: We kinda doubt the Pentagon kept forwarding addresses for all those fired gay Arabic interpreters.

Recommendation 77: "The Director of National Intelligence and the Secretary of Defense should devote significantly greater analytic resources to the task of understanding the threats and sources of violence in Iraq."

Reason it was doomed: If this really needed to be said, we are screwed even worse than we thought.

Defining Victory Down

"You know, I think an interesting construct that General Pace uses is, 'We're not winning, we're not losing.' " This was President Bush's response to the question "Are we winning in Iraq?" in an interview with *The Washington Post* in December 2006. Let us stipulate at this point in the sad story of the Right's Iraq adventure that no one likes to admit a mistake. In the TV era, we've had John F. Kennedy's mea culpa for the Bay of Pigs, Bill Clinton's teary remorse over Rwanda, and, perhaps, whatever it was that Ronald Reagan meant to say about Iran-contra (historians are still reviewing the videotape). But, historically, presidential apologies are rare.

Frankly, those of us who opposed the war would have tolerated George Bush's refusal to publicly apologize if there had been any indication that, privately, he was aware of what was going on and was taking steps to change course. But, as it turned out, all the character traits of the Right's warmongers—their hubris, their pigheadedness, their grandiosity, their contempt for facts, and their preposterous tendency to take the "long view" whenever the short-term news is bad—conspired to compound the gathering tragedy in Iraq. Somehow, no matter how bad the news was, the Right managed to rewrite the narrative so that everything was going according to plan.

"Sweets and flowers" became "exceedingly complex and very tough," a "heavy lifting," and a "long, hard slog" intoned with an extra measure of the old soldier's grit to which Cheney (of the five deferments) and Bush (of the incredible shrinking military record) were spectacularly unentitled. Pressed on whether he had made any mistakes or would have done anything differently, Bush resolutely stayed the course, shrugging and rambling as only he can to evade the question.

"In the last campaign, you were asked a question about the biggest mistake you'd made in your life, and you used to like to joke that it was trading Sammy Sosa," *Time*'s John Dickerson had asked at a 2004 press conference. "You've looked back before 9/11 for what mistakes might have been made. After 9/11, what would your biggest mistake be, would you say, and what lessons have you learned from it?" After a pause, a stumped President Bush had replied: "Hmm. I wish you would have given me this written question ahead of time, so I could plan for it."

With the eventual purge of some of the neocon war planners and, eventually, Rumsfeld himself, after the 2006 election Bush hunkered down in his personal Green Zone protected by the handpicked minions of the vice president, who never stopped selling the war.

When Bush tapped Cheney for the vice presidency—or, rather, when, after an exhaustive search, Cheney chose himself for the vice presidency—the message went forth from Meme Central that, after eight years of sax and sex under Bill Clinton, the adults were finally in charge. And, in a pinch, that's always how Cheney's message wranglers have played defense. "War is hell!" "History will judge!" As if somehow opposition to the war was a side effect of the permissive instant-gratification attitudes engendered in the 1960s.

Amid the debris of an imploding war effort in the summer of 2006, Cheney sought refuge in history, telling CNN: "History will judge this president as a very successful, very effective leader."

Karl Rove, writing in *National Review* a year later, agreed: "History demands much of America and its leaders and I am confident it will judge the 43rd president as a man more than worthy of the great office the American people twice entrusted to him."

"History is going to have to judge," Bush echoed, whether he had restored honor and dignity to the office of president as originally promised.

Of all the ways the Right is wrong, resorting to some indeterminate future assessment is probably a pretty minor sin. But regardless of what the future may hold, tough decisions had to be made in the here and now, and phony tough guys Bush and Cheney routinely chickened out from making them.

The Last Hurrah:
Don Rumsfeld's Farewell Tour

One thing you can say about Don Rumsfeld is that he was consistent. Contemptuous and arrogant right up until the very end of his disastrous tenure. Or, to put it in Rumsfeldese: Am I Don Rumsfeld? Sure. Am I going to continue to put the needs of my own preening ego above the interests of the United States? You bet!

His "surprise" farewell visit to the troops in Iraq in early December 2006, just as he was cleaning out his office, had little to do with the troops and a lot to do with Rummy. Had Rumsfeld put the same amount of energy and thought into providing sufficient resources for them as he did into his rhetorical gymnastics, a lot more of them would have been around for his last cynical photo op.

And what exactly was the point of his farewell tour?

Apparently, so the Pentagon could post a "news article" on its defenselink.mil site with the headline: "Troops Haven't Lost Faith in Rumsfeld."

The trip was about Rumsfeld showing the country that while he may have been fired he was going out the same way he came in—strutting, pompous, and self-serving. The horrors caused by his failures hadn't dimmed his arrogance one iota. And that, in Rumsfeld-speak, was a known-known.

Karl Rove's Remorseless, Soulless
Attempt to Rewrite History

It was clear from Karl Rove's appearance on *Charlie Rose* in November 2007 that the erstwhile Boy Genius knew—contrary to his public pronouncements—that history would not be kind. So he pulled out his bucket of whitewash and audaciously claimed that "one of the untold stories" about the war in Iraq is that the Bush administration had been "opposed" to Congress holding the vote authorizing the president to use military force in Iraq just a few weeks prior to the 2002 elections because "we thought it made it too political."

Too political? For Karl Rove? That's like saying something was too bloody for Count Dracula.

He went on to paint a picture of a White House pushed into war, and laid the blame for much of what has happened since on a Congress that had "made things move too fast." If not for Congress, you see, there would have been more time for weapons inspections, and to build a broader coalition.

It was a satiric tour de force worthy of Jonathan Swift or Stephen Colbert—but Rove wasn't joking. He actually expected us to buy his load of BS. Watching Rove, two things were perfectly clear: his disdain for the truth and his contempt for the American people know no bounds.

Rove's appearance was the work of a shameless, remorseless, soulless political animal taking the first steps on what will no doubt be a high-profile and lucrative march toward historical revisionism. He knows that he stands shoulder to shoulder with the fanatics responsible for the worst foreign policy disaster in American history—not exactly the best thing to put on your post-government résumé—so he is hell-bent on replacing reality with the latest incarnation of the Big Lie.

A student of history, Rove is obviously also up on his Orwell: "Who controls the past, controls the future."

Unfortunately for Rove, this isn't 1984; we now live in the Age of Google, and YouTube, and LexisNexis searches. So the refutation of his lies is just a click away.

The evidence that it was President Bush and Vice President Cheney—and not Congress—who were hungry for war is overwhelming. For starters, we have Bush's own words before the vote, when he explicitly told Congress that "it's in our national interest" to get the vote "done as quickly as possible." And the insistence of Secretary of Defense Rumsfeld that "delaying a vote in Congress would send the wrong message." And the words of Senate Majority Leader Tom Daschle, who says that when he asked Bush in September 2002 why there was such a rush for a vote on Iraq, the president "looked at Cheney and he looked at me, and there was a half-smile on his face. And he said: 'We just have to do this now.' "

And there is the insider evidence provided by Richard Clarke, who wrote that within hours of the 9/11 attacks, this administration had its heart set on heading into Iraq. And corroborating evidence from Paul O'Neill, who made it clear that invading Iraq had been Bush's goal from the beginning.

Even now, with his approval ratings scraping the bottom of the historical barrel, Bush still dominates the congressional agenda on the war. And Rove wants us to buy the idea that back in the heady days of 2002, when the president was still riding a wave of support forged by 9/11, his desire for caution and reasoned action were overridden by a war-hungry Congress? "We don't determine when the Congress votes on things," Rove told Rose. "The Congress does." I guess he and Bush landed on the whole "I'm the Decider" thing later (maybe after they orchestrated that triumphal landing on the *Abraham Lincoln*).

Let's remember, this was the time when the administration had pulled together the White House Iraq Group (which included Rove himself) with the express mission of marketing the war. These people weren't in the mood to wait, they were in the mood to sell, sell, sell. The Downing Street Memo showed that by July of 2002 they were fixing the intel to sell the war. By August 2002, the White House was already using Judy Miller and *The New York Times* as prime advertising space. And by September 2002, Condi Rice was warning of smoking guns turning out to be mushroom clouds, and Cheney was using aluminum tubes to make the case that Saddam was "actively and aggressively seeking to acquire nuclear weapons."

So the record is irrefutable: the drumbeat of war coming from the White House couldn't have been louder. And no amount of five-years-down-the-road spinning by Karl Rove can change that.

Cut and Run

Although the administration found itself increasingly isolated by its conduct of the war, it did not find itself entirely lacking for company in its closed-minded little world. The loyal media shock troops— Limbaugh, Hannity, et al.—stayed on message, helped spread the pro-war theme, and repeated again and again that suggesting any sort of withdrawal was somehow cowardly. As George Carlin said of Vietnam, "Pull out? Not a very manly thing to do, is it? You gotta stay in there." "Cut and run," a phrase that evokes the image of American troops throwing down their M-16s and bolting for the border shrieking like schoolgirls, was another piece of evil genius from the Right. After all, who could be in favor of "cutting and running" or, for that matter, who could support "cutting and walking" or "cutting and strolling while whistling"? Once "cut and run" was brought into the debate, the cowardice card was on the table. We would stay in Iraq no matter what, just because we don't want to let anyone call us names. It is schoolyard politics at its worst and, the sad thing is, it soon spread from talk radio to the mainstream media.

As the linguist George Lakoff put it, "What cut and run says is, 'You're a coward,' and moreover it presupposes that the opposite is to stand and fight. Then they repeat it over and over until it becomes part of people's brains."

As early as December of 2003, Ivo Daalder, senior fellow at the Brookings Institution, and James Lindsay, vice president at the Council on Foreign Relations, co-wrote an op-ed for *Newsday* entitled "Whatever We Do, We Can't Cut and Run."

On November 18, 2005, Congresswoman Jean Schmidt (R-OH) used the phrase in the House: "A few minutes ago, I received a call from Colonel Danny Bubp, Ohio representative from the 88th District in the House of Representatives. He asked me to send Congress a message: Stay the course. He also asked me to send Congressman Murtha a message: that cowards cut and run, Marines never do."

In June 2006, the phrase popped up during a Senate debate on the Iraq war: "Cutting and running is bad policy that threatens our national security and poses unacceptable risks to Americans," declared Bill Frist, then Senate majority leader.

Wordplay

Besides pushing "cut and run" into the mainstream, the Right remained on the offensive against certain words—"civil war" and "quagmire"—and against certain people—the liberal media and the Party of Treason, i.e., the Democrats. And it continued to play word games with the supposed link between Saddam and 9/11.

Here's Bush on "quagmire" in November 2007:

Reporter: So what about Iraq? Can France, for instance, help to get us out of the Iraqi quagmire? And President Bush, where do you stand on Iraq and your domestic debate on Iraq? Do you have a timetable for withdrawing troops?

Bush: I don't—you know, "quagmire" is an interesting word. If you lived in Iraq and had lived under a tyranny, you'd be saying, God, I love freedom—because that's what's happened.

Here's the president attempting a little misdirection on the question of whether Iraq was involved in a civil war:

Reporter: Do you believe it's a civil war [in Iraq], sir?

Bush: I can only tell you what people on the ground whose judgment—it's hard for me, you know, living in this beautiful White House, to give you a firsthand assessment. I haven't been there.

Why do we have to keep talking about such unpleasant subjects when we could just be enjoying another lovely day in the Rose Garden? And, by the way, did you know that the modern White House has 132 rooms and 35 bathrooms, 412 doors, 147 windows, 28 fireplaces, 8 staircases, 3 elevators, 5 full-time chefs, a tennis court, a bowling alley, a movie theater, a jogging track, a swimming pool, and a putting green? Just beautiful!

In keeping alive the "lest we forget" 9/11 linkage, Condi Rice gave this existential answer to the question "When is a tie not a tie?" back in the fall of 2003.

"Oh, indeed there is a tie between Iraq and what happened on 9/11. It's not that Saddam Hussein was somehow himself and his regime involved in 9/11, but, if you think about what caused 9/11, it is the rise of ideologies of hatred that lead people to drive airplanes into buildings in New York."

And here she is in May 2005, fitting the elusive linkage between Saddam and terrorism into the larger plan to remake the Middle East and build a shining City on a Hill along the Euphrates: "You see, this war came to us, not the other way around. The United States of America, when it was attacked on September 11, realized that we lived in a world in which we cannot let threats gather, and that we lived in a world in which we had to have a different kind of Middle East if we were ever to have a permanent peace."

Thanks to this kind of mushy lumping together of bad things, the Right's public relations arm was able to suggest that we were engaged in an even larger enterprise, a World War Against Evil. The talk radio hit men made sure the public remained confused about whether Saddam had anything to do with 9/11 and whether there were weapons of mass destruction in Iraq despite the fact that Bush finally acknowledged the truth about both. In fact, a Program on International Policy Attitudes study in 2004 revealed that a startlingly large percentage of the general public still believed that Saddam was responsible for 9/11 and that weapons of mass destruction had actually been found in Iraq. Among Rush Limbaugh's listeners the misinformed percentage was even higher and Limbaugh was in no rush to set his dittohead followers straight.

Part of the problem comes from stories like the following one from Fox News, which ran on June 22, 2006:

Report: Hundreds of WMD Found in Iraq

WASHINGTON—The United States has found five hundred chemical weapons in Iraq since 2003, and more weapons of mass destruction are likely to be uncovered, two Republican lawmakers said Wednesday.

Senator Rick Santorum, who lost his seat in the 2006 election, was one of the two Republican lawmakers in question. He set off a national flutter among the fact-based part of the public by throwing this kind of red meat to the faith-based right-wing core. Never mind that the "weapons" were inert, unusable, and had nothing to do with the supposedly ongoing and very dangerous program of WMD that was used to justify the war in the first place. They were technically "WMD," right? Hooray!

After the Santorum report hit the air, Fox News host John Gibson breathlessly endorsed the find: "Senator Rick Santorum announcing a startling find. . . . In fact, WMD *were* found in Iraq."

It's no wonder the "Saddam *did* have WMD" myth has been so hard to kill.

As complicated as the Right's relationship with WMD was, it was nothing compared with its relationship with democracy. Wasn't democracy in the Middle East what the entire Iraq adventure was all about? Or, I should say, wasn't it the reason of last resort when the other 217 reasons turned out to be lies? Well, apparently, the idea of bringing the Iraqis democracy was about as real as Saddam's WMD.

Just listen to John McCain—the biggest supporter of the war outside of Dick Cheney—in May 2007 on *Meet the Press*. Tim Russert asked him about the fact that 144 members of the 275-person Iraqi parliament had recently signed a legislative petition calling on the United States to set a timetable to withdraw:

> **Russert:** The duly elected people's bodies, the U.S. Congress and the Iraqi parliament, say they want a troop withdrawal. That's more than a poll. Isn't that the voice of the people?

> **McCain:** . . . There is a certain amount of domestic political calculations involved there in what the Iraqi, quote, "parliament" said.

You could hear the contempt dripping off McCain's lips: "The Iraqi, quote, 'parliament.' "

So what, pray tell, is the difference between a "parliament" and a parliament? To McCain it's apparently whether the parliament agrees with him. And, by the way, Senator, there is another word for "domestic political calculations": democracy. But McCain, like Bush, was too arrogant to believe that real democracy could ever include disagreement with his wishes.

The syllogism goes something like this:

a) I'm right.
b) Democracy is right.
c) Whatever I agree with is therefore "democracy" and whatever I don't agree with, isn't.

At least McCain didn't attack the Iraqi legislators as being "un-American."

Bush's lack of respect for democracy runs even deeper than McCain's and is topped only by his cynical use—and abandonment—of the concept.

Throughout the Iraq debacle, Bush insisted that Iraq is a sovereign country ("Let Freedom Reign!") and that if the Iraqis didn't want us there we would leave. Indeed, in January 2005, on the eve of the Iraqi election, the president was asked if America would pull out of Iraq if the new government asked him to do so. "Absolutely," he replied. "This is a sovereign government. They're on their feet."

But when a majority of that government called for a withdrawal date, what was the president's response? Silence. Which is standard operating procedure in this administration. Any time they fail at their stated goals, they just make up new ones. Any time a fact comes out that belies their increasingly skewed view of reality, they just deny it. And as the circle of war supporters got smaller and smaller, the last dead-enders—which, unfortunately, included every major GOP candidate for president—grew more detached.

The danger for them, of course, is that it's a lot easier to discount democracy in Iraq than democracy back here at home.

Sunnis and Shiites Step Up Violence in Iraq to Affect the 2006 Election

As the violence escalated in Iraq in the fall of 2006, the president and the Pentagon put the whole Iraq mess into perspective: the deadly violence was, in essence, an extended campaign for the Democrats! That's right, Sunnis and Shiites were supposedly killing each other— and American soldiers—in growing numbers because they were out to influence the 2006 election.

According to Major General William Caldwell, the senior spokesman for the U.S. military in Iraq, it was "no coincidence" that the increase in killings took place in "the run-up to the American midterm elections. The enemy knows that killing innocent people and Americans will garner headlines and create a sense of frustration."

President Bush had a similar take when he told George Stephanopoulos, "There's certainly a stepped-up level of violence, and we're heading into an election. . . . My gut tells me that they have all along been trying to inflict enough damage that we'd leave."

There you have it: Sunnis and Shiites were not killing each other over centuries-old religious conflicts; they were killing each other because they disagreed about who should be Speaker of the House, Denny Hastert or Nancy Pelosi.

But which party was the violence supposed to help? Did the Sunnis want the Democrats to win, hoping they'll be quicker to pull the troops out? Did al Qaeda want the GOP to maintain control of Congress, since "staying the course" has been such a boon for terrorist recruitment? And where did the Shiites stand? Were they pro-Republican, since the invasion has been their ticket to power? Or did they want the Democrats to win and withdraw the troops? And were they even clear about whether a Democratic or a Republican victory will make it easier for them to consummate their flirtation with the mullahs in Tehran?

Can't you just picture a gathering of Sunni leaders, huddled over their computers, checking out the latest poll numbers from Virginia and thinking, "George Allen is still hanging in there against Jim Webb in Virginia. We've got to have a suicide bomber drive his car into a market crowded with Shiites"?

Or a cabal of black-clad Shiite militiamen kidnapping and assassinating a busload of Sunnis because Rep. Curt Weldon needed a bump in the polls after the FBI raided his home and office?

Who needs bumper stickers, lawn signs, or volunteer phone banks when you've got IEDs? Push polls are so 2004.

All politics may be local, but, according to the GOP spin, sectarian bloodletting was intercontinental.

In the Rear with Gear

Besides generating its own fog of war to obscure the monumental scope of the administration's failure in Iraq, the Right readily resorted to the despicable strategy of hiding behind the troops. To answer the war's critics, the outraged reply "how dare you say that about our brave fighting men and women?" quickly proved most effective in reducing the hapless Democratic opposition to sputtering retreat.

This kill-the-messenger (or at least make him or her apologize) strategy proved to be a rhetorical weapon of mass destruction, obliterating any effort to shorten the war or call the president to account.

A frequent target of the rally-'round-the-troops attack was then House Minority Leader Nancy Pelosi, who, in introducing a very tepid amendment to the defense appropriations bill in 2005, called on the president to produce a report detailing his strategy for success in Iraq and offered a stinging—and wholly accurate—indictment of the war: "This war in Iraq is a grotesque mistake; it is not making America safer, and the American people know it."

She clearly hit a nerve, because the GOP rolled out its big guns and started blasting away, with Majority Leader Tom DeLay, Majority Whip Roy Blunt, and Speaker Dennis Hastert all releasing similar press releases condemning Pelosi. DeLay said she "owes our military and their families an apology for her reckless comments." Blunt said

2006: The Right Reaps (Politically) What It Sowed

After the 2006 midterm elections, everywhere you looked, "experts" were sifting through the rubble and offering standard-issue, conventional-wisdom-approved explanations for the GOP's defeat. For a perfect example, you could have read Ron Brownstein, who divined that the "GOP ceded the center and paid the price." Or Democratic Leadership Council founder Al Fromm, who claimed November 2006 as "a victory for the vital center of American politics over the extremes."

Nonsense. The GOP lost for three reasons: Iraq, Iraq, and Iraq. Period. End of discussion.

Election day 2006 was an unambiguous repudiation of the Bush administration's failed, tragic policy in Iraq. In race after race after race, Democrats who were unequivocal on Iraq prevailed. Democrats who ran campaigns by the book, listened to their consultants, and veered to the "center," lost.

A perfect example of this can be found in Pennsylvania, where Joe Sestak and Patrick Murphy both made strong anti-Iraq positions a key part of their congressional campaigns. Sestak, a retired three-star admiral, called the war a "tragic misadventure" and advocated withdrawing U.S. troops by June 2007. Murphy, an Iraq war vet, said, "We need to start bringing our men and women home now." Both men won.

Conversely, Lois Murphy, whom many pegged as a surefire Democratic House pickup from Pennsylvania, avoided putting Iraq front and center—and lost. She didn't even mention Iraq in the "On the Issues" or "Making Us Safer" pages of her campaign website.

Then there is Ned Lamont, who paid the price for trying to play it both ways on Iraq. He initially, and courageously, ran against incumbent Connecticut Democrat and noted warmonger Joe Lieberman on the need to leave Iraq—and came from nowhere to win the Democratic primary. He then put the war on the back burner for months—giving Lieberman time to not just get off the mat but to learn his lesson on Iraq and begin muddying the waters by also using antiwar rhetoric. By the time Lamont went back to pounding Lieberman on Iraq, it was too late.

The Iraq dynamic played itself out across the country. In New Hampshire's 1st District, social worker Carol Shea-Porter, who unequivocally said, "We have to leave Iraq," defeated incumbent Jeb Bradley, despite no financial support from Rahm Emanuel and the Democratic Congressional Campaign Committee. In Kentucky, anti-Iraq progressive

John Yarmuth, who said that Americans are no longer fighting terrorists in Iraq, "we're fighting Iraqis," unseated five-term incumbent Anne Northrup.

And here were some other senatorial and congressional winners on Iraq:

Sherrod Brown, elected to the Senate from Ohio, who defeated two-term incumbent Mike DeWine: "From the beginning, I have been an outspoken critic of the Iraq war."

Jay McNerney of California, who defeated seven-term incumbent Richard Pombo: "I'm 100 percent in favor of Congressman [Jack] Murtha's plan."

Chris Murphy of Connecticut, who beat twelve-term incumbent Nancy Johnson: "We must leave Iraq as soon as possible."

Gabrielle Giffords of Arizona, who defeated ardent anti-immigration candidate Randy Graf: "My priority is to bring our troops home safe and soon."

Baron Hill of Indiana, who defeated incumbent Mike Sodrel: "We stand for getting our boys and girls out of Iraq sooner rather than later."

Dave Loebsack of Iowa, who defeated fifteen-term incumbent Jim Leach: "Complete disengagement from Iraq in the next year will serve to enhance America's security."

Sheldon Whitehouse, senator-elect from Rhode Island, who was even more strongly antiwar than antiwar incumbent Lincoln Chafee: "I support a rapid and responsible withdrawal of our troops from Iraq."

The 2006 election was not a mandate for the Democratic Party to run to the middle. It was a mandate for the Democratic Party to do everything in its power to get us out of Iraq—rapidly and responsibly. That's why it's such a shame the Democrats failed to use the power of the purse given to them by the Constitution to get the job done.

Pelosi's comments had "emboldened . . . the enemy." Hastert played the "support our troops" card.

"I think that our military is the finest military on the face of the earth. They are the best trained, they are the best equipped, they're the best led, and they're doing a fine, fine job for our country and for the Iraqi people," said Donald Rumsfeld. Fine, agreed. But how did that absolve him from the countless avoidable mistakes he made and the countless course corrections he did not? He used the same tired (but shockingly effective) rhetorical trick when asked about falling recruitment levels: "The people running around saying that the army is broken are wrong. We've got the best-trained, the best-equipped and the best-led army on the face of the earth and the best one in the history of our country." Who said otherwise? The question was about recruiting, not the quality of our fighting forces. Rumsfeld was, of course, by no means the only one in the administration using rah-rah language about the superiority of the U.S. military as an evasive maneuver. At a town hall meeting, when Vice President Cheney was asked about the possibility that a military draft might be needed to ensure our safety at home and abroad, he trotted out this non-answer answer: "This question on the draft is . . . hogwash is the best way I can think of to describe it. Anybody who has been associated with the all-volunteer military in recent years . . . that all-volunteer force has given us the most magnificent military in the world today. It's superb."

It is a fact that we have a superb military. But it is also a fact that recruitment has been dangerously affected (army recruits with high school diplomas dropped to a twenty-five-year low in 2007).

And our National Guard has become collateral damage in this war, a fact that became most evident after Hurricane Katrina's crash landing in Louisiana.

In his absurd and insulting "flypaper theory," Bush liked to posit an intrinsic connection between what was going on in Iraq and what was going on here at home. His version of the theory was completely wrong, but he's right that there is a connection. And it is a tragic one, and 100 percent airtight: every national guardsman who was in Iraq is one fewer guardsman who could have helped out in Mississippi and Louisiana.

About 40 percent of Mississippi's National Guard and 35 percent of Louisiana's—a combined total of roughly six thousand troops— were unavailable to help out because they were in Iraq. And despite official protestations that "this had not hurt the relief effort," did any-one really believe that having an additional six thousand well-trained citizen-soldiers on hand would not have made a huge difference?

As Lieutenant Andy Thaggard, a spokesman for the Mississippi National Guard, put it: "Missing the personnel is the big thing in this particular event. We need our people."

And it was not just the manpower; it was the allocation of resources. The truth is that the Army Corps of Engineers was desperately trying to get the funds to prepare for just the kind of flooding that left 90 percent of the homes in New Orleans underwater. Why didn't they get this much-needed funding? As *Editor & Publisher* explained: "At least nine articles in the *Times-Picayune* from 2004 and 2005 specifically cite the cost of Iraq as a reason for the lack of hurricane- and flood-control dollars." The damning article went on:

> In early 2004, as the cost of the conflict in Iraq soared, President Bush proposed spending less than 20 percent of what the Corps said was needed for Lake Pontchartrain, according to a Feb. 16, 2004, article, in *New Orleans CityBusiness*. On June 8, 2004, Walter Maestri, emergency management chief for Jefferson Parish, Louisiana, told the *Times-Picayune*: "It appears that the money has been moved in the president's budget to handle homeland security and the war in Iraq, and I suppose that's the price we pay. Nobody locally is happy that the levees can't be finished, and we are doing everything we can to make the case that this is a security issue for us."

To see it boiled down even more, *Think Progress* did the math:

2004: Army Corps request: $11 million
        Bush request: $3 million
        Approved by Congress: $5.5 million

2005: Army Corps request: $22.5 million
        Bush request: $3.9 million
        Approved by Congress: $5.7 million

The administration's distorted priorities deeply affected FEMA too. According to Eric Holdeman, the director of the Office of Emergency Management in King County, Washington, "the country's premier agency for dealing with such events—FEMA—is being, in effect, systematically downgraded and all but dismantled by the Department of Homeland Security." His "obituary" for FEMA warned that we, as a country, are "to an unconscionable degree, weakening our ability to respond" to the "tornadoes, earthquakes, volcanoes, tsunamis, floods, windstorms, mudslides, power outages, fires" that are inevitably coming our way. Don't those affect our national security too?

Civil War, Insurgency, and "Last Throes"

For his part, Dick Cheney remained resolutely on message—quite simply "Mission Accomplished"—long after most of his compadres had decided that that position was no longer tenable. The man who didn't have the *cojones* to fight when he was called during the Vietnam War displayed quite a pair when he told Larry King, on Memorial Day 2005, no less, that the insurgency was "in the last throes." And later in the year he told U.S. troops that Iraq "had turned the corner." After a while, we had turned so many corners that it began to feel like we were going in circles.

On the same day Cheney made his "last throes" pronouncement, 31 people were killed and 108 were wounded in yet another of the daily suicide bombings rocking Iraq, bringing the total for the previous month to over 700. And this was the month during which we were supposed to be celebrating Iraq's new government.

Cheney also told Larry King: "America will be safer in the long run when Iraq and Afghanistan as well are no longer safe havens for terrorists or places where people can gather and plan and organize attacks against the United States." What he left out was that Iraq wasn't a safe haven for terrorists before we invaded, and it wasn't organizing attacks against the United States.

So "When do we leave?" Larry King asked. "We'll leave as soon as the task is over with," the vice president replied. "We haven't set a deadline or a date. It depends upon conditions. We have to achieve our objectives, complete the mission." In other words, we have no plan. We'll leave when we finish. Or more accurately, Cheney and Bush will decide to leave when they have decided we're finished—which will not be before the country is finished with them.

Accountability?

Wherever you've got a siege, you'll find a siege mentality. And, as the quagmire in Iraq grew quaggier, the White House was definitely under siege—from the press, from the public, from a growing number of voices in Congress, including a few Republicans, and from undeniable, incontrovertible facts.

What are the hallmarks of a siege mentality? Denial, defensiveness, double-talk, wild counterattacks, a pathological fear of admitting mistakes, and an utter inability to change course—even when the current course is taking you right over the cliff. It reads like an employee manual for Bush administration staffers, doesn't it?

Even temporary forays into accountability quickly ran into the brick wall of obstinacy that has come to define the Bush approach to Iraq.

Spring 2007 was quite a time in Washington—you could practically smell the accountability in the air.

Days after *The Washington Post* helped expose the deplorable conditions at the Walter Reed Army Medical Center, Major General George Weightman, the hospital's commander, was dismissed. Then Army Secretary Francis Harvey was forced to step down.

According to Defense Secretary Robert Gates, the conditions appeared "to be problems of leadership." I couldn't have agreed more. But why did we stop there?

Once we'd had an accountability moment for incompetent leadership in the care of wounded soldiers, why not one for the incompetent leadership responsible for getting the soldiers wounded in the first place? Because the same kind of callousness about wounded soldiers that got Harvey and Weightman fired was (and still is) running rampant in the White House when it comes to the training of our troops.

Typical of this was the late February 2007 decision by the army, rushed by the president's "surge" plans to have two of the units being shipped to Iraq forgo their usual training session at the National Training Center in the Mojave Desert, which had been specifically designed to help soldiers prepare for the conditions and enemy tactics they would face in Iraq.

Asked in the same month to explain how this jibed with the president's "I support the troops" mantra, then White House Press Secretary Tony Snow explained: "They can get desert training elsewhere. Like in Iraq."

On-the-job training may be great for vocational students looking to learn a trade, but it's a devastating strategy for our soldiers fighting—and dying and getting wounded—in Iraq.

Bush and company were all for the troops . . . except when it came to, you know, actually supporting them.

So instead of accountability at the highest levels of government, we got denial and robotic reiteration of stale talking points. Take this scene from a Pentagon press conference:

When asked about how they're defining success, Pentagon spokesperson Larry DiRita replied: "There is no military definition of success." Then how is the military expected to deliver a nonmilitary definition of success?

Denial? *Yes.*

And here is Lieutenant General James Conway, director of operations for the Joint Chiefs of Staff: "We have a plan for growing the force. We are on track with projection of numbers. . . . I'm confident that the trends are moving in the right direction." Robotic reiteration? *Yes.*

And here is an exchange that shows definite signs of CSM (Creeping Siege Mentality):

Conway: The actual mission, I suppose, is classified but I can paraphrase it to say that it's a safe and secure Iraq that we're able to turn back over to the Iraqis.

Reporter: Can you give us a better sense of what that means, "safe and secure"?

Conway: There are metrics associated with it. And, again, I think we'll know it when we see it.

Kinda like porn, eh General? In other words, you have no idea. As for when U.S. troops might be coming home, the administration party line was clearly set. In the words of General Conway: "If we have a deadline [the insurgents] can wait us out."

Won't they wait us out anyway?

And here's the answer to questions about the drop in public support for the war.

Conway: Obviously, the public support of these kinds of operations is critical, which is why we spend a lot of time trying to make sure that the public has full access to all the information.

Add to the signs of CSM the telling of comically unbelievable lies? *Yes.*

The most dramatic—and literal—example of a siege mentality came in July of 2006 from U.S. Secretary of Energy Sam Bodman. "The situation seems far more stable than when I was here two or three years ago," he told *The New York Times* in an interview in the heavily fortified Green Zone. "The security seems better, people are more relaxed. There is optimism, at least among the people I talked to."

Raising the question: just who the hell was he talking to? "People are more relaxed"? "There is optimism"? "The security seems better"? What country was he describing? Surely not the one he was sitting in.

Security in the meeting rooms of the garrisoned Green Zone might have been better than it was in 2003, but the rest of Iraq was descending into what one Sunni leader described as "nothing less than an undeclared civil war."

"God knows what comes next," read a statement released by the Iraqi Islamic Party, the major Sunni political organization, in reaction to the escalating violence. The group urged the nation's leaders "to lead Iraq out of this dark tunnel."

But while those in the midst of the mayhem saw a dark tunnel, those in the Bush administration continued to see nothing but blue skies. Even as suicide bombs exploded and the death count rose, for the Right it was all relaxation and optimism.

Unbelievable. And sickening. And delusional.

Psychiatric literature defines delusional thinking as "false or irrational beliefs maintained despite clear evidence to the contrary."

The truly deranged are often so committed to their delusions, and so insistent, that part of your brain actually starts thinking: Hmm, maybe this person really is Napoleon! Maybe that woman really is a fried egg! Maybe the "surge" really will lead to victory in Iraq!

Meanwhile, the other part of your brain—the rational part—is reminding you that, no, in fact, that person is not Napoleon or any part of a Denny's Grand Slam Breakfast. They are simply delusional.

Symptoms of "false or irrational beliefs maintained despite clear evidence to the contrary" are found in ample supply in the Right's displays of magical thinking—a belief that merely wishing for something can make it so—and its ongoing claims that we're fighting them over there so we won't have to fight them over here even though there isn't a shred of evidence that the war in Iraq has made us safer, and a great deal of evidence that it has, in fact, had the opposite effect.

A new Iraq talking point emerged from the Bush administration shortly before the 2006 election: We're number one!

Looking for a bright spot amid all the gloomy assessments, the president, the vice president, and the top U.S. commander all seized on the military's perfect win-loss record in Iraq.

"The men and women of the armed forces have never lost a battle in over three years in the war," said President Bush during a fall 2006 news conference on Iraq.

"We've never been defeated in a stand-up fight in Iraq in over three years," Dick Cheney told NPR.

"The men and women of the armed forces here have never lost a battle in over three years of war. That is a fact unprecedented in history," said General George Casey at a press conference in Baghdad.

Meanwhile, after touting the military's unbeaten streak, the president admitted that Iraq "is a different kind of war. . . . This war is an ideological conflict between a radical ideology that can't stand freedom and moderate, reasonable people that hope to live in a peaceful society."

Do you win an ideological war with guns and soldiers—even undefeated ones? Bush seemed to think so, saying the key to victory in Iraq is "refining our training strategy for the Iraqi security forces, so we can help more of those forces take the lead in the fight and provide them better equipment and firepower to be successful."

The siege mentality extended beyond the government and the military to the politically well-connected firm of mercenaries ominously known as Blackwater.

In October 2007, Congressman Henry Waxman fired off a letter to Condoleezza Rice asking why a Blackwater guard who, while drunk, shot and killed one of the Iraqi vice president's bodyguards, was allowed to go back to the region.

Rice and the White House have had years of reports of misdeeds by Blackwater personnel ranging from the shooting of unarmed Iraqi civilians to a cover-up of a gang-rape of one of their own employees.

But apparently the administration's version of a get-tough oversight policy is the installation of video cameras on Blackwater vehicles and assigning State Department monitors to Blackwater patrols. Monitors that, of course, will have to be guarded by even more Blackwater guards.

The Blackwater hearings of early October 2007 provided yet another instance of how the Bush presidency forced us to examine what kind of nation we are. Already on the table were questions like: Are we a nation that tortures? Are we a nation of laws? Are we a nation where the judgment of the chief executive is beyond the reach of the law? And the hearings brought up yet another: Are we okay with a bunch of lawless mercenaries being the public face of the United States?

The events of September 16, 2007, in which, according to a military report, Blackwater guards opened fire on unarmed civilians in Baghdad, killing seventeen, were just the latest in a long line of incidents that had been enraging the Iraqi people (and the Iraqi government) since Blackwater first landed in Iraq.

As one unnamed military official put it in *The Washington Post*: "They tend to overreact to a lot of things. . . . When it comes to shooting and firing, they tend to shoot quicker than others."

Strange that we're not winning the hearts and minds of the Iraqis, isn't it?

Blackwater may be keeping the State Department individuals they guard in Iraq safe, but every day they're representing America in the Middle East, they're endangering the other 300 million of us.

But how is it that the private contracting force in Iraq came to outnumber the actual soldiers?

"The hearing," wrote Peter Singer, author of *Corporate Warriors: The Rise of the Privatized Military Industry*, "revealed a fascinating, but also disturbing, lack of awareness in Congress about the private military industry. Members on both sides repeatedly struggled with the most basic facts and issues that surrounded the over 160,000-person contractor force in Iraq: Everything from the number and roles of contractors to their status and accountability, or lack thereof. What I found especially telling, given the consistently weak grasp of the issues, was that multiple representatives opened their remarks by talking about how Blackwater contractors protected them while on visits to Iraq. They often meant this as a compliment to the firm, and also as a way of establishing their credentials on the issue. But it usually backfired, revealing a lack of simple curiosity. It showed that they've known about the massive use of contractors for years—they just didn't bother to ask any questions, even when the issue was in their faces."

At this point, we might as well call this war Operation Not Bothering to Ask Any Questions.

And though it was promising that a bill that would close legal loopholes that have allowed Blackwater guards to kill innocent civilians with impunity passed the House, it's still not enough. As critics of the bill noted, prosecution would depend on the executive branch, which, so far, has shown little interest in investigating Blackwater.

One of the sponsors of the bill, Jan Schakowsky (D-IL), also introduced a measure that would phase out private contractors altogether over the next five years.

In the Senate, Barack Obama introduced a bill similar to the one the House approved. As Obama put it, "We cannot win a fight for hearts and minds when we outsource critical missions to unaccountable contractors."

Of course, Blackwater's defenders say that they're just filling a need, because the military doesn't have the personnel to do what Blackwater is doing. Well, if the military could afford to pay its soldiers six-figure salaries, I imagine recruiting might be a bit easier.

But at the end of the day, it's not really about money. It's about what kind of country we are. Do we really want to contract out one of the primary functions of government?

Why the Right Was Wrong About Iraq

For anyone who sets out to prove that the Right is wrong, Iraq has become a barrel in which to shoot fish. Feith, Perle, Garner, Bremer, and Rumsfeld are perfect subjects for a "Where Are They Now?" special on Fox News—all probably collecting speaking or lobbying fees, writing books, or, perhaps, biding their time for the next geopolitical chess move in Iran or North Korea or Taiwan or Tajikistan. Though it is tempting to regard the Right's armchair generals as a spent force, like nuclear waste they require careful monitoring.

Contrary to the rosy assertions of a cheap, easy, and kinda fun war followed by an epidemic of Middle Eastern democracy, it soon became clear that the war was going to be "a long hard slog."

The World Bank:
Where Architects of War Go Nesting

While his former bosses Bush and Cheney paid the price in public disapproval for leading us into the debacle in Iraq, Paul Wolfowitz was successfully repackaged as the warm and fuzzy poverty-fighting president of the World Bank, and treated like an elder statesman.

There he was in 2005, weighing in on fighting poverty around the globe at Bill Clinton's Global Initiative summit and at Teddy Forstmann's Aspen weekend gathering of movers and shakers (where he said not one word about Iraq).

Talk about your Extreme Political Makeover. Wolfie went from war hawk to the second coming of Mother Teresa—all without having to make any kind of redemptive pit stop in political purgatory or having to apologize for being so wrong about Iraq. I guess love means never having to say you're sorry for helping launch an unnecessary and disastrous war.

And isn't it interesting how the World Bank became the go-to nesting spot for the architects of such wars? Back in 1968, fresh from leading America deep into Vietnam, Robert McNamara resigned from the Pentagon and headed to the World Bank, where he served as president for the next thirteen years (often weeping while delivering his annual reports about the world's poor).

No tears from Wolfie, but he quickly began saying things like "Nothing is more gratifiying than being able to help people in need" and "A clear message from modern history is that this is a small world . . . and that leaving people behind is a formula for failure for us all." Is this the same neocon zealot who, under the direction of Cheney, oversaw the drafting of the 1992 "Defense Planning Guidance" statement—a bellicose blueprint for establishing a "world order" under American authority that included the toppling of Saddam Hussein (and which became the intellectual foundation for the preemptive invasion of Iraq)?

Wolfowitz preferred to keep all that messy Iraq business locked away in his past. His official bio at many events skipped right over his role in the war.

Soon after taking office, he said, "I had quite honestly hoped to leave the Pentagon behind me in this job." And, at an appearance in Japan in October 2005, he told reporters: "I'm not here any longer as a Bush administration official and I don't have to defend their record." Oh, so it's "their" record now, is it?

Well, World Bank Wolfie may have wanted to forget all about Wartime Wolfie—but we can't.

We remember that it was Wolfowitz who, in the run-up to the war, mocked General Eric Shinseki as "wildly off the mark" for saying the United States would need at least 200,000 troops on the ground in Iraq. "It's hard to conceive," Wolfowitz told Congress three weeks before the invasion, "that it would take more forces to provide stability in post-Saddam Iraq than it would take to conduct the war itself and to secure the surrender of Saddam's security forces and his army. Hard to imagine." That failure of imagination has led to the death and mutilation of thousands of Americans and tens of thousands of Iraqis.

And we remember how Wolfowitz pooh-poohed the idea that the United States would be saddled with the bill for the occupation and reconstruction of Iraq. "The idea that [cost of war estimates are] going to be eclipsed by these monstrous future costs ignores the nature of the country we're dealing with," he lectured Congress, going on to explain that Iraq had "$10 to $20 billion in frozen assets from the Gulf War," and generated "on the order of $15 billion to $20 billion a year in oil exports." "To assume that we're going to pay for it is just wrong," he insisted.

"Just wrong," indeed. The taxpayer tab for Iraq will in fact exceed three trillion dollars.

No wonder World Bank Wolfie wanted to leave Wartime Wolfie in the past and move on—without being held accountable.

Ironically, what finally brought down one of the primary architects of the biggest foreign policy disaster in our nation's history was his girlfriend. Getting a country to go to war based on lies and being partially responsible for the needless deaths of thousands barely slowed Wolfie down. But using his position at the World Bank to help his girlfriend, Shaha Riza, land a cushy job at the State Department led to his ouster from the World Bank in May 2007. Sort of like Al Capone going to prison for tax evasion.

But a few short months later he reappeared as Chairman of the Secretary of State's International Security Advisory Board.

That must be one hell of a guardian angel Paul Wolfowitz has looking out for him.

Quagmires, like quicksand and perfect storms, are one of those natural phenomena that exist more as metaphor than reality. "I don't do quagmires," Rumsfeld famously said at the beginning of the war.

But in Iraq, metaphor has become reality. We're stuck in a quagmire. And because the prevailing right-wing ideology obscures facts and because the Right was determined to be right at all costs, we wasted years and lives that are lost forever, disagreeing on something that should have been obvious to anyone with a brain: that it was time to change course in Iraq, even if some draft-dodging radio crackpot wanted to call the new course "Cut and Run." Unfortunately, when the president finally came to this inevitable conclusion, the new course he chose to follow didn't entail troop withdrawal, or increased involvement from our allies, or a tougher stance with the Iraqi government, or more resources dedicated to reconstruction—or any combination of these measures. No, instead he chose to send more of our already depleted military into the fray. Enter the surge . . .

8

Iraq: Petraeus Ex Machina

An Escalation by Any Other Name

In the Orwellian skirmish over language taking place on the political front lines, the Right has been winning hands down. In recent years, framing gurus have manufactured insidious formulas like Frank Luntz's "death tax," the hideous-sounding "partial birth abortion," and the juvenile but effective substitution of "Democrat Party" for "Democratic Party."

As the plan to salvage the president's political fortunes by escalating the war in Iraq took shape, some cynical wordsmith coined the term "surge" as a replacement for the heavily tarnished "escalation," which never quite recovered its stature after Lyndon Johnson and William Westmoreland had to wear it around their necks on the way to early retirement. Whereas an "escalation" sounded costly and permanent, a "surge" sounded upbeat: an energetic but short-lived phenomenon, maybe having to do with surfing or college football. It would seem almost unsporting to be against a surge.

The origins of the surge plan started one day back in late 2006, when Karl Rove was sitting in his office reading the latest polling data and sticking pins in a Joe Wilson voodoo doll. I can't prove that but I wouldn't bet against it. The president's numbers were at such historical lows that Rove, who had been fighting off the unwelcome attentions of special prosecutor Patrick Fitzgerald, had to take decisive action.

The steadily deteriorating situation in Iraq and the president's stubborn refusal to change course (as well as his stubborn refusal to acknowledge that he was stubbornly refusing to change course) had

I Never Said "Stay the Course"

In October 2006, during an interview with George Stephanopoulos, President Bush made the astounding claim that "stay the course"—an oft-repeated White House mantra on the war—had not, in fact, been an oft-repeated White House mantra on the war.

George Stephanopoulos: James Baker says that he's looking for something between "cut and run" and "stay the course."

George Bush: Well, hey, listen, we've never been *"stay the course,"* George. We have been—we will complete the mission, we will do our job, and help achieve the goal, but we're constantly adjusting to tactics. Constantly. (George Stephanopoulos interview with President Bush, October 22, 2006)

A quick Lexis/Nexis search reveals the truth, raising the question: can Bush even tell when he's lying about Iraq anymore, or has it become an involuntary reflex?

"Iraq is the central front in this war on terror: If we leave the streets of Baghdad before the job is done, we will have to face the terrorists in our own cities. We will *stay the course*, we will help this young Iraqi democracy succeed, and victory in Iraq will be a major ideological triumph in the struggle of the twenty-first century." (President Bush's remarks at Utah Air National Guard, August 30, 2006)

"We will *stay the course*, we will complete the job in Iraq." (President Bush, Crawford, Texas, August 4, 2005)

"It's a wonderful feeling to have a strong ally in believing in the power of free societies and liberty. And that's why we're going to *stay the course* in Iraq. And that's why when we say something in Iraq, we're going to do it, because we want there to be a free society." (President Bush, Rose Garden, April 16, 2004)

threatened the Right's rapid ascendancy post-9/11 and jeopardized Rove's grand project of installing a permanent Republican government in Washington.

It was a foregone conclusion that a change in course would not include any acknowledgment of fault or error at any point in the con-

duct of the war. Whatever the administration decided to do, no matter what it was, would be presented as a logical, flexible response to a
changing situation on the ground in accordance with the recommendations of the senior military commanders blah-blah-blah. But having spat the words "cut and run" in the face of anyone who had dared
to suggest anything ranging from an immediate withdrawal of all
forces to a gradual redeployment over the horizon, any move that
reduced forces would spell surrender to the Right.

So the plan was hatched for an *increase* in the size of the American
forces in Iraq, a possibility that would have seemed like an absurd
joke if it had been suggested a few months earlier. Someone on Rove's
team must have hauled out a well-thumbed copy of *Roget's Thesaurus*
and the midnight oil began burning in the West Wing: not in order to
decide what to do but, rather, what to call it. After some other possi-
bilities, like, perhaps, "the wave," "the plunge," "the swell," "the
spring cleaning," and "Operation Aladdin" were considered and dis-
carded, some bright spark suggested the word my dictionary defines
as "any sudden, strong increase, as of energy, enthusiasm, etc." The
surge was born.

The President Listens to His Generals . . .
So Long as They Agree with Him

The president had repeatedly insisted that he was running the war by
listening to his generals, and that he doesn't "make decisions based
upon politics about how to win a war," choosing to "trust our commanders on the ground to give the best advice about how to achieve
victory." As he put it in the run-up to the midterm elections: "I
believe that you empower your generals to make the decisions—the
recommendations on what we do to win."

But when his generals were lukewarm at best about the surge, the
military commanders were poked, prodded, pushed, and bribed into
backing it. For months senior military staff—including General
John Abizaid, commander of U.S. Central Command, and General
George Casey, senior coalition commander—had been unwavering
in their opposition to sending more troops to Iraq, arguing that it
would increase Iraqi dependency on Washington, attract more foreign jihadists to Iraq, increase the appearance of an American occupation, and, in the evocative words of one military official, "be like
throwing kerosene on a fire."

Testifying at a Senate Armed Services hearing in late 2006, General Abizaid said unequivocally that he did not "believe that more American troops right now is the solution." But, with Rove supporting it, the surge was inevitable. So much for "trusting" and "empowering" your commanders. Eventually, Abizaid and Casey ended up providing cover for Bush by caving to White House pressure and acting like they supported the move—albeit in the most unenthusiastic terms possible.

"I'm not necessarily opposed to the idea," said Casey in December 2006, speaking like a man who feared that if he actually said that he thought it was a good plan, God—or someone in close personal contact with him—would strike him down. "What I want to hear from you is how we're going to win, not how we're going to leave," the president had told his military experts on the cusp of announcing his troop escalation strategy in January—and on the cusp of rewarding General Casey for good conduct by kicking him upstairs to the post of army chief of staff. Yet more play-acted success in Iraq. The general did so well over there, let's put him in charge of the whole shebang!

And check out the verbal contortions of the senior Defense Department official who told *The New York Times* that Casey and Lieutenant General Raymond Odierno, who at that point was overseeing day-to-day operations in Iraq, were open to "the possible modest augmentation in U.S. combat forces." Not exactly a ringing endorsement of a surge—but nowhere near the honest expression of the military's reported "firm stand" against it.

How "firm" a stand was the military taking? *The Washington Post* reported the difference of opinion between Bush and his top generals this way:

> The Bush administration is split over the idea of a surge in troops to Iraq, with White House officials aggressively promoting the concept over the unanimous disagreement of the Joint Chiefs of Staff, according to U.S. officials familiar with the intense debate. Sending 15,000 to 30,000 more troops for a mission of possibly six to eight months is one of the central proposals on the table of the White House policy review to reverse the steady deterioration in Iraq. The option is being discussed as an element in a range of bigger packages, the officials said. But the Joint Chiefs think the White House, after a

month of talks, still does not have a defined mission and is latching on to the surge idea in part because of limited alternatives, despite warnings about the potential disadvantages for the military, said the officials, who spoke on the condition of anonymity because the White House review is not public.

The president has often summarized his point of view as, "You can't fight a war from Washington. . . . You can't make the tactical decisions necessary to win. It just won't work." But that's precisely what happened with the troop surge plan—and what has been the modus operandi since the beginning of the war. General Shinseki's fate has obviously been a factor in his successors' subsequent acquiescence, and helps explain why the catastrophe in Iraq has been masterminded from Washington every step of the way—the honest advice of our military commanders be damned.

Surgin' General

With the packaging now complete—this was to be an energetic and enthusiastic "surge" during which we'd keep doing all the great things we had been doing in Iraq and keep having all those successes only *more so*—all that was left was the casting. Clearly, the Hamlet-like hemming and hawing of Abizaid and Casey disqualified them from consideration for the task of leading the surge.

David Petraeus is nothing if not a good soldier. So it doesn't seem likely that we'll know what he really thinks of the idiots he's working for for a long time, if ever. Petraeus, as his many fans like to point out, quite literally wrote the book (or, rather, a dissertation) on counterinsurgency warfare while getting his Ph.D. at Princeton's Woodrow Wilson School, "The American Military and the Lessons of Vietnam, A Study of Military Influence and the Use of Force in the Post-Vietnam Era." Petraeus's military career included commanding the 101st Airborne Division during its shock and awe attack on Baghdad, and subsequently during the campaign to subdue Ninawa province. Then he served as the de facto military governor of Mosul, Iraq's third largest city, where, *Newsweek* reported, "no force worked harder to win Iraqi hearts and minds than the 101st Air Assault Division led by Petraeus."

There's been a great deal of fruitless speculation about Petraeus's personal politics but what we know about his efforts in Iraq before the surge indicates that he had no stake in validating anyone's agenda. It was the administration that cast him in the role of *deus ex machina*, the god who suddenly arrives and solves a seemingly insolvable crisis.

For Bush, "Petraeus" became a magic word. The president publicly mentioned Petraeus's name over 150 times in the first six months of 2007.

Frank Rich took a chisel to the notion that Petraeus was the second coming of Grant, Patton, MacArthur, and Halo's Master Chief all rolled into one Ivy League package. According to Rich, Petraeus's purported military infallibility was as much a shimmering desert mirage as the Iraqi throngs who were going to greet us as liberators, throwing flowers at our soldiers' feet. Rich laid it out chapter and verse: Petraeus was wrong about Mosul, he was wrong about the competency of newly trained Iraqi troops, he was wrong about what he wishfully referred to as "the astonishing signs of normalcy" in Baghdad.

And he had also shown a special gift for thunderingly misguided comparisons, likening the political standoff in the Iraqi parliament to disputes among our Founding Fathers, and straining to make the case that the civil war raging in Iraq was akin to the struggles Britain faced with the IRA in Northern Ireland. There were many problems with this last comparison, not the least of which is the fact that the IRA was never more than a thousand strong, and never embraced suicide bombing.

Given all the hype surrounding him, no one would have been surprised if Petraeus had walked across the Potomac on his way to testify to Congress and be anointed as the savior of Iraq. James Fallows took the metaphor a step further, pointing out in *The Atlantic* that Petraeus had become Bush's New Jesus: "The New Jesus is the guy the boss has just brought in to solve the problems that the slackers and idiots already on the staff cannot handle. Of course, sooner or later the New Jesus himself turns into a slacker or idiot, and the search for the next Jesus begins. . . . Petraeus is a serious man, but the expectations being heaped on him are simply laughable."

The New, Improved Iraq War

With the brand identity in place and a persuasive celebrity spokesperson on board, the product launch for the new and improved Iraq war was set. For those who believe that the only sensible course of action in Iraq is the withdrawal of all American military forces, debating the particular merits of the surge strategy is a little like deciding whether you think the *Titanic*'s deck chairs would be more conducive to a pleasant shipboard atmosphere if they were side by side or facing each other.

The surge was an increase in local troop strength (not, it should be said, to the levels advocated in the army's newly revised counterinsurgency field manual, another book on counterinsurgency co-written by David Petraeus) from 132,000 to a politically tolerable 152,000 soldiers and marines. These new troops were to pacify the neighborhoods and provinces where either Shiite or Sunni sectarian fighters had gained control and then set up camp, holding the recaptured ground until the Iraqi military was able to relieve them. "Clear, hold, and build."

This mission improbable was, notwithstanding Petraeus's undeniable appeal, a tough sell for two obvious reasons. First of all, there was no denying the fact that we were sending more troops and increasing our involvement in Iraq—even if the increase was promised to be temporary. Second, the Iraqi military was proving to be an unsteady ally, to say the least. Having been thoroughly infiltrated by sectarian militias, it was widely suspected of causing much of the mayhem in Iraq. But for the Right, the surge was manna from heaven. It offered the glittering prospect of eking out a "win" in Iraq, not by achieving an actual victory—that hope was long dead for all but the certifiably delusional members of the Right—but by creating a situation in which a victory-of-sorts could be claimed.

Selling the Surge, Surging the Sell

Since the start of the war, President Bush had been relentless about shielding Americans from its cost. Oh sure, he'd use the sacrifice of the fallen as a political backdrop during a State of the Union speech or to buttress his smears of any dissent as evidence of not "supporting the troops." But from Day One of this war he tried to keep Americans from coming face-to-face with the gruesome reality.

That's why he has avoided the funerals of soldiers killed in action. That's why for so long he refused to allow photographs of caskets arriving on American soil. The president continued to kid himself that by keeping his game face of smug "What, Me Worry?" optimism—

what CIA veteran John McLaughlin called his "idyllic vision" of the war—he could get the public to buy into his fantasy of leading us to victory.

Nor was this attitude limited to public appearances. *New York Times* columnist David Brooks recounted a meeting with the president in the summer of 2007: "Far from being beleaguered, Bush was assertive and good-humored. While some in his administration may be looking for exit strategies, he is unshakably committed to stabilizing Iraq. . . . I left the 110-minute session thinking that far from being worn down by the past few years, Bush seems empowered. His self-confidence is the most remarkable feature of his presidency."

To maintain this fragile self-delusion, Bush promoted the surge by treating the general public to the sort of reassurance that he undoubtedly wanted for himself.

Though the surge's proponents continued to try to have it both ways—the surge was something both new ("we're constantly adapting our tactics") and improved ("we're sticking with our overall strategy")—the surge was clearly a Plan B solution to the problems that had developed under Plan A. So, trying to extend this line a little further, was there a Plan C in case Plan B didn't work? That's the kind of logical question that just made Condi Rice a bit sad (even when asked by the Senate Foreign Relations Committee): "It's bad policy to speculate on what you'll do if a plan fails when you're trying to make a plan work."

Okay, Madam Secretary, if you say so, but it sure would be nice to know that you do have a Plan C, even if you don't want to tell us what it is.

Besides the "Plan C dooms Plan B" argument, there was also the "grown-ups are in charge" approach, which remains the vice president's default setting. And here's Cheney managing expectations: "This is an existential conflict. It is the kind of conflict that's going to drive our policy and our government for the next twenty or thirty or forty years. We have to prevail and we have to have the stomach for the fight long term."

Well, no one said it was going to be quick and easy—except the Right. (By the way, it would be a delicious irony, considering how he likes to suggest that the war's critics don't have "the stomach" for it, if Cheney had avoided service in Vietnam because of an intestinal ailment. In actuality, he skipped the war by finagling several deferments, the last for marriage. As he put it, "I had other priorities in the sixties than military service"—such as not getting shot at.)

With the surge now in motion, the Right could again claim that it was made up of forward-looking big thinkers unlike the pettifogging Monday morning quarterbacks on the other side. The subject had been changed, the past was finally past, and not a minute too soon.

The past and the future. There are some—mostly those inside the White House and their shills in the media and on Capitol Hill—who would have you believe the two have nothing to do with each other. Richard Perle offered his spin on the "don't look back" mind-set on *Meet the Press* in the spring of 2007:

> **Russert:** Mr. Perle, is the war in Iraq worth the price we've paid?
>
> **Perle:** Forgive me for saying it, but I think it's the wrong question. It's a bit academic for one thing. But the question is what is in our national interest now, what is going to make Americans safer.

"Academic"? Looking back at how we got to where we are is anything but academic. Especially when the same people responsible for this disaster are still in power. Or still on *Meet the Press* telling us what to do next.

And, if Perle's cerebral approach leaves you a little, well, *cold*, there's always good old-fashioned nostalgia to sell an unpopular idea. Continuing to excavate a political mine that many thought had long been exhausted, George Bush repeatedly invoked 9/11 in batty peace-through-escalation speeches as our troops' overseas deployments were extended and their stateside ones shortened.

Speaking in front of American Legionnaires in Fairfax, Virginia, in April 2007 the president brought to mind a played-out wedding band, dragging out the moldy-oldie hits from days long past. There were the four mentions of September 11, the nod to the heroism of the passengers on United Flight 93, and the reminders of his tough-talking, dead-or-alive glory days: "I vowed that day that we would go on the offensive against an enemy. . . . I vowed that if you harbor a terrorist you're equally as guilty as the terrorist. That's a doctrine." He even threw in a Cheneyesque "It's hard work." One half-expected one of the Legionnaires to toss the president a megaphone so he could re-create his Ground Zero "I hear you" smash hit. And, remarkably, he offered four different versions of his classic flypaper rationale for continuing the war (c'mon, everyone, sing along, you know the words):

> "We want to defeat them there, so we don't have to face them here."

> "The best way to defeat this enemy is to find them overseas and bring them to justice so they will not hurt the folks here at home."

> "What's interesting and different about this war is that the enemy would follow us here."

> "It's in our interests . . . to pursue the enemy overseas so we don't have to face them here."

If the news ticker at the bottom of the TV screen hadn't been filled with stories about Don Imus, Attorney General Alberto Gonzales's subpoena, and Anna Nicole Smith's baby, you would have thought you were watching a presidential speech from 2002.

Having been briefed on what they were selling, the media brigade dutifully got with the program—not just on Fox but on CNN. Here's Glenn Beck: "This U.S.-led plan to help Iraqis protect their own is saving upwards of twenty-five innocent people, just like you and me, every single day. Jane Fonda, is twenty-five not enough for you? Hollywood morons like Sean Penn, Susan Sarandon, you can argue all the political strategy, foreign policy, and ideology you want all day long. If Nancy Pelosi and her pals had their way, they will impose something called military readiness standards. They're going to screw this thing up six ways to Sunday."

Clouds Still Outnumber Silver Linings

The first reports on the surge cannot have been encouraging to its champions despite their careful efforts to downplay expectations, oiling a blame-the-Iraqis trapdoor if the whole thing went south.

In the punch-in-the-gut words of the *New York Times*'s Damien Cave: "Iraq's political leaders have failed to reach agreements on nearly every law that the Americans have demanded as benchmarks, despite heavy pressure from Congress, the White House, and top military commanders." And the Pentagon admitted "some analysts see a growing fragmentation of Iraq."

Putting his finger on the essence of the political problem, Prime Minister Nuri al-Maliki gave this bleak assessment: "There are two mentalities in this region, conspiracy and mistrust." Not exactly the cornerstones for reconciliation. (In a PR exercise on the op-ed page of *The Wall Street Journal*, Maliki compared the situation in Iraq to America in the 1860s and our own "civil war that took hundreds of thousands of lives but ended in the triumph of freedom and the birth of a great power." Maybe Maliki sees himself as Lincolnesque, but a Pentagon report recounted his failures to deliver on his promises of progress.)

As for the administration's Petraeus *ex machina*, the general quickly reached the point where he began grasping for silver linings. He told *USA Today* the surge is working, citing as proof of "normalcy" "professional soccer leagues with real grass field stadiums, several amusement parks—big ones, markets that are very vibrant." And while calling the attack on the Samarra mosque a "serious blow" to U.S. efforts, he tried desperately to stay positive, telling ABC News: "There is even some hope, perhaps, that al Qaeda may have overplayed its hand."

The carnage intensified to the point where the first six months of the surge were the deadliest six-month stretch of the war, with 586 Americans killed. On average, we lost more than three U.S. soldiers a day—and more than one hundred a month. And more than one hundred Iraqi civilians were being killed every day.

Petraeus's civilian partner, American Ambassador Ryan Crocker, also struggled to paint a rosy picture of the surge. Appearing on *Meet the Press* in June 2007, Crocker demonstrated that along with the surge in troops, there had also been a surge in BS.

Crocker served up his crock in a bizarre, robotic manner that made him look like he had been animated by Disney Imagineers— a genuine possibility since the administration was running out of actual human beings willing to defend the war. So instead they rolled out the Crockerbot2000.

Crocker's talking points previewed the spin the administration would use come September. Here's what he said—and what it really means: "America could not ask for a finer, more experienced and more able military leader than they have in General Petraeus. I have heard him give tough, clear assessments to the president, to congressional visitors as they come through, and you've heard him in the open media. . . . He calls it as he sees it." *Translation: So, in September, when he tells you that the surge is working, you had better believe him!*

"The other thing I think we're going to do [in September], because we owe it to our leadership at both ends of Pennsylvania Avenue, is also try to provide an assessment of what the consequences might be if we pursue other directions." *Translation: Even if the surge isn't going so well come September, we are going to tell everyone—especially those in Congress—that if we leave Iraq we will unleash a genocidal bloodbath and war across the planet and, indeed, the entire galaxy. So we really need to give it more time.*

"The surge buys time for a political process to get some legs under it." *Translation: We really, really need to give it more time.*

"There is nothing easy about the task in front of [Iraq's leaders], and I have certainly been struck since I've been here at the amount of commitment and effort that senior Iraqi officials have demonstrated to try and get the job done." *Translation: We really, really, really need to give it more time.*

"It's definitely not by any means a universally negative picture." *Translation: Don't believe the facts, believe us!*

You know the soft bigotry of the Bush administration's low expectations for Iraq had finally hit bottom when "Hey, we're doing slightly better than universally negative!" became the rallying cry.

Looking at the facts on the ground, deceiving the American people about them, and making decisions based on those deceptions had been the White House's MO for the entire run of the war. Why would anybody think the administration was suddenly going to change when it came to reporting on the surge?

The Highly Offensive Optimism Offensive

Meeting "benchmarks" was supposed to be a way out of the quagmire, but they proved to be nothing more than a shiny distraction. In May 2007, if you'd been given a dollar for every time "benchmarks" was bandied about in Washington, you could have outbid Rupert Murdoch for control of *The Wall Street Journal.*

But amid all the benchmark babble, there was precious little clarity on whether they represented an acceptable compromise position—or were just another Bush mirage shimmering in the Iraqi desert.

Thank goodness for Michael Ware, CNN's Baghdad-based war correspondent. Amid all the media hot air, his reporting was like a bracing splash of ice-cold water to the face. A jolt of from-the-belly-of-the-beast reality. A wake-up call delivered via jackhammer. With an Australian accent.

I caught Ware on May 1, 2007, on *Anderson Cooper 360°*, discussing the latest from Iraq with Cooper and David Gergen. Now, it's hard not to like David Gergen, but the contrast between his safely-ensconced-in-the-Beltway take on benchmarks and Ware's boots-on-the-ground no-BS approach couldn't have been starker.

> **Cooper:** Well, Michael Ware, let's talk about those benchmarks. . . . The benchmarks, I guess, are to pressure Maliki. Has pressure worked on him in the past?

> **Ware:** No, never. This is such an old scenario, Anderson. I mean, this word "benchmark" has been used over and over and over. And no matter what conditions have been set for Maliki to meet, he's never once lived up to them. So, now Washington is trying to up the ante, increase the pressure upon him in what most likely will be the vain hope that he will deliver.

Woosh, sting (that's the sound of ice-water truth hitting face). He later added this, the verbal equivalent of taking a pair of White House–designed rose-colored glasses and grinding them into the sidewalk with your heel:

> **Cooper:** Is this notion of a unified democracy of Sunni and Shia, is there any real support for it within the Iraqi government?

> **Ware:** No, no, none that I have seen, Anderson. And I have dealt a lot with all of the important factions within the Iraqi government. It's simply in no one's interest whatsoever to pursue a true reconciliation.

Then there was Gergen, and this gem of waffling:

> **Gergen:** While the benchmarks may seem like sort of a Washington game, in some ways, they're a very important prelude to the United States beginning to look for a way to disengage.

A prelude to beginning to look for a way to disengage? In other words, let's wait six more months to see how things are going, then, if this latest in a long line of unmet benchmarks also goes unmet, we can begin to commence to initiate the starting of thinking about the mulling over of the consideration of a possible path that could, in time, lead us to begin to commence to start looking for a means that could, with any luck, result in America beginning to commence to start withdrawing from Iraq. Eventually.

The truth is, we kept putting forth key benchmarks for the Iraqis—on Iraqi troops, on oil revenue sharing, on reversing de-Baathification, on amending Iraq's new constitution—and they kept failing to meet them. Time after time after time.

Indeed, as of January 2008, the one-year anniversary of Bush's State of the Union presentation of his "New Way Forward" in Iraq, only three of the eighteen benchmarks had been met. And when the fractured Iraqi government was able to set aside its differences—as it did in February 2008, agreeing on a budget, setting dates for provincial elections, and approving amnesty for thousands of jailed Sunnis—there was great doubt over whether these agreements would ever be implemented. Even Petraeus and Crocker, while hailing the passage of the provisional powers legislation as "a landmark law," warned that there could be poison pills hidden in the fine print. And counting these three measures—which were passed because most of the contentious details were tabled for a later date—only four of the eighteen benchmarks had been fully met, with another five only partially accomplished. Which left the surge far from having met its objectives.

Nothing new there. For example, in July 2007, an interim report on Iraq had shown that progress on eight of the eighteen benchmarks set by Congress in May of the same year had been "satisfactory," while eight others had been "unsatisfactory." Two others were too close to call.

To hear the president and the White House spin it (and the media dutifully report it), the interim progress report on Iraq the administration submitted to Congress in July was "a mixed bag."

That's like a doctor telling you that your acne has cleared but you have a brain tumor—and you coming away thinking the doctor's report is "a mixed bag."

Indeed the president called the report "a cause for optimism." As expected, he asked for more time, said the military had achieved "great things," and blamed the rising unpopularity of the war on "war fatigue." That and restless leg syndrome.

In June, the White House had labeled progress in Iraq a mixed bag. In July it also said it was a mixed bag. The stage was set for General Petraeus to tie his white horse up outside the White House and report that Iraq was something of a mixed bag. But coming from a fresh face who could be counted on to accentuate the positive, this was expected to play as good news.

By the way, there was none of this mixed baggery for Dick Cheney. He stuck his fingers in his ears and never stopped humming, telling Wolf Blitzer at the start of the surge, "The reality on the ground is, we've made major progress. We've still got a lot of work to do. We've got a lot of provinces in Iraq that are relatively quiet. There's more and more authority transferred to the Iraqis all the time. . . . Bottom line is that we've had enormous successes and we will continue to have enormous successes."

And the president made the claim that "there is a convergence of visions between what Iraqi leaders want . . . and the vision articulated by my administration." Tell that to the majority of the members of the Iraqi parliament who in May, by signing a legislative petition, rejected the ongoing occupation of their country by U.S. forces. Mr. Bush must also have missed the contemporaneous poll showing that only 22 percent of Iraqis support the presence of coalition troops in their country.

Petraeus Storms Capitol Hill, Congress and the Press Surrender Without a Fight

As the drum roll for the surge began to swell, Bush continued to pretend to be taking a hands-off approach to Iraq, claiming: "I'm going to wait to see what David has to say." But in reality Bush was cherry-picking the military commanders to listen to just as diligently as he cherry-picked prewar intel.

The same administration that didn't know the difference between Sunni and Shiite before the war—and now doesn't know the difference between al Qaeda and al Qaeda in Iraq—has somehow been incredibly effective at weeding out "insurgent" thought in the Pentagon. The "clear, hold, and build" strategy has been a smashing success in Washington.

He came, he saw, he conquered. As George Lakoff wrote, "Bush took advantage of certain conventions of etiquette and politeness when he sent Petraeus to testify before Congress. Those conventions hold that one does not criticize the symbolic stand-in for the military, even when the uniform-wearing stand-in is on an overt political mission that is at the heart of the administration's continuing betrayal of trust."

By repeatedly politicizing the military—while militarizing our politics—Bush has betrayed those in uniform. Again and again. But because of the conventions Lakoff alluded to, the gambit worked. Petraeus's opening salvo during his much anticipated September testimony was delivered while barely looking up from his script and was barely grounded in reality. But it was treated as though it had come down from the mountaintop. And all of humanity suddenly knew the way forward in Iraq.

The problem was that many of Petraeus's numbers were (excuse my impoliteness, General) flat-out wrong. *The Washington Post* and the *Los Angeles Times* documented how the White House and Petraeus used questionable methodology to arrive at their stats. So the general's numbers for civilian violence varied widely from the numbers produced by congressionally mandated studies.

Petraeus's conclusions about "sectarian violence" were also highly speculative and subject to challenge. Yes, in certain areas of Baghdad violence has gone down, but that's partly because of the ethnic-cleansing in those neighborhoods.

And Anbar province, cited by both Petraeus and Bush in his follow-up address to the nation, actually wasn't such a glittering success after all. A *New York Times* piece by Gary Langer, ABC's pollster, reported several rare cases of 100 percent unanimity among respondents to a survey conducted in Anbar—unanimity in their hostile feelings toward the United States. And every respondent called attacks on coalition forces "acceptable" and called the U.S.-led invasion wrong.

Most important, the purpose of the surge wasn't to prove that more troops could increase security; it was that the increased security produced by the surge would lead to political conditions in which increased security could be had without U.S. troops. And that clearly wasn't happening. At the time of Petraeus's triumphant appearance on Capitol Hill, the Iraqi government had returned from a one-month summer recess, taken without regard for the Bush administration's urgent appeal that they keep working.

Dept. of Misdirection:
With Iraq a Disaster,
GOP Goes Crazy over a Newspaper Ad

The GOP, in a desperate search for a position more inspiring than "We have to continue endorsing a failed war mounted under false pretenses," seized on a September 11, 2007, MoveOn.org ad going after General Petraeus: "General Petraeus or General Betray Us?"

Does anybody really believe the problem with the war in Iraq is too much questioning of those in authority, too much bluntness, and not enough deference to those who have been in charge of the war for the last four years? Rather than focus on the content of the ad, the Right came down with the vapors over its headline, which had the temerity to question General Petraeus. Tens of thousands of dead civilians, nearly four thousand dead American soldiers, a three-trillion-dollar war, and the squandering of America's moral authority—none of that seems to have ruffled their feathers very much. But the ad? Now, that got them royally steamed.

Rudy Giuliani was up in arms, railing against "character assassination on an American general who is putting his life at risk." John McCain declared that "MoveOn.org ought to be thrown out of this country." Even Don Rumsfeld popped his head out of his spider hole to blast the ad.

It's the political version of the old lawyer's axiom: When the law is against you, argue the facts. When the facts are against you, argue the law. When both are against you, attack the plaintiff. And when the war is an unmitigated disaster, the facts on the ground are against you, and your only plan for the future is "more of the same," go crazy over a newspaper ad.

Was the MoveOn ad blunt? Yes. Did it go for the jugular? No doubt. But while the way it chose to make its points can be debated, the accuracy of those points cannot. Does anyone really doubt that the president hid behind Petraeus's medals and sent him on a week-long talk-show tour to sell a policy he could no longer peddle himself?

There was at least one member of the Republican Party who was willing to truly stick up for the military. Here's Senator Chuck Hagel on *Real Time with Bill Maher* on September 14, 2007:

Maher: "Isn't it a dirty trick on the American people when you send a military man out there to basically do a political sell-job?"

Hagel: "It's not only a dirty trick, but it's dishonest, it's hypocritical, it's dangerous and irresponsible. The fact is this is not Petraeus's policy; it's Bush's policy. The military is—certainly very clear in the Constitution—is subservient to the elected public officials of this country . . . but to put our military in a position that this administration has put them in is just wrong, and it's dangerous."

Someone should have put that in an ad.

And yet, thanks to the media, Petraeus's blinding chestful of medals, and a postmodern devaluation of the very notion of truth, the Right managed to fool some of the people all of the time into thinking that the war in Iraq is still winnable and that victory is just a simple matter of choosing the proper time frame in which to consider what's happened and what will happen. If you pick the right three months in the right three places, everything's going great, and, at the same time, if you look at the situation from some infinitely distant point in the future, the setbacks and disasters start to flatten out.

"Surge Mission Accomplished"

Everything that has happened in Iraq before and after the surge has only confirmed the monstrous folly of the Right. I wish there were some way to redeem the sacrifice of all who have died in the real-life game of Risk that the Right has been playing with our troops. But the only way to honor them now is to stop more of them from dying. In answer to John Kerry's famous question posed during his testimony to Congress as a young officer during the Vietnam War, "How do you ask a man to be the last man to die for a mistake?" I would say let's make sure that the last person who *has* died in Iraq is the last person who *does* die. Only when we've brought the last soldier home will we really be able to speak rationally about the war, without the Right hiding behind the pretense of "supporting the troops."

A decrease from one unacceptable level of violence to another smaller but still unacceptable level of violence is not progress. If you are headed for a brick wall at two hundred miles an hour and your speed is cut in half you are still doomed. The time until you meet your fate has been doubled, but the result is, in the end, the same. In other words, there is no military solution in Iraq.

The perceived security gains under the surge are the result of three temporary circumstances. The first is that radical anti-American cleric Moqtada al-Sadr has temporarily withdrawn his heavily armed fundamentalist militia, the Mahdi Army, from the field. They will return once the surge is over and the surge, by definition, will be over sooner rather than later. The second is that influential Sunni sheikhs and elders have renounced al Qaeda–influenced terrorists and begun to fight them. They are doing this to consolidate their own power and because of hefty payments from the United States. Their forces are becoming professionalized, it is true, but their loyalty is to their sect and tribe and they will become a force for instability, not unity, once the surge winds down.

Finally, there are the direct effects of the troop increase. It surely isn't surprising that in the immediate vicinity of the thirty thousand troops involved in the surge, attacks temporarily decrease. Just as it's not surprising, for instance, that the crime rate inside the gates of the White House is lower than the rate in NE Washington. The point of the surge was that it would have a political spillover effect. But since that hasn't really happened, the White House is once again attempting to move the goalposts, and the media enablers are there to help with the heavy lifting.

Indeed at the end of November, Ambassador Crocker was quoted in *The New York Times* saying Iraq was "going to be a long, hard slog."

Sound familiar?

It should, because here was Rumsfeld almost five years ago: "It will be a long, hard slog."

This thing has been going on for so long, the administration is recycling excuses. But hey, at least the administration can claim it's no longer hostile to recycling—at least when it comes to messages.

The ambassador also conceded that "with American military successes outpacing political gains in Iraq, the Bush administration has lowered its expectation of quickly achieving major steps toward unifying the country."

But the purpose of the surge was not more "military success" but political stability. As Matt Yglesias put it in *The Atlantic*, "Its goal was to create an improvement in the security situation in Baghdad which (it was hypothesized) was the necessary precondition for a political resolution to Iraq's fundamental conflicts. The surge was tried, and American casualties went up and violence stayed at the same level and then violence declined and then U.S. casualties declined and then it turned out that the surge had failed and the political situation was the same as it had been at the beginning."

Instead of actual political gains, in Iraq the new goal became convincing everyone political progress is being made.

Here's how *The New York Times* described it: "Instead, administration officials say they are focusing their immediate efforts on several more limited but achievable goals in the hope of convincing Iraqis, foreign governments and Americans that progress is being made toward the political breakthroughs that the military campaign of the past 10 months was supposed to promote."

Now the surge was apparently implemented so "American officials" could focus on "pragmatic goals like helping the Iraqi government spend the money in its budget."

That's right: our new definition of success in Iraq had become helping the Iraqi government spend money.

The administration and John McCain give high fives to each other and declare "surge mission accomplished" because only thirty to fifty American soldiers were being killed every month—and because separating Sunnis and Shiites with massive conrete walls had led to a dip in sectarian violence. But opponents of the surge were not skeptical that it would pay military dividends. They were skeptical that the surge would magically translate into political success.

But, of course, war supporters are off the hook, because every four years one of them comes out to tell the American people that Iraq is going to be "a long, hard slog." Indeed, to hear John McCain tell it, we could be sloggin' in Iraq for "a thousand years."

Why the Right Is Still Wrong About Iraq

In the summer of 2005, I traveled to Palermo, Sicily, and on my way over, I decided to brush up on my Sicilian history—and that meant delving into Thucydides and his epic chronicle of the disastrous Sicilian Expedition.

Of course, I had been forced to read all that as a Greek schoolgirl. But oh what a difference the passage of many, many years and one

Iraq war have made in my reading of the great Athenian soldier-historian. The parallels between his rendering of the Sicilian Expedition—a case study in imperial power gone awry—and our current situation in Iraq were inescapable and chilling. And Santayana's old saw about those unable to remember the past being condemned to repeat it kept leaping to mind. Or, as Thucydides himself put it back in the day: "It will be enough for me, however, if these words of mine are judged useful by those who want to understand clearly the events which happened in the past and which (human nature being what it is) will, at some time or another and in much the same ways, be repeated in the future." Boy, are they ever.

For those of you who slept through your Ancient History 101 class, here's a quick refresher, courtesy of Wikipedia:

The Sicilian Expedition was an Athenian expedition to Sicily from 415 B.C. to 413 B.C., during the Peloponnesian War. It was an unmitigated disaster for the Athenian forces. As Thucydides recounts wryly in his *History of the Peloponnesian War,* the generals leading the campaign had scant knowledge of Sicily, or of its population, and thus the forces marshaled for its conquering were woefully inadequate.

Sound familiar?

But that was just the tip of the hubris iceberg when it came to ancient analogies to the modern mistakes being made in Iraq.

For starters, the Athenian warmongers, led by Alcibiades, were convinced that conquering Sicily would be a cakewalk, leading to easy control of its grain and trade routes—and would serve as a great warning to other enemies of Athens. Those on the other side, led by Nicias, argued that the resources needed to conquer Sicily would be much greater than what the hawks were advertising (perhaps Nicias was an ancient relative of General Shinseki). Nicias also correctly predicted that the ancient equivalent of the Coalition of the Willing wouldn't be all that willing (or, rather, about as willing as they were almost twenty-five centuries later).

The invasion of Sicily was part of a larger war—against Sparta—which was the first great "clash of civilizations" and it, too, was sold as a war of liberation. But instead of rolling over (and tossing flowers at the Athenians' feet?), the previously divided and ethnically diverse Sicilians were drawn together by the invasion and attracted anti-Athenian forces from throughout the region (no word on whether that included any gimpy Jordanians).

In the end, Athens' ill-fated invasion of Sicily helped bring about the end of the Athenian empire, proving Toynbee's dictum: "An autopsy of history would show that all great nations commit suicide."

And in the end, the Right is wrong about Iraq because by displaying the same imperial hubris twenty-four centuries later it has had a catastrophic impact on America's position in the world and on our long-term safety.

9

Casualties of War: Neglecting Afghanistan, Empowering Iran

Axis of Error

Einstein defined insanity as doing the same thing over and over again while expecting different results. Long after the war in Iraq had become a debacle of truly historic proportions, the radical Right still nurtured the fond hope of a doppelgänger war in Iran, undertaken for almost identical reasons and aims but with an even lower chance of success. Until December of 2007, when *The New York Times* leaked the news that the National Intelligence Estimate, the consensus opinion of all our nation's intelligence-gathering agencies, had been revised and that Iran had, in fact, halted its secret nuclear weapons program, there was the genuine possibility that we might have found ourselves entangled in a third foreign war.

The similarities in our dealings with both Iraq and Iran are striking proof that, apart from everything else, the Right has a one-track mind (which it may have lost). Ever since the fall of one of the Right's favorite repressive dictators, the Shah, from his Peacock Throne in 1979, Iran has been something of an obsession in neocon quarters. The neocon narrative holds that Jimmy Carter allowed America to be publicly humiliated by the prolonged hostage crisis and that on the day Ronald Reagan took office, the Iranian "students" at the American embassy got the message that recess was over and released the over fifty hostages after more than a year. It was a proud moment for the crowd that believes the most significant problem America faces in the world today is that it puts up with too much nonsense. Not only did it sharpen the Right's disdain for diplomacy and world opinion, it convinced them that the world's reciprocal disdain was actually a good thing, validating their decisions. The more the world disliked what we were doing, the more right we must be.

Since then, Iran has been on the Right's short list of places where the natives need to be taught a stern lesson, losing the top slot to Iraq only when Bush 41 left Saddam in power at the end of Desert Storm. Among the most ardent of Tehran's foes was the American Enterprise Institute's Michael Ledeen. In 2002, he wrote an influential opinion piece in *The Wall Street Journal* titled, "The War on Terror Won't End in Baghdad," which called for the toppling of "terror regimes." And, in 2005, he contributed a delectably demented commentary to *National Review Online* that outlined a vast conspiracy of Arab and European appeasers with Iran at the center. "Everything we know about Iran," he wrote, "demands that we take action. Every day we learn more. It is hard to explain why we, and the rest of the Western world, continue the farce of negotiations and do nothing to bring down a regime that will surely kill as many of us and our allies as possible."

Ledeen speculated in 2003 that France and Germany might have "struck a deal with radical Islam" to use "extremism and terrorism as the weapons of choice" to foil American geopolitical aims. "It sounds fanciful, to be sure," he wrote in the most accurate statement in the entire article, but "if this is correct, we will have to pursue the war against terror far beyond the boundaries of the Middle East, into the heart of Western Europe. And there, as in the Middle East, our greatest weapons are political: the demonstrated desire for freedom of the peoples of the countries that oppose us." Notice that nowhere in his cheerleading for wars in Iran and the "heart of Western Europe" does Ledeen ever volunteer for duty himself.

A fun fact you may not know about Michael Ledeen is that while he was serving as a consultant to the National Security Council in 1985, he helped engineer the arms-for-hostages deal with Iran. Apparently, his views on the virtues of expediency have shifted in the last two decades. Now he wants to go to war—or, rather, wants other people to go to war—to topple the Iranian regime.

In 2002, in George Bush's famous saber-rattling State of the Union speech, he lumped Iran in an "Axis of Evil," an idea that suggested the world was choosing sides for a coming world war. In fact, having fought a devastating war with Saddam Hussein from 1980 to 1988, Iran was about as likely to join forces with its longtime rival for regional power as it was to rename its central mosque after Caspar Weinberger.

Bartlett's Familiar Quotations edition of 2058 may well have but a single entry for George W. Bush: "Axis of Evil." This is how Bush introduced the world to the supervillain Axis: "Iran aggressively pursues these weapons and exports terror, while an unelected few repress the Iranian people's hope for freedom. . . . States like these, and their terrorist allies, constitute an axis of evil, arming to threaten the peace of the world. By seeking weapons of mass destruction, these regimes pose a grave and growing danger. They could provide these arms to terrorists, giving them the means to match their hatred. They could attack our allies or attempt to blackmail the United States. In any of these cases, the price of indifference would be catastrophic."

What is clear in retrospect is that the Axis of Evil construct was intended to make sure that our foreign policy aims, which were redefined as eliminating the world's evildoers, were sufficiently general and vague to include any number of the neocons' pet projects. Basically, it was a request for a blank check from the rest of the world, with some fine print that read, "trust us." The only question was, which part of the Axis would get taken down first? In the end, the "bomb Iraq first" school of thought won over the "bomb Iran first" crowd.

At the time, you'll recall, there was a shared delusion making the rounds at the American Enterprise Institute and the vice president's office that an immediate collateral benefit of the invasion of Iraq would be that repressed peoples throughout the region would rise up to demand democracy and freedom. This "reverse domino theory" was summarized by foreign policy clairvoyant Richard Perle, who, on the eve of the Iraq war, said: "It is the beginning of the end for the Iranian regime." Freedom-loving Iranians would be inspired, like the French after the American Revolution, to throw their theocratic dictators out and, in their place, install a truly representative government that would actually honor the will of the majority while respecting and protecting the rights of minorities through independent democratic institutions. One wonders how our allies in Saudi Arabia felt about that prospect.

Another part of the Iran backstory the Right would probably like to forget is Dick Cheney's own dealings with the country during his private sector interregnum. When President Clinton signed an executive order in 1995 barring American firms from investing in Iran's energy sector, Cheney's employer, Halliburton, simply set up shop offshore in order to be able to continue dealing with the ayatollahs, unimpeded by annoying American laws. Cheney, in typical fashion, was unapologetic. "The problem is that the Good Lord didn't see fit to always put oil and gas resources where there are democratic governments," he groused.

In any event, the Saudi princes needn't have worried. Iran, which was supposed to be the first of these dominoes to fall into the democratic camp, instead tumbled in the opposite direction. While it's important to keep in mind that the definition of a "moderate" or a "reformer" in Iranian politics is different from ours, President Mohammad Khatami, who had come to power in 1997, had stuck his neck out in Iran—and defied many hard-line critics within his own government—by being open to America and the West. But the Right had defined anything other than war as "appeasement," and so Khatami's 2003 diplomatic overture through a Swiss intermediary was not even responded to.

When asked before Congress in early 2007 about the Swiss overture, Condi Rice couldn't remember whether she had seen the terms proposed by the Iranians. But as Michael Hirsh and Maziar Bahari wrote in *Newsweek*, "the faxed two-page proposal for comprehensive bilateral talks" was a "dramatic offer. . . . To the National Security Council's [Hillary] Mann, among others, the Iranians seemed willing to discuss, at least, cracking down on Hizbullah and Hamas (or turning them into peaceful political organizations) and 'full transparency' on Iran's nuclear program. In return, the Iranian 'aims' in the document called for a 'halt in U.S. hostile behavior and rectification of the status of Iran in the U.S. and abolishing sanctions.' "

Although Khatami was ignored by the Bush administration his efforts were not ignored inside Iran. Anti-American hard-liners were gleeful at Khatami's humiliating failure, which vindicated their claims that nothing good could come from working with the West and that America's stated desire for peace in the Middle East was a sham.

And so, with nothing to show for his more moderate approach, Khatami was replaced, in 2005, by a genuine headcase, Mahmoud Ahmadinejad. As has often been the case, the Right's claims about Iran proved self-fulfilling. Rebuffed in its tentative efforts to rejoin the community of nations, politically united in the face of an outside threat from the United States, and suffering under decades of economic sanctions imposed largely at the insistence of the United States, Iran became the sort of rogue state that Bush had said it was when he prematurely made it a member of the Axis of Evil.

Ahmadinejad, by the way, had run for office principally as an economic populist—not as a Holocaust-denying, America-hating champion of Islam. (That came later.) But he did trounce his comparatively moderate opponent, Akbar Hashemi Rafsanjani, by repudiating the foreign policy of Khatami. And it shows just how wrong the Right was about the effect the invasion of Iraq would have on regional politics that, when Ahmadinejad realized he was unable to deliver on his promises to provide a chicken in every pot, he successfully changed the subject by easily directing the public's anger at a big soft target: the United States. Iranian dissident groups and anyone remotely pro-America were cowed. Rather than being emboldened by regime change in Iraq, pro-democracy Iranians slumped down in their chairs to avoid even being associated with the lumbering, ham-fisted American colossus. And then came the administration's noises about direct attacks on Iran.

Flynt Leverett, a former senior director for Middle East Affairs for the National Security Council under President Bush, ridiculed the notion floated by the neocons of an Iranian variation of "sweets and flowers." "The idea that an American attack on Iran's nuclear facilities would produce a popular uprising is extremely ill informed," he told Seymour Hersh in *The New Yorker*. "You have to understand that the nuclear ambition in Iran is supported across the political spectrum, and Iranians will perceive attacks on these sites as attacks on their ambitions to be a major regional player and a modern nation that's technologically sophisticated." He further predicted that any American belligerence "will produce an Iranian backlash against the United States and a rallying around the regime." It turned out that just the threat of an attack was enough to cause this "rallying around" to happen even without an actual attack.

Since the Right has always discounted (been unaware of) the significance of the sectarian divisions between Sunnis and Shiites, it was a foregone conclusion that they would also squander the opportunity that the Khatami regime had offered to engage with Iran's moderates. Unlike every other Muslim country except Bahrain and, importantly, Iraq, Iran is predominantly Shiite. This, coupled with Iran's ambitions to be a regional power broker, inevitably pushed it into a close association with the various Shiite political and paramilitary groups in post-Saddam Iraq, including, among others, Moqtada al-Sadr and his Mahdi Army.

If we had used skillful diplomacy—two words that will never be attached to the Bush administration—it would be possible to imagine a different course of events following the fall of Baghdad. Instead, with the Bush administration and its neocon lackeys breathing down their necks, the Iranians not only encouraged the Shiites to turn on the Americans but provided them with the weapons to better achieve their lethal goals.

Like every other country in the world, Iran needs access to American markets and goods. In addition to the oft-used sticks, we've also got bunches of carrots we could have offered—as we have done for our former enemy Vietnam. How different things might have been if we had sought to empower, embolden, and vindicate Iran's moderates by talking to them rather than by attacking their neighbor and engaging in Axis of Evil rhetoric.

Iran-dioactive Dreams

On November 14, 2006, President Ahmadinejad announced that Iran's semi-clandestine nuclear program had achieved a "full nuclear fuel cycle." Presumably this news of a triumph for local science played well domestically to a public starved for good news. But it also played well back at Neocon Central. The Iraq war was, by then, clearly a disaster. The original game plan—we topple Iraq and democracy blooms and unicorns prance all over the Middle East— was seeming more and more ludicrous, and voters were starting to point fingers. If only the public could be distracted by a new enemy. And voilà; like clockwork, here was a casus belli for the next item on the Imperialist Wish List: a kook with a bomb. And this guy wasn't being coy like Saddam or North Korea's Kim Jong Il. He was telling everyone who would listen about his nuclear prowess. And let's not waste any time figuring out which American foreign policy decisions may or may not have made that more likely. Bottom line: a guy who hates us became the leader of Iran and he's close to getting nukes!

Just as Saddam played into the hands of the Right by not proving to U.N. inspectors that he had no WMD, Ahmadinejad played into their hands by talking up his nuclear successes. And, yet again, the facts were being adjusted to fit the psycho-political agenda, with the post-Tenet CIA once again assigned the dirty work of making another case for war. It was as if they took the Iraq script and just replaced "unstable Saddam" with "unstable Ahmadinejad."

Groundhog Day in the Middle East

The compliant CIA obediently pumped up the Iranian threat and the United States hardened its anti-diplomacy policy, refusing to join European efforts to talk some sense into the Iranian leadership. Before you could say "overreach," the Pentagon was ratcheting up its plans for the Right's next glorious military adventure. Seymour Hersh drew on his unequaled network of sources in the defense and intelligence communities to write a series of alarming articles in *The New Yorker* calling attention to the Right's designs on Iran. The president had decided that he must do "what no Democrat or Republican, if elected in the future would have the courage to do." Bush believed "that saving Iran is going to be his legacy," according to one of Hersh's sources.

The White House's dutiful military planners began drawing up Strangelove-ian plans for all-out war with Iran, a much more complicated task than "liberating" Iraq, which has, itself, proved rather more complicated than the Pentagon anticipated. These plans included an unprecedented bombing assault on more than four hundred targets associated in one way or another with Iran's nuclear program. The saber-rattling escalated as carrier-based U.S. naval aircraft started flying mock nuclear-bombing runs within range of Iranian radar-tracking.

Here's a partial checklist of similarities between the administration's policy toward Iraq and Iran. There was, for starters, the idea of "unfinished business." For Iran, the hostage crisis, and for Iraq, the first Gulf War. *Check*. There was the looming threat of "weapons of mass destruction" supported by dubious intelligence generated by politically directed analysts and shady exile groups. *Check*. There was the misguided belief that large percentages of both populations were eagerly awaiting a U.S. invasion so that, after politely thanking the United States, they could install Jeffersonian democracy. *Check*. There was the buffoonish—and possibly mentally unstable—leader intent on provoking the West in order to increase his stature at home and in the wider Muslim world. *Check.* There was the exporting of terrorism and the alleged link with 9/11. *Check.* So we're clear, Iran certainly did take on the role of global troublemaker by support- ing and arming Shiite militias in Iraq and Hezbollah in Lebanon. But it's important to note that the tempo of these activities changed dramatically after the American invasion of Iraq. So, problematic country becomes hotbed of terrorism after Bush administration falsely claims it is one already? *Check.* Official roadblocking of foreign diplomatic efforts that might actually ease the crisis, but make the domestic exploitation of said crisis more difficult? *Check.* Regime change through military action with or without allies and partners becomes American policy? *Check*—at least on Iraq. With Iran, we shall see.

The chances of military action against Iran increase exponentially if John McCain is the next White House occupant. "There's only one thing worse than the United States exercising the military option," he has said. "That is a nuclear-armed Iran." I guess I missed the part where we found out those are our only two options.

The complete and utter lack of realistic planning for what might happen in Iran after an American bombing attack was underscored by Middle East analyst Geoffrey Kemp. In an interview in *Newsweek*, he said, "The U.S. capability to make a mess of Iran's nuclear infrastruc- ture is formidable. The question is, what then?" *Newsweek* went on to report that the CIA and the Defense Intelligence Agency had "war- gamed the likely consequences of a U.S. pre-emptive strike on Iran's nuclear facilities. No one liked the outcome. As an Air Force source tells it, 'The war games were unsuccessful at preventing the conflict from escalating.'"

Especially disturbing, the Right seemed to have learned nothing from what went wrong in Iraq and was prepared to make the same mistakes all over again. The *exact same* mistakes. Only on a bigger scale. Although we can try to explain this by looking to one or more of the Right's well-established attributes—stubbornness, arrogance, hubris, intellectual laziness—I have to go with Einstein. Planning to make the same dumb moves in Iran that have failed so spectacularly in Iraq and expecting a different outcome is, quite simply, insane.

The Persian Carpet Gets Pulled

On October 17, 2007, during a press conference intended, in part, to address concerns about Russian diplomatic support for Iran, President Bush warned that Iran's intransigence regarding its nuclear program could lead to "World War III." My more conspiracy-minded friends immediately cried "October Surprise." A war with Iran, if timed properly, would, as wars tend to do at first, rally the voting public behind the president and his party, perhaps in time to help the GOP nominee out of step with the public on the war in Iraq squeak out a win.

Less than two months after Bush's speech, the National Intelligence Estimate flatly contradicted the prior assessment Bush was hyping. "Did we say that Iran was trying to build a nuclear bomb? Oops, sorry, what we meant to say was that Iran was *not* trying to build a nuclear bomb. I mean, they were, but they stopped in 2003." When I first heard this, I figured that the president would somehow claim credit for the fact that Armageddon had been canceled, spinning Iran's voluntary disarmament as yet another positive effect of the war in Iraq. But apparently I was giving him too much credit (one of Bush's defining characteristics is his ability to continually shock you, until you realize: this guy will never bottom out). Instead, the president seemed genuinely flummoxed by the report and tried out a revised position that was highly illogical, even for him. The fact that Iran had no nuclear weapons program changed nothing, Bush said, even though the Iranian threat existed almost entirely because of its nuclear weapons program.

No nukes, no threat, or so it would seem. But it turns out that the hazard now was not that Iran had a bomb but that—having once tried to build one, failed, and stopped trying—it might . . . stop no longer trying. In other words, Iran is still a danger because it has the potential to be a danger. Um, okay, but doesn't that apply to a very large number of countries on earth? "I think it is very important for the international community to recognize the fact that if Iran were to develop the knowledge that they could transfer to a clandestine program, it would create a danger for the world," Bush said, commenting on the report, then added, "Iran was dangerous, Iran is dangerous, and Iran will be dangerous if they have the knowledge necessary to make a nuclear weapon." You see? Were Iran to decide to restart its nuclear program, and were it to succeed, and were it still an antagonist to the United States when all this came about, then, yes, to that extent, Iran is a danger for the world.

If, having been informed that Iran no longer had a nuclear weapons program, Bush was going to treat Iran the same as if it had been pursuing one, it seems reasonable that Iranian leaders would ask themselves what was the use of abandoning the program in the first place. If America is going to invade one way or another, better to have nuclear weapons than not. Could it be, yet again, that the administration, under the hawkish sway of the Right, had proved incompetent in even the most basic sort of international give-and-take? Or was it, yet again, that the administration was bringing about the situation it was ostensibly railing against but that really was the desired outcome? Or some combination of both?

Still, at least for the time being, the publicity given to the NIE meant that the military option was off the table. Not everyone, however, viewed the postponement of World War III as good news. Even though the revision of the NIE based on new intelligence was an encouraging sign that the spy agencies were beginning to learn the lessons of Iraq by challenging received wisdom and resisting group-think, for the Right this was just another betrayal by the permanent apolitical bureaucracy.

Norman Podhoretz, a bellwether for emerging right-wing orthodoxy, wrote:

> I must confess to suspecting that the intelligence community, having been excoriated for supporting the then universal belief that Saddam had weapons of mass destruction, is now bending over backward to counter what has up to now been a similarly universal view (including as is evident from the 2005 NIE, within the intelligence community itself) that Iran is hell-bent on developing nuclear weapons. . . . But I entertain an even darker suspicion. It is that the intelligence community, which has for some years now been leaking material calculated to undermine George W. Bush, is doing it again. This time the purpose is to head off the possibility that the President may order air strikes on the Iranian nuclear installations.

The critiques did not stop with Podhoretz. The editorial page of *The Wall Street Journal* opined that the revised NIE was the work of three famously "hyper-partisan anti-Bush officials" who, presumably, somehow managed to get all sixteen intelligence agencies to sign off on their "hyper-partisan" efforts. The American Enterprise Institute's Mark Falcoff dismissed the report's authors as just another pack of tweedy ivory tower dwellers, divorced from the rough-and-tumble of the real world—like, presumably, the hardscrabble think tanks of northwest Washington, D.C. "The estimates guys are mostly academic types who couldn't find a job teaching at a university when they got their Ph.D.," Falcoff wrote on the *Power Line* blog. "Politically and culturally they are absolutely indistinguishable from the career people at the State Department. You can imagine what that means in the present context of Bush-hatred." Yes, what could be worse than "career people" at the State Department?

The good news is that the system actually—finally—worked to prevent, or at least stave off, another military and political disaster overseas. And for that, we can all be eternally grateful.

Afghanistan, the Other Debacle

The Roman Emperor Nero famously fiddled as his capital burned. Although that's an all-too-handy metaphor for the Bush administration's handling of government as a whole, it fits most neatly with the intense attention the executive branch has lavished upon Iraq and Iran, while the once promising "liberated" state of Afghanistan plunged into a black hole of anti-Americanism, narcotics trafficking, and religious fanaticism.

For all the disastrous consequences of the Iraq invasion, one of the most devastating has been the way it has caused us to take our eye off the ball in Afghanistan.

More than six years after we toppled the Taliban, the first front on the global war on terror is facing a very uncertain future. Time and time again, President Bush has touted the "amazing" progress being made "on the road to democracy" in Afghanistan.

He has painted a sunny picture of Afghanistan that makes the former Taliban stronghold sound like Mayberry in *The Andy Griffith Show*. Bush described a "liberated Afghanistan" where "women are working, boys and girls are going to school, and Afghans have chosen a president and a new parliament in free elections." I could almost hear Louis Armstrong singing in the distance: "I see friends shaking hands, saying 'How do you do?'/They're really saying 'I love you . . . ' "

But deadly rioting in the last two years has revealed a seething anti-Americanism—and growing Afghan resentment at the presence of American military forces. In the spring of 2006, rioters shouted "Death to America!" and condemned Hamid Karzai (that freely elected president) as "a puppet of the Americans."

"We are against America," said one demonstrator, "all Afghans are against them."

Among the rioters carrying sticks and stones were some of those schoolchildren Bush had offered as symbols of the new Afghanistan. Apparently, they were learning a different version of the old adage about "sticks and stones." Schoolchildren were also among the dead and severely wounded in the rioting.

Although there were conflicting accounts of the event that set off one of the riots, some Afghan witnesses described it as a hit-and-run accident in which a U.S. military convoy plowed into dozens of vehicles, drove toward shops and crowds of people, then fired on enraged protesters before speeding off.

"Afghans often complain that U.S. military convoys drive recklessly," reported the *Los Angeles Times.* The Americans responded that "they drive aggressively to avoid threats such as roadside bombs and suicide attackers." Sorry, Opie, but Kabul clearly isn't Mayberry.

Wasn't Afghanistan supposed to be the big success story of the war on terror—the Mission that was actually Accomplished?

Instead, the Afghan government faces an aggressive insurgency led by a resurgent Taliban, widespread corruption, a tattered infrastructure, severe electrical shortages, a lack of trained police and army forces, and a sputtering economy still dominated by drug traffickers. And, Afghanistan's neighbor to the south and east, Pakistan, seems poised on the brink of chaos, complicating the already difficult task of policing that country's tribal badlands where the Taliban has regrouped (and al Qaeda has reconstituted itself).

Senator Chuck Hagel, the Nebraska Republican who has been so courageous in his critique of the Bush administration's handling of Iraq, was equally clear-eyed about the problems plaguing Afghanistan—drawing the unmistakable connection between the two countries. "You can't carry the same intensity in two global conflicts," he said. "Iraq is sucking the oxygen out of everything." Including our efforts to stabilize Afghanistan.

There are a few 2007 stats that the president regularly leaves out of his feel-good speeches about Afghanistan: 6,500 people killed, including 110 U.S. troops, and 140 suicide bombings set off by the Taliban. This was record violence, the average number of attacks per month having risen 30 percent, from 425 in 2006 to 548 in 2007. And the beginning of 2008 saw a 15 percent increase in violence compared with the beginning of 2007. In February 2008, a single suicide bombing took more than 100 lives.

The Afghan poppy crop, which fuels the worldwide heroin trade, now accounts for more than half of the country's GDP, according to a U.N. survey. The executive director of the U.N. agency responsible for monitoring the crop told *The Independent* that production was up 17 percent in 2007, while heroin production rose by a third. Cheaper, stronger heroin flooding the world market, with a real possibility of a global heroin glut, is just one of the catastrophic unintended consequences of the Iraq invasion.

Quoting "diplomats and well-informed Afghans," *Newsweek* reported that "up to a quarter of the new Parliament's 249 elected members are linked to narcotics production and trafficking." One source claimed that 70 percent of the drug traffic can be linked to Afghan government officials. The Afghan president's own brother has been accused of being a major player in the heroin trade (a charge he vehemently denies).

There were fresh setbacks in 2008. Canadian Prime Minister Stephen Harper phoned Bush to warn he would withdraw Canada's troops from Afghanistan in 2009 if NATO wasn't able to send reinforcements to the violent Kandahar region.

The BBC reported that the quality of Great Britain's troops was deteriorating as leave time shrank while budgets spiraled out of control. It quoted British Defence Select Committee Chairman James Arbuthnot: "The continuing pressure on our armed forces personnel is likely to have an impact on retention and there are some disturbing signs of an increase in early departure in the army. The army, the navy, the RAF are not able to do what they need to be able to do because people are leaving and that is, of itself, a strong indication of a falling morale."

And an important study cochaired by former NATO commander General James L. Jones and Thomas R. Pickering, a former U.S. ambassador to the U.N., released in January 2008, found that the Taliban had been able to take over sizable parts of southern and southeastern Afghanistan. "The prospect of again losing significant parts of Afghanistan to the forces of Islamic extremists has moved from the improbable to the possible," the study said, warning that Afghanistan could revert to a "failed state." The report called the ongoing efforts by the Bush administration, NATO, and the Karzai government "inadequate, poorly coordinated and occasionally self-defeating."

Efforts to reconstruct the war-torn nation are also proceeding very slowly. With the Iraq war draining hundreds of billions of dollars, the rebuilding of Afghanistan has had to make do with the leftovers. But despite the urgent need for more roads, schools, clinics, and reliable electricity (even Kabul gets only a few hours of power a day), the Bush administration has cut reconstruction aid to Afghanistan from $1 billion in 2005 to $802 million in 2007—an amount that falls far short of what's needed. Ronald Neumann, the former U.S. ambassador, told Congress in early 2006 that it would take over $5 billion during the next four years to get the job done.

"This is too critical to just say we want victory but we want it on the cheap," he said. But that is exactly how Bush has tried to get it.

Why the Right Is Wrong About Iran, Afghanistan, and Endless War

"There's going to be other wars," John McCain said in January 2008. "We will never surrender but there will be other wars." And, shockingly, the idea did not seem to fill him with unbearable sadness. In fact, he seemed like a grizzled football coach at the tail end of a long career, finally about to get a shot at coaching in the Super Bowl. This displaced ardor for war is part of what makes the Right so wrong about our national security.

McCain was supposed to be the grown-up. But on the most important matter a president can face—questions of war and peace—he carries himself like a cocksure teenage bully, itching for the next fight.

After insisting that future wars are just around the corner, McCain launched, during the same speech, into a creepy riff in which the suffering of our soldiers seemed to leave him almost breathless with anticipation: "We're going to have a lot of PTSD [post-traumatic stress disorder] to treat. We're gonna have a lot of combat wounds that have to do with these terrible explosive IEDs that inflict such severe wounds. My friends, it's gonna be tough, we're gonna have a lot to do."

It's a speech that could easily have been delivered by General Buck Turgidson, George C. Scott's war-loving character in *Dr. Strangelove*. ("I'm not saying we wouldn't get our hair mussed, but I do say no more than ten to twenty million killed—tops!")

The president displayed that same enthusiasm in his 2008 State of the Union speech. He seemed stuck in a time warp—tossing out applause lines from years gone by and using rhetoric drawn from the Dark Ages of the war on terror.

It appeared as if he had cobbled his address from the yellowing pages of old speeches. In lieu of new ideas, we got blasts from the past such as "jubilant Iraqis holding up ink-stained fingers," "we are engaged in the defining ideological struggle of the twenty-first century," the obligatory mentions of 9/11, and the promise that "we will deliver justice to the enemies of America" (and somewhere in the mountains of Pakistan, Osama bin Laden rolled his eyes and said, "Yeah, whatever").

Bush also pulled out a pitch for the war that could have been uttered, unchanged, five years ago (and just might have been): "A failed Iraq would embolden extremists, strengthen Iran, and give terrorists a base from which to launch new attacks on our friends, our allies, and our homeland." The only things missing were sixteen words on yellowcake from Niger and Colin Powell holding up a vial of baking soda. The problem was, our policy in Iraq had already failed, had already emboldened terrorists, had already strengthened Iran, and had already created a new terrorist breeding ground.

Then there was the president's reelection chart-topper. "Al Qaeda is on the run in Iraq" still had the crowd roaring its approval and holding up metaphorical disposable lighters even though the big news of 2007 from the intelligence community had been that al Qaeda had grown in strength. And that was another reason that the Right was wrong. By neglecting Afghanistan it had allowed al Qaeda to reconstitute.

As the president was giving his farewell State of the Union, McCain was attacking his then main rival, Mitt Romney, using the same shopworn cudgels that the Right had wielded again and again to cow Democratic opposition to the war. McCain accused Romney of once saying (in 2007) that he "wanted to set a date for withdrawal similar to what the Democrats are seeking." Heaven forbid. "I was there," said McCain at a town hall meeting held in a Florida retirement community. "He said he wanted a timetable for withdrawal." Heat up the tar! Pluck the feathers!

Let's put aside the argument that followed about whether Romney did or didn't actually say this. It tells you everything you need to know about the Right when merely suggesting that we think about getting our troops out of Iraq can be portrayed as unpatriotic, un-American, and tantamount to coming out in favor of unconditional surrender. Even mentioning "timetables" gets you branded as a "cut-and-run" peacenik.

"If we surrender," McCain told reporters at another campaign stop, "and wave a white flag like Senator Clinton wants to do and withdraw as Governor Romney wanted to do, then there will be chaos." He also compared Romney to Democratic Senate Majority Leader Harry Reid and demanded that his opponent apologize "to the young men and women who are serving in uniform." A Romney spokesperson called McCain "unhinged"—a claim that applies to the Right in general. But shortly after McCain's verbal bombardment of Romney, he effectively clinched the GOP nomination—and Romney's endorsement soon followed.

The Right's tried-and-failed approach to matters of war and peace offers an important reminder that whatever differences the Democrats may have—and however heated and divisive the party's primary race became—when it comes to endless war, the two parties are heading in wildly different directions. The Democrats are all looking to the future while the Right remains mired in a Neanderthal past.

10

Torture: America Loses the Moral High Ground

The Nea-Cons Embrace Torture

In 2004, when the hideous abuses at Abu Ghraib came to light, the Bush administration formed a defensive perimeter offering its standard excuses: the abuses were regrettable, the work of a few bad apples, these things happen in war, there will be a full investigation, and those responsible will be punished. So sorry and such a shame that the glorious victory in Iraq has been a little tarnished.

Two years later, Bush called Abu Ghraib a "terrible mistake," a two-word summary that neatly (if too kindly) describes this administration's entire foreign policy.

The nea-cons and the administration's posse on talk radio were predictably not admitting that much. Showing that he shared Lynndie England's unique sense of fun, Rush Limbaugh declared that the human pyramids of naked, terrified men or Lynndie's dog-walking antics were "no different than what happens at the Skull and Bones initiation." According to Rush, the hand-wringing over Abu Ghraib was just further proof that anyone who criticizes any aspect of the conduct of the war simply doesn't understand its overall seriousness.

And during hearings before the Senate Armed Services Committee about Abu Ghraib, Senator James Inhofe achieved a personal best when he actually said, "I'm probably not the only one up at this table that is more outraged by the outrage than we are by the treatment."

While a "what's the big deal?" defense was to be expected from Rush and a senator famous for his forays beyond the outer limits of common sense, the fact that four years later the administration has taken a position actually advocating torture of the sort that earned Private England three years in jail and a dishonorable discharge shows just how out-of-control our rightward slide has become.

Of all the twisted whack-job viewpoints that have been main-streamed by the twenty-first-century GOP, none is as repulsive to ordinary, decent people as the condoning of torture. When you call it what it is, torture, not "enhanced" interrogation techniques, the American people overwhelmingly oppose it.

The fact that one has to make a "case against torture" seems absurd. The idea of torture is viscerally repellent and should be self-refuting. Of all the important things there are to debate, are we really going to argue over the fundamental barbarity of torture? What's next? A discussion on the value of rape as a weapon? How about exe-cuting the families of Guantánamo detainees until they tell us where Osama is hiding? After all, we're at war, people!

It Depends on What Your Definition of "Torture" Is

For the Right, the defense of torture has deteriorated into a morally oily game of definitions, like Clinton parsing the meaning of "is," only about something a lot less pleasurable than a blow job: "water-boarding" and "stress positions" aren't torture, they're "enhanced interrogation techniques"; people who condemn stern measures don't understand the nature of the enemy; our policy is classified so that terrorists can't learn how to resist our techniques; or the most crazily circular argument of all—we don't torture people because the law forbids it and we don't break the law so whatever we're doing, it isn't torture.

Here's the president playing this word game in a typically jovial fashion with *Newsweek*'s Richard Wolffe:

Wolffe: Thank you, sir. A simple question.

Bush: Yes?

Wolffe: What's your definition of—

Bush: It may require a simple answer.

(LAUGHTER)

Wolffe: What's your definition of the word "torture"?

Bush: Of what?

Wolffe: The word "torture," what's your definition?

Bush: That's defined in U.S. law, and we don't torture.

Wolffe: Can you give me your version of it, sir?

Bush: No. Whatever the law says.

And finally there's the "if the president says it's okay, then it's okay" trump card, an untenable legal position that has discredited the Justice Department, which has been forced time and time again to play it in order to win a hand. The blanket argument that the boss is always right was bolstered by legal advisers—including an up-and-comer in the Justice Department's in-house legal laboratory, the Office of Legal Counsel, John Yoo—who advised Bush soon after 9/11 that the United States did not have to comply with the Geneva Conventions in handling detainees in the war on terror. As "illegal enemy combatants" they had no protections. With this rhetorical flourish, Yoo and his cohorts had given the administration the blank check on brutality they were looking for.

Waterboarding: Drowning Rational Thought

The Bush administration's tortured reasoning and rationalization of "enhanced" interrogation techniques was most clearly demonstrated by its stance on waterboarding—the forced drowning technique that has long been the subject of war-crimes trials, and that Senator Ted Kennedy called "the worldwide symbol for America's debate over torture."

At first, the administration refused to admit the technique was ever used, and refused to concede that even if it was used, it would be illegal. This led to endless verbal gymnastics by its representatives, such as Attorney General Mike Mukasey, who, while refusing to brand the procedure illegal, said he found it "repugnant" and would "feel that it was" torture if it were done to him.

Mike McConnell, Bush's Director of National Intelligence, also went the hair-splitting route, saying he did not know "whether it's torture by anybody else's definition" but that he personally considers it so, due to his teenage experiences as a lifeguard: "I'm a water-safety instructor, but I cannot swim without covering my nose. I don't know if it's some deviated septum or mucous membrane, but water just rushes in. . . . Waterboarding would be excruciating. If I had water draining into my nose, oh god, I just can't imagine how painful . . . for me it would be torture." Yet he insisted: "The United States does not engage in torture."

Bush's arrogance on the matter of torture came to a head in February of 2008 when, after years of refusing to confirm or deny the use of the technique, CIA Director Michael Hayden finally confirmed that his agency had in fact used waterboarding on al Qaeda suspects in 2002 and 2003. Hayden banned the technique at the CIA in 2006; the Pentagon and the FBI have similar prohibitions.

Following Hayden's admission, Senate Democrats demanded a criminal investigation. The White House responded by insisting that waterboarding is legal and that the president was free to authorize its use.

This despite the fact that Congress had passed two laws—including the Military Commissions Act of 2006—that prohibited extreme interrogation techniques; indeed, Republican Senator Lindsey Graham, one of the co-sponsors of the act, said he had been assured by the White House that this included waterboarding. But when it comes to torture, Bush and Cheney refused to give an inch.

White House deputy spokesperson Tony Fratto insisted that since the attorney general had approved the 2002 and 2003 uses it therefore was legal and, hence, not actually torture.

Finally, a senior intelligence official made the case that since U.S. soldiers had been waterboarded as part of their training it couldn't possibly be torture: "We don't maim as part of our training. We don't mutilate. We don't sodomize. Those are things that are always bad. . . . Intellectually there has got to be a difference between [waterboarding] and the others; otherwise we wouldn't have done it in training."

And at military training camps across the country, waterboarded but unsodomized and unmutilated soldiers said a silent prayer of thanks.

Torture According to the Right: The Criteria

It is this contempt for the rule of law, which the Bush administration no longer even bothers to hide, that Connecticut's Democratic Sena-

tor Chris Dodd described while commenting on the nomination of
Judge Mukasey:

> A lot has been made of Judge Mukasey's troubling stance on
> waterboarding and torture more broadly. While I think those
> are critically important questions, his beliefs on executive
> power are in many ways far more important. The attorney
> general must be a reliable defender of the rule of law. But Mr.
> Mukasey seems to share the exact same ideology as other mem-
> bers of the Bush administration. He thinks the President has
> the authority to ignore the rule in the name of national secu-
> rity. Mr. Mukasey doesn't seem to understand the oath we take:
> we don't swear to support and defend the Constitution or pro-
> tect the country. We defend the Constitution to protect the
> country. For that reason alone, he should be disqualified to
> serve as the highest-ranking law enforcement official in the
> United States government.

But Senator Dodd's concerns about Judge Mukasey were not
shared by his colleagues on the Judiciary Committee, Senators Chuck
Schumer and Dianne Feinstein, who voted to bring Mukasey's nomination to the floor. They did so despite clear evidence in the judge's
own letter to committee chairman Patrick Leahy and the Judiciary
Committee—which was intended to set the Senate's collective mind
at ease—that Mukasey was going to be as much of a weaseling shill
for torture as was his predecessor, Alberto Gonzales.

"Waterboarding," he wrote, "cannot be used by the United States
military because its use by the military would be a clear violation of
the Detainee Treatment Act."

Sounds great until you note, as Bob Cesca, author and *Huffington
Post* blogger, pointed out, the repeated usage of the word "military"
but no mention of the CIA or private military contractors. Ever since
Lynndie got shipped off to the stockade, the military has been very
publicly out of the torture business. It's the CIA and our rendition
partners in Egypt and Uzbekistan who do the torturing now. Fur-
thermore, the president has already dealt himself a Get Out of Jail
Free Card—in the form of yet another signing statement—for any
aspects of the McCain Amendment (which establishes uniform standards for the interrogation of detainees) that threaten to become a
nuisance. This one reads:

The executive branch shall construe Title X in Division A of the Act, relating to detainees, in a manner consistent with the constitutional authority of the President to supervise the unitary executive branch and as Commander in Chief and consistent with the constitutional limitations on the judicial power, which will assist in achieving the shared objective of the Congress and the President, evidenced in Title X, of protecting the American people from further terrorist attacks.

Make It Sound Benign

Making whatever they choose to do sound benign is the Right's number one public relations goal when it comes to torture. This supplies the rhetorical ammunition that Rush and his friends need to shoot down any objections. Sleep deprivation, loud persistent noise, and stress positions sound no worse than what most parents go through with a newborn, until you learn what really happens to a human body when they are taken to an extreme.

Menachem Begin, the late prime minister of Israel, experienced sleep deprivation firsthand in Stalin's gulag. Andrew Sullivan quotes him describing a typical victim: "Wearied to death, his legs are unsteady, and he has one sole desire to sleep, to sleep just a little, not to get up, to lie, to rest, to forget. . . . Anyone who has experienced the desire knows that not even hunger or thirst are comparable with it."

To say that acute sleep deprivation is not torture is like arguing that a severe beating is nothing more than a vigorous massage.

And stress positions, when you hear about them from the victims, start to sound a little like a crucifixion. Here is a description from a Gestapo memo from the Nuremberg war crimes trial:

Still more feared than beatings were stress positions (*Pfahlbinden*, literally "strapping to a post"). This punishment was implemented in the following manner: Hands were tightly bound to the prisoner's back with a rope, then the body was lifted up and the rope was hung from a prong which had been fastened at a height of two meters to a tree, so that the feet dangled in the air. Consequently the weight of the entire body burdened the joints which had been twisted to the back. The minimum period for which a person was suspended was half an hour. This punishment was applied at least twice a week. (Concentration Camp Document F321 in the proceedings of the International Military Tribunal in Nuremberg, 1949)

Waterboarding—which evokes a recreational activity, maybe one of those parachuting-snowboarding hybrids that are invented by bored French daredevils—is defended by the Right as only a little worse than getting some water up the nose while showering. In fact, it is a forced drowning technique that triggers the body's choking reflexes and has been around since Torquemada and the Spanish Inquisition—although its current form was perfected by Cambodia's Khmer Rouge. When you realize that the preferred torture method of the Bush administration is no different, you start to get a handle on how far things have sunk. The other tricks of the torturer's trade currently in use have been reverse-engineered from the Cold War–era training given to American pilots in how to withstand Soviet interrogation.

There is one case in which waterboarding proved highly persuasive, but Rush and the administration are unlikely to trumpet it as a great success. In 2004, Daniel Levin, who was the acting head of the Office of Legal Counsel at the Justice Department (John Yoo's old shop), decided to undergo waterboarding as part of his preparation of an opinion on the limits of interrogation techniques. His 2004 opinion, which categorized torture as "abhorrent to American law and values and to international norms," superseded a far more torture-friendly opinion from 2002 that began the unlimited expansion of presidential authority long sought by the Right.

For his pains, Levin saw his opinion emasculated by a White House–dictated footnote saying that previous lenient Justice Department opinions on torture remained in force. He was then told by the newly arrived Alberto Gonzales that his services were no longer required. He was replaced by the more agreeable Steven Bradbury, who bent over backward to justify stress positions and other harsh methods in a series of revisions of Justice Department policy in 2005.

And if you need more proof that the radical Right has infiltrated the Pentagon, here it is: Four-star General Kevin Byrnes, the third most senior of the army's eleven four-star generals, was sacked in August 2005 over allegations that he had an extramarital affair. Meanwhile, Lieutenant General Ricardo Sanchez, the senior commander in Iraq during the Abu Ghraib torture and abuse scandal, was being considered for promotion to, yep, four-star general.

Talk about utterly perverted priorities.

It became clear long ago that the Bushies inhabit a bizarro, topsy-turvy universe—a place where being utterly wrong about slam-dunk WMD earns you a Medal of Freedom, dismissing a "Bin Ladin Determined to Strike in U.S." memo earns you a promotion to secretary of state, signing off on torture makes you attorney general material, dozens more American soldiers being blown up is the mark of an enemy in its "last throes," and revealing the identity of an undercover CIA agent (and then lying about it) merits a vote of confidence instead of a pink slip.

Nevertheless, Byrnes's firing is still stunning. Consider: in modern times, no four-star general has ever been relieved of duty for disciplinary reasons; prior to this incident Byrnes had a spotless military record; he had been separated from his wife at the time and he was already set to retire in November.

Is this what it took for Rummy and company to continue seeing themselves as paragons of virtue who will do whatever is necessary to hold people accountable for their private conduct while turning a blind eye to the wanton assault on decency and morality that marked our management of Abu Ghraib and Guantánamo?

In other words, it's the s-e-x, stupid! By firing Byrnes, the Bush administration could tout its high morals, demonstrating it will not stand for a leader who breaks his marital vows—even after he's separated from his wife. The GOP base ate it up.

My only question is: was Rummy given photos of General Byrnes in flagrante delicto? Must have been. If you'll recall, Rumsfeld told Congress that it took him months to look into the reports of abuse at Abu Ghraib because, even though he'd been alerted that U.S. soldiers were humiliating and torturing naked Iraqi prisoners, "It is the photographs that give one the vivid realization of what actually took place. Words don't do it."

Not that once Rummy and the White House saw the photos from Abu Ghraib they leapt into action. They leapt into damage control—treating the worst American military scandal since Vietnam's My Lai massacre not as an international land mine that could blast our country off the moral high ground but as a PR problem that could be spun, manipulated, stonewalled, and, ultimately, swept under the rug.

And they were right—at least as far as the American electorate was concerned. The feelings of the Arab world are a whole other matter.

Here is the pathetic scorecard from the Abu Ghraib/Guantánamo outrages: Only one high-ranking officer involved was demoted (General Janis Karpinski, the former head officer at the prison). One! Indeed, many of the others involved have been promoted, including two senior officers who oversaw or advised on detention and interrogations operations in Iraq—former deputy commander Major General Walter Wojdakowski and Colonel Marc Warren, formerly the United States's top military lawyer in Baghdad. And the former top intelligence officer in Iraq, Major General Barbara Fast, was also given a promotion. Meanwhile Major General Geoffrey Miller, who had a hand in both Abu Ghraib and Guantánamo—and who, despite his continued denials, has been repeatedly accused of instigating some of the worst interrogation tactics—has yet to be held accountable.

The message is clear: overseeing a system that led to prisoners being buggered with chemical lights and having electrodes attached to their genitals will get you a leg up in Bush's military; having consensual sex with someone other than your wife will get you booted out the door.

Make Sure It Doesn't Show

So, first you label torture with benign, even playful names. Then, you make sure the methods leave no marks. Black eyes, broken arms, and brain damage might raise awkward questions or generate sympathy for the victims.

But although a lot of the damage from the Guantánamo Toolbox is psychological, that doesn't mean it isn't real. And it can be more permanent than a broken arm. Beyond the psychological damage of the torture itself, there's the underlying fact that, if the torture is going to "work," the victim must be convinced that the torturers are not going to stop, that they will kill him unless he cooperates, even if we know that they really won't—except by accident. (At least 112 detainees have died while in U.S. custody since 2002. And at least 43 of those deaths have been investigated as homicides.)

To fully understand the psychological injuries that torture inflicts (and also to see why the utilitarian opponents argue that it doesn't work), you need look no further than the Kafkaesque case of an Egyptian national named Abdallah Higazy, who was questioned by the FBI after a transmitter capable of broadcasting on aircraft frequencies was found in his hotel room. During a polygraph test, an FBI agent by the name of Michael Templeton allegedly told Higazy that if he didn't cooperate, Templeton would "make sure that Egyptian security gives [his] family hell."

Higazy was faced with a hideous Hobson's choice. "I knew that I couldn't prove my innocence, and I knew that my family was in danger," he said. He explained that "the only thing that went through my head was oh, my God, I am screwed and my family's in danger. If I say this device is mine, I'm screwed and my family is going to be safe. If I say this device is not mine, I'm screwed and my family's in danger. And Agent Templeton made it quite clear that cooperation meant saying something other than this device is not mine."

So Higazy confessed to using the transmitter to send messages to terrorists on airplanes and the Bush administration scored another victory in the war on terror—that is until the airplane pilot who had stayed in the room before Higazy showed up and asked if anyone had seen his radio.

"You Don't Understand What We Are Dealing With"

One of the all-purpose arguments the Right employs in defending any of the abuses perpetrated in the war on terror is that those who object simply "don't understand what we're dealing with." That some of the victims of American torture—though we don't know how many—may, indeed, be horrible people intent on hurting America does not justify torturing them any more than acknowledging that child molesters are evil justifies torturing them.

The "liberals just don't get it" is a tired refrain from the war on terror invoked to justify any sort of action that would previously have been universally condemned. With "that was then, this is now, we live in a post-9/11 world" as a premise, the amoral Right seems to think it can justify just about anything: that torture is okay, that civil liberties must be suspended, that invading Iraq is a good idea, that all other national priorities must be consigned to a distant second place on the national to-do list.

The challenge in selling torture is that there is a broad national consensus among Joe and Jane Six-Pack, Larry and Linda Latte, and Julio and Juanita Jugo de Naranja that our criminal justice system, for all its flaws, is capable of dealing with very, very bad people while still respecting their enshrined rights to due process and Miranda protections. For torture to be necessary to force alleged terrorists to share information but not for child murderers to admit their crimes, a constant plea of exceptional circumstances is necessary. That's where the endless war on terror comes in handy.

And because debates over whether bad things are good or bad are prima facie ridiculous, even in the war on terror era, the sensible center retreated to a variety of utilitarian counterarguments for the "case" for torture that often fell apart, as utilitarian arguments often do, on purely empirical grounds. Suddenly, we weren't just arguing about torture, we were losing the argument.

This is a key point. That the Right has put decent people on the defensive and forced them to lay out an argument against torture is proof of how strong they have become and how effective their methods are. Torture is wrong. End of story. Making any sort of a case against it is to concede that a case needs to be made. And that's the only opening the Right needs to begin using the "two sides to every argument" tactic. The utilitarian arguments outlined below are a perfect example of how the mainstream has failed to prevent the Right from running rampant. They treat them like rational people, willing to change their minds, and open to persuasion. But they're not. They made up their minds long ago and now they just want to collect converts for their cause by any means necessary.

Giving Torture the Third Degree

Torture as Payback

A person who's being drowned will say anything to make the drowning stop. Information derived from torture is riddled with false leads, which have to be expensively investigated. When these leads go nowhere, it's back to the waterboard. As a process, torture rewards convincing liars as much as it does truth-tellers. And there are far more effective means of getting people to talk that use brain power rather than bloodlust. Or so the torture-doesn't-work argument goes.

In a widely quoted (and forwarded) article in *The New York Times*,

Frank Rich brilliantly attacked the administration and its embrace of torture. The piece, titled "The Good Germans Among Us," relied for its power on every columnist's most powerful weapon: a legitimate Nazi comparison. In this case, Rich argued that by not objecting more forcefully to the government's methods, we were all as culpable as the "Germans who professed ignorance of their own Gestapo." In keeping with the Greatest Generation theme, Rich quotes Americans who obtained valuable information from German prisoners through skillful questioning rather than the third degree. (Incidentally, the Gestapo were not great believers in torture. According to testimony at the Nuremberg trials, "The Gestapo in general believed that other methods of interrogation, such as playing off political factions against each other, were much more effective than third degree methods. Third degree methods had to be approved by [the] head office.")

The problem with the practical argument that torture doesn't work is that it skates over moral thin ice and turns ethics into simple trial and error. As Professor Gordon Marino of St. Olaf College wrote on *The Huffington Post*:

> It is not enough to raise doubts about torture as a method. When the critics of Gestapo techniques base their condemnation on statistics and the testimony of selected experts, they are in peril of conceding that under certain circumstances it might be appropriate, or even obligatory, for the defenders of freedom to take out their tongs. Those of us who would swear off the kinds of practices that we have been sub-contracting to other nations have to separate the moral from the practical arguments. We have to maintain that there are some practices, like slavery, that are wrong unconditionally. The Universal Declaration of Human Rights provides the premises for this position and clearly instructs us that "there are limits to what one human being can do to another, without losing his or her humanity."

As a thought-provoking exercise, it's worth asking why torture is both historically and currently popular if it's so ineffective. Is it possible that, in addition to everything else, the radical Right has bought into a delusion shared with the Salem witch-hunters? Well, yes. The war on science that is being pursued hand in hand with the war on

terror means that there are no facts and you don't have to believe anything you don't want to believe. There's no such thing as data, just
political cant and biased opinion. So, if you're planning to cruise over
to Gitmo and tell the guy at the gate that torture doesn't work and
you can prove it, you can expect him to respond with a cheerful "Sez
you!"

In fact, an intelligence advisory group, the Intelligence Science
Board, issued a 325-page study in December 2006 titled "Educing
Information" that harshly criticized the current "enhanced" interrogation techniques as ineffective, especially when compared with the
skillful questioning of Japanese and German prisoners by American
interrogators during World War II. "It far outclassed what we've
done. [The questioners] had graduate degrees in law and philosophy,
spoke the language flawlessly," and prepared meticulously for questioning sessions, said Steven M. Kleinman, a former air force interrogator and trainer who contributed to the report. Kleinman called
the current U.S. strategy "amateurish," pointing out that today's
interrogators often have to work through interpreters and are unfa-
miliar with the culture of their prisoners.

But rather than come up with interrogation methods that work
using the particular American genius for persuasion, the administration has put far more energy into doing a limbo under the generally accepted legal and social norms that forbid torture. As one
participant in the study put it, "There's nothing like the mobilization of effort and political energy that were put into relaxing the
rules."

So if it doesn't work, there must be another explanation. And I'm
afraid that the explanation for the current vogue for torture goes further than just a difference of opinion over whether or not it works.
Torture does satisfy one need—however primitive—and that is the
need for revenge, the need to hurt the people who hurt us. Although
torturers may deny that they do what they do punitively and may
even argue they do it without malice ("Hey, thanks for the info and
no hard feelings!"), it's hard not to see the administration's harsh
treatment as a typical misdirected response to their flummoxed impo-
tence when it comes to punishing the real perpetrators of 9/11. If we
can't stop bin Laden from taunting us from his cave in the Pakistani
tribal badlands, at least we can put some of his supposed minions
through another sleepless week.

This childish lashing out at the prisoners who happen to be handy because we can't find the people we really should be questioning is yet another result of the administration's incompetence. But there's also a way in which torture is a by-product of the well-known Bush laziness: the 9–5 workday, the long summer vacations, the impatience with detail. Torture is trying to get intelligence on the cheap. Forget about analyzing gigabytes of information, forget about building networks of human sources, forget about recruiting and training new intelligence agents with language skills and cultural ties to potential terrorist groups, forget about forging productive working relationships with foreign intelligence agencies, forget the lessons of 9/11 and the recommendations of the 9/11 Commission. Forget all that. Let's just beat it out of them!

Banning Torture Is an Act of Self-Defense

Another utilitarian argument against torture is that, if we are torturing enemy combatants, how can we object if captured American soldiers are tortured? If this really is a war, then our side has a clear incentive to treat enemy prisoners the way we would insist that our own fighting men and women be treated if captured.

Our military, at least, seems to find this particular variation on the Golden Rule to be persuasive and has unequivocally opted out of the "enhanced" interrogation game by openly declaring that its members will observe all of the Geneva Conventions. And in March of 2007, General Petraeus sent a letter to the troops warning that "expedient methods" using force violated American core values.

However, the men and women of the CIA have been exempted from the relevant part of the Geneva Conventions (Common Article 3) thanks to the Military Commissions Act of 2006, another Justice Department put-up job that the Congress, always fearful of being labeled "soft on terror," obediently rubber-stamped. Subsequent secret exemptions from international law generated by the creative minds at the Justice Department have further excused the CIA from any petty concerns about Common Article 3.

As retired CIA officer Milt Bearden has written on *The Huffington Post*, the ironic outcome of giving this distasteful duty to the CIA, and then writing them a secret hall pass, is that it exposes CIA agents to the danger of prosecution overseas, where foreign governments may not be interested in whether or not Michael Mukasey thinks torture is okay: "One can expect a torrent of cases to be filed against the men and women of the CIA in the coming months and years," Bearden wrote. "They'll have to get used to either staying pretty close to home, or taking their ski holidays in North Korea. Stepping off a plane anywhere in Europe will become a little dicey. The CIA's men and women are putting themselves at enough risk already. They deserve better and we owe them more than this. The sway of feckless leadership at CIA has gone on long enough. It's time that the CIA takes the Defense Department lead and plays by the rules again."

Why the Right Is Wrong About Torture

The prohibition on torture by civilized nations is an ethical absolute not subject to the moral slippery slopery that the Right has used to keep the Loyal Opposition off-balance. To allow torture under any circumstances, no matter how exigent, is to roll off a moral cliff from which there can be no recovery.

Okay, so torture is ineffective, lazy, and dangerous. But the problem with both utilitarian arguments against torture—it doesn't work, and it may turn on us—intended as they are to appeal to the common sense of a public that may have begun to climb on the fence after having been told repeatedly that the Marquess of Queensberry Rules don't apply to the war on terror, is that, even if it were effective, torture degrades all of us. It doesn't just put our troops and our intelligence agents in danger, it puts all of us, and the society we are supposed to be fighting for, at risk. Relying on a practical counterargument allows the possibility that some interrogator might come forward and be able to cite examples when ticking bombs have been discovered thanks to the third degree. To say that it doesn't work has to mean that it *never* works, and that's not the discussion we should be having.

"There are some things worse than avoiding all casualties in warfare," Andrew Sullivan wrote.

> One of those things is abandoning the core meaning of what a country and a civilization stand for. If America does not stand against the torture of individuals seized without due process by an unchecked executive power, then America stands for noth-

ing. In fact, if this standard had applied two centuries ago, America would not exist at all. The president takes an oath not to prevent any American life from being lost in wartime, but to protect and defend the Constitution which is the sole guarantor of such liberty. Churchill upheld that rule, even as London was reduced to rubble and hundreds of thousands of mothers' children were lost. Washington made it a central hallmark of the meaning of his new republic. To destroy the Constitution, the rule of law, and habeas corpus and to legalize torture in the false hope of saving lives is the action of those who do not understand freedom and who do not understand America. It is the action of cowards and slaves.

At the South Carolina GOP primary debate, Mitt Romney suggested we should "double Guantánamo" and use "enhanced" interrogation techniques. And at a New Hampshire voters forum, the über-Christian Mike Huckabee declared that conditions at Guantánamo Bay were "amazingly hospitable," and argued that Gitmo was "too darn good" for its detainees, many of whom have been imprisoned indefinitely on meager evidence.

But to see how unmoored the Right has become from both common decency and common sense, you must look no further than the public statements of the former Macho Mayor Rudy Giuliani. When asked during a campaign stop in Iowa to clarify whether he believed that waterboarding was torture, Giuliani replied: "It depends on how it's done. It depends on the circumstances. It depends on who does it." So if you're being waterboarded by a sexy girl in a room filled with candles, it's all good? Does Rudy occasionally come home, dim the lights, open up a nice bottle of chilled Chablis, put on a little Barry White, and ask Judi to break out the waterboard? Since when is there so much wiggle room when it comes to obeying the Geneva Conventions?

Stretching Reason:
The Right Rationalizes the Rack

In 2002, George W. Bush declared in a secret memo that U.S. forces should observe the Geneva Conventions "to the extent appropriate and consistent with military necessity." How has that same flexible spirit been used to explain some of the military's favorite methods of "enhanced" interrogation? And how might it explain favorite modes of "enhanced" interrogation from the medieval past?

Torture: Waterboarding

Rationalization: It's a "dunk in water." Asked by a radio host whether "a dunk in water is a no-brainer if it can save lives," Dick Cheney responded, "Well, it's a no-brainer for me."

Torture: Sleep deprivation

Rationalization: Sleep deprivation? Torture? That's "plain silly," says Rudy Giuliani. "I mean, on that theory, I'm getting tortured running for president of the United States. That's plain silly. That's silly."

Torture: Stress positions

Rationalization: Donald Rumsfeld, who worked at a stand-up desk: "I stand for eight to ten hours a day. Why is standing limited to four hours?"

Torture: The rack

Projected Rationalization: You like to stretch out after a hard day's work, right? I sure do. And so do detainees, I bet.

Torture: The Iron Maiden

Projected Rationalization: You can't dismiss alternative medicine without trying it. If the Eastern world says acupuncture is a healing art, shouldn't we keep an open mind? Starting with detainees?

Torture: Being hit in the gonads by a hammer

Projected Rationalization: Have you ever really wanted to join a fraternity? This is pretty much the same sort of tomfoolery.

Torture: Being drawn and quartered

Projected Rationalization: It looks much, much worse than it actually is.

Music to Confess by:
A Guantánamo Playlist

Here are some of the songs played at top volume at Guantánamo and Abu Ghraib to keep prisoners awake:

Track: "Enter Sandman"

Artist: Metallica

Venue: Abu Ghraib

Sample Lyric: Hush little baby don't say a word / And never mind that noise you heard

Track: "The Real Slim Shady"

Artist: Eminem

Venue: Guantánamo

Sample Lyric: My bum is on your lips, my bum is on your lips / And if I'm lucky, you might just give it a little kiss

Track: "Bodies"

Artist: Drowning Pool

Venue: Abu Ghraib

Sample Lyric: Let the bodies hit the floor / Let the bodies hit the floor!

Track: "I Love You"

Artist: Barney the Purple Dinosaur

Venue: Guantánamo

Sample Lyric: With a great big hug and a kiss from me to you / Won't you say you love me too

11

Xenophobia 2.0:
The Immigration Fixation

The Return of the Ugly American

The Right's ever-vigilant Slogan Division focus-grouped a winner on immigration: "No amnesty for lawbreakers." No "shamnesty." And that is where the Right made its stand, right in the middle of the Minutemen fever swamps.

For the Right, any process that attempts to integrate twelve million undocumented immigrants into American life by offering a path to citizenship is a betrayal. Even President Bush was labeled a Judas when he tried to get behind a compromise immigration bill in 2007. "Amnesty" supposedly rewards illegal and immoral behavior, contrary to the stern and high-minded ethical code that the Right likes to impose on others so long as there are enough loopholes and exceptions to keep life comfortable for themselves.

The truth, as anyone who thinks about it for a minute realizes, is that undocumented immigrants already have paid a price for their pursuit of the American dream, often starting with an expensive and harrowing journey into this country and continuing with years of low-paying toil at one of those famous "jobs Americans don't want to do"—usually for the benefit of a business that would prefer to keep its labor costs to a minimum by hiring the cheapest workers. They do this work without the benefits and protections that citizens receive, even though they often pay their fair share in taxes. According to Shikha Dalmia, a senior analyst at the libertarian Reason Foundation, contributions from undocumented immigrants using fake Social Security numbers total 10 percent of the annual Social Security surplus, which is about $50 billion. The nonpartisan National Research

Council estimates that low-skilled immigrants contribute as much as $10 billion to the U.S. economy every year.

And yet they and their families are never free from the fear that whatever life they have built for themselves here is just a sandcastle that can be swept away at any moment by one of the increasingly common raids by heavily armed agents of Immigration and Customs Enforcement.

Picture the fry cook—we'll call him Pete just to avoid any stereotyping—at the back of Rush Limbaugh's favorite watering hole, the Fatted Calf. Rush and his guest, Bill Bennett, have just ordered their favorite deep-fried delicacies—chicken for Rush, pork for Bill—along with a starter of delicious golden-crisp calamari. Pete goes to the Fatted Calf early to clean the grease from the frying baskets and he'll be working late into the night, even after the last of the late-night diners have left. Rush and Bill like their food to be brought quickly, because they are busy guys with big appetites. But they don't want it to cost too much because Bill, at least, is on a very strict budget. The Calf's owner, Simone LeGree, keeps cracking the whip in the kitchen to make sure Pete is constantly frying and, if he asks for a raise or a day off or a bathroom break, not only can she easily replace Pete but she can punish him for his insolence by simply reporting him to the immigration authorities.

The lives of Rush and Bill and, especially, Simone wouldn't be anywhere near as comfortable without Pete. If she had to hire a citizen to do his job—we'll call him Luis to continue our campaign to Stop Ethnic Stereotyping in Hypothetical Examples (SESHE)—she'd have to pay him more, abide by laws giving Luis the right to reasonable hours and overtime pay and a safe working environment, and run the risk that Luis might even do something radical like join a union and win further protections through his right to collective bargaining. Simone's profit margin would be cut or she might have to pass some of her higher costs along to Rush and Bill.

So, it's a little hard to see how hardworking Pete is the one taking advantage of the system. It's really Simone and, indirectly in the form of good service at cheap prices, Rush and Bill who benefit. But, strangely, the Right is not focused on plans to punish them. "No amnesty for lawbreakers" somehow doesn't apply to those who break the law by hiring undocumented workers. Employers, large and small, are given amnesty every day in the same way that many undocumented workers are: through a lack of enforcement. The difference is that employers don't have to worry they will lose everything they've worked and sacrificed for, like their restaurant or factory or nationwide chain of big box stores, if the law were to be suddenly enforced.

We needn't even enter the hypothetical realm to understand the Republican hypocrisy on this issue, since many in the GOP—at least in private—are immediately willing to cop to it. My friend *Huffpost* editor Marc Cooper told me of just such a story. In March 2006, he was invited to attend Restoration Weekend, the annual retreat of movement conservatives organized by David Horowitz. Marc says that on opening night, several hundred guests gathered for the kick-off reception inside the swank Biltmore Hotel in Phoenix.

The highly trained hotel wait staff, all wearing nametags with Latino names and most of them undoubtedly from Mexico, efficiently served the gathered Republicans plate after plate of fajitas, guacamole, Veracruz-style shrimp, and red-hot salsa. The conservatives munched away happily and eagerly applauded as blowhard Congressman J. D. Hayworth flogged his anti-immigration book, *Whatever It Takes*, calling for a militarization of the entire southern border. When Hayworth got to the part of his spiel advocating a moratorium on even legal immigration from Mexico and expedited deportation of all the undocumented workers already here, a former chair of the California Republican Party and a former classmate of Cooper's turned to him and merrily quipped: "Please don't let the deportations begin until dinner is finished being served."

Illegal immigrants are favorite political scapegoats for the simple reason that they are not able to vote and not able to buy access and support through their campaign contributions. And since the weakest and most vulnerable are the most scapegoated, undocumented workers make perfect targets. So in an election year, the line to take a swing at the punching bag with Pete's face on it gets longer and longer, because Pete can't punch back.

The Strange Case of the
2005 CNN Leprosy Epidemic

The leading media bully on immigration issues is not to be found, as might be expected, in the more-right-than-thou world of Fox News but on the airwaves of CNN. Lou Dobbs, who walks, talks, and sounds like an actual newsman and spent years as a bland journey-man, has reincarnated himself as a blow-dried modern-day Father Coughlin, mounting a wildly anti-immigration hobby horse and rid-ing it to ratings success. Dobbs's brand of naked advocacy, becoming a veritable nightly PR agent for the Minutemen fringe, was matched on CNN's *Headline News* every night by that cutesy xenophobe, Glenn Beck.

Like Bill O'Reilly, Dobbs presents himself as a champion of the ordinary Joe, crossing ideological lines to attack overcompensated CEOs, corrupt politicians of both parties, and our flawed political system whenever the mood strikes. There's nothing wrong with that sort of muckraking if the person doing the raking is honest with the facts. But when it comes to his stock-in-trade, championing the ordi-nary Joe in Joe's constant struggle against José—sorry, I mean Pete—Lou is not above skipping over the fact-checking of any item that happens to be too good to be true.

A perfect, and perfectly reprehensible, example of Dobbs's men-dacity was his promotion—and subsequent full-throated defense—of spurious statistics about a non-existent spike in U.S. leprosy cases. A scourge Dobbs attributed to—what else—"the invasion of illegal aliens."

The facts of the story were thoroughly investigated—and deli-ciously detailed—by David Leonhardt of *The New York Times* in a May 2007 article headlined "Truth, Fiction and Lou Dobbs." Here's the gist:

During a 2007 profile of Dobbs on *60 Minutes*, Lesley Stahl con-fronted Dobbs with a snippet from the April 14, 2005, edition of his show during which Dr. Madeleine Cosman, introduced as "a medical attorney" (even though she has no medical credentials), claimed that "we have some enormous problems with horrendous diseases that are being brought into America by illegal aliens." CNN's reporter, Christine Romans, was much more specific, explaining: "There were about nine hundred cases of leprosy for forty years. There have been seven thousand in the past three years." In his intro, Lou pointed the gnarled finger of blame at "our open borders," through which previ-ously eradicated diseases were returning.

Waiter, there's an ear in my soup!

Stahl questioned the stat, telling Dobbs, "We went to try and check that number, seven thousand. We can't."

Dobbs puffed himself up and righteously declared, "If we reported

it, it's a fact" (a phrase Leonhardt dubbed an "Orwellian chestnut").
Dobbs later insisted: "We don't make up numbers, Lesley."

The day after the *60 Minutes* story, Dobbs dug himself an even
deeper hole by pompously standing by his story, with CNN reporter
Romans declaring again on his show that, after years of decline,
"Suddenly, in the past three years, America has had more than seven
thousand cases of leprosy."

But before you strap on your face mask, seal the doors with duct
tape, and demand to see the green card of anyone you come in contact with, here are the facts.

According to the National Hansen's Disease Program (because of
its pejorative and fear-mongering connotations, the disease formerly
known as "leprosy" is now called "Hansen's disease"—except, of
course, on Lou Dobbs's show), there have indeed been seven thousand cases of the disease in the United States. But not over the last
three years. Over the last *thirty* years. That's right. Dobbs exaggerated the leprosy threat by a factor of ten. What's more, the incidence
of diagnosed cases peaked in 1983. An honest reporter might also
have mentioned that Hansen's disease is one of the least contagious of
all transmittable diseases and that most people who get it catch it
from an infected person with whom they have prolonged contact.
The specter fabricated by Dobbs of filthy aliens infecting nice,
decent, hardworking middle-class people with some disfiguring mal-
ady by sharing a handshake or a bus ride with them would be laughable if it weren't so contemptible.

When the Southern Poverty Law Center, a great advocate for the
truly dispossessed, fought back by running newspaper ads demanding
a correction of Dobbs's story, Lou invited two representatives of the
group on the show and then proceeded to chew them out on his
home turf for daring to tell the truth about his lies. Nobody does that
to Lou. Never once during his blustery rampage did he acknowledge
that his show deceived its viewers with an untrue story.

His curiosity piqued by the leprosy scare, Leonhardt took a closer
look at Dobbs's program and discovered that *Lou Dobbs Tonight* has
more in common with *War of the Worlds* than it does with *The News-
Hour:*

For one thing, Mr. Dobbs has a somewhat flexible relationship
with reality. He has said, for example, that one-third of the
inmates in the federal prison system are illegal immigrants.

That's wrong, too. According to the Justice Department, 6 percent of prisoners in this country are noncitizens (compared with 7 percent of the population). For a variety of reasons, the crime rate is actually lower among immigrants than natives. Second, Mr. Dobbs really does give airtime to white supremacy sympathizers. Ms. Cosman, who is now deceased, was a lawyer and Renaissance studies scholar, never a medical doctor or a leprosy expert. She gave speeches in which she said that Mexican immigrants had a habit of molesting children. Back in their home villages, she would explain, rape was not as serious a crime as cow stealing. The Southern Poverty Law Center keeps a list of other such guests from *Lou Dobbs Tonight.* Finally, Mr. Dobbs is fond of darkly hinting that this country is under attack. He suggested last week that the new immigration bill in Congress could be the first step toward a new nation—a "North American union"—that combines the United States, Canada and Mexico. On other occasions, his program has described a supposed Mexican plot to reclaim the Southwest. In one such report, one of his correspondents referred to a Utah visit by Vicente Fox, then Mexico's president, as a "Mexican military incursion." When I asked Mr. Dobbs about this yesterday, he said, "You've raised this to a level that frankly I find offensive."

"Offensive" is certainly the right word for the self-righteous indignation of a supposed journalist who has been allowed, night after night, in the guise of concern for the little guy, to preach reverse class war of the privileged against the weak and disadvantaged. Lou Dobbs probably doesn't even think of himself as a right-winger. He probably thinks he has too much "integrity" to be a partisan hack. Indeed, to the extent he thinks at all it must be only about ratings and to hell with any collateral damage from his bombastic rantings. He built his TV career as a supine interviewer and full-time tout for corporate America. Only after the Internet bubble broke and the public mood began to sour on the economy did Dobbs experience his public-minded fight-for-the-little-guy epiphany.

And like the politicians who attack immigrants because they know they can't vote, Dobbs knows that they aren't usually Nielsen families either.

Denying Drivers' Licenses:
A Head-On Collision

Although it rouses the rabble, the Right's stance on immigration is, in many respects, counterproductive and—there's no other way to put it—stupid. For starters, although it can be popular in congressional races, anti-immigrant rhetoric could cost the GOP nationally by alienating the country's largest minority—Hispanics. According to a study by Americas Majority, a conservative group, Latino voters will reach tipping point numbers in several key red states in this election year. The whole "kick 'em out" tone has been so nasty that Republicans might experience a reciprocal kick-'em-out action themselves. Some of those Republicans still capable of strategic thinking painfully recall their California debacle. After former Governor Pete Wilson successfully got reelected by shamelessly surfing an anti-immigrant wave in 1994, Latino voters surged and, ever since, with the sole exception of Governor Schwarzenegger, Republicans have been banished from statewide office.

The immigration issue descends to the darkest zones of dumbness in the debate over providing drivers' licenses to illegals. Governor Eliot Spitzer of New York made a proposal to do so subject to all the usual DMV testing that American citizens have come to know and love. In proposing the bill, Spitzer made the point that issuing drivers' licenses would dramatically increase traffic safety and lower insurance costs, both by reducing accidents and by giving the newly licensed immigrant drivers access to car insurance. Unlicensed illegal immigrant drivers are more than five times as likely to get into fatal car crashes than are licensed drivers. But Spitzer soon found himself dancing a merry jig when he was attacked by both the alarmist Right and some less-than-courageous Democrats. Bowing to political reality, Spitzer revised his proposal twice and then withdrew it. The result? A lot more untested, unregulated drivers making our roads a lot less safe.

The Spitzer saga is a tale of political courage snuffed out by political reality. In trying to change the policy on drivers' licenses, Spitzer was swimming against the national tide. Since 9/11, most governors, including Spitzer's predecessor, George Pataki, have put up roadblocks that make it effectively impossible for illegal immigrants to obtain licenses. Only five states—Hawaii, Washington, Maine, New

Mexico, and Utah—allow drivers to get a license without proving their legal status. And those five are under growing pressure to toughen their laws.

The Spitzer proposal, and others like it, are designed with built-in safeguards to prevent immigrants from using their drivers' licenses for any purpose other than driving. A valid ID like a foreign passport would be required and photo comparison technology would be used to prevent terrorists from stocking up on phony documents. The licenses given to undocumented workers would also have looked dramatically different from regular drivers' licenses to make it clear that the bearer was not a citizen. These licenses are not the same as Social Security cards or passports. The New York proposal also included a residency requirement that would have prevented illegals from neighboring states flooding New York's DMV with license applications. Like any sensible immigration policy that has a chance of success, licensing programs for undocumented workers merely acknowledge a reality, which is that undocumented workers are already on the roads driving to their jobs frying Rush Limbaugh's chicken or landscaping Mitt Romney's governor's mansion. When every high school student in the country seems able to get a fake driver's license in order to buy beer, doesn't it make sense to give real drivers real licenses?

Apparently not. Or, at least, not to a coalition of disparate groups hastily assembled by the Right to beat down the Spitzer plan. More than a dozen county clerks—including at least one appointed by Spitzer—declared that they would not comply with the governor's order. Peter Gadiel, the father of a World Trade Center victim and the president of 9/11 Families for a Secure America, declared, "terrorists here illegally used licenses to kill my son and thousands of others in the World Trade Center; if they do it again using New York licenses issued by the governor, the blood of the victims will be on Mr. Spitzer's hands." Lou Dobbs, naturally, spearheaded the campaign against the policy, calling Spitzer an "idiot."

Ronald Reagan, an icon of the Right despite the occasional tax increase here and there, the ballooning deficits he spurred, and the legalization of abortion while he was California's governor, was one of the first to realize that highway safety is the most expendable of all national objectives. As California governor, he won the hearts and votes of the biker constituency (a group even more strongly defined by a single issue than gun owners) by repealing helmet laws, even though, apart from the damage helmetless motorcycle crashes do to bikers' heads, they also cost the taxpayers a pretty penny in emergency response and medical costs. And in his campaign for president, he lured an astonishingly large group of indifferent and previously nonvoting voters to his camp by promising to eliminate the national 55-mile-per-hour speed limit, a bit of Carter-era nanny-statism hated by the libertarian Right.

Given the choice, then, between the very real danger of unlicensed drivers who have not had their eyes, their ability to read, or their knowledge of the who-goes-first-at-a-four-way-stop-sign rule (okay, I'm a little fuzzy on that too) tested and the ignorant fear of giving noncitizens the uniquely American privilege of standing in line at the DMV, the Right goes for the potent symbolism every time. They get away with it because a mother whose child has been killed in an accident involving an unlicensed illegal immigrant is unlikely to acknowledge that such a tragedy is actually an argument *for* granting undocumented workers licenses. Instead, she'll likely play into the Right's hands by asking bitterly what the driver was doing in this country in the first place—a question that will not make any of us safer on the road tomorrow.

Giant Barbed-Wire Fences Make for Great Neighbors

Even many of those who decry the terrible vice of sneaking into the United States in order to better oneself admit that we can't simply round up all twelve million undocumented immigrants and ship them home. And yet, amazingly, that is the position—or, at least, the inevitable consequence of the position—advocated by the Right.

Amnesty for illegal aliens as defined by the Right is any plan that is short of sending all illegal immigrants home and making them start over from the beginning, applying for citizenship or work visas from abroad. Let me dignify that preposterous position with some commonsense objections for just a moment. Remember, the consensus estimate of the number of undocumented immigrants in this country stands at about *twelve* million. Apart from the economic devastation caused by depriving American business of millions of workers, the cost of rounding them up and shipping them home is estimated at around $200 billion. And one can't calculate the moral and emotional cost of armed men arresting families in their homes or workplaces and marching them onto trains or buses. Whatever your idea is of what's "American," this can't be it. And it simply isn't going to happen. But this un-American nightmare would be the logical consequence of the Right's "no exceptions" pandering.

If you want to punt on the question of what exactly you would *do* about the illegal immigrants already here, you can always change the subject to what you would do to prevent more from coming in. One of the recent solutions, patrols by armed militia groups like the Minutemen, seems to make even the Right nervous, since the pistol-packing kooks who turn up for the TV cameras aren't exactly in keeping with the sober, adult image the Right likes to project. Although their effect on border safety is negligible, we can thank the Minutemen for one thing: shining a little daylight on the anti-immigrant movement's ugly xenophobic, conspiracy-minded underbelly, which acts as if Mexico and the minimum- and subminimum-wage-earning Mexicans have a secret plan to take back and annex the Southwest. Even though it has to pander to them, the Right will not be inviting the Minutemen to join its country club any time soon.

But there is another idea, already materializing, that seems to have come more from Wile E. Coyote's Acme catalogue than from the Minutemen's well-thumbed copy of *The Turner Diaries*. I refer, of course, to the erection of Lou Dobbs's most arousing fantasy: that double, or triple (or is it a four-ply?) super-fence from San Diego to Brownsville across America's entire southern border that will seal us off from the hordes who wash our dishes and mow our lawns and injection-mold our widgets forever. (And it has the additional advantage of "keeping out the terrorists"—even though many terrorists have actually entered the country legally.) As many a late-night comedian has wondered, how is the government going to build such a huge fence at a reasonable cost unless it hires illegal aliens to do the job? I guess they'll have to build it from the southern side. And, perhaps more to the point, as Arizona's Democratic Governor Janet Napolitano wryly put it: "You show me a fifty-foot wall and I'll show you a fifty-one-foot ladder at the border. That's the way the border works."

The Jobs Americans Don't Want to Do?

A limp and rather clichéd response to the Right's chest-thumping about immigration and the foreigners "stealing" American jobs is to point out that most illegal immigrants do *not* work as astronauts, movie stars, CEOs, or "news" anchors. What we really need to do is ask ourselves why there are so many millions of jobs that Americans don't want to do. If our standard of living is based on hiring people illegally, on "rewarding people for breaking the law" by sneaking in here to work for us, is it a standard we can claim any sort of moral right to? The Right would like to punish illegals for their sins, but will the Right also ask us to share the sacrifice of a diminished quality of life? Unlikely. We need an immigration policy that allows people already here who broke one big rule in the past but who have played by the rules ever since to come out of the shadows.

People of goodwill certainly have work to do reconciling our consumption-driven economy with the fact that it depends on so many poorly paid men and women doing dirty and sometimes dangerous work at low pay with no benefits. If you restrict the labor pool to just citizens for, say, jobs cleaning peep show booths, then the sacred free market will set the wage to the level where a citizen will take the job. Under those circumstances, I'm confident the *Wall Street Journal* headline would read, "Peep Show Cleaners' Wages Expected to Rise Sharply." Okay, so maybe a peep show parlor or two has to go under. No tears there. But when the labor market is freed from the distortions of the current insider-outsider configuration, wages would rise as demand increased, and so would inflation. And we'd all have to pay the price.

While we're on the subject of playing into the Right's hands, the rather less than noble stand of some Democrats must be noted. After remaining mostly silent on the issue for the last two decades, some Democrats and their allies came up with some bold initiatives for comprehensive reform over the past few years. Even some powerful unions, including the Service Employees International Union, joined the sensible reform movement, breaking with organized labor's long-time demand of closing down the borders. But as soon as the Right began flexing its congressional muscle to block any reform, too many Democrats quickly began backtracking and sounding remarkably similar to the nea-cons, swooning over the very idea of some Berlin-like wall cutting through El Paso. And just as a handful of more rational Republicans joined with enlightened Democrats to reach agreement on a much needed guest worker program, the more ossified industrial labor unions went right back to the old-time religion of blocking reform.

Why the Right Is Wrong on Immigration

The Right is wrong on immigration because they favor continued tough talk over policy reform. One suspects that a hidden reason the Right is wrong on immigration is their need for a scapegoat to divert attention from their massive failures in domestic and foreign policy.

There's a simple way to transform all these jobs Americans don't want to do into jobs Americans would love to do: raise the wages for them. At a certain price, anyone will clean a toilet. But the Right doesn't like that idea either, opposing increases in the minimum wage and even suggesting that the correct minimum wage is zero.

The Right is wrong about immigration because while they want to pay workers as little as possible, they believe that only U.S. citizens should be entitled to American jobs. They are in for a very rude awakening.

12

The Right's Recession

Poverty as a Punch Line

During the 2004 presidential campaign, George Bush promised the Right that the good times would keep on rolling. More tax cuts for the rich, less industry-constraining regulation, and continued prosperity—at least for loyal Republican donors. When Bush's challenger, John Kerry, suggested that economic policy should serve larger social goals that benefit everybody, he was instantly ridiculed.

"Senator Kerry says he sees two Americas," said Dick Cheney at the 2004 GOP convention. "It makes the whole thing mutual. America sees two John Kerrys." At the same convention, Rudy Giuliani joked that Democrats needed "two Americas—one where John Kerry can vote for something and another where he can vote against the same thing." Hardee-har-har.

The laugh riot came just days after the release of a devastating report from the Census Bureau showing that over 12 percent of the American people—35.9 million, 12.9 million of them children—were living below the poverty line, and that the number of Americans with no health insurance had increased during Bush's first term by 5.2 million, bringing the total to 45 million. Hilarious, right? I bet they got a good chuckle out of that up at the White House.

The growing chasm between the Two Americas was chillingly documented in another report released in 2004 by the Economic Policy Institute, which revealed that over the last few years "income shifted extremely rapidly and extensively from labor compensation to capital income (profits and interest)." As Jared Bernstein, co-author of the report, put it: "The economic pie is growing gangbusters and the typical household is falling behind."

The 2004 GOP convention chose not only to render the increasing pain of increasing millions invisible but to use it as a punch line.

The 2008 Democratic convention needs to link the reality of the Two Americas with Bush's miserable failures in Iraq. Iraq and the economy are two topics the media talk about as though they have nothing to do with each other. But it's the Other America that's paying the opportunity costs in forgone investments in education, health care, and job training.

And it's the Other America that's also paying the highest price of all in lost lives and maimed bodies. There are precious few denizens of Bush's America slogging through the bloody streets of Najaf and Fallujah—other than the occasional Halliburton executive, there to check on the company's no-bid contract for democracy.

Subprime Chickens Home to Roost

I don't know about you, but I kind of like the Blame Game. Although people who are being blamed for something tend to complain about it, I think if they won't take responsibility for their actions and mistakes, well, sometimes you've just got to help them out a little bit. So, let's play the Blame Game over the current economic slump.

The downturn was triggered by a collapse in the booming subprime mortgage business, that latest form of legal loan-sharking to come into vogue in the capital markets. Subprime mortgages are risky loans to borrowers with low credit ratings. These loans are a good business for lenders only when high rates of interest can be charged, which typically happens after an initially low bait-and-switch "adjustable rate" mortgage "adjusts" to a higher rate after a year or two. Thanks to the Right's relentless campaign against government regulators, unscrupulous mortgage brokers were free to peddle these risky loans to vulnerable customers tempted by the traditional American dream of owning a home. After junk bonds, the S&L crisis and bailout, and now the mortgage collapse, is there anyone outside of a few country miles in Greenwich, Connecticut, who still believes that financial institutions need less regulation?

The president, who had bragged endlessly about how robust the economy was, saw on his watch 2.2 million foreclosure filings in 2007. And it wasn't just the little guys who got hosed. Blue chip investment banks like Citigroup and Goldman Sachs were forced to take staggering write-downs against anticipated losses. And all because they bought into the Looney Tunes theory that bundling up risky loans into exotic derivative commodities somehow magically eliminated the risk.

Mortgage mayhem happened not because the government was caught off-guard, but because the government kept looking the other way and because the Right kept insisting that this negligence was a virtue.

The Iraq Recession

Beyond the subprime mortgage bubble, there's another factor at work in the current economic downturn. The war in Iraq has a three-trillion-dollar price tag. And the money wasn't spent on body armor. Much of that money has been lost in the desert sands due to waste, fraud, or mismanagement. And even more has gone to war profiteers—the corporations that put profit over patriotism.

There are quite a few things we could have done with that money.

With three trillion dollars (and rising) we could have solved two thousand billion-dollar problems; we could have invested in our crumbling infrastructure (and saved billions down the road), in education, or in health care. All that stuff the Right says we can't afford looks pretty cheap compared to the cost of their cherished Iraq misadventure.

The fact is, spending on Iraq, which the Democrats have proven unwilling to curtail, has deprived our policymakers of the flexibility they need to tame the business cycle. Then there's the little problem of $100-a-barrel oil. As Nobel laureate and former chief economist of the World Bank Joseph Stiglitz put it, "The soaring price of oil is clearly related to the Iraq war. The issue is not whether to blame the war for this but simply how much to blame it."

And he's not alone. Other economists warned back in 2002 about possible economic fallout from the war in Iraq.

"The Bush administration has not prepared the public for the cost or the financing of what could prove to be an expensive venture," said William Nordhaus, Sterling Professor of Economics at Yale. "Perhaps it worries acknowledging the costs will endanger the large future tax cuts, which are the centrepiece of its domestic policy. . . . One way or another, Americans will pay for the war."

"If the conflict wears on or, worse, spreads, the economic consequences become very serious. Late last year, George Perry at the

Rewarding Failure

One person who may have lost his job—but almost certainly will not lose his house or, more likely, houses, as a result of the housing bubble is Angelo Mozilo, the CEO of the teetering Countrywide Financial Group, the death star of the subprime mortgage debacle.

In the year before the market downturn, Mozilo exercised his options on $130 million in Countrywide stock, actually making money as his company was imploding and was about to announce plans to lay off 12,000 workers.

Along with the $161 million golden handshake for Merrill Lynch's Stanley O'Neal, who was sent packing after his bank declared an $8.4 billion write-down, and the nearly $100 million handed to Citigroup's CEO Charles Prince on his way out the door after Citi said it expected up to $11 billion in mortgage-related losses, Mozilo's soft landing proves once again, as AP's Ellen Simon put it, "that chief executives are the only ones with nothing at risk if their companies slump."

For all the Right's preening talk about "personal responsibility," the CEO class seems strangely immune from any sort of genuine reckoning for its failures. The rise of the Right has meant that any efforts to link executive pay to performance are now regarded as radical ideas, akin to demanding the nationalization of the oil industry or preaching the dictatorship of the proletariat. And as a result, CEOs walk away from the smoking wreckage of their businesses not only unscathed but very rich indeed.

Brookings Institution ran some simulations and found that after taking into account a reasonable use of oil reserves, a cut in world oil production of just 6.5 percent a year would send the United States and the world into recession," said Robert Shapiro, former undersecretary of commerce in the Clinton administration.

Katrina Relief:
Iraq on the Bayou

Even in the unlikely event that the Right would admit that their selfishness, arrogance, and stupidity contributed to the current recession (and they won't), it would still not temper their instinctive pursuit of misery dollars. The perverted form of capitalism at the core of the

Right's philosophy dictates that when others are suffering there is money to be made.

For the Right, crisis begets opportunity, not to solve problems but to profit from their perpetuation. Just think of Halliburton and Blackwater sopping up juicy profits from the bloodshed in Iraq, a market closed to them while Saddam was still calling the shots.

To see how even the worst disasters can make the Right's eyes gleam with the prospect of pushing their agenda past the complacent Democrats, take a look at Hurricane Katrina, where disaster relief instantly became a policy and patronage boondoggle—and a profit engine.

After the disaster, Tony Snow, the soon-to-be White House Press Secretary, crowed: "This would be a marvelous time to push in a serious way for school choice, dramatic regulatory reform . . . even more thoroughgoing tort reform, privatization of everything from the Department of Commerce to many FEMA duties, and so on."

Political journalist David Sirota spotlighted a few of the top opportunities the GOP saw arising from Katrina, including the suspension of the seventy-six-year-old Davis-Bacon Act requiring federal contractors to pay workers "prevailing wages," the chance to offer more giveaways (and fewer regulations) to oil companies, and—proving that no issue was too tangential to link to Katrina—the chance to try to get the president's derailed attempt to privatize Social Security back on track.

Everybody wanted to get in on the act. Pete Domenici, the senior senator from hurricane-free New Mexico, began looking to ease environmental requirements on oil refineries, and George "Macaca" Allen, at the time the U.S. senator from Virginia, tried to repeal parts of the Clean Air Act.

Within two weeks, the aftermath of Katrina had turned into an all-you-can-eat right-wing-policy buffet.

As is so often the case with these tireless champions of crony capitalism, the main course at this opportunistic smorgasbord was "privatization." And the target du jour was the hapless Federal Emergency Management Agency (FEMA), then still run by "Heckuva job, Brownie." The new talking point was that the government's disastrous response to Katrina proved that disaster relief is no business for the government to be in, and should therefore be turned over to the Halliburtons of the world (after all, they've done such a great job supplying our troops and reconstructing Iraq, right?).

Of course, FEMA's Katrina failures had less to do with big government bugaboos and much more to do with the way Bush and the partisan hacks he installed there turned a successful cabinet-level agency (one that Governor George W. Bush took time to praise in a debate with Al Gore in 2000) into a denuded and incompetently managed afterthought run by a former commissioner of the International Arabian Horse Association.

In fact, the piecemeal privatization of FEMA started soon after Bush took office. FEMA's response to Katrina was simply the logical conclusion of the process. "The car broke because Bush slashed its tires and now his allies are trying to convince us that the real problem lies with the whole 'car' concept," is how *American Prospect*'s Ezra Klein described the chutzpah of the GOP attempt to use the Katrina fiasco to further privatize FEMA.

David Brooks wasted an entire post-Katrina column attempting to make that very case. Let me distill its essence for you: government sucks! According to Brooks, "the Army Corps of Engineers had plenty of money"—so the problem wasn't that Bush had slashed funding to fortify the levees, the problem was government. And according to Brooks, "there were ample troops nearby to maintain order"—so the problem wasn't that nearly 40 percent of Louisiana's and Mississippi's National Guard was deployed in Iraq, the problem was government. And the problem certainly wasn't that Bush had filled five of the eight top slots at FEMA with incompetent political cronies . . . no, the problem was (all together now!) government. Which is partially true—the fuller version being: government-as-run-by-George-W.-Bush-and-the-Right.

The fault lies not in the platonic idea of government but in the crummy reality of particular leaders with a particular theory of how to run it. Leaders with one-track minds like Katrina-era Treasury Secretary John Snow, who claimed: "Making the [Bush] tax cuts permanent would be a real plus in a situation like this." So the lives of people in New Orleans would be salvaged if a few of the richest Americans became even richer? Peculiar logic.

The Katrina relief effort was Iraq-on-the-bayou. The list of the companies awarded clean-up and reconstruction contracts was the same old gang from Baghdad: Halliburton, Bechtel, Fluor, and the Shaw Group (which put up a tasteful notice on its website saying "Hurricane Recovery Projects—Apply Here!"). It was a veritable bacchanalia of crony capitalism. Even *The Wall Street Journal* got an uneasy sense of déjà vu, pointing out that "the Bush administration is importing many of the contract practices blamed for spending abuses in Iraq." These included contracts awarded without competitive bidding, and cost-plus provisions "that guarantee contractors a certain profit regardless of how much they spend." As Naomi Klein wrote: " 'Where has all the money gone?' ask desperate people from Baghdad to New Orleans, from Kabul to tsunami-struck Sri Lanka. One place a great deal of it has gone is into major capital expenditure for these private contractors. Largely under the public radar, billions of taxpayer dollars have been spent on the construction of a privatized disaster-response infrastructure: the Shaw Group's new state-of-the-art Baton Rouge headquarters, Bechtel's battalions of earth-moving equipment, Blackwater USA's six-thousand-acre campus in North Carolina (complete with paramilitary training camp and six-thousand-foot runway)." So, no, Katrina did not prove the failure of government, it proved the success of the Right's version of government—which again and again fails the American people.

The Tax Cut Cult

With the fall of the Berlin Wall, the Right lost its lodestar. Opposition to communism was the most basic of all conservative beliefs. The acid test of true right-wing faith was not whether you were against communism (and looking back, who besides a few unreconstructed radicals wasn't?), but how much? Did you want to poison Fidel's underwear, nuke Hanoi, give the bomb to Taiwan, deal with every dirty dictator on Earth, so long as they weren't communist, and keep your finger on the button assuring Mutual Assured Destruction? If so, then you might be admitted to the club—after a thorough background check and the signing of proper loyalty oaths, of course.

It may be some comfort when listening to our modern right-wing nuts to remember that cooler heads did ultimately prevail in those Cold War days. Perhaps they will again during our current war against terrorism, thwarting other bizarre causes célèbres of the Right, like promoting skepticism on global climate change and keeping Glenn Beck on the air.

The Right may have wandered aimlessly for a week or two after the break-up of the Evil Empire, wondering what to get worked up about next. The Mafia? Too many nude scenes in Hollywood movies? Legionnaire's Disease?

It settled on an enemy that this time around was not a foreign government or system of government. It was our own government and our own system of government. The Right had seen the new enemy, and it was us!

The enhancements to the concept of Western democracy made during the New Deal era were the new threat. It was very existential. Somehow, our way of life had become a danger to our way of life. The Right had a seductive little pitch all worked out for the ordinary working stiff:

"No one likes paying taxes, right? But people do it because they believe that it's the right thing to do and that they eventually get their money's worth through public works, national defense, clean water, roads, a stable banking system, a police force, and some assistance to the poor, all of which holds us together as a society. But what if we told you that paying taxes was actually unpatriotic because it simply feeds cash to our bloated government, which, instead of using the money for good works, simply perpetuates itself by creating ever more byzantine bureaucracies? Paying taxes does not result in a better, fairer, more cohesive society but one in which we're only equal in that we are all slaves of the same master. Thus, the right thing to do is not just to evade paying taxes through offshore tax dodges and other sheltering schemes—which have always had a distasteful criminal feeling about them—but to simply cut off the flow of nourishing dollars, to starve the monster, so that it can go on minimal life support."

With this simple but juicy piece of bait, the tax cut cult, the Right's new high priesthood, snagged converts by the millions. Imagine how seductive the message that our base impulses are actually civic virtues might be if alcoholics were told that booze would keep them young and healthy or if philanderers were told that they were doing their wives a favor by cheating. The pitch proved effective, but the ordinary taxpayers who jumped at the chance for financial and moral salvation all wrapped up in a convenient little bundle (you didn't have to actually do anything illegal—just support certain candidates) quickly found themselves betrayed.

Government as the Enemy

It's never terribly hard to find stupid, wasteful, and unnecessary things that our super-sized government does with our money. Bridges to nowhere, highways to nowhere, museums in the middle of nowhere, squadrons of tanks in the sand . . . we're all familiar with the classic examples of government waste and inefficiency because they're invariably played for laughs. The very size of government may bother some. And, of course, there's the phenomenon that many of the things we should like about government, such as, say, building codes that protect us from fire or aid for working mothers or air-sea rescue operations by the Coast Guard or an untainted food supply, are invisible to most of us on a daily basis, while many of our direct dealings with government, from waiting in line at the DMV to getting a traffic ticket to sending our check to the IRS on April 15, are frustrating and unsatisfactory.

The Right took this emerging idea that government was the problem, laundered it of its origins in the fever swamps of the political fringes, and called it "reform." By taking a radical anti-government position and advocating that government be starved of tax revenues at its roots and that its regulatory branches be ruthlessly pruned, the Right veered from the conservative course of championing the status quo onto a course of radical change.

And there was Mike Huckabee during the 2008 presidential campaign running ads while America was at war, promising to be "the president who nails the 'Going out of Business' sign on the door of the IRS. . . . I'll lead the fight to abolish the IRS, and we'll keep our jobs, and paychecks." Tearing up a 1040 tax form during his rallies, and railing against the IRS, Huckabee sounded more like Lenin than a slow, steady, reliable Old School Republican like Dwight Eisenhower, who refused to support his party's move to cut taxes in 1953 in the middle of the Cold War.

And John McCain, who sold his soul to the Right to win the GOP nomination, now rarely makes a campaign stop without mentioning his bedrock commitment to making George Bush's tax cuts permanent. These, of course, are the same tax cuts that he spoke so eloquently against before hopping in bed with the Right: "I cannot in good conscience support a tax cut in which so many of the benefits go to the most fortunate among us, at the expense of middle-class Americans who most need tax relief."

So though we're told over and over again that we are currently engaged in an all-consuming war on terror in which the very idea of civilization is at stake, the seemingly contradictory ideas of cutting taxes and defeating terrorists have remained at the top of the Right's priorities list. You'd think an enormous deficit and a recession might strike them as not very desirable during our fight for civilization. But you'd be wrong.

The New Robber Barons

Here's *New York Times* columnist Paul Krugman on the truth of who benefits from the Bush tax cuts: "The reality is that the core measures of both the 2001 and 2003 tax cuts mainly benefit the very affluent. The centerpieces of the 2001 act were a reduction in the top income-tax rate and elimination of the estate tax—the first, by definition, benefiting only people with high incomes; the second benefiting only heirs to large estates. The core of the 2003 tax cut was a reduction in the tax rate on dividend income. This benefit, too, is concentrated on very high-income families."

One of the Right's refrains is that taxing the rich somehow stifles economic growth because the rich need constant incentives to make more money. So just imagine you're sitting at the very bottom of the Forbes 400 with an even $1 billion in net worth. Do you think that a few million dollars one way or the other in taxes would make any difference at all in how you conduct your business life? If you're a highly competent (or even incompetent—it makes little difference these days) CEO, would you really pack it in and retire to Boca if you could make only $97 million a year instead of $100 million? Would you really throw in the towel? Similarly, if you're a lazy heir do you think you'd convert your investments into gold bars and bury them in your backyard just because you might have to pay taxes if you tried to increase your inheritance?

When the Right realized that it would have to come up with a better argument as to why taxing the rich was somehow bad for the non-rich, they turned as they often do to the dark wizard of the Right's anti-tax cult, Grover Norquist. Norquist has popularized the idea of the "burden" of "double taxation." Supposedly, the estate tax—or "death tax" as Norquistians call it—is a form of double taxation because the estate was already taxed as income when it was earned. But for the rich, estates consist largely of investments that are not taxed unless they are realized.

Apart from helping fund the government, the estate tax has the added benefit, deemed essential to our democracy, of impeding the creation of a permanent aristocracy, defined not by birth but by wealth. Michael Kinsley has written of this tension between capitalism and democracy:

> Separation of the spheres of democracy and capitalism also depends on an unspoken deal, a nonaggression pact, between democracy's political majority and capitalism's affluent minority. The majority acknowledge that capitalism benefits all of us, even if some benefit a lot more than others. The majority also take comfort in the belief that everyone has at least a shot at scoring big. The affluent minority, meanwhile, acknowledge that their good fortune is at least in part the luck of the draw. They recognize that domestic tranquillity, protection from foreign enemies, and other government functions are worth more to people with more at stake. And they retain a tiny yet prudent fear of what beast might be awakened if the fortunate folks get too greedy about protecting and enlarging their good fortune.

(A word on the idea that everyone has "a shot at scoring big." While this is definitely true, the odds for most people are very long and, under the Right, growing longer. But, like lottery ticket salesmen, the Right have used this idea to enlist broader support for tax cuts, convincing American Dreamers to vote contrary to their own current financial interest in favor of their imagined future interest.)

During the Bush years the number of billionaires boomed—along with the number of poor and middle-class families without health insurance. The United States is now the third most unequal industrialized society after Russia and Mexico.

And wealth inequity is not just a boo-hoo issue for soak-the-rich ex-hippies or a matter of envy or social-leveling. Sure, capitalism has winners and losers. But when the winners lap the losers so many times around the track because they are being driven in a souped-up limousine while the rest are hobbling along on foot as fast as they can, the social costs start to mount and we become a poorer society.

Right-Wing Foxes Guarding the
Regulatory Henhouse

With the growth of the federal government actually accelerating under Bush despite almost eight years of tax-cutting, the Right's mission to reduce the size of government—at least the part that doesn't feed Halliburton—has been pursued with a special zeal.

In addition to social programs, the Right expanded its targets to include a whole host of government agencies that were not much more popular than the IRS. Because of the same paradox that causes such image problems for government as a whole, which is that when it's working effectively you don't notice it but when it's a nuisance, you do, individual agencies are even more susceptible to the Right's tried-and-true rhetoric about "cutting red tape."

Since closing down EPA headquarters altogether or turning the Consumer Product Safety Commission's offices into a Home Depot might reveal the radical extent of their plans, the Right embarked upon a sneak attack: put the foxes in charge of the henhouses and let them eat the chickens so gradually that no one would notice. Free markets are inherently self-regulating, the reasoning goes, so why can't businesses be? Irresponsible or incompetent corporate behavior produces poor results and, in turn, a change in management or management strategy. At least that's how it's supposed to work. In the Right's mind, the best way to put these wonderfully self-regulating forces into play is to put an industry stooge in charge of "enforcing" legal regulations, the ones intended to protect people *before* a toxic spill takes place or a dangerous product hits the supermarket shelves. A reliable hack will know when to back off and let industries police themselves. And when the profit motive becomes paramount, things like product safety become expendable luxuries.

For a prime example of this, look no further than Nancy Nord, the acting head of the Consumer Product Safety Commission, who has fought valiantly to eliminate all that excess government spending by demanding lower and lower budgets for her own agency. But it's not like she's regulating the length of buggy whips or air traffic control for zeppelins. Nancy Nord actually has a job to do, whether she wants to do it or not. She was named to head the agency after Michael Baroody, the son of a former president of the conservative American Enterprise Institute and the former chief lobbyist for the National

Association of Manufacturers—a group that's basically the anti–
Consumer Product Safety Commission—withdrew his name from
consideration under heavy Democratic fire. Here's how Robert
Borosage, president of the Institute for America's Future, told the
tale:

> Even where regulations do apply, conservatives and the corpo-
> rate lobby have succeeded in disemboweling the regulatory
> agencies. So George Bush names Nancy Nord, a former
> Chamber of Commerce lobbyist against regulation, to head
> the Consumer Product Safety Commission. Between industry-
> financed junkets, Nord declaims loudly on the effectiveness of
> corporate self-regulation. She opposed more resources and
> staffing for an agency that has half the size and budget it had
> when it was founded in 1974. Toxic toys are regulated. But
> with 80 percent of our toys imported from China, the CPSC
> has about 90 field investigators, most of whom work from their
> homes and are based on the East Coast, tracking 15,000 prod-
> ucts. It has, although Nord denies it, exactly one staffer—a guy
> named Bob—tasked full time to test toys.

And—believe it or not—Bob's primary method of testing toys is
by dropping them to see if they break.

I guess you could call the recent suicide of Zhang Shuhong, the
owner of a plant in China that manufactured Big Bird and Elmo toys
for Mattel's Fisher-Price brand—some of the dangerous toys that
slipped past Bob—a perfect example of the market's genius for self-
regulation. You'd think you might be able to get the Right to support
the idea that someone in our government should at least keep an eye
on products from China—even if they're going to turn a blind eye to
shoddy workmanship and reckless corner-cutting here at home—on
strictly old-fashioned xenophobic grounds. But Nancy Nord is nothing if not fair. She wants her agency to pay as little attention to haz-
ardous foreign products as it does to domestic ones. The best way to
make sure the agency doesn't do its job is to make sure that it can't, by
eliminating its resources. And she won't stop until she's fired herself.

Deregulation Disasters

The Right has been so successful at placing industry insiders in charge of dismantling regulatory agencies that you have to wonder if some of their less successful causes, like outlawing abortion, are simply diversions to keep us from figuring out what they are really up to.

Here's just a few of their greatest hits.

As Chinese products have flooded the market and NAFTA-juiced trade has increased imports to record levels—despite the weakness of the dollar, thank you, Mr. President—the Consumer Product Safety Commission has had a number of conspicuous failures. The best known of them was the unprecedented double recall of both a lead-tainted Thomas the Tank Engine toy and the toy sent to consumers to replace it. The Product Safety Commission has fought for more flammable mattresses and dropped prevention of child-drowning from its list of strategic goals. Its overworked inspectors didn't catch an obvious defect in the Simplicity Crib that killed nine-month-old Liam Johns. None of this is any surprise, since the stooges Bush has installed to lead the agency spend most of their time trying to cut its throat, reducing its staff from a high of 978 in 1980 to less than half that today.

A partial list of products recalled for high lead levels—over just a two-week period in October 2007—after they had slipped past the CPSC and into the market reads like Satan's Christmas List:

55,000 skull pails filled with Halloween candy mix

350,000 bookmarks and journals

5,400 tabletop puppet theaters

2,400 Breyer 2006 Stirrup Christmas ornaments

19,000 Deluxe Wood Art Sets

49,000 Disney Deluxe Winnie-the-Pooh 23-Piece Play Sets

7,800 Princess Magnetic Travel Art Set Lap Desks

10,000 bendable dinosaur toys

2,500 collectible Jeff Gordon Mini Helmets

2,400 Kidnastics balance beams

1.6 million Cub Scouts Totem badges

11,200 Alpine design aluminum water bottles

192,000 key chains

15,000 children's toy decorating sets

63,000 Frankenstein tumblers

79,000 *Pirates of the Caribbean* medallion squeeze lights

35,000 Baby Einstein Discover and Play color blocks

10,000 wooden pull-along alphabet and math blocks wagons

Ah, the beauty of the self-regulating marketplace . . .

After failing to protect the public from numerous drugs—including the herbal supplement ephedra and the arthritis drug Vioxx—the Food and Drug Administration has actually taken the side of drug-makers in a series of lawsuits intended to prevent states from stepping in to regulate drugs in the agency's stead and limit the liability of the manufacturer for a dangerous product. This is the bleeding edge of the deregulation craze, described this way by Laurie Beacham and Amy Widman of the Center for Justice and Democracy:

> Agencies are regulating industries less vigorously while erod-ing the ability of the civil justice system to protect citizens from unsafe products created by those industries. Under the Bush administration, agencies unduly influenced by industry are using their power to preempt—or override—laws, including liability or "tort" laws that protect the public health and safety, which have always been regulated by the states. The methods vary. Sometimes agencies claim that their safety standards are the final word and, therefore, that no tort claims should be allowed in state courts. Sometimes an agency intervenes in a lawsuit on behalf of a corporate defendant, such as Pfizer, claiming that if its own standards have been met, the case should be thrown out.

The FDA has long been under the thumb of the very pharmaceu-tical companies it is supposed to oversee. This dysfunctional dynamic has proved especially deadly, with numerous drugs being pulled off the market only after causing serious injuries and deaths. Take the case of the drug known as Trasylol, marketed by Bayer. On the market for fourteen years, it was eventually found to be causing as many as one thousand deaths per month. But even after scientific studies in 2006 conclusively proved its dangers, the FDA dragged its heels for two years before restricting its use. Only after Germany banned the drug was the FDA embarrassed into action.

Big Pharma spent over $170 million on lobbying in 2006, and has contributed over $66 million to federal candidates since 2002, with over $46 million of that going to Republicans.

In return, the Bush administration has served up FDA commissioners like Lester Crawford, who was forced to resign after failing to disclose that he owned stock in companies regulated by his agency, and current FDA commissioner Andrew von Eschenbach, a vocal supporter of faster drug approvals. The Bush administration has also given back to big business interests by taking away: the FDA is conducting only half the food inspections it was doing in 2003, and safety-testing of U.S.-produced food has dropped nearly 75 percent since 2003. This despite an upswing in highly publicized food recalls and outbreaks of food poisoning. And with more and more of our food coming from other countries, how appetizing is it to know that just 1.3 percent of food imports were physically examined by FDA inspectors in 2006?

The bracing truth is that we now have a regulatory system in which corporate greed, political timidity, and a culture of cronyism are the order of the day.

The FDA is also partly to blame, along with the Department of Agriculture and the Centers for Disease Control, for another unwelcome import from China: pet food made from wheat gluten tainted with poisonous melamine and cyanuric acid that killed thousands of dogs and cats at the end of 2006 and the start of 2007.

After assuring the public that, while regrettably some pets had died, humans were in no danger, the USDA and FDA learned that, in fact, 23 million chickens and 56,000 hogs had been exposed to these two industrial chemicals. Looking on the bright side, the two agencies issued a press release reporting that there was "no evidence of harm to humans" thus far: "While the Centers for Disease Control and Prevention systems would have limited ability to detect subtle problems . . . no problems have been detected to date." Who needs inspections? We'll just keep our fingers crossed.

The Occupational Safety and Health Administration has been a thorn in the side of cost-conscious business leaders for years. Under the current administration, OSHA has been forced by budget cuts (Bush used a rare veto to block a modest budget increase of 7 percent for the agency) to reduce the scope of its inspections by 70 percent. It has been forced to back off on a number of initiatives, including regulating chemicals used in the manufacture of semiconductors that are believed to cause miscarriages.

According to *The New York Times,* "Since George W. Bush became president, OSHA has issued the fewest significant standards in its history, public health experts say. It has imposed only one major safety rule. The only significant health standard it issued was ordered by a federal court. . . . The agency has killed dozens of existing and proposed regulations and delayed adopting others."

Indeed, over the seven years Bush has been president, OSHA has been more intent on providing protection to employers than workers. "They've simply gotten out of the standard-setting business in favor of industry partnerships that have no teeth," said Peg Seminario, director of occupational safety and health at the AFL-CIO.

OSHA has also gone to incredible lengths to reduce the categories of recognized workplace injuries. Even with those lowered standards, in 2005, 4.2 million workers were injured or became ill from on-the-job causes. And more than 6,800 workers died from workplace injuries.

In place of regulation, OSHA has shown whose side it is on by calling for, yes, greater "personal responsibility." Edwin Foulke Jr., the head of OSHA, has advocated a "voluntary compliance strategy" of self-policing to encourage careless workers to be a little more cautious, especially when handling company property. Foulke, the quintessential anti-regulation regulator, calls himself a "true Ronald Reagan Republican" who "firmly believes in limited government."

"Early in his tenure at OSHA," the *Times* reports, "Mr. Foulke delivered a speech called 'Adults Do the Darndest Things,' which attributed many injuries to worker carelessness. Large posters of workers' making dangerous errors, like erecting a tall ladder close to an overhead wire, were displayed around him." See, we don't need a regulatory agency at all—just a poster of a mother shaking her finger and saying, "Be careful!"

Microwave popcorn will never taste quite the same once you learn that OSHA declined to mandate any new safety rules for food plants after learning that diacetyl, a food flavoring, was giving workers at a popcorn plant in Jasper, Missouri, a rare and sometimes fatal lung ailment. According to Foulke, the science linking diacetyl and "popcorn worker's lung," or bronchiolitis obliterans, is "murky." Much like, one supposes, X-rays of the workers' lungs. OSHA, which apparently feels that protecting workers doesn't include protecting their lungs, also shelved rules to shield health workers from tuberculosis, a preventable but stubborn disease that is on the rise again, in scary, drug-resistant forms. They should just be more careful not to catch it.

A little-known agency, the Federal Motor Carrier Safety Administration, has also been in the vanguard of deregulation by loosening rules covering the politically connected trucking industry regulating how long truck drivers could drive without a break and how much training new drivers must have. You can guess which way the rules were adjusted. Trucking is America's most dangerous industry in terms of overall deaths and accidents. That is, no pun intended, no accident, as safety standards, such as logbooks filled out by the drivers themselves (called "comic books" by insiders) have been among the most relaxed, thanks to the industry's extreme eagerness to pay hard cash to stay in a regulatory blind spot. The trucking industry donated more than $14 million to Republicans in the first six years of the twenty-first century and has been rewarded with almost unprecedented freedom to police itself on the honor system.

Indeed, one of the heads of the Federal Motor Carrier Safety Administration, picked by Bush, was Joseph Clapp, who, according to *The New York Times*, was "the former chairman of Roadway, a trucking company, and the leader of an industry foundation that sponsored research claiming fatigue was not a factor in truck accidents, a conclusion at odds with government and academic studies." The Right's views on trucking regulations come down to, that's right, that drivers should just be more careful. And the rest of us should be more careful not to be in that 18-wheeler's way when it comes careening across the highway divider.

Another exceptionally dangerous business, mining, is supposed to be regulated by the Mine Safety and Health Administration, which has also seen its budget cut under Bush. If there's one industry that has consistently proven itself unworthy of the trust required to look over its own shoulder, it's mining. The Crandall Canyon Mine disaster exposed the critical weakness of the Mine Safety and Health Administration when it came to the most basic part of its job: protecting miners.

It is truly chilling to connect the dots between Karl Rove's politics über alles strategy and the Utah mining disaster.

Rove's unprecedented use of federal assets for political gain meant that every tool at his disposal was employed to help foster his goal of a permanent Republican majority. "It was all politics, all the time," as Representative Henry Waxman put it.

"It was total commitment," marveled Representative Thomas Davis III, who worked closely with Rove in 2002 on the GOP's House reelection campaign. "We knew history was against us, and [Rove] helped coordinate all of the accoutrements of the executive branch to help with the campaign."

These accoutrements included, according to *The Washington Post*, "enlisting political appointees at every level of government in a permanent campaign that was an integral part of [Rove's] strategy to establish electoral dominance." But Rove's plan involved much more than having cabinet officials make election year visits bearing federal goodies to the districts of embattled Republicans; it also meant using the government's regulatory mechanisms to reward major GOP contributors. Major contributors such as Big Coal.

Coal-mining interests have donated more than $12 million to federal candidates since the Bush era began with 88 percent of that money—$10.6 million—going to Republicans.

And what did that largess buy the industry? It produced mine safety regulators who were far more interested in looking out for the financial well-being of mine owners than for the physical well-being of miners.

Exhibit A: Bush's mine safety czar, Richard Stickler, whose agency both approved the controversial mining technique used at the Crandall Canyon Mine before the collapse and oversaw the rescue operation.

Stickler is a former coal company manager with such an abysmal safety record that his nomination as head of the Mine Safety and Health Administration was twice rejected by senators from both parties, forcing Bush to sneak him in the back door with a recess appointment.

In other words, the guy the White House tapped to protect miners is precisely the kind of executive the head of the Mine Safety and Health Administration is supposed to protect miners from.

Industry-friendly regulators like Stickler have been the rule under Bush, not the exception. Bush's first mine safety czar was Dave Lauriski, a former mining executive who had earned a reputation for aggressively defending the interests of mine owners. Lauriski took office promising owners that he would "collaborate more with stakeholders on regulatory initiatives" and become "less confrontational" with mine operators.

Exactly what did he mean by "less confrontational"? And are the workers whose lives are on the line not "stakeholders" in the system? According to the *Washington Monthly*, during his tenure, Lauriski "filled [MSHA's] top jobs with former industry colleagues, dropped more than a dozen safety proposals initiated during the Clinton administration, and cut almost 200 of the agency's 1,200 coal mine inspectors. Mine-safety experts have linked many of these actions to the causes of deadly mine safety accidents since 2001." Among the mine safety regulations Lauriski dropped was one that would have deepened investigations of mining accidents.

And since Lauriski gutted those safety regulations, 170 miners have died in mining accidents.

Lauriski resigned after *60 Minutes* revealed that MSHA had improperly awarded no-bid contracts to coal industry companies to which he was tied.

J. Davitt McAteer, appointed by Bill Clinton to head MSHA, had been a key force behind the 1969 Coal Mine Health and Safety Act, had worked with Ralph Nader on workplace safety reforms, and was running a public interest law firm focused on occupational safety when Clinton chose him. He came to the job with a very different perspective from the one required by Rove's objective of using government agencies as "accoutrements" for the GOP's permanent campaign.

The long list of industry hacks given key slots at federal agencies will forever stand as the ultimate tribute to Rove's effectiveness in turning the federal government into a patronage arm of the Republican Party—and a payback machine for those who fund it.

These cynical appointments, which put the party's interest above the public interest, have left our country less safe, our environment more polluted, our fellow citizens less healthy—and, in the case of the Crandall Canyon Mine, nine of them dead, six entombed in the mine forever.

Karl Rove may be gone, but the destructive legacy of his politicization of the federal government will be with us for many years to come—its tentacles reaching far and wide.

The Federal Communications Commission, for instance, has sided with wireless companies in a class action suit about radiation emissions from cell phone towers that may be linked to cancer hotspots, and the Forest Service has allowed logging on federal lands without environmental reviews. And, as we all know, nothing makes a red-blooded right-winger madder than that bastion of hippie tree-huggers, the Environmental Protection Agency. The administration has eviscerated agency rules on what triggers new source reviews, the process by which plants and factories that replace old equipment are brought into compliance with current regulations.

Not every case of reckless deregulation is due to lax oversight by a government agency. In some cases, privileged industries have been exempted from oversight altogether thanks to artful lobbying. Take the theme park industry. Why would the government back away from tightening up a business that just seems to cry out for close scrutiny? Well, it seems that the theme park operators would prefer not to be regulated, and twenty-seven years ago they convinced the Reagan-era Congress to exempt them from this onerous burden. Robert W. Johnson, president of the Outdoor Amusement Business Association, told *The Washington Post*, "Amusement parks need less taxes, less government oversight. But they need federal support." And they get it to the tune of $200 million. Buckle up, close your eyes, and enjoy the ride.

The Right's background music to this deregulation extravaganza is the beating of drums for tort "reform," which actually means limiting the ability of those harmed by employer negligence to file civil lawsuits. There is, naturally, no shortage of industry groups willing to bankroll the Right's efforts at this "reform."

Why the Right Is Wrong About the Economy

Although inevitably couched in high-minded blather about principles and fairness and markets and responsibility, what the Right has done with the economy is to have turned government from an engine of democracy that creates opportunities for all and acts on behalf of the greater social good into an agent of privilege greasing the wheels of greed. Like a business that strikes the mother lode by exploiting an underserved niche, the Right has mined millions from wealthy people who, instead of simply paying their fair share to maintain a system that allowed their wealth creation, would rather pay a think tank to come up with ways for them to get even richer without having to risk playing in a fair marketplace—and then come up with reasons to feel morally superior about it. In answer to Reagan's famous reductive question, "Are you better off than you were four (or eight) years ago?" the answer for the campaign donor class is, "Hell, yes!"

Those on the Right have been able to contain their outrage over the growth of government and our gargantuan deficit because they really don't care about the growth of government as much as they love their tax cuts. Psychologists say that cognitive dissonance, the belief in conflicting ideas, is resolved through rationalization and, as rationalizations go, the virtue of self-interest—greed is good—is a very powerful one.

We can hope that the housing and subprime mortgage crash, the credit crunch, and the recession might humble the Right a bit, since their policies have been rendered so transparently bankrupt. But as long as they have their own private bubbles to live inside, bursting bubbles elsewhere will have little effect. That's what tax cuts and deregulation do: they widen the gulf that separates the two Americas.

For most people, quality of life isn't about counting money in a private fortress. It's about living in a just and fair society where people share burdens and benefits and are a part of something bigger than themselves. Taxes and government regulation, despite some inevitable inefficiencies, make this possible, and the legacy of government action is visible all around us, if we only choose to see it. Cue the violins, if you like, but countries, like people, can be rich in both material and nonmaterial ways. The gospel of Matthew asks, "For what is a man profited, if he shall gain the whole world, and lose his own soul?" And we may ask the same question about how a nation profits if it loses its soul. And Matthew, as Mike Huckabee will tell you, knew what he was talking about. He was, after all, a tax collector.

13

Sick, Sick, Sick: The Right's Unhealthy Approach to Health Care

Budget Cuts Bleed the Old, the Poor, and the Ill

In his final budget, delivered in February of 2008, George Bush made history, of a sort, by requesting more than $3 trillion from the Congress and the American people for the first time ever. The president's new budget is larded with the usual Bush-era excesses: corporate welfare, pet projects for special interests, and lobbyist-generated windfalls for the politically connected. What's more, this red-ink budget does not include a full funding request for Iraq and Afghanistan, which is bound to exceed the $70 billion that has been allocated.

The $3 trillion budget is an outright acknowledgment that, under the sway of the Right, George Bush will leave office with the American economy in ruins. The president claims that his plans will balance the budget in 2012 but, since his own economic forecasters say that the deficit will continue to grow for at least the next two years, this is hardly likely. Fiscal restraint and smaller government have become nothing more than slogans for the Right, to be used as cheap applause lines, like praising the meatballs at a Knights of Columbus dinner.

Despite its enormity, the 2008 budget includes a number of mind-boggling cuts, primarily in two of the most popular and successful programs of the federal government: Medicare, which pays for health care for older Americans, and Medicaid, which provides health insurance for the poor. Indeed, the only piece of Medicare the president doesn't cut is a windfall for the drug monopolies—the dreaded Part D, which leaves millions of older Americans falling through its now infamous donut hole in drug subsidies. That's right. When our leaders gathered around the big table to decide who was going to take the heat for the falling dollar and ballooning government, they decided to cut funds for teaching hospitals, nursing homes, hospices, ambulances, and home health care, while keeping in the pork for their corporate pals. The budget, for example, did not include any cuts in payments for Medicare Advantage Plans, which are run by large insurers, a group that has always been given a sympathetic ear from this president.

The president's budget axe fell directly on the elderly, the indigent, the ill, and the three million Americans currently receiving Medicaid's home health care. "Under the proposal, 75 percent to 80 percent of home health agencies would be doomed," said William Dombi of the National Association for Home Care and Hospice. "They would not be able to meet payroll. They would not be able to operate."

The biggest Medicare savings were in cuts in the funding of our nation's hospitals. According to *The New York Times*, the cuts included "$15 billion from an across-the-board reduction in the annual updates for inpatient care; $25 billion from special payments to hospitals serving large numbers of poor people; and $20 billion from capital payments for the construction of hospital buildings and the purchase of equipment." An additional $23 billion would be cut from payments to teaching hospitals.

And these cuts were announced at a time when medical costs triggered almost half of all personal bankruptcies.

Emergency in the ER

President Bush, when last I checked, seems to be a pretty healthy guy. At least, physically. He jogs, he doesn't drink, and he is adamant in demanding a solid eight or nine hours of sleep every night. He goes on an extended annual vacation like clockwork every August, taking precautions to ensure that his restorative "me time" is not disturbed by inconsiderate war protesters. He gets an annual checkup and, if he were to choke on another pretzel or tumble off his mountain bike while dodging some pesky reporter, he would instantly be transported to the finest local hospital—or have the hospital's best doctors and equipment transported to him.

The president of the United States has a platinum health insurance plan—as he should. And, even if he didn't, Bush's many business ventures, successful and, strangely enough, unsuccessful, have made him a wealthy man. So even without his government-funded health care plan he could afford to pay cash and buy the best.

And beyond all that, George Bush has always been a lucky guy. Besides his material wealth and the number of people genuinely concerned with his health, Bush speaks English—after a fashion, it's true—and is a U.S. citizen. And he's white and male, two other attributes that still have their advantages when it comes to getting full service from our health care system. Which is all to say: there's no health care crisis inside the White House.

So maybe the president was steered astray by the subjective fallacy when he said something as offensively ignorant as, "I mean, people have access to health care in America. . . . After all, you just go to an emergency room." As if 47 million Americans without basic health care insurance was actually happening in a different country, or perhaps in just a different—and more sound—state of mind.

Sure, the president's dad didn't know what a supermarket scanner was, but has Dubya never heard the kitchen table laments of tens of millions of Americans who know they are one heart attack, or failing kidney, away from total economic ruin? I know the president is consumed by his splendid little war in Iraq, but has he not heard that health care is the number one domestic concern of Americans of both parties?

It's not just that millions are uninsured, it's that even more are underinsured, with big business on a binge of retracting retiree health care promises, leaving the most vulnerable medically stranded.

Yes, Mr. President, it's true that, most of the time, emergency rooms will treat a baby with croup, a man with a broken arm, or an old lady with chest pains—even if they have to wait hours to be seen and be turned back out on the streets as quickly as possible. Ever since the passage of the Emergency Medical Treatment and Active Labor Act in 1986, hospitals have been required to treat all patients who turn up at their emergency rooms, regardless of the patient's ability to pay. The Emergency Treatment Act, sadly, is not a guarantee. Even if you arrive at the emergency room waving your copy of the act with one hand and bleeding profusely from the other, you still may not get immediate care. You still have to get past a triage nurse, who, under orders from hospital administrators to turn away as many nonpaying customers as possible, often makes Nurse Ratched seem like Florence Nightingale. Worse, Presidents Reagan and Bush 41 chose not to enforce the act and, after Clinton briefly tightened up the rules, Bush 43 has again loosened them, though not enough to satisfy the Right.

Mandating emergency room care as a safety net for the poor isn't, of course, the best way to provide medical care for them—though the reasons why are not the ones front and center in the objections of the Right. If your only option is to go to the emergency room, then you'll only get medical care when you have an emergency and not receive the regular checkups, vaccinations, and preventive care that help avoid emergency room visits and, for the seriously ill, extended hospital stays. By turning the emergency room into the neighborhood physician, you also compound the difficulty of providing efficient urgent care because the ER becomes the first point of contact with a health care provider for that many more people.

Our Sick Society

But this isn't just about the poor—89.6 million people were uninsured for at least part of the 2006–2007 period. Seventeen million of these uninsured have been added to the rolls since 2000, according to Families USA, a tireless advocate for health care and a cornucopia of information on the subject. Nearly 80 percent of those without health care are from working families. And, of the balance, 4 percent are looking for work and the remaining 16 percent are unable to work, often for health reasons. In short, most Americans don't have health insurance not because they are irresponsible, reckless, or lazy but because they simply can't afford it.

The message from average citizens is unambiguous: something must be done. Something must change so that America is no longer the lone industrialized nation on earth that doesn't have a universal national health care system.

Though the Right doesn't want to hear it, France, Germany, Great Britain, and two dozen other countries do a better job of keeping their citizens healthy than we do. The facts, as gathered by the World Health Organization, are incontrovertible. We pay more for health care ($6,102 per person) and yet live shorter lives (77.3 years) compared to, say, Britain, which spends $2,508 per person with a life expectancy of 78.5 years.

We could learn from all the other countries that provide some sort of national health insurance—public or private or a hybrid. And we can draw from our own positive history with Medicare and Medicaid. The success of the Right's health care propaganda machine is captured in the apocryphal tale of an agitated senior citizen collaring a politician and begging him not to "let the government get its hands on Medicare."

Ironies abound in politics, partly because of the growing disconnect between campaigning and governing. The two activities have become increasingly incompatible, with candidates making promises they don't keep or denying they did what they did or said what they said at previous points in their careers. A great irony of this political season is that there was a candidate in the race with a laudable record of success on health care that he was forced to disavow as though it were a youthful indiscretion. As governor of Massachusetts, Mitt Romney managed to provide health care for every man, woman, and child in his state (at least on paper) using a public-private partnership that is a model for what is politically achievable in the health care arena. It wasn't perfect, and some people fell through the cracks, but it was an enormous step forward.

But when it came time, as a candidate for president, to pander to the Right, Romney tried to pretend it never happened, using the old "um . . . uh . . . wow, look at that over there!" technique of misdirection.

On no other single policy issue is the Right as far out of step with the vast bulk of the American people. But beyond sharing the loose consensus that no one is completely happy with our current health insurance system and that something needs to be done to change it, the Right has carved out a position that, like a third-rate Vegas comic, has a lot of threadbare premises and few, if any, satisfying punch lines. There's the ritual railing against both taxes like the levy on cigarettes that funds SCHIP—the State Children's Health Insurance Program—and taxes like the "hidden tax" imposed by the Emergency Treatment Act. There's the blind faith in the wisdom and kindness of the market. And there's the fussing and fuming about entitlements and government programs. And there are the ominous warnings about a "government takeover" of our health care system. You can just see the muscle-bound goons and pencil-pushing bean-counters barring the door at your pediatrician's office—or the pediatrician's office you'd go to if you could afford health insurance. Take Romney's most oft-repeated line from the stump opposing "government-run" health care: "You don't want the guys who ran the Katrina clean-up running our health-care system." A heckuva line, if you forget that those people were Republicans!

Behind those rallying the mob with tried-and-true claims about untried-and-untrue "socialist" policies—as Romney called them—are the usual suspects whispering in their ears: powerful special interests with something to lose from reform and the money to buy an audience with the Right's opinion-leaders.

But the business community is by no means united in opposition to health care reform. Many employers have found themselves overwhelmed by the responsibility to provide health care for their workforce. Any company that can get out of insuring its employees is doing just that. As the economy becomes increasingly global, it's harder and harder for American businesses to compete with those of other countries that don't have this bottomless money pit affecting their bottom line. Since Bush 43 came into office, the percentage of insured Americans getting coverage through their employers has declined from 64 percent to 59 percent, and the drop-off appears to be accelerating.

Businesses feeling the strain of providing health benefits for their workers got the equivalent of a B_{12} shot from another formerly independent government agency brought to heel by the Right after being packed with Bush appointees. The Equal Employment Opportunity Commission announced in the middle of Christmas week (a favored release date for information you'd rather no one notices) that employers are now able to discriminate between retirees and younger employees and deny continued health coverage to the former group once they become eligible for Medicare at sixty-five.

The commission acted, in part, because companies threatened that if they couldn't get out of providing health care for their more expensive older employees, they would simply stop paying for it for employees of any age. The result of the decision was that the approximately ten million retirees who rely primarily on health plans provided by their former employers were suddenly added to the Medicare books at taxpayer expense.

In order to institute the new policy, the commission had to expressly exempt businesses from the Age Discrimination in Employment Act of 1967, which an appeals court in Philadelphia has ruled it is entitled to do—a complete reversal of the commission's historic role in fighting discrimination. And if you don't find that development scary, just imagine what might happen if other discrimination statutes were similarly picked apart. Remember, the Right doesn't like any of these rules. They came for the old people this time, but you may be next.

Opposition to national health care from the medical profession has also faded, as doctors who might see their fees decline have found their financial imperatives in greater and greater conflict with their charge as healers to "do no harm." Even the traditionally conservative American Medical Association, tired of watching its members hamstrung in their duty by insurance companies, ratified a proposal aimed at helping low-income individuals afford health insurance.

Two industries have been relentless in their opposition to any changes in the current system and, if you follow the money, it's not hard to figure out why. Insurance companies make a profit on you only if you pay for health care you don't use, so any plan to force them to cover everyone regardless of risk factors would cut into their truly sick margin of profit. And the big pharmaceutical companies would prefer not to have to haggle with the government over drug prices. As of January 2008, the drug industry had injected over $9 million into various federal races this election cycle just to make sure the political class is kept sufficiently sedated. It's worth noting that, as a GOP bloodletting looms, Big Pharma has altered its long-term trend of giving mostly to Republican candidates and is doling out its green-tinged sugar pills almost evenly to candidates of both parties. The amount of campaign cash spooned out by insurance companies and their employees is even larger: over $15 million for the 2008 cycle.

But the antagonism of a few big industries doesn't alone explain why the Right is so rabidly against universal health care. Nor does the Gospel According to Rush, which preaches that life is tough and some people lose. The view that health care is a fundamental right is so well established that no one on the Right dares to seriously argue that the poor don't deserve health care. No, the Right will tell you that the free market and individual savings accounts will take care of everyone. Or it's back to the ER.

The real answer to why the Right objects so strenuously to the notion of universal health care and why they continue to fight it in the face of overwhelming popular support was revealed in a telling

Wall Street Journal opinion piece by neocon big thinker and newly minted *New York Times* columnist William Kristol. It was written in 1994 as the ill-fated Clinton health care plan headed for Capitol Hill. "Passage of the Clinton plan in any form," he wrote, "would be disastrous. It would guarantee an unprecedented federal intrusion into the American economy. Its success would signal the rebirth of centralized welfare-state policy." Kristol wasn't afraid that the Clinton plan would fail. He was afraid that it *would* succeed, and that its success might pave the way for other enlightened government programs. There it is, Kristol-clear: the unadulterated lunacy of the Right exposed for all to see. I mean, where would it end? If health care succeeded, then who knows what the government might successfully fix next: public education, the environment, our crumbling infrastructure? The mind reels.

It was Kristol who mobilized Republicans to fight the Clinton plan and who developed the right-wing dogma that any changes to the system would inevitably lead to the enslavement of American taxpayers by a faceless bureaucratic Health Politburo. Today the hospitals, comrade, tomorrow the classrooms. Enter, stage right, "Harry and Louise" (remember them?), a nice-looking couple who, in a series of ads produced by the insurance lobby, expressed the view that, gosh, they just weren't so sure about this newfangled idea of universal health care, especially if it might somehow limit their "freedom of medical choice." Since Harry and Louise were, in fact, actors and didn't actually exist, nobody got a chance to ask them what the hell they were talking about or to grab them by the shoulders and shake a little sense into them. And, as Hillary Clinton and, more importantly the American people, learned the hard way, television advertising can be a powerful force—sometimes for better (selling us wonderful new products that we desperately need like erectile dysfunction pills and super-caffeinated energy drinks) and sometimes for worse (Harry and Louise).

As it happens, Harry and Louise came back to bite Kristol in 2002 when the same actors returned in ads opposing a ban on human cloning, a cherished cause of the *Weekly Standard* editor, who chaired a group called Stop Human Cloning. (A notion we can get behind if we imagine that there could actually be two Bill Kristols in this world! Though, when you watch Fox News, it seems that we might already be too late.)

Harry and Louise, middle-aged and consumed by vague but very strong fears back in 1993, are entering their golden years now. Like many senior citizens they're probably even more fretful and easily terrified by the Kristol Klones on cable news who, on behalf of the insurance industry, the drug lobby, and the Right's project to discredit effective government, are still wearing their "socialized medicine" Halloween masks.

SCHIP Crumbles

Some small shred of decency must have survived in George Bush because when the time came to veto the reauthorization of the State Children's Health Insurance Program, he made sure that the Oval Office door was locked and that reporters and television cameras were nowhere to be found. So maybe the guy who once promised to leave no child behind and popularized the linkage between "compassionate" and "conservative" felt a little guilty about kiboshing a plan to provide health care assistance for the children of working parents with low to modest incomes.

Started in the Clinton years, the State Children's Health Insurance Program (SCHIP) provides federal money to help states cover uninsured children in the growing number of families of modest means who cannot afford private health insurance but are not poor enough to qualify for Medicaid. The states have flexibility to set their own rules depending on particular local circumstances. The program has proved remarkably effective, providing coverage for millions of children who would otherwise remain unshielded by that invisible and notoriously fickle hand of the marketplace. It's also wildly popular.

Insurance companies hate SCHIP because it siphons potential customers (including a significant percentage of highly lucrative healthy ones) away from the private insurance pool. The Right hates it because it's another effective government program. But since SCHIP protects kids, the Right's argument of first resort, which is that all government spending (except military spending and corporate welfare) undermines a "culture of personal responsibility," doesn't fly. Although children are expected to learn about responsibility as they grow up, denying a three-year-old whooping cough medicine probably isn't going to teach him a valuable lesson. Without this tired refrain at their disposal, the Right went to their standard catalogue of distortions and deceptions to attack a successful program that is a matter of basic human compassion.

Because the proposal Bush vetoed would have expanded SCHIP to cover an additional 4 million poor kids beyond the 6.6 million already covered, the Right Chicken Littled the issue by shouting it was unaffordable and irresponsible budget-busting. Sorry, kids, Senator Stevens needs a bridge to nowhere, so no eye exam for you. The truth was that Senator Stevens could still have his bridge, Cargill could still have its corn subsidies, Richard Mellon Scaife could still have his tax cut, and we could still spend $10 billion a month in Iraq without having any effect on SCHIP expansion, which was entirely funded by an increase in the—cough, cough—cigarette tax. I know, I know, tax increases are something the Right hates even more than providing health insurance to poor kids, but light up a ciggie and think about it for a moment. Cigarette taxes are a proven way to reduce smoking, which causes health problems for millions of Americans (including many nonsmokers) and raises health care costs for all of us. According to Centers for Disease Control statistics, more than 400,000 Americans die prematurely each year due to smoking, meaning that one in five deaths in the United States is smoking-related. Unlike state lotteries—a revenue-generator that encourages addictive, self-destructive behavior—the proposed tobacco tax would have a double health care benefit by funding SCHIP and discouraging smoking.

Besides the phony "it would be nice but we can't afford it" routine, the SCHIP debate provoked another deceptive right-wing refrain: "it's not necessary because they can afford it." Although they seem to love handouts for the rich, the Right are implacably opposed to providing health care assistance for families that earn as much as $83,000 a year. According to the Annenberg Public Policy Center of the University of Pennsylvania, the president's claim that this bill "would result in covering children in families with incomes up to $83,000 per year, isn't true. . . . No state sets its cut-off that high for a family of four and the bill contains no requirement for any such increase. The Bush administration, in fact, just denied a request by New York to set its income cut-off at $82,600 for a family of four."

But even if the limit were $83,000 of gross income, what would that mean? Take away the normal bite of taxes and Social Security and Medicare withholding and would it really signal that we had suc-

cumbed to godless socialism if we did provide some economic relief
for that middle-class family?

The Right also took a swipe at a favorite punching bag, claiming
SCHIP would provide health insurance for illegal aliens when, in
fact, it specifically excludes undocumented immigrants and even legal
immigrants who have been in the country for less than five years. But
what's a few lies if we can save a few bucks on kids' health care, right,
Harry and Louise?

The Right Swift-Boats a Twelve-Year-Old

When twelve-year-old Graeme Frost and his nine-year-old sister,
Gemma, were severely injured in an SUV crash—caused by a patch of
black ice—in 2004, they were taken to a hospital with severe brain
trauma. For an entire week, Graeme languished in a coma and to this
day requires physical therapy. But it turned out that the accident and
the children's difficult recovery weren't the end of the Frosts' misfor-
tunes. Their second round of trouble started when Senator Harry
Reid's office called looking to put a mediagenic human face—or human
voice, at any rate—on the SCHIP issue by having someone who had
relied on the program deliver the Democrats' weekly radio address.

Reid chose the Frosts because they were a perfect example of
how the program works. Halsey Frost, a woodworker, and his wife,
Bonnie, who works for a medical publishing company, raise their
four children on a total income of $45,000 a year. A private health
insurance plan would have cost them over $14,000 per year, more
than the mortgage on their home. Because their home state of Mary-
land permits families earning up to three times the federal poverty
level to participate in SCHIP, the Frosts were enrolled in the program. It was one positive glimmer in an otherwise grim family
tragedy.

Reid's Senate staffers, engaged in a furious battle to renew and
expand the program against the resistance of the Right, wrote the
script for Graeme: "My parents work hard and always make sure my
sister and I have everything we need, but the hospital bills were
huge," the twelve-year-old brain trauma survivor said in his radio
address. "We got the help we needed because we had health insurance for us through the SCHIP program. But there are millions of
kids out there who don't have SCHIP, and they wouldn't get the care
that my sister and I did if they got hurt."

Judging by the instantaneous response of the Right's attack dogs, you'd think Graeme had delivered an address promoting the nationalization of all means of production, distribution, and exchange while burning an American flag printed on a copy of the Declaration of Independence. Graeme and the Frosts were blogged within an inch of their lives by right-wing goons determined to show that they were proof not of SCHIP's value but of its potential for abuse by greedy freeloaders. Although to look at them you'd think the Frosts were every right-winger's dream—a hardworking, white, heterosexual couple running a small business—SCHIP's opponents ginned up an impressive smear campaign that made them out to be hypocritical limousine liberals. Our health care system has been sputtering, but the Right's hate machine hums away, fine-tuned and well lubricated.

Here are the supposedly damning facts: Gemma and Graeme attend private school (shock!); their dad, a self-employed woodworker (hippie!), owns the building he works out of (horror!); and the reason the Frosts' mortgage is so expensive is that the house they live in is valued at half a million dollars (scandal!). And what about that gas-guzzling SUV (hypocrite!) that flipped over? Those things don't come cheap. And why were the kids so badly injured? Weren't they wearing seat belts? By the time the Right had chewed them up, the Frosts were lucky to keep custody of their children and not find themselves deported.

It got so crazy that pictures of the Frosts' house and of Gemma and Graeme's school were posted on the Web, and Halsey and Bonnie Frost's wedding announcement from *The New York Times* (liberal media!) was scrutinized with a fine-tooth comb. Graeme's story was probed with proctological intensity, and Reid and the Democrats wound up on the defensive. The blog *Wake Up, America* posted a spittle-soaked item headlined, "Democrats Use Terrorist Tactics: Hiding Behind Children," that compared congressional leaders to Hezbollah and al Qaeda and declared: "It is well known and documented that terrorists hide behind innocent men, women and children, knowing that when those that they are attacking fight back, those innocents will get hurt, but it doesn't matter to them, because when the innocents get hurt they create a media frenzy of 'look, they attacked innocent people!' "

In all of this, the underlying facts of Graeme's story were never in dispute. What SCHIP did for the Frosts was enable them to weather a catastrophic blow without losing their home or their business—eventualities that, writ large, are not good for communities. The fact that, at various times, the Frosts may have been prosperous enough to start a business, get a mortgage, buy a car, and, who knows, honeymoon in Barbados, does not change the fundamental fact that few Americans can pay the out-of-pocket expenses for the sort of care that Graeme and his sister needed after the accident. Does the Right really want American families to choose between pursuing the American Dream—with things like a business and a mortgage—and paying to save their children's lives? That might sound reductionist, but that's literally what their campaign against the Frosts and SCHIP amounted to. When the government can offer a solution that keeps a family like the Frosts from going bankrupt and costs the taxpayer zilch, can anyone seriously argue that it shouldn't?

America's Top Doc Gets Quarantined

While we all have our favorite government officials (I go back and forth between the deputy acting undersecretary for intergovernmental affairs and the governor of Guam), the surgeon general is probably at or near the top of most people's lists. The unique stature of the surgeon general has enabled recent holders of the office, including C. Everett Koop—he's the one with the rocking, babe-magnet Amish beard—and the avuncular David Satcher to speak out effectively on controversial issues like the AIDS crisis and needle exchange programs. While never entirely free from political pressure—as Joycelyn Elders found out when she made some sensible observations about masturbation, a topic still considered taboo by the Right—the surgeon general, beloved as "America's Family Doctor," has remained largely above the fray.

That is, until George W. Bush became president.

Dr. Richard Carmona, who served four years as surgeon general under the current president, must have seemed like an ideal candidate for the job. Quite literally a good soldier, Carmona had served in the army's Special Forces and been awarded two Purple Hearts in Vietnam. He was not only a trauma surgeon but also a former law enforcement officer, having served as a leader of the Pima County, Arizona, SWAT team.

Despite Carmona's heroic résumé, the Right clearly felt it could push him around. After being squeezed out of office, Carmona was subpoenaed by that tireless watchdog of the people, Henry Waxman. Appearing before Waxman's House Oversight Committee, Carmona said:

> During my first year as Surgeon General, I was still quite politically naive in the ways of the Beltway. As I witnessed partisanship and political manipulation, I was astounded but also unsure of what I was witnessing—for I had no reference point. I asked myself whether this was just happening to me as the new Surgeon General, or whether this was the norm for all Surgeons General. I turned to my fellow Surgeons General, the men and women who came before me and had made tremendous positive contributions to the science and practice of public health, who had saved and improved millions of lives through their work and dedication. They became my mentors. They said that they had all been challenged and had to fight political battles in order to do their job as "the doctor of the nation." But each agreed that never had they seen Washington, D.C., so partisan or a new Surgeon General so politically challenged and marginalized as during my tenure. . . . The problem with this approach is that in public health, as in a democracy, there is nothing worse than ignoring science, or marginalizing the voice of science for reasons driven by changing political winds. The job of Surgeon General is to be "the doctor of the nation"—not "the doctor of a political party."

Here is the astonishing exchange between Representative Waxman and Dr. Carmona during his testimony:

Rep. Waxman: You've testified you were prevented from speaking out on stem cells, abstinence education, and Plan B emergency contraception, is that correct?

Dr. Carmona: That's correct.

Rep. Waxman: You testified you were prohibited from preparing reports on mental health preparedness and emergency preparedness, is that correct?

Dr. Carmona: And global health.

Rep. Waxman: You testified that you couldn't release the report on global health.

Dr. Carmona: Correct.

Rep. Waxman: You testified that your report on the dangers of secondhand smoke was delayed for years while you fought efforts to weaken your science-based findings. Is that correct?

Dr. Carmona: That's correct, and I was not aware of it at the time. I didn't find out about the scientific assault until later on, because the staff was trying to protect me . . . fighting their own battles, if you will, for scientific integrity.

It's a wonder they didn't try to get him to take that warning off the side of cigarette packages while they were at it.

Besides the major public health dust bunnies that the administration tried to sweep under the rug, there was also a comical side to the effort to police the former policeman. Carmona was instructed, based on some mysterious formula, to mention President Bush exactly three times per page in his speeches and was discouraged from any involvement in the Special Olympics because of its connection with a "prominent family."

"I was specifically told by a senior person, 'Why would you want to help those people?' " he testified. Assuming that "those people" referred to the political family and not the disabled athletes, a reporter asked Dr. Carmona if he was referring to the Kennedys, who have a long history of involvement with the Special Olympics. "You said it. I didn't," he replied.

The New York Times, reporting on Carmona's testimony, described an all-too-familiar scenario:

On issue after issue, Dr. Carmona said, the administration made decisions about important public health issues based solely on political considerations, not scientific ones.

"I was told to stay away from those because we've already decided which way we want to go," Dr. Carmona said.

He described attending a meeting of top officials in which the subject of global warming was discussed. The officials concluded that global warming was a liberal cause and dismissed it, he said.

"And I said to myself, I realize why I've been invited. They want me to discuss the science because they obviously don't understand the science," he said. "I was never invited back."

Wading into the waters where Joycelyn Elders had vanished a decade before, Carmona attempted without success to promulgate the scientific consensus that effective sex education includes a discussion of contraception. "However, there was already a policy in place that did not want to hear the science but wanted to preach abstinence only, but I felt that was scientifically incorrect," he said.

When invited to testify in the government's racketeering case against the tobacco industry, Carmona was told not to appear. And, incredibly, the administration, taking no chances, also told the government prosecutor that Carmona, despite his office, was not competent to testify in the matter. Carmona appeared anyway and not only immediately proved his competence but was declared by Sharon Y. Eubanks, director of the Justice Department's tobacco litigation team, as "one of the most powerful witnesses."

Having shown an uncompromising penchant for truth-telling—for which the Right has a zero-tolerance policy—Dr. Carmona was not asked to serve a second four-year term as surgeon general. As his successor, the administration nominated Dr. James Holsinger, the sort of team player the Right could be more certain of. Among his other qualifications, Holsinger is the author of a report that described homosexual sex as "unnatural and unhealthy." A perfect fit for the Right.

The Flat-Earth Anti-Condom Chorus

Amazingly, you can still drum up a rather potent contingent on the Right—even as the global death toll from AIDS soars into the tens of millions—to argue that encouraging sexually active young people to use a condom is a pernicious idea.

The flat-earth anti-condom chorus has been singing fortissimo for quite a while. Back at the beginning of 2002, Secretary of State Colin Powell gave a worldwide audience of MTV viewers this eminently sensible advice: "Condoms are a way to prevent infection. . . . It's the lives of young people that are put at risk by unsafe sex, and, therefore, protect yourself."

General Powell was not ordering his audience to arm themselves with condoms and go out and start humping like bunnies. Indeed, Powell and his wife, Alma, have long been strong supporters of Best Friends, a highly successful youth abstinence program. Rather, he was telling his listeners that if they were going to have sex they should at least be smart and safe about it.

But that didn't stop the throbbing anti-condom cabal from reacting as if Powell had come out in favor of mandatory underage bestiality. Their attacks were as spurious as they were condescending. "Colin Powell is the secretary of state," harrumphed Focus on the Family's James Dobson, "not the secretary of health. He's talking about a subject he doesn't understand."

As if only the secretary of health and human services should be allowed to comment on a subject that every parent in America should be discussing with their teenaged kids. Not that Dobson would have admitted that the health and human services secretary was qualified to comment if he had something to say Dobson disagreed with. As one of the self-appointed sheepdogs of the Right, Dobson's real job is to patrol the ideological perimeter and bark the strays back into the herd.

Rather than come out and admit that he was attacking Powell on moral grounds, Dobson tried to pretend his problem with condoms was purely "scientific," claiming that Powell "clearly doesn't understand the science regarding condom efficacy."

Picking up the science baton—and trying to bash in Powell's head with it—was Kenneth Connor, then president of the Family Research Council, an offshoot of Focus on the Family, also founded by James Dobson. His tactic was twisting a National Institutes of Health finding that condoms are more effective in preventing HIV infection than other STDs, such as chlamydia, into "proof" that condoms don't really work and that the idea of "safe sex" is a myth. A few mosquitoes sometimes get through my window screens, but that doesn't invalidate the idea of window screens altogether—nor of malaria treatments.

Connor's claims were another instance of the Right's war on science. This became clearer when you read the actual report, which found condoms, when used properly, to be effective in preventing the transmission of the virus that causes AIDS almost 100 percent of the time. The problem is that in Africa, where the majority of HIV infections are occurring, only a scant minority of the sexually active population uses condoms.

In the end, the attack on Powell wasn't about "condom efficacy" or which cabinet post qualifies you to comment on premarital sex. It was about trying to roll back the clock to the 1950s—or at least the sitcom version of the 1950s—where Ricky and Lucy slept in separate beds, and where if Ozzie gave Harriet the clap, it was a polite round of applause for the yummy pot roast.

Instead of being excoriated, Powell should have been celebrated for abandoning the double-talk that is the lingua franca of the Right, and confronting the condom issue head-on. With AIDS claiming 2.1 million victims in 2007, and an additional 33 million people currently infected with HIV, Powell's message is one that can't be repeated often enough.

America's Real Drug Problem

Although Medicare is a model for the sort of public health plan that could be extended to cover all Americans, thanks to the Bush administration's reform of so-called Part D, it is forbidden by law from bargaining with drug manufacturers to lower prices and is unable to get the best deal for the millions of senior citizens who use its drug plans. On average, the prices for the most commonly prescribed drugs are 58 percent higher when obtained through Medicare than through the Department of Veterans Affairs, which is allowed to negotiate prices with drug companies. That gaping hole through which millions of Americans now fall thanks to Part D could easily be plugged if Medicare were allowed to bargain. But the free market is worshipped by the Right, it seems, only when it doesn't interfere with the mega-profits of the monopolies that fund it.

It's not terribly surprising that Big Pharma would prefer to be shielded from the enormous buying power of Medicare. The artificially high prices goose their profit margins. In the campaign to preserve their windfall profits, the drug companies have enlisted the Right. And to justify its egregiously laissez-unfaire position, the Right does a little rhetorical yoga. Here's how Ron Pollock of Families USA explains it: "Opponents of Medicare bargaining make two contradictory claims. First, they claim that private market competition under Part D is more effective in reducing prices than Medicare bargaining; and second, they claim that Medicare bargaining would reduce prices so significantly it would harm research and development. These arguments cannot both be true—and, indeed, neither is true."

Actually, the top drug companies spend two to three times as much on marketing as they do on research. At Abbott Laboratories—

the people who dispense Humira, Vicodin, and Depakote—24.6 percent of revenues is spent on marketing while a mere 8.2 percent goes to their eponymous laboratories. Money they could spend on finding the next miracle drug is instead spent hawking cures for once unheard of medical conditions like Restless Leg Syndrome. Commercial breaks of network newscasts are now filled with someone reading side effects of various drugs in a brisk monotone. By the time Charlie or Brian or Katie has signed off, the warning that is stuck in my brain is to contact a physician if you suddenly experience shortness of breath, dizziness, elevated heart rate, fainting, intestinal bleeding, and sudden cardiac arrest.

And it's not as if the government is picking up the slack. In late 2007, Bush used another of his rare vetoes to block a bill that would have allocated $30 billion for the National Institutes of Health, where cutting-edge research is done, and an additional $6.3 billion for the Centers for Disease Control and Prevention.

Medicare Mess: Part D Gets an F

For the last three months of 2005 and the first three months of 2006, the 43 million Medicare recipients, all older or disabled Americans, were invited to sign up for a new prescription drug benefit known as Medicare Part D. Part A covers hospital care and Part B outpatient treatment. Part C is an alternative to Parts A and B that allows private insurers to take over the government's role. Formerly known as Medicare Choice, Part C started the ball rolling toward Medicare Part D, a full-blown attempt by the Right to privatize a highly effective program.

If the government had simply enrolled all Medicare patients in a prescription drug program it would not only have vastly simplified an extremely confusing sign-up process that presents eligible patients with multiple choices in a bewildering array of combinations of deductibles and co-payments, it would also have been able to use its enormous market share to demand lower prices from the drug companies. Which is exactly why the Right did not allow that to happen.

Part D was the Right's prescription for sabotaging a major entitlement program and, while they were at it, giving away billions to drug-makers and insurers. Because Part D invites insurance companies into the transaction as middlemen, it gives them a piece of the action.

To add to the cost and complexity for thinly stretched seniors, patients have their drug costs covered only up to a certain point (currently about $2,400 a year). After that there is a "coverage gap"—known as the "donut hole"—until a new threshold of about $3,850, above which Medicare begins covering some share of the cost again.

Who would come up with such a cumbersome and wasteful arrangement? For the answer, we have to look at Beltway back-alley transactions involving Representative Billy Tauzin, a Republican from Louisiana, who fast-tracked the bill through the House and then almost immediately retired to take a $2-million-a-year job as president of the Pharmaceutical Research and Manufacturers of America; and Tom Scully, the head of Medicare, who muzzled the program's chief actuary during the bill's passage, and then also took a high-paying lobbying job.

The actuary, Richard Foster, had come up with some truly startling cost figures. Although the administration had said over and over that Part D would cost no more than $400 billion (without explaining where that number came from), Foster, who describes his job as providing "technical assistance to the administration and Congress on a nonpartisan basis," calculated a much higher figure of $551 billion (the actual cost seems to be around $534 billion). "The administration seems to have a habit of suppressing information to serve its political purposes," said Congressman Pete Stark at the time. "Tom Scully told my staff that Rick Foster would be 'fired so fast his head would spin' if he released this information to us." Foster came forward to reveal what had happened to him, thus bringing Diogenes' multi-millennial search for an honest man to an end but not, unfortunately, in time to block the passage of the disastrous bill.

Lowering Costs: Hooray for the VA

Notwithstanding the fact that the VA came under scrutiny following the scandal at Walter Reed (which is run by the Defense Department, not the VA), the Department of Veterans Affairs hospital system actually provides good care to the five million patients in its vast network of 163 hospitals, 859 clinics, and 134 nursing homes. In particular, the VA's care-driven rather than cost-driven approach to hospital administration has cut the length of hospital stays while improving outcomes, an extremely rare feat in health care management.

"At a time when the rest of the country has been going to unfettered access to specialists and little actual management of care on the part of health plans or physicians' groups, the VA is going in the opposite direction," says Dr. Elliott Fisher, a professor at Dartmouth Medical School and the co-director of the VA's Outcomes Group.

The VA has also pioneered a system of electronic health care records that is now considered the state of the art and for which it received an award for government innovation from Harvard's Kennedy School. The system reduced both costs and errors and cut waste by eliminating unnecessarily repeated tests and other procedures.

For these reasons (and 292 others), a study by the RAND Institute found that the "VA outperforms all other sectors of American health care across a spectrum of 294 measures of quality in disease prevention and treatment." And for the last seven years the VA has come out ahead of private sector health care in the independent American Customer Satisfaction Index.

Like Medicare and Medicaid, the VA hospital system is proof that government-managed health care is not the chaotic bureaucratic nightmare portrayed by the Right but rather a system that is here already and doing a better job than the private hospitals run for the benefit not of patients but of drug companies and insurers. More reasons, we suppose, that the Bush administration has had to be pressured and cajoled by Democrats and military families to spare the VA the sort of cuts the Right keeps on proposing.

The VA system is perhaps most widely admired not for its innovative record-keeping, its adoption of outpatient care as a preferred option, or the cutting-edge research it conducts in its facilities. For those who are eligible for its services, the VA is beloved for its low-cost prescription drugs, which it is able to provide by using its enormous buying power to demand fair prices from the drug companies, an option specifically forbidden to Medicare.

The difference between the lowest annual VA price and the lowest annual Medicare drug plan price of the top seven drugs prescribed to seniors, according to Families USA, is shown in the following table:

Drug	Amount/Function	Lowest VA Price	Lowest Medicare Price	Difference
Plavix	75 mg, anti-clotting agent	$989.36	$1,323.24	$333.88 (38.6%)
Lipitor	10 mg, cholesterol-lowering agent	$520.49	$785.40	$264.91 (50.9%)
Fosamax	70 mg, osteoporosis treatment	$250.32	$763.56	$513.24 (205%)
Norvasc	5 mg, calcium channel blocker	$315.84	$486.48	$170.64 (54%)
Protonix	40 mg, gastrointestinal agent	$214.52	$1,148.40	$933.88 (435.3%)
Celebrex	200 mg, anti-inflammatory agent	$632.09	$946.44	$314.35 (49.7%)
Zocor	20 mg, cholesterol-lowering agent	$127.44	$1,485.96	$1,358.52 (1,066%)

Considering what we owe our veterans, it's good to know that the VA is doing some things right. And considering how vehemently those on the Right oppose letting our senior citizens get the benefit of the same sort of free market transaction for drugs through Medicare that the VA gets, it makes you wonder if the Right would make the VA pay inflated prices if they could. What's that word that Ann Coulter seems to like so much? Shameless?

The Right's Health Care Elixir: Another Tax Cut

The Right does, however, have a health care plan of its own—and talk about a placebo.

The Right's preferred solution to the health care crisis is one more tax-cutting plan. Health Savings Accounts are available to taxpayers enrolled in a high-deductible health plan. But a third of the uninsured are poor, earning less than $25,000 per year, and another third have very modest incomes, earning less than $50,000, so they simply can't save enough to make Health Savings Accounts a viable option. Faced with the task of choosing between necessities (food, shelter, clothing) and the "luxury" of being insured, they will find it very difficult to save the $2,100 necessary to fund their Health Savings Accounts on an annual basis. For the poorest, that's close to 10 percent of their annual income. And keep in mind that once the deductible is consumed, additional medical costs are only partially paid by the insurers. Cost-sharing could easily reach $10,000 per year for a family requiring simple routine medical care. And, of course, the tax break wouldn't help the poorest, since they pay no federal income taxes.

The enormous but hidden cost of uninsured Americans is that they don't get preventive care and wind up needing much more expensive emergency treatment. Health Savings Accounts would not change this.

Another touted benefit of Health Savings Accounts, according to the Right, is that they encourage consumers to shop for the best health care plan and thereby spur competition among insurers. (This from the same people who bar Medicare from receiving competitive bids on prescription drugs!) It's this kind of bewildering nonsense that sometimes makes you wonder if the Right's think tank commanders are wolfing down a few too many free samples sprinkled around by Big Pharma. For starters, individual consumers just don't have the buying power to negotiate prices with big insurers.

Can you imagine? "Press one to make a payment, two to file a claim, and three to bargain with our accounting and legal departments for a cheaper rate." And as every Heritage Foundation fellow knows, the best time to go on a comparison tour of all the major medical providers is when you're sick or injured. Also, many are uninsured because they have chronic conditions and no one will cover them—at least at an affordable price. In many cases, this is one of the major reasons they're poor, seeing how a large percentage of bankruptcies are caused by medical problems. According to a Harvard study, a chronic health condition or a sudden illness or injury is a major factor in 46.2 percent of personal bankruptcies.

A basic flaw in the market-based solutions of the Right, like Health Savings Accounts, is that they require low-income consumers to behave like Warren Buffett. If they behaved like Warren Buffett, they'd be . . . Warren Buffett instead of having to confront the intimidating hurdles that the uninsured face now—and would continue to face with Health Savings Accounts—in getting their families covered.

But if the shoe were on the other foot, if the Right's constituent base were forced to jump through the same hoops, it wouldn't take long before we got health care reform.

Insurance companies don't want to cover the uninsured for a simple reason: it's not profitable to do so. And attempts to get them to do what is clearly in society's best interests, via contrived mechanisms with dozens of moving parts like Health Savings Accounts, are doomed. The insurers evaluate and manage risk based on reams of data. That's their business. Convincing them to voluntarily make a civic-minded choice that costs them is a fool's errand. Meaningful health care reform will take place over the objections of the insurance companies—and only after we overcome their political will and financial clout.

Why the Right Is Wrong About Health Care

The Right would rather be right about the ineffectiveness of large government programs than be wrong about health care reform that would improve and prolong the lives of millions of Americans. That's why, despite the overwhelming popularity of the idea and despite the fact that covering everyone would generate almost immediate cost savings for the nation, the Right remains adamantly opposed to universal health care. Administrative costs would be reduced through the application of universal standards, and strapped businesses would finally be excused from their crippling dual role as businesses and health care managers. It is nothing less than a disgrace that the United States is unable to do for its citizens what every single other wealthy nation on the planet manages to do.

For the Right, national health care is dangerous because it will almost certainly be a success and will validate the sort of worthwhile expansion of government services that the nea-cons mortally fear. That's not a reason on its own to do it, but it's going to be fun to watch it happen.

The public is telling us that health care reform is an idea whose time has come, which, as Victor Hugo—who knew a little something about the tides of history—pointed out, is quite a powerful thing. The current state of the debate over health care in this country offers real hope for a major defeat for the Right. That's why they will fight it to the last—and why they must be overruled. Paul Krugman, the

Sage of Princeton, wrote about health care's key position in the struggle to show how wrong the Right really is:

> Universal health care could, in short, be to a new New Deal what Social Security was to the original—both a crucially important program in its own right, and a reaffirmation of the principle that we are our brothers' keepers.

14

God, Guns, and
the Right's New Democracy

Democracy for Dummies

In the Right's version of America, currently being beta-tested on unwilling subjects across the country and around the world, fanatical nea-con programmers have been working overtime to iron out all those bothersome bugs and kinks they think have been holding the United States back for the last 230 years—exasperating glitches like openness, integrity, accountability, responsibility, an informed public, and that annoying Constitution.

I have to admit, this new version has been a little hard for me to get used to; it's a lot different from the America I grew up studying—and revering.

For those of you having a similar problem, I've decided to provide this helpful primer to democracy as conceived by the Right: America 2.0.

In the Right's rebooted democracy, the messy concept of the public's right to know has been replaced by the far more user-friendly "don't worry, we know what's right for you." Why clutter up the citizenry's hard drive with all sorts of unimportant facts and information? The government, by contrast, at least when it's being run by the Right, seems to have the right to know everything.

Which is why, just to be on the safe side, the Right's New Democracy (to give it an appropriately Orwellian name) comes with a helpful, one-step fact-check-and-delete program. No need to bother with taping or even transcribing important meetings like the president's three-hour appearance in front of the 9/11 Commission—in the Right's New Democracy, your leaders decide what's pertinent and discard the rest into the unrecoverable trash bin of history.

That's why the White House helpfully confiscated the notebooks of the 9/11 commissioners as they were leaving the Oval Office. Hard copies are so twentieth century. If you do happen to record something you wind up wishing you hadn't, like those CIA interrogations, then it's "quick, into the shredder before someone finds out."

The slogan that would best sum up their attitude toward your right to know would be: Because we said so. How do you know nothing worth knowing was said in this or that testimony? Because we said so. How do you know that there were no private sector attendees in a government policy meeting who shouldn't have been there? Because we said so.

To see how liberating this kind of updated democracy can be, look no further than the reports of the frequent laughter that occurred during the 9/11 Commission's two-birds-with-one-stone questioning of Bush and Cheney. No longer burdened with having to fill the public in on whether our leaders did all they could to prevent 9/11 and the deaths of 2,973 people—and have done all they can to make sure something like it never happens again—the president and his inquisitors were free to trade quips and zingers like a bunch of second bananas at a Friars Roast. It was a true Inside-the-Borscht-Beltway gathering.

"The president got off a couple of good shots," said commission member John "Shecky" Lehman, while Commissioner Jim "Soupy" Thompson labeled the president a "bit of a tease." I'm sure the families of the 2,973 dead would have found it hilarious. We don't know the specifics of anything important that was said, or if anything important was said at all, but, hey, at least they had some fun. But I'm sure nothing was said that we need to know. Why? Because they said so. Or, to borrow from Ronald Reagan for a second slogan: trust, don't verify.

For his part, the president stressed the importance of his testifying in tandem with his beloved veep: "I think it was important for them to see our body language . . . how we work together." Body language experts confirm that subtle shifts in physical positioning—such as Cheney sticking his hand up the president's back and making his mouth move—can often provide significant behavioral clues.

The Right's New Democracy also automatically eliminates a number of pesky problems historically associated with the greatly overrated First Amendment. For example, one convenient feature allowed President Bush and his then Man in Mesopotamia, Paul Bremer, to tout the freedom of speech now permitted in post-Saddam Iraq while simultaneously shutting down Iraqi-run newspapers and radio and television stations. And whereas previous versions of democracy were systemically incompatible with the quashing of dissent, New Democracy makes clamping down on the free flow of information as easy as hitting a hot key and issuing a Pentagon ban on media coverage of flag-draped coffins arriving at Dover Air Force Base.

And when there *is* a public record of what the government's doing? No worry, because state-of-the-art media manipulation software makes it incredibly easy to get away with misstatements, half-truths, and out-and-out lies.

Witness the lack of outrage in the coverage of Paul Wolfowitz's astounding assertion in front of a congressional committee back in 2004, when he was deputy defense secretary, that the U.S. death toll in Iraq was "approximately 500"—when, in fact, at the time of his testimony, the correct number was 722. But what are a couple of hundred dead Americans among friends and chickenhawks? Especially when they're other people's children? And round numbers are so much easier for congressmen and the media to work with.

Or observe the scarcity of critical voices when, on the anniversary of Bush's infamous "Mission Accomplished" photo op, the president boldly declared that, as a result of the removal of Saddam, "there are no longer torture chambers or rape rooms or mass graves in Iraq"—a statement directly contradicted by a top-secret army report completed two months before the president congratulated himself. And by the release of enough vile photographs, including from our own torture chambers in Abu Ghraib, to stock an x-x-x S&M website.

But the true killer app of the Right's New Democracy has to be its ability to retain the outward appearance of unabashed flag-waving patriotism while sacrificing the lives of American soldiers on the altar of tax-cutting fanaticism. Thus, Bush was able to cloak his reelection campaign in red, white, and blue at the same time, according to a defense industry study, that a major budgetary shortfall was leaving U.S. soldiers seriously underequipped—leading to the *preventable deaths* of close to two hundred brave Americans, and the maiming of thousands more. While many of our soldiers have had to make do without body armor, combat helmets, and properly protected vehicles, America's millionaires were receiving an average tax cut of $127,661. Yet Bush was able to win a second term by painting himself as the war president.

The guiding principle behind the Right's New Democracy is a deep mistrust, bordering on contempt, of the American people, which is in inverse proportion to their undying faith in the ability of overprivileged, undertaxed elites to decide what is best for America—and the world. Call me old-fashioned, but I prefer the old 1776 version, where We the People get to make up our own minds.

Executive Power Run Amok

In a revealing piece in *The Boston Globe*, Charlie Savage laid out the results of a questionnaire the *Globe* sent to the presidential candidates on the limits of executive power, asking their opinions on the Bush administration's all-encompassing view of presidential authority. It's hard to think of another issue in which the importance-to-the-public/attention-paid-by-the-media ratio is as out of whack.

As Savage—who won a Pulitzer for his coverage of Bush's abuse of signing statements, and wrote *Takeover: The Return of the Imperial Presidency and the Subversion of American Democracy*—put it: "Bush has bypassed laws and treaties that he said infringed on his wartime powers, expanded his right to keep information secret from Congress and the courts, centralized greater control over the government in the White House, imprisoned U.S. citizens without charges, and used signing statements to challenge more laws than all predecessors combined."

He has wielded executive power in a manner that has greatly increased the ability of the executive branch to do damage. And the problem is, even well-intentioned executives don't like to give up power. So Bush has opened Pandora's box. It's easy to imagine the next president saying: Sure, Bush used his increased prerogatives irresponsibly but, trust me, I'll use them to do good.

The Constitution is a monument of wisdom about the intoxicating qualities of unfettered power. The Founding Fathers' greatest fear was tyranny. Sure, Mr. President, maybe you are a good person, and maybe you do have our best interests at heart, but don't take it personally if we double-check you with a few laws.

That is not a popular reading of the Constitution on the Right.

Which is why the next president's approach to executive power is so crucial if we are to put the brakes on the Right's takeover. "Legal specialists," writes Savage, "say decisions by the next president—either to keep using the expanded powers Bush and Cheney developed, or to abandon their legal and political precedents—will help determine whether a stronger presidency becomes permanent."

The *Globe* questionnaire was sent to all the presidential candidates. Even though it no longer matters what most of them replied, Mitt Romney's answers are emblematic of the Right's philosophy on executive power, which was summed up in his assertion that "our most basic civil liberty is the right to be kept alive"—the excuse for undermining civil liberties through the centuries. Turns out Mitt's not so hot on that whole "Give me liberty or give me death" thing.

Then there was his response to a question about whether the president can use an interrogation technique that Congress has "prohibited under all circumstances."

Romney's answer: "A President should decline to reveal the method and duration of interrogation techniques to be used against high value terrorists who are likely to have counter-interrogation training. This discretion should extend to declining to provide an opinion as to whether Congress may validly limit his power as to the use of a particular technique." Glenn Greenwald, writing in *Salon*, called Romney's stance "an astonishing assertion—that the terrorists will win if Mitt Romney expresses his views on whether the President must obey the law."

And in answer to a question about the president's power to detain U.S. citizens without charges, Romney allowed, "All U.S. citizens are entitled to due process, including at least some type of habeas corpus."

I actually didn't know there were different types.

Justice on Earth and in Heaven

In December 2005, New York's mayor, Michael Bloomberg, was on TV discussing the New York City transit strike. "We live in a country of laws," he said, "where there can be severe consequences for those who break them." But during George Bush's two terms we saw a two-tiered approach to American justice: mass transit workers live in a country of laws, but many on the Right reside in high-end suburbs with very different zoning.

In the spring of 2007, multiple scandals and cover-ups started unraveling.

Scooter Libby was found guilty of perjury and of obstructing justice in order to encumber the Plame investigation—and keep secret the White House's efforts to intimidate its critics.

In the same week that the Libby jury returned its guilty verdict, Capitol Hill was the scene of sickening testimony about the way we'd been treating our wounded troops at Walter Reed Army Medical Center, and continuing congressional hearings investigating the firing of eight U.S. Attorneys for being too zealous in their prosecution of GOP corruption or too sluggish in their prosecution of Democrats.

Unraveling the cover-ups revealed that the evidence trail on the firings went all the way to the White House. In an interview with McClatchy Newspapers, Alan Weh, chairman of the New Mexico Republican Party, admitted that, in 2005, he asked a White House staffer who worked for Karl Rove for help in getting rid of New Mexico U.S. Attorney David Iglesias. Weh, unhappy that Iglesias refused to rush a showy investigation of Democratic officials in time for the 2006 election, followed up directly with Rove in 2006.

According to Weh, his conversation with the Boy Genius went like this:

Weh: Is anything ever going to happen to that guy [Iglesias]?

Rove: He's gone.

You can almost picture Rove letting out a satisfied laugh and pressing a button on his desk, à la Dr. Evil, causing a trapdoor thousands of miles away to open under Iglesias's chair. "He's gone."

It's just one more example of how the Right treats every part of the executive branch: instead of protecting the environment, the Environmental Protection Agency is used to weaken it; the State Department campaigns against diplomacy; the Food and Drug Administration undermines food safety. And then came the injustice at Justice. It's Borat politics: everything has a "not" appended to it. The Environmental Protection Agency . . . Not! The Justice Department . . . Not!

It's an outrage that eight U.S. Attorneys were fired because of their unwillingness to go along with the abuse of the judicial system being imposed from the top. But the real scandal could be found in those who did go along with the abuse. According to a study reported by TPMmuckracker.com, 79 percent of elected officials and candidates under federal investigation between 2001 and 2006 were Democrats, and only 18 percent were Republicans. Hard to believe that's just a coincidence.

There was an illuminating moment on *Meet the Press*. Considering how Tim Russert avoids illuminating moments as a general rule, it might even have been a moment of divine intervention. Russert was interviewing David Iglesias, the guy Rove sent through the trapdoor, and asked him about a Bible verse, Proverbs 19:25, that he had referred to at the end of one of his recently released e-mails:

> **Russert:** Proverbs 19:25, it caught my attention and I went to the Good Book and looked it up. "Smite a scorner, and the simple will beware: and reprove one that hath understanding, and he will understand knowledge." Explain why you cited that Proverbs.
>
> **Iglesias:** It's interesting that you would pick that up. Actually, that's a typo. I meant to say Proverbs 19:21, which is "Many are the plans in a man's heart, but it's the Lord's purpose that prevails." In other words, all this mess may seem chaotic and without reason, but ultimately there's a bigger plan, there's a providential plan. So I meant to put Proverbs 19:21, not Proverbs 19:25.

I say both passages are relevant. The Lord may have an ultimate purpose that involves the meting out of justice, but that doesn't absolve us from doing what we can here on earth with the tools we've been given.

Like the ability to smite a scorner.

The U.S. Attorneys' story revealed how extensively the Bush rot had spread throughout the Republican Party.

Iglesias testified that New Mexico Senator Pete Domenici had "leaned on" him, pressuring him over the phone to move forward on the investigation of a state Democrat before the November election. When Iglesias told the senator that the cases wouldn't be filed before November, Domenici said, "I am very sorry to hear that," and hung up on Iglesias, who testified that he was physically sickened by the exchange.

Republican Representative Heather Wilson, her eyes set on inheriting Domenici's Senate seat, made a similar coercive call to Iglesias, one that raised more ethics red flags in his mind.

Another of the fired prosecutors, John McKay of Seattle, testified that the chief of staff to GOP Representative Doc Hastings had called, fishing for information on McKay's investigation of possible election fraud in Washington state's highly contentious 2004 governor's race. McKay was uneasy about the call and ended it as quickly as he could. He said that White House counsel Harriet Miers later suggested he had "mishandled" the voter fraud inquiry.

It's worth noting that Hastings was the ranking Republican on the House Ethics Committee. And that four of the fired prosecutors were looking into corruption charges against Republicans when they were handed their pink slips. And let's not forget that Bush felt Harriet Miers—and her heart, which he knew so well—belonged on the Supreme Court.

Trying to control the bleeding, Justice Department spokesman Brian Roehrkasse dismissed the dismissed prosecutors as "disgruntled employees grandstanding before Congress."

Apparently Roehrkasse hadn't read the news reports that the fired U.S. Attorneys had refused to voluntarily appear before Congress, and only did so after being subpoenaed by the House Judiciary subcommittee.

Bush's and Cheney's mendacity and fondness for bullying tactics—put on repellent display in the Libby trial and then in the vicious campaign against the uncooperative attorneys—hadn't just contaminated the White House staff. The disease had infected the entire Republican Party.

The USA PATRIOT Act

"Uniting and Strengthening America by Providing Appropriate Tools Required to Intercept and Obstruct Terrorism"—USA PATRIOT, quite the unforced acronym. The act, which erodes essential civil liberties and rights that Americans have fought and died for, expands the capacity of government to do pretty much whatever it feels like as long as it can link its actions, no matter how tenuously, to the fight against terrorism. It allows searches, seizures of people and evidence, wiretaps, and e-mail taps without probable cause. Through a revision of grand jury rules, it erodes the wall that bars the CIA from domestic spying. It allows the FBI unimpeded access to financial and medical records and to information from public libraries about suspicious book borrowing. And it clarifies the status of noncitizens detained on national security matters: they have no status. With the Senate quivering in fear, the USA PATRIOT Act passed almost unanimously. Only Russ Feingold voted against it.

Since passing, the act has come under repeated fire, but the administration has always held firm. During the 2004 campaign, President Bush famously defended the PATRIOT Act by telling voters, "By the way, any time you hear the United States government talking about wiretap, it requires—a wiretap requires a court order . . . When we're talking about chasing down terrorists, we're talking about getting a court order before we do." This was some two years after he had authorized wiretaps without a court order. In that same speech he also assured the crowd, "We value the Constitution." Perhaps the biggest lie of all the many he has told during his time in office.

A Terror Top Ten List

Looking to bring back the Fear Factor that worked so well in the 2004 campaign, in October 2005 the president boldly declared that the United States and its partners had "disrupted at least ten serious al Qaeda plots since September 11—including three al Qaeda plots to attack inside the United States. We have stopped at least five more al Qaeda efforts to case targets in the United States or infiltrate operatives into our country." Holy Moly—that sounds impressive . . . and effective . . . and scary. That's enough counterterrorism to fill at least three seasons of *24*.

That is, until the details of these "serious" plots the president was referring to started to dribble out. Just hours after the speech, the White House released a helpful worksheet . . . and the experts started scratching their heads.

For instance, one of the three U.S.-targeted plots cited by the president involved plans to use hijacked airplanes to attack targets on the West Coast in 2002—plans hatched by 9/11 mastermind Khalid Sheikh Mohammed. This was part of the so-called second wave of suicide attacks disclosed by the 9/11 Commission, attacks that never materialized because Mohammed became "too busy" to see them through. The 9/11 Commission reported that the hijacking plot never got beyond the theoretical stages. Which raises the philosophical question: If a plot never moves beyond the spitballing stage, is it possible to foil it? And does a terrorist abandoning his plans because he has too much on his plate planning other successful attacks qualify as the CIA having "disrupted" him?

The *Los Angeles Times* quoted a federal counterterrorism official as saying of the hijacking plots: "I don't think we ever resolved these . . . [they] were on the boards, but they never got anywhere." Yet the White House listed them as the top two "serious" plots that had been thwarted. And it went downhill from there.

Serious plot number three cited by the White House was the case of reputed "dirty bomber" Jose Padilla. But the senior federal law enforcement officials interviewed by the *Los Angeles Times* said "they hadn't found any evidence . . . that the plot had developed into any kind of operational plan." As for the remaining "serious plots," here is *The New York Times*'s assessment: "It was not immediately clear whether other items on the list represented significant threats."

In other words, it was a Top Ten list you'd expect to hear from David Letterman, not the president.

Well, what about those five instances of "casings and infiltrations"? Unfortunately, these were even less detailed than the ten plots, including one "in which an unnamed person was said to be given the task of collecting information on unspecified tourist targets." We are, of course, glad those ten plots were stopped. But they are hardly compelling evidence to support the case to stay the course in Iraq.

When asked why the White House would include so many alleged, vague, and seemingly half-baked schemes in a list of thwarted major terrorist plots, yet another federal counterterrorism official said: "Everyone is allowed to count in their own way." I guess that's how they can sleep at night, counting in their own way how many lives and dollars the war is costing.

Fear as an Applause Line

True to form, when President Bush spoke in February 2008 to the annual jamboree of political conservatives, he offered up another round of Fear Factor. He told a wildly cheering crowd of two thousand at the Conservative Political Action Conference in Washington that it was crucial they elect a Republican to the White House in November because "prosperity and peace are in the balance"—the clear implication being that Democrats were so weak they would drive us into recession and lead us into war. Thank God we avoided that. No one at the convention, of course, bothered to raise a hand and say, "Excuse me, Mr. President, but under your administration we currently have neither peace nor prosperity. We have two flagging wars in Iraq and Afghanistan and this week the stock market experienced its biggest drop in five years as we head into recession. What the hell are you talking about?"

But that would have meant the Right dealing with actual facts instead of projected fears. And then it would not have been a political conference of the Right.

When it comes to naked, cynical manipulation of fear, however, the Joe McCarthy Memorial Tail Gunner Award goes to Mitt Romney. When Romney spoke before that same CPAC event and announced his withdrawal from the '08 presidential race, the spirit of old Joe must have been nearby. He uncorked a vintage serving of good old red-meat red-baiting, only this time, as if in a perverse game of Mad Libs, swapping "Jihadist" for "Communist." Take a whiff of this:

> If I fight on all the way to the convention, I forestall the launch of a national campaign and, frankly, I would be making it easier for Senator Clinton or Obama to win. Frankly, in this time of war, I simply cannot let my campaign be a part of aiding a surrender to terror. . . . Today we are a nation at war. And Barack and Hillary have made their intentions clear regarding Iraq and the war on terror: They would retreat, declare defeat. And the consequences of that would be devastating. It would mean attacks on America, launched from safe havens that would make Afghanistan under the Taliban look like child's play. About this, I have no doubt.

The only McCarthyite flourish missing from Mitt's exit performance was his reaching into the breast pocket of his finely cut jacket and pulling out a secret list of the one hundred sites he had "no doubt" would be attacked if the Defeatocrats were elected.

Gun Crazy

A few days before the Iowa caucuses in 2008, Mike Huckabee was all over our TVs in a bright orange parka holding a twelve-gauge shotgun, pheasant-hunting—and hunting for votes by parading his gun-loving credentials.

Have you ever found yourself wondering what our country's obsession with guns is all about? Indeed have you ever found yourself watching the news and wondering what kind of country makes it so easy for a madman to arm himself with weapons that allow him to blithely mow down his human prey from up to five hundred yards away? The answer is found in the TiVo-worthy solution disgraced former House majority leader Tom DeLay offered to Charlie Rose a few days after the Virginia Tech massacre, in which thirty-two people were gunned down by a mentally ill student armed with a Glock 19 and a Walther P22 loaded with hollow point ammunition. DeLay's answer to avoiding future campus carnage was one I've heard echoed by other pistol-packing members of the Right: allow students to bring concealed weapons to class with them. Yes, the answer to gun violence is . . . more guns!

For DeLay and his fellow gun-lovers, the Second Amendment guarantees not only a well-regulated militia, but a well-armed student body. It brings a whole new dimension to school supplies. Ruler? Protractor? Glock 19 with ankle holster? Target practice will be a freshman prerequisite. It's Mutual Assured Destruction Goes to College. *Animal House* meets *Death Wish*. Shoot-out at the O.K. Dorm.

Do we really want our institutions of higher learning to become ivy-covered versions of the Wild West? Didn't DeLay and company ever watch *Deadwood*?

DeLay's ideas were not new. Less than two weeks after the Columbine tragedy, the National Rifle Association held its annual meeting in Denver. One year later, standing in front of a cheering crowd, the NRA's leading man, Charlton Heston, raised a vintage rifle over his head and bellowed that he would only give it up if it were pried away: "From my cold, dead hands!"

That's the mind-set of the Right: any evidence contradicting their position simply reinforces it. After the sniper shootings in the Washington, D.C., area in October 2002 inspired a push to create a national database of ballistic "fingerprints," the NRA adopted a scattershot, drive-by-shooting approach to mowing down the idea, despite powerful evidence that such a system would be a boon to law

Tom DeLay Has the Answer to Gun Violence: More Guns

The bizarro-world exchange between Charlie Rose and Tom DeLay:

Rose (holding up a newspaper photo of Cho Seung-Hui): The picture on the other side is the gunman at Virginia Tech. This is an old debate, and we don't have time to talk about it, but does it make you rethink guns? What he did was all legal. He went in and got a handgun, bought a handgun, was checked, had no criminal record. Went back a month later, got another gun. Do we need to do something about this?

DeLay: Yeah. We need to remove the ban of guns on the Virginia Tech campus, and allow people to defend themselves, and allow people to get concealed carry licenses. Maybe if there was one person in there that had a concealed carry license, was carrying a gun, he wouldn't have killed as many people.

Rose: So if there was a student in the classroom or a professor in the classroom that had a gun, they could have defended those students?

DeLay: That's right.

Rose: Do you think that's the answer?

DeLay: That is the answer.

Rose: More guns?

DeLay: It's been proven over and over again.

Rose: More guns in the hands of students in this case, or in the professors', is the answer to—

DeLay: It has been proven as such. The criminal doesn't know that you have a gun.

enforcement. The technology isn't foolproof, the organization's mouthpieces obediently repeated. Ballistic fingerprints can be tampered with. Guns get stolen. What about the 200 million guns already in circulation? And the always popular: "Guns don't kill people, people kill people."

Then White House spokesman Ari Fleischer parroted this bumper sticker cop-out when he helpfully explained why the president didn't support a federal ballistic fingerprinting database: "In the case of the sniper," he said, "the real issue is values." Yeah, like the value of being able to pick off unsuspecting victims at long range with a military-style weapon versus the value of sending your kids to school without having to worry about whether they'll come home.

You would have thought that the war on terror and fear of another domestic attack might have convinced Bush and those on the Right who pay so much lip-service to security to rethink their position on the availability of certain kinds of weapons. Yet in September 2004 they allowed the federal ban on assault weapons to expire, making the job of al Qaeda sleeper cells, domestic terrorists, school shooters, David Koresh wannabes, and bloodthirsty lunatics everywhere a whole lot easier.

Since then it has been perfectly legal to buy, sell, and own a new line of domestically produced rapid-fire killing machines. Combat-ready weapons like the AK-47, the Uzi, and the TEC-9 assault pistol—weaponry designed to kill large numbers of people as efficiently as possible—are flooding the American market. And thanks to the gaping loopholes in our gun laws, everyone from unhappy teens to Osama bin Laden's henchmen can legally obtain this kind of ferocious firepower at gun shows without even having to undergo a background check. It's an invitation to cash-and-carry mayhem.

After the U.S. Army toppled the Taliban in Afghanistan, our soldiers found an al Qaeda training manual that included an entire section lauding the ease with which prospective terrorists in the United States could legally stock up on assault weapons, "preferably an AK-47 or variations."

Bowing to the demented demands of the no-gun-law-is-a-good-gun-law crowd at the National Rifle Association, Republican congressional leaders shot down the assault weapons ban. And the president refused to put any pressure on Congress to extend it. This despite the fact that, during the 2000 campaign, he said, "It makes no sense for assault weapons to be around our society," and despite White House spokesman Scott McClellan's protestations that the president "supports reauthorization of the current law."

Given his much touted commitment to keeping us safe, you'd think the renewal of the assault weapons ban would be a high priority for the president. Polls showed that over 70 percent of Americans supported keeping the ban on the books, as did every major police organization in the country. Even 64 percent of gun owners supported the ban because they realized that outlawing weapons that feature flash suppressors, silencers, folding stocks, bayonet mounts, and large-capacity ammo magazines is not an attack on the Second Amendment—it's self-preservation.

Instead of using his bully pulpit to push for the ban's renewal, Bush feigned support for the measure while effectively ensuring its demise. The reason was as simple as it was craven: it was all about placating the NRA branch of the Right. By playing politics with our safety, the president showed where he really stands on his signature issue of national security.

While law-abiding citizens have their toenail clippers confiscated at airport safety checks before being allowed to board, the Right has made it even easier for the real bad guys to arm themselves with weapons of massive destruction.

The Good Lord thought "Thou shalt not kill" was important enough to qualify for his Ten Commandments. If he'd had a little more room on those tablets, he might have added: ". . . and, while you're at it, thou shalt not grant immunity to those who help arm killers."

Yet that is exactly what the Right, which has so aggressively claimed the biblical high ground, did by backing a deeply immoral bill shielding reckless gun dealers and gun makers from lawsuits, and denying the victims of gun crimes their day in court and recompense for their injuries.

Here's a nasty little stat: Just 1 percent of gun dealers supply 57 percent of the guns used in crimes. These are dealers like Washington's Bull's Eye Shooter Supply, which sold the assault rifle the D.C. snipers used to gun down their victims—as well as guns traced to fifty-two other crimes including homicides and kidnappings.

Under the guise of protecting our civil liberties, the Right has been doing the bidding of the gun lobby while sabotaging homeland security.

Witness the astonishing refusal of John Ashcroft when he was attorney general to allow FBI agents to scan the National Instant Criminal Background Check System to see if suspected terrorists had recently bought a firearm. How's that for perverse priorities? The

Right has absolutely no problem with the government snooping around in the private medical records of law-abiding women, but a G-man wanting to make sure suspected terrorists have not gotten their hands on a gun was somehow seen as waging an unconstitutional assault on the Second Amendment.

I guess the Right skipped reading that al Qaeda training manual. Osama and his murderous charges must have been brushing up on their Lenin: not only will capitalists sell you the rope with which to hang them, they will also set up a nice gun show to sell you the Uzis and TEC-9s with which to mow them down.

Putting the Good Book to Bad Use

The Right took their Bible-thumping ways to a whole new level in 2004 by using the Good Book to try to bash in the skulls of their opponents. Less than two months before election day, the Republican Party sent out an incendiary mass mailing warning that, if elected, "liberals" will try to—I kid you not—ban the Bible. The full-color flyer featured a picture of the Bible with the word "Banned" stamped across it, and a photo of a man, on bended knee, placing a wedding band on the hand of another man, accompanied by the word "Allowed."

This "God is on our side" attack was all the more outrageous because it was not coming from some shadowy 527 committee that the GOP could publicly—albeit disingenuously—distance itself from, but, rather, from the Republican National Committee. The president's team had undoubtedly "approved this message."

They also used the official Georgewbush.com campaign website to attack John Kerry, a Roman Catholic, as being "Wrong for Catholics," while an RNC website, KerryWrongForCatholics.com, slammed him for not being loyal enough to the pope. We've certainly come a long way since JFK had to assure voters in 1960 that he wouldn't take orders from the Vatican.

The idea that Democrats are anti-Bible and that Republicans have a hotline to The Man Upstairs is both offensive and patently absurd. And, contrary to their claims, the Right does not hold a copyright on the Bible and has grotesquely perverted its core teachings. (For proof, take a look at statistics showing the rise in the number of Americans living in poverty during the Bush presidency.)

As Reverend Jim Wallis, the founder of Sojourners, told me: "It's a bitter irony: these people accuse Democrats of wanting to ban the Bible, then proceed to utterly ignore the vast majority of its contents when it comes to questions of social justice, war and peace, and protecting the environment." Indeed, if you removed every reference to helping the poor in the New Testament, the Good Book would be reduced to little more than a Not Bad Pamphlet. "The Prophets would be decimated," Wallis said, "the Psalms destroyed, and the Gospels ripped to shreds."

Perhaps the holy rollers on the Right should crack open a Bible and see what it has to say about caring for the poor ("Whatever you did for one of the least of these brothers of mine, you did for me."—Matthew 25:40), caring for the earth ("The Lord God took the man and put him in the Garden of Eden to work it and take care of it."—Genesis 2:15), and caring for human rights ("So God created man in his own image, in the image of God he created him."—Genesis 1:27). I've got a hunch Jesus wouldn't be too thrilled with what the Right has been doing in His name.

And while it's acquainting itself with the book it purports to defend, the Right might also have a look at John 8:32 ("Then you will know the truth, and the truth will set you free") to see what it has to say about the moral imperative of telling the truth. Telling voters that a vote for Democrats is a vote for Osama bin Laden is *not* telling the truth.

But for the Right, the truth, like religion itself, is nothing but a tool to achieve power. And if you doubt that, recall the Republican establishment's state of near-apoplexy about Mike Huckabee's short campaign surge at the start of 2008. They should have been happy. After all, they'd been cultivating evangelicals and fundamentalists for thirty years. Now they finally had a candidate who was truly part of the movement, whose religious beliefs are virtually identical to those of George Bush—he's anti-choice, born-again, against gay marriage, and gets political advice directly from God. He's perfect!

Actually, that is the problem. The evangelical crowd was fine when it was just a resource to be cynically exploited every few years in demagogic anti-gay get-out-the-vote campaigns. But when the monster the GOP has created threw off the shackles, fled the lab, and scored a shocking win in Iowa, the party didn't know what to do. Huckabee taught the Right a modern political lesson: it's not enough to "be careful what you wish for." You have to "be careful what you say you wish for" too.

It was actually fun to watch them squirm. *The Atlantic*'s Ross Douthat dubbed this feeling "Huckenfreude," which he defined as "pleasure derived from the outrage of prominent conservative pundits over the rising poll numbers of Mike Huckabee."

And there was certainly no shortage of outrage among hyperventilating conservative columnists across the country. *National Review*'s Rich Lowry coined a neologism of his own: "Huckacide." This is when a national party commits suicide by nominating an "under-vetted former governor who is manifestly unprepared to be president of the United States."

That would certainly be crazy, wouldn't it? Makes you wonder where these people were for the last seven years.

Over at *The Washington Post*, Charles Krauthammer was wringing his hands about an "overdose of public piety," "scriptural literalism," and how the 2008 campaign is "knee-deep in religion."

At *The Weekly Standard*, Stephen Hayes worried about the fact that Huckabee "told a producer for Pat Robertson's Christian Broadcasting Network that his religious background made him most qualified to lead the war on terror," and that he "seems to believe the best foreign policy is one guided by the Golden Rule." Scoffing at the Golden Rule? What's next, attacking the Boy Scout Oath? The *Standard*'s headline writers couldn't resist, dubbing his perceived foreign policy shortcomings "The Perils of Huckaplomacy."

At *The Wall Street Journal*, Peggy Noonan fretted that the Republican Party of today wouldn't like Ronald Reagan much now that "faith has been heightened as a determining factor in how to vote," and warned that voters in Iowa and elsewhere were "deciding if Republicans are becoming a different kind of party."

If? *If?*

Turns out that when you define your party in a certain way for two or three decades, people actually start to believe it, and that definition can, in fact, become your party.

According to Andrew Sullivan, "It is certainly too late for fellow-traveling Christianists like Lowry and Krauthammer to start whining *now*. This is their party. And they asked for every last bit of it."

The Republican establishment tied itself in knots trying to land on a publicly acceptable rationale for their Huckabhorrence (I told you, it's irresistible). Some criticized his "fair tax" plan—but since when have nutty economic plans ever disqualified a Republican presidential candidate? (Huckabee's sales-tax-only plan, like his deeply felt religious views, is simply the full extension of what the Republicans have been saying for years that they believe. Eliminating the IRS in favor of a national sales tax is about as regressive a tax policy as can be, since a poor person has to pay the same percentage of tax on a quart of milk as a rich person does on a Rolls-Royce.)

No, the real reason for the Establishment's rejection of Huckabee was, as *Washington Monthly* blogger Kevin Drum put it, that "mainstream conservatives are mostly urban sophisticates with a libertarian bent, not rural evangelicals with a social conservative bent. They're happy to talk up NASCAR and pickup trucks in public, but in real life they mostly couldn't care less about either. Ditto for opposing abortion and the odd bit of gay bashing via proxy. But when it comes to Ten Commandments monuments and end times eschatology, they shiver inside just like any mainstream liberal."

Bingo.

Steve Benen wrote on *Talking Points Memo*, "The Republican Party's religious right base is supposed to be seen, not heard. Candidates are supposed to pander to this crowd, not actually come from this crowd."

The Right wants their base to be a kind of electoral cicada: wake up every four years, vote, and then go underground and shut up.

One other hazard for the Huckabee-haters was that right-wing social positions aren't the only thing they've been nurturing for thirty years—there's also that aggrieved, martyred hatred of "the elites." Of course, in the past it was completely manufactured. The Right's elite is as insular and clubby as any. But this time, there really was a group looking down its nose at the evangelicals—and it wasn't the godless liberals. It was the supporters of Romney, McCain, Thompson, and Giuliani.

Republicans have been running on a faux populist/religiously conservative platform ever since Richard Nixon. It was refined and heightened by Bush 41's Lee Atwater and again by Bush 43's Karl Rove. And when they got a rising candidate who truly represented that platform, the party's movers and shakers did all they could to kneecap him.

But, as the Good Book says: "Whatsoever a man soweth, that shall he also reap."

The Right's Perverted Priorities

I don't know whether it has something to do with their toilet training or an awkward conversation they had with their parents about the facts of life, but it seems to me that commentators on the Right are always more upset by blatantly sexual language than by the blatantly fraudulent language we're constantly fed by our leaders. Make a joke about blow jobs and the public finger-waggers come pouring out of the woodwork, complaining about the coarsening of our culture. But let President Bush say that Brownie is doing "a heck of a job" or Dick Cheney say that the insurgency is in its "last throes" and the morality cops on the Right don't raise an eyebrow. Yet those kinds of lies are the real obscenity.

Don't forget, it took less than two weeks after the unveiling of Janet Jackson's right boob at the 2004 Super Bowl before the president's congressional cronies were holding hearings on the matter—but it took fourteen months before Bush bowed to public pressure and allowed the 9/11 Commission to be formed. Again, you pick the real obscenity.

Another particularly glaring example of misplaced priorities was the administration's reenergized War on Porn, which included the formation of an FBI squad exclusively devoted to cracking down on sexually explicit material involving consenting adults.

That's right, with the war on terror in full swing, our commander in chief commanded a group of FBI agents to do nothing but work the porn beat when they could have been tracking down—oh, I don't know—terrorist sleeper cells. Good to know he's got his eye on the prize.

I don't know about you, but I certainly feel safer knowing the feds are devoting resources to keeping close tabs on Jenna Jameson and Peter North. Let's just hope the next round of al Qaeda terrorists looking to attack the United States are particularly interested in sex shops and porn shows because that increases the chances they'll come to the FBI's attention.

This blast from our bluenosed past was labeled "one of the top priorities" of former Attorney General Alberto Gonzales. Along with the FBI's anti-porn squad, Gonzo also created an Obscenity Prosecution Task Force in the Justice Department that pulled away prosecutors working on organized crime and racketeering, money-laundering, and computer crime cases and had them focus on the War on Porn.

Of course, getting obscenity convictions in today's climate—where Jameson's *How to Make Love like a Porn Star* was a *New York Times* best-seller and all the big hotel chains make a mint off sexually explicit movies—won't be as easy as it was in Ed Meese's day.

The indecency of spending precious resources on making it harder to watch the plethora of video celeb sexcapades was not lost on federal and local law enforcement officials, who reacted to the anti-porn push with a mixture of scorn and anger. *The Washington Post* quoted an experienced national security analyst who called the culture war initiative "a running joke for us," while the *Daily Business Review* cited high-level Justice Department sources as saying that prosecutors were being assigned porn cases over their entirely understandable objections.

For the moral relativists in the Bush administration, the definition of sin seems to depend on whether the sinner is on their side or not.

Justin exposing Janet's boob is a sin, but White House staffers exposing Valerie Plame is a win. Profiting from porn is a sin, but Halliburton's wartime profiteering is a win. Two men getting hitched is a sin, but Tom DeLay and Jack Abramoff playing with each other's clubs is a win. And telling students condoms can prevent STDs is a sin, but lying about WMD is a win.

The Real Obscenity

"This isn't an isolated situation. It is only the most recent example of Republican House leaders doing whatever it takes to hold on to power. If it means spending billions of taxpayers' dollars on questionable projects, they'll do it. If it means covering up the most despicable actions of a colleague, they'll do it."

Quick Quiz: Can you name the source of this damning quote?

(A) MoveOn.org
(B) Harry Reid
(C) Nancy Pelosi
(D) *Daily Kos*
(E) *New York Times* editorial

Actually, it's (F) None of the Above. The stinging words were delivered by Richard Viguerie, one of the founding fathers of the modern conservative movement, in an e-mail to his supporters in the midst of the Mark Foley pervy IMs scandal. You know the Grand Old Party's in trouble when its Grand Old Men start questioning its leaders' morals.

The "despicable actions of a colleague" Viguerie referred to were the lecherous e-mails and instant messages of Representative Mark Foley, who was the Republicans' most prominent hyper-hypocrite until Larry Craig strolled into a Minneapolis airport men's room. Sure, it's sickening that Foley enjoyed salacious images of young boys, but the really scandalous behavior was the Republican congressional leadership covering its own naked posterior.

The public's outrage was more about the loss of trust than about sordid IMs. So the American people can't trust these guys to look after the interests of vulnerable young people. We can't trust them to tell the truth about the war in Iraq. We can't trust them to tell the truth about who really benefits from their tax cuts. We can't trust them to tell the truth about what they are doing to protect us at home. And we can't trust them to tell the truth about the predatory actions of their point man on child porn.

From the beginning, the Foley scandal was loaded with You Can't Make This Stuff Up details, starting with his co-chairmanship of the Missing and Exploited Children Caucus. In this same spirit, here is a trio of actual Foley quotes:

On the crackdown on child predators: "If I were one of those sickos, I'd be nervous."

On teen nudist camps: "It's putting matches a little too close to gasoline."

On Bill Clinton (circa 1998): "It's vile. It's more sad than anything else, to see someone with such potential throw it all down the drain because of a sexual addiction."

Paging Dr. Freud!

And the craziness wasn't confined to Foley or his congressional protectors.

As the Foley scandal was breaking in the fall of 2006, I was part of a panel discussion in which author David "Rush's Brother" Limbaugh tried to make the case that the Foley story actually "could backfire" on Democrats by making them "too cocky" and by causing Christian voters "to realize just how poorly Democrats, secular Democrats, safeguard values issues. They are the party that promotes the radical homosexual agenda. They're the party connected with NAMBLA and the ACLU, which enables NAMBLA, the National Association of Man/Boy Love."

I'm not sure how Republican House leaders covering up the story of a Republican congressman preying on teenage pages would cause Christian voters to make the Democrat–Man/Boy Love connection but, as frantically grasping at straws goes, Limbaugh was actually on to something: the fact that our electoral choices are frequently based on completely irrational feelings (see George Bush, circa 2004).

No one understood this better than a past master of the political martial art of headline-wielding, Newt Gingrich. The classic example of his trying to exploit unrelated news events came just days before the 1994 election, when Gingrich sought to make political hay out of the story of Susan Smith, the South Carolina mother who drowned her young sons by rolling her car into a lake with them strapped in the backseat.

Throwing logic and coherent thought to the wind, Gingrich called the crime "a sign of how sick the system is," adding: "And I think people want to change. The only way you get change is to vote Republican."

Gingrich was roundly criticized for making this crude and illogical connection. But, on a gut level, he understood the impulse to lump all the bad things happening in our country together and seek a simple solution: vote for the party not in power. Anything that makes voters feel—rationally or not—that things are going to hell in a handbasket (or in an IM) intensifies the longing for change.

Fourteen years later, the shoe is jammed tightly onto the other foot. Mark Foley—and the Right's see-no-buggery, hear-no-buggery, speak-no-buggery handling of him—was one more "sign of how sick the system is." And that it's time for a change.

The Real Moral Values of Values Voters

The media generated a myth in the wake of the 2004 election that what voters cared most about was "moral values." It was a myth based on a poorly worded exit poll question that tried to turn "moral values" into a concrete issue like health care or the war in Iraq, which they clearly are not. Even Karl Rove, the architect of the president's evangelical strategy, conceded that security was that election's most galvanizing issue. It far surpassed red-state concerns about gay marriage. Fear of gay couples saying "I do" didn't carry George Bush back into the White House; fear of Osama saying "Take two" did.

Indeed in the eleven states with gay marriage ballot initiatives in 2004, Bush's share of the popular vote increased 2.6 percent from his 2000 totals. In states with no gay marriage initiative, he went up 2.9 percent. And as for Republicans ruling rural America, exit polls found that Bush was up 13 percent in big cities, while Kerry was down 11 percent from Al Gore's totals. On the other hand, in towns with populations between ten thousand and fifty thousand, Bush went down 9 percent, while Kerry gained 10 percent over Gore. So Kerry's problem wasn't small-town America seeing red over gay marriage. More importantly, the values debate is not about triangulating on gay marriage. It's about bringing focus and urgency to the creation of a more fair, just—and, yes, moral—society. Franklin Roosevelt expressed this moral imperative when he said that "the test of our progress is not whether we add more to the abundance of those who have much; it is whether we provide enough for those who have too little." Isn't this the exact opposite of the immoral credo that has animated the Right?

And although it hardly got any ink compared with the passage of the gay marriage initiatives, voters in Florida and Nevada—red states both—approved initiatives in 2004 calling for big hikes in the minimum wage. This was incontrovertibly a moral values initiative. It's a disgrace that low-wage workers who work full time are not paid enough to lift their families out of poverty. Real values voters know this, and there are enough of them out there that you don't have to sell your soul to get elected.

America's Founding Fathers understood the connection between statecraft and soulcraft. They were not political men engaged in a spiritual enterprise. They were deeply spiritual men engaged in a political enterprise. After all, the premise that "all men are created equal"—which Abraham Lincoln called "the father of all moral principle"—is true and self-evident only in spiritual terms. We are clearly not self-evidently equal by any other criteria, including brains, looks, and talent. And by bringing soul into American politics, our leaders will be able to galvanize voters in Kansas no less than in California.

With 36 million people living in poverty, and 47 million with no health insurance, what we need is the resolute conviction to transform data into narratives and economic issues into moral ones. From real moral values spring clear political priorities that can counter the Right's divisive religiosity—and win back America's values voters.

Why the Right Is Wrong About Civil Liberties and Moral Values

The Right is wrong about civil liberties because in the name of keeping us safe it has abused executive power, bypassed laws and treaties, quashed dissent, and withheld information both from Congress and from the American public.

And it is wrong about American values because it has reduced them to guns, gays, and abortion and has ignored both the moral imperative of fighting poverty and the biblical admonition that "we shall be judged by what we do for the least among us."

15

John McCain:
Hijacked by the Right

Has there ever been a more repugnant example of political pandering than John McCain's decision in February 2008 to vote against a bill banning waterboarding, putting hoods on prisoners, forcing them to perform sex acts, subjecting them to mock executions, or depriving them of food, water, and medical treatment?

That's right, John McCain, the former POW who has long been an outspoken critic of the Bush administration's disturbing embrace of extreme interrogation techniques.

But that was before his desperate attempt to win over the Right, lowlighted by his unconscionable surrender on torture. It revealed how outdated the media's favored image of McCain as an independent-thinking maverick had become.

McCain the maverick had been unequivocal in his condemnation of torture, and eloquent in expressing why. "We've sent a message to the world that the United States is not like the terrorists," he said at an Oval Office appearance in December 2005, after he had forced the president to endorse a torture ban McCain had authored and pushed through (a ban the president quickly subverted with a signing statement). "What we are is a nation that upholds values and standards of behavior and treatment of all people, no matter how evil or bad they are. And I think that this will help us enormously in winning the war for the hearts and minds of people throughout the world in the war on terror."

He made a similar case on the campaign trail in Iowa in October 2007: "When I was imprisoned, I took heart from the fact that I knew my North Vietnamese captors would never be treated like I was treated by them. There are much better and more effective ways to get information. You torture someone long enough, he'll tell you whatever he thinks you want to know."

And there was this pithy and powerful summation of why torture should never be an option: "It's not about who *they* are, it's about who *we* are."

Of course, all that was before he put his conscience in leg irons— and before caving to the would-be Torquemadas on the Right became part of his campaign strategy.

Taking to the Senate floor to justify his vote against the torture ban, McCain twisted himself in knots trying to explain how he could sponsor a bill—the 2006 Detainee Treatment Act—that prohibits the use of any cruel, inhumane, or degrading treatment by the military while voting against a bill that would extend that ban to the CIA and other intelligence agencies: "It was never our purpose to prevent the CIA from detaining and interrogating terrorists. On the contrary, it is important to the war on terror that the CIA have the ability to do so. At the same time the CIA's interrogation program has to abide by the rules, including the standards of the Detainee Treatment Act."

Got that? The CIA has to abide by rules prohibiting torture but we can't tie the CIA's hands by making it abide by rules prohibiting torture. Straight talk, RIP.

What's more, McCain said he voted against the bill because it would be a mistake to "tie the CIA to the Army Field Manual"—the manual he gave a ringing endorsement to in a November debate: "I just came back from visiting a prison in Iraq. The army general there said that techniques under the Army Field Manual are working and working effectively, and he didn't think they need to do anything else. My friends, this is what America is all about."

But not apparently once you have the White House in your sights. Then all bets—and deeply held convictions—are off.

Watching McCain hang a For Sale sign on his principles and embrace the shibboleths of the Right like this has been a profoundly sad thing. Especially for me. I've long admired, respected—indeed loved—John McCain. I've written many columns about him citing his courage and integrity, traveled with him on the Straight Talk Express, and invited him to keynote the 2000 Shadow Convention I helped organize to address issues left unaddressed by the two main parties—poverty, campaign finance reform, and the failed war on drugs. I introduced him at the convention in the summer of 2000 as "the most prominent voice for reform within the political system." Indeed, the fact that he agreed to be the keynote speaker was an enormously courageous act in defiance of the wishes of George W. Bush and the GOP establishment.

McCain's opening speech that day, featuring his vow to clean up a system that no longer served the people, captured the imagination of much of the crowd. And McCain was unbowed by the catcalls and boos from a splinter of the audience who couldn't see past their narrow partisanship. He accepted the risk of appearing at our Shadow Convention to denounce what he called the "iron triangle of lobbyists, big money, and legislation," in part because that same alliance, led by George W. Bush, had crushed his candidacy just a few months before in South Carolina.

Out of the fiery crash of 2000, McCain reassembled his political vehicle. Unfortunately, the value of talking straight took a distant backseat to the value of getting elected. During his 2008 campaign, the old John McCain has become almost unrecognizable, desperate to make himself at home in the middle of that iron triangle he once denounced. Did some sinister force place a soul-snatching pod under his bed? In any case, the old McCain is as gone as our budget surplus.

He clearly convinced himself that the only way he could become president was to sell his soul—making a pact with the devils of the religious right and turning into what columnist Jim Pinkerton dubbed "a born-again Bushophile." He's now BFFs with the same religious bigots he once denounced as "agents of intolerance." As the Reverend Falwell departed for that great direct-mail convention in the sky, he ascended with the knowledge that McCain had finally been converted. Indeed, McCain told Falwell that he had spoken "in haste" in 2000.

At the end of February 2008, when he was asked in Rocky River, Ohio, what would happen if he couldn't convince the American public that the war in Iraq is succeeding, he replied, "Then I lose. I lose." He quickly tried to retract his prediction, but the fact remains that no political leader is as identified with the president's surge in Iraq as John McCain. McCain's role as head cheerleader for the surge was preceded by his tragicomic stroll through a Baghdad market, which he claimed was proof you could "walk freely" through parts of the city. Subsequent TV news footage revealed that he'd been accompanied on his leisurely stroll by one hundred armed U.S. soldiers, three

Blackhawk helicopters, and two Apache gunships, proving beyond a doubt that he had traded his signature straight talk for deceptive triumphalist blather. But the walk wasn't the beginning. Even before that, at the end of 2005, he was spouting nonsense like this on *Meet the Press:* "I do believe we were greeted as liberators in many respects in many parts of Iraq. We really were. I remember the statue coming down and people being freed from prisons, etc. . . ."

I guess he did not remember the stories about that statue event being staged. Or some other prison stories that weren't so happy. Did he forget Abu Ghraib? And what would the old McCain have said about the new McCain justifying as "standard procedure in Iraq" the Pentagon practice of paying Iraqi newspapers to publish articles favorable to the U.S. position? So anything that was "standard procedure" in Iraq is now okay? Isn't Iraqi standard procedure what we've sacrificed thousands of lives and squandered hundreds of billions of dollars trying to get rid of? Or was it to get rid of that statue?

Going over the list of policy backtracks and rightward swerves that McCain has undertaken is enough to make Faust blush. He endorsed a constitutional amendment in Arizona to ban gay marriage and deny benefits to unmarried couples of any kind. He has expressed a newfound support for teaching "intelligent design" in schools. He's a fearsome opponent of lottery gambling but a big supporter of Indian gaming, especially by Arizona-based tribes who also contribute to his campaigns. He has supported an amendment to limit the right to habeas corpus. He didn't show up for a 2008 vote on a bill that included tax incentives for clean energy, even though he was in Washington—and then his staff misled environmentalists who called to protest, telling them that he had voted for it. He even appeared at a fund-raiser for Alabama lieutenant governor candidate George Wallace Jr., who has given four speeches to the Council of Conservative Citizens, a white supremacist group. And the tireless 2000 champion of campaign finance reform and critic of the influence of money and lobbyists on our politics has been replaced by a candidate who thinks nothing of doing favors for big donors and flying around with lobbyists, like Vicki Iseman, representing clients with business in front of the Senate commerce committee he chaired.

McCain's capitulation on immigration has been especially dramatic. He once stood tall as a fearless leader on bipartisan, comprehensive reform—having built an impressive alliance that included the Chamber of Commerce, Big Labor, and Ted Kennedy. Indeed, the McCain-Kennedy bill became the template for the most enlightened, humane, and sensible approach to solving our border problems. But once he became a presidential contender, he shrank himself to a moral pygmy on the issue. Count McCain, now, as one more Minuteman fence-builder.

When he addressed the 2008 CPAC meeting, he effectively apologized for having supported sensible reform:

> And while I and other Republican supporters of the bill were genuine in our intention to restore control of our borders, we failed, for various and understandable reasons, to convince Americans that we were. I accept that, and have pledged that it would be among my highest priorities to secure our borders first, and only after we achieved widespread consensus that our borders are secure, would we address other aspects of the problem in a way that defends the rule of law and does not encourage another wave of illegal immigration.

Translation: Start building that wall, which I know won't work.

The ultimate flip-flop came during the CNN presidential debate at the Reagan Library in California when he was asked by *Los Angeles Times* reporter Janet Hook, "At this point, if your original proposal came to a vote on the Senate floor, would you vote for it?"

"No," he responded, "I would not, because we know what the situation is today. The people want the borders secured first."

Could there be a better illustration of pandering? In other words, "I was McCain before I wasn't McCain."

Like many a religious parable, the tale of McCain's evolution—sorry, deliberate "intelligent design" transition—on the subject of religion in politics goes way back. In February 2000, in response to a taped phone message by Pat Robertson sent to Michigan residents accusing a McCain aide of being antireligious, McCain said: "The political tactics of division and slander are not our values. They are corrupting influences on religion and politics, and those who practice them in the name of religion or in the name of the Republican Party or in the name of America shame our faith, our party, and our country. . . . Neither party should be defined by pandering to the outer reaches of American politics and the agents of intolerance."

In the years since then—and especially since he began running for the 2008 GOP nomination and courting "the outer reaches of American politics"—McCain has, to be generous, rethought his take on pandering quite a bit.

McCain's conversion on the religion-in-politics front has, however, not been without a few moments of bewilderment—not of the Mother-Teresa-questioning-her-faith kind, but rather of the comical hard-time-keeping-his-stories-straight kind.

In May 2007, in the midst of a spring he spent kissing the rings of those "agents of intolerance," McCain's campaign told the AP that he was an Episcopalian, while noting that his four younger children are Baptists and that he attends a Baptist church when at home in Arizona. Barely a month later, McCain told the McClatchy Newspapers that he found the Baptist church more fulfilling than the Episcopal church, but still considered himself Episcopalian.

By the fall he was still at it with his Solomon-worthy answer. When asked by an AP reporter about how his Episcopal faith affects his political life, McCain replied: "It plays a role in my life. By the way, I'm not Episcopalian. I'm Baptist. Do I advertise my faith? Do I talk about it all the time? No." I guess it depends on what your definition of "all the time" is.

Of course, this being McCain, a clarification of the clarification of the Episcopalian/Baptist flip-flop soon followed: "The most important thing is that I am a Christian, and I don't have anything else to say about the issue." And it's true, he didn't. Until he gave an interview to Beliefnet and made the head-scratching claim that "the Constitution established the United States of America as a Christian nation." McCain also delivered this gem: "I just have to say in all candor that since this nation was founded primarily on Christian principles . . . personally, I prefer someone who I know has a solid grounding in my faith."

When the predictable uproar ensued, McCain responded with a clarification. Followed by another clarification to clarify his clearly not-clear-enough original clarification. (If nothing else, we can rest assured that a McCain White House would be second to none in clarifying things.)

Though McCain's charge through the GOP primaries sent the

Right—spearheaded by Rush Limbaugh, Laura Ingraham, and Ann Coulter—into fits of lamentation and teeth-gnashing, he has been demonstrating every day that he will be more than right-wing enough come November. In fact, he already is. (The fire from the talk radio blusterers shows that the "outer reaches" of the Right have such a stranglehold on the party that they even feel comfortable taking shots at the GOP standard-bearer.)

Like Bush, McCain has never hesitated to make cynical use of the 9/11 tragedy when he finds it politically convenient. During an appearance at the Virginia Military Institute on April 11, 2007, McCain took on the role of Bush cover band, trotting out note-for-note renditions of the president's Iraq war favorites. He gave us 9/11 nostalgia ("In the early days after 9/11, our country was united in a single purpose: to find the terrorists bent on our destruction"); he gave us the Iraq–9/11 link ("the potential consequence of allowing terrorists sanctuary in Iraq is another 9/11—or worse"); he gave us the be-very-afraid guitar solo ("In Iraq today, terrorists have resorted to levels of barbarism that shock the world . . . and we Americans are their ultimate target"); he gave us the exploitation of America's fallen soldiers ("Let us honor them by doing all we can to ensure their sacrifices were not made in vain"); and, of course, he closed with the classic attack on Democrats "who deny our soldiers the means to prevent an American defeat."

We can safely predict that the Republicans and their nominee will continue to desperately sell the war in Iraq by shamefully tapping into the wellspring of 9/11 emotion and playing directly to our fears of "another 9/11—or worse."

I hate to be the one to break up a love affair, but the John McCain the media and independent voters fell in love with in 2000—the straight-shooting, let-the-chips-fall-where-they-may maverick—is no more. He's been replaced by a man willing to say or do anything to win the affection of his newfound object of desire, the radical Right.

In February 2008, we got the money shot of his betrayal on tape: McCain singing the praises of Karl Rove, calling him "one of the smartest political minds in America," and saying, "I'd be glad to get his advice."

Yet many in the media can't bring themselves to stop acting as if McCain is still the dashing rebel who made knees buckle back in the day. Indeed, some are so reluctant to give up their entrenched view of McCain that "principled" and "pandering" are no longer seen as mutually exclusive terms. That was the animating premise of a February 2008 column by Nicholas Kristof in *The New York Times:* that McCain had become the world's most principled panderer.

"Mr. McCain truly has principles that he bends or breaks out of desperation and with distaste," wrote Kristof. In Kristof's through-the-looking-glass world, it's apparently a higher order of pandering if you start with deeply held core convictions that you trash in the name of political expediency while feeling really bad about it.

And it's not just journalists. With McCain well on his way to securing the Republican nomination, Newt Gingrich, in full stand-up comedy mode, made the claim that McCain's looming nomination represented "the victory of the moderate wing" of the GOP—of which he now counts himself a member!—and that with McCain, "for the first time since Eisenhower, you have someone who has clearly not accommodated the conservative wing winning the nomination. That is a remarkable achievement."

The Right's stranglehold on the Republican Party is now so strong that Newt Gingrich, the original barbarian at the GOP gate, is considered a voice of moderation. And that capitulating on torture and tax cuts and immigration and "the agents of intolerance" and going full throttle on Iraq can be seen as "not accommodating" the Right.

What is it going to take for us to face reality? McCain verbally stroking Rove while caving in on torture should be the equivalent of that great scene at the end of *The Godfather* in which Diane Keaton's Kay watches in horror as Al Pacino is transformed, in the kiss of a ring, from her loving husband Michael into the next Don Corleone. This ain't the same man you married.

The old John McCain once tried to take the mantle of true conservatism away from George W. Bush. The new John McCain is now essentially running to give America a third Bush term—and, indeed, will out-Bush Bush when it comes to staying the disastrous course we're on in Iraq.

He even got Bush's blessing: "I know his convictions," Bush said on Fox News early in 2008. "I know the principles that drive him. And no doubt in my mind he is a true conservative."

There you have it: John McCain, a Bush conservative. If you love George W. Bush, and all that he's brought you over his two terms in office, you're gonna love John McCain. "I'm very honored and humbled," John McCain said, standing next to George Bush in the Rose Garden the day after he had clinched his party's nomination, "to have the opportunity to receive the endorsement of the president of the United States, a man [for whom] I have great admiration, respect and affection." The metamorphosis of the Maverick into the Successor was now officially complete.

Don't forget, in 2000 Bush himself was presented as something of a maverick—a Republican who espoused "compassionate conservatism," got along with Democrats in Texas, and was going to win over Latinos, end his party's long-standing hostility toward minorities, and govern from the center.

"My friends, this is going to be a different kind of convention for a different kind of Republican," said 2000 Republican National Committee Chairman Jim Nicholson. Of course, that different kind of Republican evaporated the moment W's hand hit the Bible on inauguration day. McCain hasn't waited that long. He's already offered his proof of fidelity to the Right.

As it turns out, the 2008 John McCain doesn't need any advice from Karl Rove. He's already internalized the Boy Genius's lessons.

If you think the problem with the United States right now is that we haven't given Bush enough time to finish his agenda, then John McCain is your man. If not, it's time to stop running on the fumes of romantic notions past and find a good divorce lawyer.

The Thousand-Year War Express is careering along the road to the White House, and the new John McCain is gunning the engine. And he has to be stopped.

Righting the Wrongs of the Right

In Dante's *Inferno*, deceivers are sentenced to have their souls encased in flames, hypocrites are forced to wear cloaks weighted with lead, and those who use their powers of persuasion for insidious ends are doomed to suffer a continual fever so intense that their bodies sizzle and smoke like a steak splayed upon a George Foreman grill. But the worst affliction is reserved for those who know better and don't act on that knowledge. If we are going to avoid that fate, we need to purge ourselves of the media toxicity that has allowed the Right to flourish, and encourage those who know better to stand up and speak the truth.

Why have we been so vulnerable to such a brazen takeover of our foreign policy—allowing the launch of an immoral, unnecessary, and ultimately catastrophic war? Why have we tolerated staying on this disastrous course despite all evidence that it is leading us over a cliff? Why have we allowed the shredding of our Constitution—warrantless mass eavesdropping on American citizens, firing of U.S. Attorneys, quashing of dissent? Why have we enabled the corruption of American values—allowing torture to become policy, and permitting such obscenities as Abu Ghraib and Guantánamo to replace the glory of Omaha Beach and the bold vision of the Marshall Plan? Why have we capitulated to the undermining of science—the suicidal denial of scientific reports on global warming and stem cell research? And nearly a century after the Scopes trial, why are we once again allowing the armies of ignorance to assail Darwin and evolution?

With the consequences of the media's failure to do their job over the last seven years raining down on us every day, it's easy to point the finger of blame at our toothless journalistic watchdogs. It is indeed beyond time for reporters to become intrepid again and for the pundits to free themselves from the conventional wisdom. And it is just as easy to put the blame on our Democratic leaders who again and again became enablers, behaving more like loyal lackeys than the loyal opposition. It is also beyond time for them to stop being so easily cowed by attacks on their patriotism and by the cynical exploitation of fear and the now ritual waving of the banner of national security. But, ultimately, to put an end to the madness inflicted on us by the Right, we need to address the root causes of the rot afflicting our politics. And nothing is more central to this task than character. After all, not everyone is equally affected by the fear-mongering and the pressure to capitulate. Some—whether in the media or in elected office—manage to remain uncontaminated, or recognize their contamination earlier than others and join the fight against the forces polluting their judgment and their courage.

Otherwise, why did Jack Murtha change course on the war in 2005 while Joe Lieberman never managed to see through the fog of lies and manipulation? What made the late Paul Wellstone, even though he was facing a tough reelection battle, immune to the fears that led so many of his colleagues to vote for a war authorization resolution they knew was wrong? And what made Chuck Hagel stand up to his own party once the overwhelming evidence convinced him that the war was wrong?

In a word: leadership.

In this time of Lilliputian public figures it's clear that to end the hijacking of America by the Right each one of us needs to take up the gauntlet and stand up for the truth, no matter how many in the corridors of power or at the top of the media food chain would prefer to maintain the status quo. Leadership is a risky business requiring wisdom, courage, and fortitude—and as my compatriot Socrates put it, courage is the knowledge of what is not to be feared. Leadership has always been about seeing clearly while most around you have their vision clouded.

The American genius is about bringing out the extraordinary in ordinary people. Picture Jimmy Stewart's Jefferson Smith going to Washington or Gary Cooper's Longfellow Deeds going to town. It wasn't elected officials who led the struggle for civil rights or the drive for women's rights or the fight to end the war in Vietnam or the war in Iraq. It was the people. And once again it will be the people trusting the truth they see—no matter how often it is denied by those in power—that will put America back on the road to goodness and to greatness.

The Right's orgy of greed, hubris, and arrogance will go down as an era marked by the celebration of selfishness and naked brute force. Over this past year it seemed, thankfully, that America was poised to turn a new page and close the book on this tragic chapter of our history. The nomination of John McCain, however, will change this. McCain is the Trojan Horse the Right desperately needed to put a faux maverick, faux independent, faux straight-talker imprint on the same ruinous policies that have taken us down this dark road. Though the era of the Right has exhausted its historic course, collapsing in moral, political, and economic bankruptcy, the transformation and co-opting of McCain shows the durability of the Right and the lingering danger it poses. There is nothing automatic about its disappearance from the stage. Not unless we, together, give it—and John McCain—a mighty push into the wings and out the stage door.

Source Notes

Chapter 1: The Right Goes Wrong

4 somewhere between one hundred years: CBS *Face the Nation*, January 6, 2008.

4 "the rare opportunity": Ryan Lizza, "Can John McCain Reinvent Republicanism?," *The New Yorker*, February 25, 2008.

4 "They are, if anything": *This Week with George Stephanopoulos*, ABC News, November 4, 2007.

5 In April of 2007: William F. Buckley, "The Waning of the GOP," *National Review*, April 28, 2007.

5 "The party is in a funk": *This Week with George Stephanopoulos*, ABC News, November 4, 2007.

5 "The dead-enders": Speech, Donald Rumsfeld, San Antonio, TX, August 25, 2003 (www.defenselink.mil/speeches/speech.aspx?speechid=513).

6 "President Bush's statements": Zachary Coile, "Pelosi Backs Away from Rep. Stark's Criticism of Bush," *San Francisco Chronicle*, October 20, 2007.

6 believe in the science of evolution: "USA Today/Gallup Poll results," *USA Today*, June 7, 2007.

6 don't want *Roe v. Wade* overturned: Report, "Support for *Roe v. Wade* Increases Significantly, Reaches Highest Level in Nine Years," Harris Poll, November 9, 2007.

6 bring our troops home: Susan Page, "Poll 63% Want All Troops Home by End of '08," *USA Today*, February 12, 2007.

7 The TV spot: Adam Nagourney and Robin Toner, "Strong Charges Set New Tone Before Debate," *The New York Times*, September 27, 2004.

7 "These people want": Thomas Edsall, "After Late Start Republican Groups Jump into the Lead," *The Washington Post*, October 17, 2004.

7 "al Qaeda wants Kerry": Dana Milbank, "Tying Kerry to Terror Tests Rhetorical Limits," *The Washington Post*, September 24, 2004.

7 "best recruiting": "UK Envoy's Bush Barb Made Public," BBC News, September 20, 2004.

8 Newt Gingrich: Michael Kramer, "The Political Interest," *Time*, January 16, 1995.

9 Even Bush's good buddy: *Paula Zahn Now*, CNN, September 24, 2004.

10 "There will always be": Wolf Blitzer, "Search for the 'Smoking Gun,'" CNN.com, January 10, 2003.

10 "The biggest threat": "Full Transcript of the Debate Between the Vice Presidential Candidates in Cleveland," *The New York Times*, October 5, 2004.

10 "biological weapons": Transcript of George W. Bush's State of the Union Address, CNN, January 28, 2003.

10 "Matt, I'm just telling": *Today*, September 11, 2006.

11 "It's a dangerous world": Press Conference of the President, September 15, 2006 (www.whitehouse.gov).

11 "The real threat": *Meet the Press*, MSNBC, September 10, 2006.

11 Then, before the 2006: Michael Kranish, "GOP Ad Puts Focus on Terror," *The Boston Globe*, October 20, 2006.

11 "mass death": Peter Baker, "Cheney Back Delivering the Grim Campaign Speech," *The Washington Post*, October 8, 2006.

11 "These are the stakes": "Republicans Launch Terrorism Ad," WSJ.com, October 19, 2006.

11 "The dictionary definition": *Countdown with Keith Olbermann*, MSNBC, October 23, 2006.

12 "If Democrats take over": Huma Zaidi, "It's the Economy," *First Read*, MSNBC.com, October 23, 2006.

12 "Harold, call me": Alex Johnson, "Tennessee Ad Ignites GOP Squabbling," MSNBC.com, October 25, 2006.

12 "His memory": George Orwell, *1984*, p. 34 (Signet Classic, 1950).

12 Before a week had passed: "Bush Details Foiled 2002 al Qaeda Attack on L.A.," CNN.com, February 9, 2006 (http://www.cnn.com/2006/POLITICS/02/09/bush.terror/index.html).

16 Frances Townsend: Elisabeth Bumiller and David Johnson, "Bush Gives New Details of 2002 Qaeda Plot to Attack Los Angeles," *The New York Times*, February 10, 2006.

16 Listening to Bush's speeches: "President Discusses Progress in War on Terror to National Guard," speech, National Guard Building, Washington, D.C., February 9, 2006 (www.whitehouse.gov/news/releases/2006/02/20060209-2.html).

16 This is precisely: "White House Defends Rove over 9/11 Remarks," Associated Press, June 24, 2005.

17 Chutzpah doesn't even begin: Interview of the Vice President by Wire Service Reporters, via Telephone, Jackson, WY, August 9, 2006 (www.whitehouse.gov/news/releases/2006/08/20060809-2.html).

17 So Cheney went: Ibid.

17 In a survey: "The Terrorism Index," *Foreign Policy* / The Center for American Progress, July/August 2006.

17 "stay in the fight": Office of the Vice President, Interview with Wire Service Reporters via Telephone, August 9, 2006.

17 four thousand lives: Iraq Coalition Casualty Count, January 22, 2008 (www.icasualties.org/oif/BY_DOD.aspx).

17 over 2 trillion dollars: Joseph Stiglitz and Linda Bilmes, *The Three Trillion Dollar War* (New York: W. W. Norton, 2008), p. 24.

17 Indeed when: William Neikirk, "Bush and Pols React, Starkly," The Swamp, *Chicago Tribune*, August 10, 2006.

18 It's worth noting: Spencer Hsu, "House Passes Bill to Implement More of 9/11 Panel's Suggestions," *The Washington Post*, January 10, 2007.

18 "After six years": Anne E. Kornblut and Sheryl Gay Stolberg, "In Latest Push, Bush Cites Risk in Quitting Iraq," *The New York Times*, September 1, 2006.

Chapter 2: The Media: Equal Time for Lies

20 1,420-calorie Monster Thickburger: Kevin Tibbles, "Hardee's Unveils the 'Monster Thickburger,' " NBC News, November 16, 2004.

23 "I used to spread the blame": Jim Hansen, "The Threat to the Planet," *The New York Review of Books*, vol. 53, no. 12, July 13, 2006.

24 A September 2007 report: "Securing, Stabilizing, and Rebuilding Iraq: Iraqi Government Has Not Met Most Legislative, Security, and Economic Benchmarks," GAO, September 2007 (http://www.gao.gov/new.items/d071195 .pdf).

24 A signature case was: "Petraeus, Crocker to Say Stay the Course," CBS News, September 8, 2007.

25 there had been numerous stories: Dan Froomkin, "White House Watch," Washingtonpost.com, August 16, 2007 (www.washingtonpost.com/wp-dyn/ content/blog/2007/08/16/BL2007081601003.html).

25 veteran GOP operative Ed Gillespie: Peter Baker et al., "Among Top Officials, 'Surge' Has Sparked Dissent," Washingtonpost.com, September 9, 2007 (www.washingtonpost.com/wp-dyn/content/article/2007/09/08/AR20070908 01846_pf.html).

25 According to a *Washington Post*–ABC News poll: Washingtonpost.com, September 9, 2007 (actual poll: http://www.washingtonpost.com/wp-srv/politics/ polls/postpoll_090907.html).

26 "What Senator Kennedy is going to do": "Kennedy Demands Accountability in Iraq War," *CNN Newsroom*, January 9, 2007 (http://transcripts.cnn .com/TRANSCRIPTS/0701/09/cnr.04.html).

26 And there was Judy Woodruff: *Meet the Press*, NBC, January 7, 2007.

26 Was Republican Senator Chuck Hagel: "Text of the Resolution on Iraq," *The New York Times*, January 17, 2007.

26 the proud possessor of: James Pinkerton, "Walter Jones Meets Rudyard Kipling," *The Huffington Post*, January 18, 2007 (www.huffingtonpost.com/ james-pinkerton/walter-jones-meets-rudyar_b_39022.html).

26 "I do not believe": "Brownback Comments on Troop Surge," January 10, 2007, Sam Brownbeck Press Office (http://brownback.senate.gov/pressapp/ record.cfm?id=267419&&days=365&).

26 liberal has: "ACU Releases 2005 Congressional Ratings," American Conservative Union, April 5, 2006 (http://www.conservative.org/pressroom/2006/ 0604052pr.asp).

26 Soon after: "Brownbeck, Hunter to Join Blogs for Life Conference," Family Research Council, January 16, 2007 (http://www.frc.org/get.cfm?i=PR07A03).

27 "We need to quit refereeing": Democratic Primary Debate in Coral Gables, Florida, transcript, September 9, 2007 (http://media.miamiherald.com/smedia/ 2007/09/09/23/English_transcript.source.prod_affiliate.56.pdf).

27 A CBS/*New York Times* poll: Dalia Sussman, "U.S. Opposition to War at All-Time High, Poll Shows," *The New York Times*, May 24, 2007.

27 In *The New York Times*: Michael R. Gordon, "Hints of Progress, and Questions, in Iraq Data," *The New York Times*, September 8, 2007.

27 "cherry-picking positive indicators": Karen DeYoung, "Experts Doubt Drop in Violence in Iraq," *The Washington Post*, September 6, 2007.

27 "Data on car bombs": Gordon, "Hints of Progress and Questions in Iraq Data," *The New York Times*, September 8, 2007.

27 "The figures that have emerged": Ibid.

28 The NIE represented: "Trends in Global Terrorism: Implications for the United States," National Intelligence Estimate, April 2006 (http://hosted.ap .org/specials/interactives/wdc/documents/terrorism/keyjudgments_092606.pdf).

28   The report also highlighted: Michael Abramowitz, "Intelligence Puts Rationale for War on Shakier Ground," *The Washington Post*, July 18, 2007.

29   "both sides in the Iraq debate": *Anderson Cooper 360°*, CNN, July 17, 2007.

30   "My main beef": Larry C. Johnson, *No Quarter*, June 30, 2007 (http://noquarter .typepad.com/).

30   Take Tim Russert: *Meet the Press*, NBC, July 1, 2007.

31   the plot's ringleader: Mark Coultan, "JFK airport plot foiled—and flawed," *The Age* (Melbourne, Australia), June 4, 2007.

31   "one of the most chilling": Adam Goldman, "Authorities Say 'Unthinkable' Devastation Possible in NYC Plot to Blow Up JFK Airport," Associated Press, June 3, 2007.

31   "unfathomable damage": No byline. "4 Charged with Terror Plot at JFK Airport," CNN.com, June 4, 2007.

31   "Such an attack": Goldman, "Authorities Say 'Unthinkable' Devastation Possible," Associated Press, June 3, 2007.

32   burned onto a DVD: "Informants' Actions Key in Fort Dix Terror Plot Case," Associated Press, May 10, 2007.

32   And we traveled a similar path: Tony Karon, "The Miami Seven: How Serious Was the Threat?" *Time*, June 23, 2006.

32   It was almost comical: Michael Cooper, "Giuliani Says Successes Surpass Kerik's Mistakes," *The New York Times*, November 6, 2007.

32   "You can't sit there": Marcia Kramer, "Bloomberg on JFK Plot: 'Stop Worrying, Get a Life,' " CBS, June 5, 2007.

32   San Francisco Mayor: Lisa Leff, "San Francisco Mayor Admits Affair with Aide's Wife," Associated Press, February 1, 2007.

33   January 2007 set a deadly record: *CRS Report for Congress, Iraqi Civilian Deaths Estimates*, Congressional Research Service, September 5, 2007.

33   "If there is one thing": G. K. Chesterton, *On Lying in Bed and Other Essays* (Bayeaux Arts, 2000), p. 35.

33   Wolf Blitzer followed up: *The Situation Room*, CNN, February 1, 2007.

33   On a day that saw Iraq: Bryan Bender, "US advisers warn threat of civil war mounting in Iraq," *The Boston Globe*, March 1, 2006.

34   "It wasn't a sexual": Amy Reiter, "It Isn't Easy Being in the Green," Salon.com, January 31, 2001 (archive.salon.com/people/col/reit/2001/01/31/npwed/index .html).

34   "The U.S. Supreme Court is": "Anna Nicole Smith Takes Case to U.S. Supreme Court," *CBS Evening News*, February 28, 2006.

34   With Anna Nicole's Supreme Court victory: "High Court Victory for Anna Nicole," CBS News, May 2, 2006.

34   True, but the stories: The White House, "President Bush Announces Major Combat Operations in Iraq Have Ended," May 1, 2003 (www.whitehouse.gov/ news/releases/2003/05/20030501-15.html).

35   "Who knows what draws": "Anna Nicole Smith Wins Right from Supreme Court to Continue Battle for Husband's Fortune," *CBS Evening News*, May 1, 2006.

35   "what many thought at the time": "Iraq Three Years After 'Mission Accomplished' Speech by President Bush," *CBS Evening News*, May 1, 2006.

35   2,266 American soldiers killed: Iraq Coalition Casualty Count (continuously updated) (http://icasualties.org/oif/).

35   16,927 American soldiers wounded: Ibid.

35 and the $241 billion: Jonathan Weisman, "Projected Iraq War Costs Soar," *The Washington Post*, April 27, 2006.

35 And if the CBS report: Survey of Iraqi Public Opinion, International Republican Institute, March 23–31, 2006 (www.iri.org/mena/iraq/pdfs/2006-04-27 -Iraq%20poll%20March%20March.ppt).

36 by the way: *NBC Nightly News*, NBC, May 1, 2006.

36 "a turning point for the citizens": "Iraq Three Years After 'Mission Accomplished' Speech by President Bush," *CBS Evening News*, May 1, 2006.

36 "News stories have": Jay Rosen, "The Downing Street Memo and the Court of Appeal in News Judgment," *The Huffington Post*, June 20, 2005.

37 an eighteen-year-old girl: Matthew Davis, "Missing Teen Case Grips US Media," BBC News, June 25, 2005.

38 the deaths of: CNN.com, "U.S. and Coalition Casualties," June 2005 (www.cnn.com/SPECIALS/2003/iraq/forces/casualties/2005.06.html).

39 The commutation of: "Grant of Executive Clemency," Statement by the President on Executive Clemency for Lewis Libby, July 2, 2007 (www.whitehouse .gov/news/releases/2007/07/20070702-4.html).

39 "outrage from the left": "No Prison for Libby," *American Morning*, CNN, July 3, 2007.

39 "criticism from the left": "No Prison for Libby; U.K. Terror Plot; Airport Attack Witness," *Anderson Cooper 360°*, CNN, July 2, 2007.

39 "will further drive": Carla Marinucci, "What Decision on Libby Means for White House. Bush Commutes Sentence, but Lets Fine Stand," *San Francisco Chronicle*, July 3, 2007.

39 In a Gallup poll: Susan Page, "Poll: Bush Approval Drops to a New Low of 29%," *USA Today*, July 9, 2007.

39 *Time* Magazine/SRBI poll: *Time* magazine/SRBI, March 13, 2007 (www .srbi.com/TimePoll4083-Final%20Report-2007-03-15.pdf#page=7).

39 Tom Tancredo and Sam Brownback: "Third G.O.P. Debate," *The New York Times*, June 5, 2007.

40 "You do the crime": *Patterico's Pontifications*, July 2, 2007 (http://patterico .com/2007/07/02/bush-commutes-libbys-prison-sentence/).

40 "I find Bush's action": Orin Kerr, *The Volokh Conspiracy*, July 2, 2007 (http:// volokh.com/archives/archive_2007_07_01-2007_07_07.shtml#1183422066).

40 Bush's imperial chutzpah: Michael Abramowitz, "A Decision Made Largely Alone," *The Washington Post*, July 3, 2007.

40 "I don't believe my role": as quoted in Paul Kergor, *God and George W. Bush: A Spiritual Life* (New York: HarperCollins, 2004), p. 39.

41 Brit Hume took the the attacks: *Fox News Sunday*, February 18, 2007.

41 During a panel discussion: Ibid.

42 "They must have the equipment": Ibid.

42 "Do you support the idea": Ibid.

42 There was Republican Senator Chuck Hagel: *Meet the Press*, NBC, February 18, 2007.

43 "We're not in the business": Ibid.

43 "best format": Dana Milbank, "In Ex-Aide's Testimony, a Spin Through VP's PR," *The Washington Post*, January 26, 2007.

43 Like Cathie Martin: Ibid.

43 "I have been told": Daniel Schulman, "Leakers Who Lunch," *Mother Jones*, January 30, 2007.

46   On August 16, the story: *American Morning*, CNN, August 17, 2007.

46   Case in point: Martin Stolz, "Workers at Mine Plan a Third Rescue Hole," *The New York Times*, August 13, 2007.

46   "with a coal-blackened face": Ibid.

46   "Conditions are the most difficult": Martin Stolz, "Workers at Mine Plan a Third Rescue Hole," *The New York Times*, August 13, 2007.

47   "There are many reasons": Dan Frosch, "No People in Pictures from Mine," *The New York Times*, August 14, 2007.

47   If the media had mined: Joe Milicia, "Utah Mine Owner Pushes for Safety," *Associated Press*, August 9, 2007.

47   And of the 324 violations: Kirk Johnson, "Safety Issues Slow Mine Rescue Efforts," *The New York Times*, August 8, 2007.

47   The media's infatuation: Robert Sanders, "Seismologists Confirm Utah Mine Collapse Probably Caused Temblor," Berkeley Press Release, August 9, 2007.

48   So we continued to get cloying coverage: "Desperate Search for Utah Miners Continues," *Anderson Cooper 360°*, CNN, August 13, 2007.

48   "to damage Murray Energy": Frank Langfitt, "Utah Mine Owner Defends Safety Process," *Morning Edition*, NPR, August 9, 2007.

48   "anti-American": Thomas Burr, "On TV and Before Congress, Mine Owner Railed Against More Regulation," *Salt Lake Tribune*, August 7, 2007.

48   "the destruction of American lives": "Murray's Meltdown: Angry, Rambling Briefing Draws Rebukes," *Aggregate Research*, August 8, 2007.

50   Murray had abruptly pulled: Mike Gorrell, "Faint 'Noise' from Deep Inside Mine Brings Flicker of Hope for Crandall Canyon 6," *Salt Lake Tribune*, August 16, 2007.

50   "focus like never before": Pat Reavy, "Governor Calls for Underground Rescue at Utah Mine to Cease Immediately," *Deseret Morning News*, August 17, 2007.

50   Congress launched a series: "Crandall Canyon Families Testify at House Labor Committee Hearing," U.S. House of Representatives Committee on Education and Labor press release, October 3, 2007 (www.house.gov/apps/list/speech/edlabor_dem/rel100307.html). And "Enzi, Help Committee Republicans Call for Inspector General Investigation of Crandall Canyon Mine Oversight" press release, August 27, 2007 (help.senate.gov/Min_press/2007_08_27_a.pdf).

51   Take the way that: Manuel Roig-Franzia and Spencer Hsu, "Many Evacuated, but Thousands Still Waiting," *The Washington Post*, September 4, 2005; Evan Thomas, "The Lost City," *Newsweek*, September 12, 2005.

52   "Anderson Cooper: Getting It Right": *Anderson Cooper 360°*, CNN, September 1, 2005.

54   In December 2005: Bob Marshall and Mark Schleifstein, "Firm Blames Corps for Short Piling," New Orleans *Times-Picayune*, December 3, 2005.

54   having spent almost $60 million: Foon Rhee, "Giuliani's $59 million delegate," *Boston Globe*, January 31, 2008.

55   "She was a strong supporter": *Anderson Cooper 360°*, CNN, December 27, 2007.

55   "This is a time to be focused": *Lou Dobbs Tonight*, CNN, December 27, 2007.

56   Exhibit A came: *Meet the Press*, NBC, December 30, 2007.

Chapter 3: The Media: Snoozers, Losers, and the Honor Roll

67 Kristol is a founder: Project for the New American Century, www.new americancentury.org/williamkristolbio.htm.

67 "Dick Cheney does send": David Carr, "White House Listens When Weekly Speaks," *The New York Times*, March 11, 2003.

67 hired by the *Times*: "*The Times* Adds an Op-Ed Columnist," *The New York Times*, December 30, 2007.

67 Kristol's truth-shattering piece: William Kristol, "Why Bush Will Be a Winner," *The Washington Post*, Outlook section, July 15, 2007.

68 " 'Precipitous withdrawal' ": Press Conference by the President, James S.Brady Briefing Room, July 12, 2007 (http://www.whitehouse.gov/news/releases/2007/07/20070712-5.html).

68 "Silent Majority" speech: Nixon's Silent Majority Speech, November 3, 1969, CNN Historical documents (www.cnn.com/SPECIALS/cold.war/episodes/11/documents/nixon.speech/).

68 "I'm a little amused": Carr, "White House Listens."

69 "The war in Afghanistan has gone": Kristol, "Why Bush Will Be a Winner."

69 Indeed, 2007 saw the highest number: Jonathan Karl and Luis Martinez, "Afghanistan Now Most Dangerous for U.S. Troops," ABC News, November 30, 2007.

69 The Taliban is making a comeback: "Afghanistan Opium Survey 2007," Council on Foreign Relations, August 2007 (www.cfr.org/publication/14099/).

69 "al-Qaeda may once again have a place": Kristol, "Why Bush Will Be a Winner."

69 But, according to the National Intelligence Estimate: Karen DeYoung and Walter Pincus, "Al-Qaeda's Gain Keeps U.S. at Risk, Report Says," *The Washington Post*, July 18, 2007.

69 "These Waziristan havens": Kristol, "Why Bush Will Be a Winner."

70 "Saddam Hussein would be alive": Ibid.

70 "He might well have restarted": Ibid.

70 "We are routing al-Qaeda in Iraq": Ibid.

70 Actually, a growing: "Syria, Jordan Left in Lurch on Iraq Refugees—U.N.," Reuters, July 6, 2007.

70 "Political progress is beginning": Kristol, "Why Bush Will Be a Winner."

70 "It would help if the administration": Ibid.

70 "It would help if Bush": Ibid.

70 "If the president": Ibid.

71 "Following through to secure": Ibid.

71 "What it comes down to is this": Ibid.

71 "this is a group of people": Department of Defense News Briefing, November 29, 2005 (www.defenselink.mil/transcripts/transcript.aspx?transcriptid=1492).

71 "a combination of rejectionists": "President Outlines Strategy for Victory in Iraq," United States Naval Academy, November 30, 2005 (www.whitehouse.gov/news/releases/2005/11/20051130-2.html).

71 "as Iraqi security forces stand up": John D. Banusiewicz, " 'As Iraqis Stand Up, We Will Stand Down,' Bush Tells Nation," American Forces Press Service, June 28, 2005 (www.defenselink.mil/news/newsarticle.aspx?id=16277).

71 "we will never back down": "President Discusses War on Terror at National Endowment for Democracy," speech given at Ronald Reagan Building and International Trade Center, Washington, D.C., October 6, 2005 (www .whitehouse.gov/news/releases/2005/10/20051006-3.html).

72 "reject an Iraq in which": "President Discusses War on Terror and Rebuilding Iraq," speech given at Omni Shoreham Hotel, Washington, D.C., December 7, 2005 (www.whitehouse.gov/news/releases/2005/12/20051207-1 .html).

72 "by far the largest" portion: "President Outlines Strategy for Victory in Iraq," speech given at United States Naval Academy, November 30, 2005 (www .whitehouse.gov/news/releases/2005/11/20051130-2.html).

72 "still harbor dreams of returning": Ibid.

72 "share the same ideology": Ibid.

72 "responsible for most of the suicide bombings": Ibid.

73 "WMD—I got it totally wrong": Don Van Natta Jr., Adam Liptak, and Clifford J. Levy, "The Miller Case: A Notebook, a Cause, a Jail Cell and a Deal," *The New York Times*, October 16, 2005.

73 "at least four non-Miller stories": Jack Shafer, "The Exorcism of the New York Times," *Slate*, October 20, 2005.

73 "And a lot of others": From personal conversation with author, October 21, 2005.

74 "In October 2005": Howard Kurtz, "Reporter, *Times* Are Criticized for Missteps," *The Washington Post*, October 16, 2005.

74 "I told her there was unease": Van Natta, Liptak, and Levy, "The Miller Case."

74 "During the run-up": Franklin Foer, "The Source of the Trouble," *New York*, May 31, 2004.

75 "We have to stop Jayson": Carl Swanson, "The Battle for the Newsroom," *New York*, May 19, 2003.

75 "kept kind of drifting": Van Natta, Liptak, and Levy, "The Miller Case."

75 "After weeks of investigation": Joby Warrick, "U.S. Claim on Iraqi Nuclear Program Is Called into Question," *The Washington Post*, January 24, 2003.

76 "The head of the International Atomic Energy Agency": Colum Lynch, "U.N. Finds No Proof of Nuclear Program," *The Washington Post*, January 29, 2003.

76 "It seems that what you're suggesting": Bob Simon, "Selling the Iraq War to the U.S.: Does Bush Administration Use Misleading Data?," *60 Minutes*, CBS News, December 6, 2002.

77 "Demetrius Perricos, chief inspector": Ian Williams, "Missing Evidence: Poking Holes in the Case for War," *LA Weekly*, January 30, 2003.

77 "Despite the Bush administration's claims": Walter Pincus, "U.S. Lacks Specifics on Banned Arms," *The Washington Post*, March 16, 2003.

78 "Take the case of staff reporter": John MacArthur, "All the News That's Fudged to Print: If You Think Jayson Blair Was Loose with the Facts, Look at How *The Times* Covered Iraq," Toronto *Globe & Mail*, June 6, 2003.

79 "After two months": Bob Drogin and Maggie Farley, "Hard Claims but Only Soft Proof So Far in Iraq," *Los Angeles Times*, January 26, 2003.

79 "President Bush's case against Saddam Hussein": Julian Borger, "Threat of War: US Intelligence Questions Bush Claims on Iraq: President's Televised Address Attacked by CIA," *The Guardian*, October 9, 2002.

79   "Top American scientists": Dafna Linzer, "No Evidence Iraq Stockpiled Smallpox," Associated Press, September 18, 2003.

80   Michael Massing wrote: Michael Massing, "Now They Tell Us," *The New York Review of Books*, February 26, 2004.

80   And in August: Steve Ritea, "Going It Alone," *American Journalism Review*, August 2004.

80   On October 8, 2002: John Walcott, Jonathan S. Landay, and Warren P. Strobel, "Some in Bush Administration Have Misgivings About Iraq Policy," Knight Ridder Newspapers, October 8, 2002.

80   On October 27, 2002: Warren P. Strobel and Jonathan S. Landay, "Infighting Among U.S. Intelligence Agencies Fuels Dispute Over Iraq," Knight Ridder Newspapers, October 27, 2002.

81   "We consider the story of Iraq's weapons": "*The Times* and Iraq," *The New York Times*, May 26, 2004.

81   "With any luck": Howard Kurtz, "The Judy War," *The Washington Post*, October 18, 2005.

81   "What makes [Special Prosecutor] Patrick Fitzgerald's": Frank Rich, "It's Bush-Cheney, Not Rove-Libby," *The New York Times*, October 16, 2005.

82   "the question was no longer": Daniel Eisenberg, "We're Taking Him Out," *Time*, May 5, 2002.

82   "Rumsfeld has been so determined": Ibid.

82   "It was all about finding": Paul O'Neill, "Bush Sought Way to Invade Iraq," *60 Minutes*, CBS News, January 11, 2004.

82   " 'I know you have a lot to do' ": Richard Clarke, *Against All Enemies: Inside America's War on Terror* (New York: Free Press, 2004), p. 32.

83   "the intelligence and facts": Walter Pincus, "British Intelligence Warned of Iraq War," *The Washington Post*, May 13, 2005.

83   "I've spent my life": *Larry King Live*, CNN, November 21, 2005.

83   "wrongdoing in the executive branch": Frank Rich, "Dishonest, Reprehensible, Corrupt . . ." *The New York Times*, November 27, 2005.

83   "Each day," wrote Rich: Ibid.

84   "scrupulous passivity": Joan Didion, "The Deferential Spirit," *The New York Review of Books*, September 19, 1996.

84   "everyone in the end": *Larry King Live*, CNN, November 21, 2005.

84   *Plan of Attack*: Bob Woodward, *Plan of Attack* (New York: Simon & Schuster, 2004), p. 11.

84   "This is very good indeed": Murray Waas, "Bush Intelligence Briefing Kept from Hill Panel," *National Journal*, November 22, 2005 (http://nationaljournal.com/about/njweekly/stories/2005/1122nj1.html).

85   "told Tenet several times": Woodward, *Plan of Attack*, p. 250.

85   "The Iraqi regime possesses": "President Bush Discusses Iraq with Congressional Leaders," press release, September 26, 2002 (www.whitehouse.gov/news/releases/2002/09/20020926-7.html).

85   "You can't distinguish between al-Qaeda and Saddam": "President Bush, Colombia President Uribe Discuss Terrorism," press release, September 25, 2002 (www.whitehouse.gov/news/releases/2002/09/20020925-1.html).

85   "Simply stated, there is no doubt": "Vice President Speaks at VFW 103rd National Convention," press release, August 26, 2002 (www.whitehouse.gov/news/releases/2002/08/20020826.html).

85   "We do know that [Saddam]": Anton La Guardia, "Saddam 'Is Months Away from a Nuclear Bomb,' " *The Daily Telegraph*, September 9, 2002.

85   "[Saddam has] amassed": "Testimony of U.S. Secretary of Defense Donald H. Rumsfeld Before the Senate Armed Services Committee Regarding Iraq," September 19, 2002, U.S. Department of Defense (www.defenselink.mil/speeches/speech.aspx?speechid=287).

85   "moral determination, which we've not seen": *The NewsHour with Jim Lehrer*, PBS, April 21, 2004.

86   "At a juncture in history": Carl Bernstein, "History Lesson: GOP Must Stop Bush," *USA Today*, May 23, 2004.

86   "I blame myself mightily": Howard Kurtz, "The Post on WMDs: An Inside Story," *The Washington Post*, August 12, 2004.

86   "The Joint Chiefs of Staff's staff": Bob Woodward, *Plan of Attack* (New York: Simon & Schuster, 2004).

87   "the best excavator of inside stories": Evan Thomas and Richard Wolffe, "The Woodward War," *Newsweek*, October 9, 2006.

87   "U.S., Iraqi, and allied forces": "Bob Woodward: Bush Misleads on Iraq," *60 Minutes*, CBS News, October 1, 2006.

87   "a damning conclusion": Ibid.

88   "a passive, impatient, sophomoric": Michiko Kakutani, "A Portrait of Bush as a Victim of His Own Certitude," *The New York Times*, September 30, 2006.

88   "I found out new things": Howard Kurtz, " 'State of Denial,' Lands Early and Hits Harder," *The Washington Post*, September 30, 2006.

89   "In this period of difficulty": *Larry King Live*, CNN, October 2, 2006.

90   "I don't weaponize my words": Marie Brenner, "Plame Gate: Lies and Consequences: Sixteen Words That Changed the World," *Vanity Fair*, April 2006.

90   take a leave after admitting: Howard Kurtz, "Woodward Apologizes to *Post* for Silence on Role in Leak Case," *The Washington Post*, November 17, 2005.

90   It's October 27, 2005: *Larry King Live*, CNN, October 27, 2005.

91   On November 17, 2005: Ibid.

91   as "laughable": *Fresh Air*, WGBH Boston, July 7, 2005.

91   "an accident": *Hardball*, MSNBC, July 11, 2005.

91   "a junkyard dog": *Larry King Live*, CNN, October 27, 2005.

91   "This investigation," he told me: Personal conversation with Carl Bernstein, November 16, 2005.

Chapter 4: Dim Bulbs: Congress's Low-Wattage Energy Bill

93   Last December: "Oil Climbs on Central Bank Plan," BBC News, December 13, 2007.

93   George Bush finally signed an energy bill: Zoe Lipman Charle, "New M.P.G. Rule Will Put Detroit on High Ground," *Detroit Free Press*, January 27, 2008.

93   And even this bill: John M. Broder, "Industry Flexes Muscle, Weaker Energy Bill Passes," *The New York Times*, December 14, 2007.

93   It seems that the Edison Electric Institute: John M. Broder, "Senate Approves Energy Bill Without Tax Increase," *The New York Times*, December 13, 2007.

93   They got out their red pens: Editorial, "Bringing an Energy Bill Home," *The New York Times*, December 4, 2007.

93   Gone was a tax increase: John M. Broder, "Senate Approves Energy Bill Without Tax Increase," *The New York Times*, December 13, 2007.

94   Brent Blackwelder: Broder, "Industry Flexes Muscle, Weaker Energy Bill Passes," *The New York Times*, December 14, 2007.

94   This other deal: Carl Hulse, "House Passes Sprawling Spending Bill," *The New York Times*, December 18, 2007.

94   oil finally hit triple digits: Jad Mouawad, "Wider Troubles Trickle Down to Oil Sector," *The New York Times*, January 24, 2008.

94   Bush, Hastert, and Frist: Press gaggle aboard Air Force One, April 24, 2006.

94   There was Frist: Bill Saporito, "Who Wins and Loses When Gas Prices Skyrocket?" *Time*, April 30, 2006.

95   carpool, and use mass transit: Mark Halperin, Teddy Davis, Sarah Baker, Angie Hu, and Emily O'Donnell with Mike Westling and Dan Nechita, "Political Pump," ABC News, April 25, 2006.

95   But Frist's patent-medicine cure: Chris Isidore, "Bush Seeks to Curb Oil Tax Breaks," CNNMoney, April 25, 2006.

95   "And the easiest way": "President Discusses Energy Policy," April 25, 2006 (www.whitehouse.gov/news/releases/2006/04/20060425.html).

95   ExxonMobil's earnings: James R. Healey and Matt Krantz, "Gas Costs: Pain at Pump, Gain to Industry," *USA Today*, April 25, 2006.

95   With profits like that: "Oil: Exxon Chairman's $400 Million Parachute," ABC News, April 14, 2006.

95   Our oilman president: Chris Isidore, "Bush Seeks to Curb Oil Tax Breaks," CNNMoney, April 25, 2006.

95   Dick Cheney's secret Energy Task Force: Dana Milbank and Justin Blum, "Document Says Oil Chiefs Met with Cheney Task Force," *The Washington Post*, November 16, 2005.

95   They also doled out over $4.5 million: In 2000 it was $1.9 million (www.opensecrets.org/2000elect/indus/P00003335.htm), and in 2004 it was $2.6 million (www.opensecrets.org/presidential/indus.asp?id=N00008072&cycle=2004), thus $1.9 + $2.6 = $4.5 million.

95   According to Public Citizen: Public Citizen, "Skyrocketing Gasoline Prices and Record Oil Company Profits: No Coincidence" (www.citizen.org/cmep/energy_enviro_nuclear/articles.cfm?ID=13912).

96   *The New York Times* estimated: Jad Mouawed, "Exxon Sets Profit Record: $40.6 Billion Last Year," *The New York Times*, February 2, 2008.

96   Or, to put it another way: Ibid.

96   Yet John McCain voted: Senate Roll Call Votes, November 17, 2005.

96   seriously raising mileage standards: William Neikirk, "The $4 Gallon of Gas," *Chicago Tribune*, May 4, 2006.

96   "Patriot Tax": Thomas L. Friedman, "Coulda, Woulda, Shoulda," *The New York Times*, November 14, 2007.

96   "This isn't supporting markets": David Roberts, "Grading on a Curve," *The Huffington Post*, October 11, 2007.

97   $3.25: Energy Information Administration, www.eia.doe.gov/oil_gas/petroleum/data_publications/wrgp/mogas_history.html.

97   33: Jim Efstathiou, "Refinery Mergers, Approved by Bush, Play Price Role," *Los Angeles Business Journal*, May 24, 2004.

97   41: Ralph Nader, "Oil and the War Against Iraq," statement released on www.nader.org, February 4, 2003.

97   67%: US Weekly Total Crude Oil And Petroleum Products Imports, and US Weekly Petroleum Products Supplied. Energy Information Administration,

US Department of Energy (http://tonto.eia.doe.gov/dnav/pet/hist/wttimus24 .htm and http://tonto.eia.doe.gov/dnav/pet/hist/wrpupus24.htm).

97   $25,000: Danny Hakin, "Senate Moves to Restrict Incentives for Big SUVs," *The New York Times*, February 21, 2004.

97   $13 billion: Tom Incantalupo, "Bush Expected to Approve Energy Bill," *Newsday*, December 19, 2007.

97   $3.4 billion: Dan Joling, "Alaska: Chukchi Sea Lease Sale Draws Record Bids, Protesters," Associated Press, February 7, 2008.

97   $31.6 billion: "Big Oil, Bigger Giveaways Ending Tax Breaks, Subsidies and Other Handouts Lavish Billions on Oil and Gas Companies," U.S. Climate Emergency Council, www.climateemergency.org/joomla/index.php?option= com_content&task=view&id=211&ltemid=165.

97   $27.6 billion: Michael Erman, "Exxon and Chevron Earnings Soar on Record Oil Prices," Reuters, February 1, 2008.

97   $40.61 billion: Ibid.

98   2020: John M. Broder, "House, 314–100, Passes Broad Energy Bill; Bush to Sign It Today," *The New York Times*, December 19, 2007.

98   "In fact, there is no such thing": Robert F. Kennedy Jr., "Coal's True Cost," *The Huffington Post*, November 29, 2007.

98   Just ask Kansas governor Kathleen Sebelius: Steven Mufson, "Coal-Funded Ad Is Called Misleading," *The Washington Post*, November 7, 2007.

99   Perhaps my favorite right-wing proposal: "$100 Gas Rebate Checks Not in the Mail," CBS News, May 2, 2006.

99   business of the feudal Wahhabi autocrats: "Official: 15 of 19 Sept. 11 Hijackers Were Saudi," *USA Today*, February 6, 2002.

99   Instead it buys the explosive charges: Eric Schmitt, "Some Bombs Used in Iraq Are Made in Iran," *The New York Times*, August 6, 2005.

99   In 2003, the Detroit Project: Katharine Seelye, "TV Ads Say SUV Owners Support Terrorists," *The New York Times*, January 8, 2003.

100   a satiric response: Ibid.

101   Even before they were released: Jeff Plungis et al., "Anti-SUV Movement Grows," *USA Today*, January 9, 2003.

101   while being rejected: George Raine, "Gas-Hogging SUVs Aid Terrorism," *San Francisco Chronicle*, January 9, 2003.

103   The Short Life of the Electric Car: Justin Hyde, "Documentary Slams GM for Ending EV1; 'Who Killed the Electric Car?' to Roll Out Next Week," *Detroit Free Press*, June 23, 2006.

104   Sales of models including the Hummer H2: Cordell Koland, "2007 Hummer H3 Sales Not Humming Along," *San Diego Business Journal*, May 14, 2007.

104   GM's sales dropped 6 percent: "Toyota Falls Short of GM in Global Sales," Associated Press, January 24, 2008.

104   And, at the beginning of 2008: Nick Bunkley, "In Global Race GM Wins by a Day of Pickup Sales," *The New York Times*, January 24, 2008.

104   Other U.S. car companies: Tom Krisher and Dee-Ann Durbin, "Ford Shares Slip to Two-Decade Low," *USA Today*, January 4, 2008.

104   Chrysler's sales also dipped in 2007: "Chrysler CEO Sees $1.6 Billion Loss This Year," Reuters, December 6, 2007.

104   Karl Wizinsky: Jeff Plungis, "SUV, Truck Owners Get a Big Tax Break," *Detroit News*, December 12, 2002.

105   By contrast, tax credits: Sandra Block, "Money: Some Hybrid Tax Credits About to Expire," *USA Today*, August 13, 2007.

105   President Bush announced: State of the Union Address, January 31, 2006 (www.whitehouse.gov).

105   Samuel Bodman: White House press briefing, www.whitehouse.gov, February 1, 2006.

106   The day after the president: "Bush Blames 'Mixed Signals' for Energy Lab Layoffs," *USA Today*, February 21, 2006.

106   Apollo Alliance: The Apollo Alliance, www.apolloalliance.org, accessed March 2, 2008.

107   The use of the term "addiction": "Bush Has Plan to End Oil 'Addiction,' " CNN.com, February 1, 2006.

107   In the quick-fix category: "Bush Renews Call for Alaskan Oil Drilling as Oil Prices Spike," CNN.com, March 9, 2005.

107   There's Alaska ecocidal madman: Paul Salopek, " 'Caribou People' Wage Last Stand in the Arctic," Knight Ridder/Tribune News, October 7, 2005.

107   and fought vigorously to preserve: "A Bridge Too Far," *The Wall Street Journal*, November 21, 2005.

108   And the ever-reliable Rush Limbaugh: *The Rush Limbaugh Show*, March 16, 2005.

Chapter 5: The Right's War on Science

110   In 1995, two small islands: John Vidal, "Pacific Atlantis: First Climate Change Refugees," *The Guardian*, November 25, 2005.

110   It was the beginning: Ibid.

110   eventually, the evacuation: Ibid.

110   The waters that will soon: Andrew C. Revkin, "Analysts See 'Simply Incredible' Shrinking of Floating Ice in the Arctic," *The New York Times*, August 10, 2007.

111   still impoverished Ninth Ward: Robin Pogrebin, "Brad Pitt Commissions Designs for New Orleans," *The New York Times*, December 3, 2007.

113   "Theologians as ancient as St. Augustine": Lawrence M. Krauss, *The New York Times*, March 29, 2005.

115   "Indisputable evidence—long hidden": Jeremy Redmon, "Anti-Evolution Memo Stirs Controversy," *The Atlanta Journal-Constitution*, February 15, 2007.

115   "the second greatest hoax": Charles P. Pierce, "In Praise of Oklahoma," *The American Prospect*, February 23, 2005.

115   Inhofe has compared environmentalists: Jim Myers, "Heat Wave Has Senator Sticking to Beliefs," *Tulsa World*, July 22, 2006.

115   EPA to the Gestapo: Chris Mooney, "James Inhofe Proves 'Flat Earth' Doesn't Refer to Oklahoma," *The American Prospect*, April 13, 2004.

115   "We all know the Weather Channel": Associated Press, "Lawmakers Hear Global Warming 'Spin' Allegations," *USA Today*, January 30, 2007.

116   the Arctic Climate Impact Assessment: Arctic Climate Impact Assessment, http://amap.no/acia/, accessed March 2, 2008.

116   Don Young waxed sarcastic: Sean Cockerham, "Alaska Congressional Delegation Doubts Scientists' Conclusions," *Anchorage Daily News*, November 21, 2004.

116 Ted Stevens, the senator: Ibid.

116 "It's a problem that George Bush": Personal interview with author, May 31, 2007.

117 "Despite the hysterics of a few pseudo-scientists": James Wolcott, "Rush to Judgment," *Vanity Fair,* May 2007.

117 In his 2004 best-seller *State of Fear*: Michael Crichton, "Author's Message," *State of Fear* (New York: HarperCollins, 2004), p. 569.

118 "I recognize the surface of the earth": Caroline Daniel and Fiona Harvey, "Bush Admits to Role of Humans in Global Warming," *Financial Times*, July 7, 2005.

118 "When the Bush Administration's": Elizabeth Kolbert, "Global Warning," *The New Yorker,* December 12, 2005.

119 Take the revelation: Andrew C. Revkin, "Bush Aide Edited Climate Reports," *The New York Times*, June 8, 2005.

119 It was June 2003: Andrew C. Revkin with Katherine Q. Seelye, "Report by EPA Leaves Out Data on Climate Change," *The New York Times*, June 19, 2003.

119 And so was the revelation: Juliet Eilperin, "EPA Wording Found to Mirror Industry's," *The Washington Post*, September 22, 2004.

119 And so was the disclosure: John Vidal, "Revealed: How Oil Giant Influenced Bush," *The Guardian*, June 8, 2005.

119 On June 10, 2005: Andrew C. Revkin, "Editor of Climate Reports Resigns," *The New York Times*, June 10, 2005.

120 "Editing Out Inconvenient Facts": *The Carpetbagger Report* (www.thecarpet baggerreport.com/archives/4399.html).

120 "Hating on the Lab": Ezra Klein, *The American Prospect*, June 8, 2005 (www .prospect.org/csnc/blogs/ezraklein_archive?month=06&year=2005&base_name =hating_on_the_lab).

121 "On Purpose": The Road to Surfdom, June 8, 2005 (www.roadtosurfdom .com/2005/06/08/on-purpose/).

122 54 percent back research: A. J. Hostetler, "Views Shift on Stem-Cell Research," *Richmond Times-Dispatch*, December 23, 2007.

122 "The ethics of medicine": United States Department of Health and Human Services Fact Sheet, July 14, 2004 (www.hhs.gov/news/press/2004pres/ 20040714b.html).

122 Late in 2007, two teams: Michael Kinsley, "Why Science Can't Save the GOP," *Time*, November 28, 2007.

123 "besieged by political pressure": letter to Stephen L. Johnson, May 24, 2006 (www.peer.org/docs/epa/06_25_5_union_ltr.pdf).

123 undermining the Food Quality Protection Act: Paul Raeburn, "Slow-Acting," *Scientific American*, August 14, 2006.

123 "not supported": letter from Melanie Marty, March 8, 2006 (http:// yosemite2.epa.gov/ochp/ochpweb.nsf/f99fd8877fb4269e85256ad30045bb5b/ 85256d1f007027ad85257132006b1844/$FILE/30806_3.pdf).

124 the National Cancer Institute says: National Cancer Institute, NCI Information Tip Sheet for Writers, "Cancer and the Environment," undated.

124 Nine million kids in America: Report by Centers for Disease Control, released March 31, 2004 (www.cdc.gov/od/oc/media/pressrel/r040331.htm).

124 children are seven times more likely: survey conducted by the Coalition for West Oakland Revitalization, the Prescott Joseph Center, the West Oakland Asthma Coalition and the Pacific Institute, November 2004 (www.pacinst.org/ reports/health_survey/west_oakland_health_survey.pdf).

124 "But any Republicans": Kingsley, "Why Science Can't Save the GOP," *Time*, November 28, 2007.

125 "If human beings follow": Jim Hansen, "The Threat to the Planet," *The New York Review of Books*, July 13, 2006.

Chapter 6: Iraq: The Beginning of a War Without End

127 a study by two nonprofit: Charles Lewis and Mark Reading-Smith, "False Pretenses," Center For Public Integrity, January 22, 2008.

128 "It is now beyond dispute": Ibid.

130 "People do not realize": Alan Greenspan, *Charlie Rose*, September 20, 2007.

131 "the stupidest fucking guy": Chris Suellentrop, "Douglas Feith, What Has the Pentagon's Third Man Done Wrong? Everything," *Slate*, May 20, 2004.

131 "Then, you have the phenomenon": Nicholas Lemann, "After Iraq: The Plan to Remake the Middle East," *The New Yorker*, February 17, 2003.

131 "First it will inspire": "Richard Perle Interview," *Frontline*, PBS, January 25, 2003.

132 In Saudi Arabia: Rasheed Abou-Alsamh, "Ruling Jolts Even Saudis: 200 Lashes for Rape Victim," *The New York Times*, November 16, 2007.

132 "One of the principal reasons": Nicholas Lemann, "After Iraq: The Plan to remake the Middle East," *The New Yorker*, February 17, 2003.

133 "why the post-Hussein occupation": Karen Kwiatkowski, "Pentagon decision-making seriously flawed," *The Record*, August 3, 2003.

133 "He was very arrogant": Laura Rozen, "Ye of Little Feith," *The American Prospect*, May 18, 2004.

133 Poor George Tenet: "George Tenet: At the Center of the Storm," *60 Minutes*, CBS News, April 29, 2007.

133 "I became campaign talk": Ibid.

134 "It's the most despicable thing": Ibid.

134 "I am resigning because": John Brady Kiesling, "Iraq: A Letter of Resignation," *The New York Review of Books*, April 10, 2003.

134 "At the end of the day": "George Tenet: At the Center of the Storm," *60 Minutes*, CBS News, April 29, 2007.

135 "I do think Bush also went": *Frontline*, PBS, January 14, 2003.

136 "It is entirely possible that in Iraq": *Meet The Press*, NBC, April 6, 2003.

136 "I really do believe": *Meet the Press*, NBC, September 14, 2003.

136 "Well, I think we *have*": Ibid.

136 "I think there is a potential civic culture": "Richard Perle: The Making of a Neoconservative," *Think Tank with Ben Wattenberg*, PBS, November 14, 2002.

137 "There's a lot of money": "Questions for Paul Wolfowitz," *American Progress*, April 20, 2004.

137 "I mean, when you talk about 1.7": "Project Iraq," *Nightline*, ABC News, April 23, 2003.

138 Andrew Natsios: Joseph Stiglitz and Linda Bilmes, *The Three Trillion Dollar War: The True Cost of the Iraq Conflict* (New York: W. W. Norton, 2008), p. 24.

139 "Freedom's untidy, and free people": Sean Loughlin," Rumsfeld on Looting in Iraq: 'Stuff happens,' " CNN, April 12, 2003.

139 On May 1, 2003, First Lieutenant George Bush: "Poll: Vast Majority Believes Iraq Mission Not Accomplished," CNN, May 1, 2006.

141 "There's been a certain amount": *Fresh Air*, WHYY FM, April 1, 2003.

142 In a speech he gave in December: "President Discusses War on Terror and Upcoming Iraqi Elections," December 12, 2005, (www.whitehouse.gov/news/releases/2005/12/2005).

143 "I believe the President": "Rice Praises Kuwait for Extending Voting Rights to Women," U.S. Department of State, May 19, 2005. (www.america.gov/st/washfile-english/2005/May/20050519185957cpataruko.7482111.html).

145 "I think in this case international law": Oliver Burkeman and Julian Borger, "War Critics Astonished. as US Hawk Admits Invasion Was Illegal," *The Guardian*, November 20, 2003.

145 "Saddam Hussein won't change": Bush-Aznar transcript, *The New York Review of Books*, Vol. 54, No. 17, November 8, 2007.

147 "Trying to get a single": Donald Rumsfeld, Defense Department briefing (www.defenselink.mil/transcripts/transcript.aspx?transcript=3190), July 20, 2005.

147 "I never estimated the cost": *Meet the Press*, June 26, 2005.

148 "As we know, there are known knowns": Hart Seely, "The Poetry of D. H. Rumsfeld," *Slate*, April 2, 2003.

149 "much of the intelligence": Sumi Das and Suzanne Malveaux, "Bush Takes Responsibility for Invasion Intelligence," CNN Special Report, December 14, 2005.

149 "My son told us": Johanna Neuman, "Marine Backed Mission If Not Bush's Election," *Los Angeles Times*, December 15, 2005.

150 150,000 Iraqis: "U.N. Survey Puts 3-Year Iraqi Toll at 151,000," *Los Angeles Times*, January 10, 2008.

Chapter 7: Iraq: The Long Hard Slog Gets Longer and Sloggier

151 After months of mounting U.S. losses: Susan Page, "Poll: USA Is Losing Patience on Iraq," *USA Today*, June 12, 2005.

151 "The president takes seriously": Jim VandeHei, "Bush Is Expected to Address Specifics on Iraq," *The Washington Post*, June 16, 2005.

152 Iraqi troops are "more prepared than others": Ibid.

152 "difficult choices and additional sacrifices": Sheryl Gay Stolberg and John Holusha, "Bush Says Victory in Iraq Is Still Possible," *The New York Times*, December 20, 2006.

152 "Administration officials say": Jim Rutenberg and David E. Sanger, "Bush Aides Seek Alternatives to Iraq Study Group's Proposals, Calling Them Impractical," *The New York Times*, December 10, 2006.

152 "Announce that whatever new approach": "Rumsfeld's Memo of Options for Iraq," *The New York Times*, December 3, 2006.

154 Recommendation 4: James A. Baker III and Lee H. Hamilton, *The Iraq Study Group Report* (New York: Alfred A. Knopf, 2008), p. 36.

154–5 Recommendations 23, 32, 64, 73, 77: Ibid.

155 "You know, I think an interesting": Peter Baker, "U.S. Not Winning War in Iraq, Bush Says for 1st Time," *The Washington Post*, December 20, 2006.

155 "exceedingly complex and very tough": Tom Bowman and Alex Cohen, "Iraq Situation 'Very Tough' Gen. Petraeus Says," *Day to Day*, National Public Radio, April 26, 2007.

155 "heavy lifting": Interview with Jim Lehrer, *NewsHour with Jim Lehrer*, PBS, September 19, 2006.

155 "long, hard slog": "Rumsfeld Predicts 'Long, Hard, Slog In Iraq,' " CNN .com, October 22, 2003.

156 "In the last campaign": White House press conference, interview question to George W. Bush by Jim Dickerson, April 13, 2004 (www.msnbc.msn.com/ id/4734348/).

156 "Hmm. I wish you would have given me": Ibid.

156 "History will judge this president": Dick Cheney interviewed on CNN by John King, the Vice President's Residence, June 22, 2006 (www.whitehouse .gov/news/releases/2006/06/20060622-8.html).

156 "History demands much of America": Karl Rove, "The Long View," *National Review*, August 31, 2007.

156 "History is going to have to judge": Dan Froomkin, "Pick Your Bush," washingtonpost.com, November 14, 2007.

157 Apparently, so the Pentagon: Jim Garmone, "Troops Haven't Lost Faith in Rumsfeld," December 9, 2006 (www.defenselink.mil/news/newsarticle.aspx? id=2366).

157 It was clear from Karl Rove's appearance: "An Hour with Senior Political Advisor Karl Rove," *Charlie Rose*, PBS, March 11, 2002.

158 "Made things move too fast": Ibid.

158 "Who controls the past, controls the future": George Orwell, *1984* (New York: New American Library, 1961), p. 32.

158 "it's in our national interest": Press realease, "President Bush Discusses Iraq with Reporters," New York, September 13, 2002 (http://www.whitehouse.gov/ news/releases/2002/09/20020913.html).

158 "delaying a vote": Thom Shanker and David E. Sanger, "Rumsfeld Says Other Nations Promise to Aid Attack on Iraq," *The New York Times*, September 19, 2002.

158 "Looked at Cheney": Dan Froomkin, "The White House 'After Party,' " washingtonpost.com, November 28, 2007.

158 "We just have to do this now": Ibid.

158 provided by Richard Clarke: "Clarke's Take On Terror," *60 Minutes*, March 21, 2004.

158 And corroborating evidence: "Bush Sought 'Way' To Invade Iraq?," *60 Minutes*, CBS, January 11, 2004.

159 "We don't determine": *Charlie Rose*, PBS, March 11, 2002.

159 The Downing Street Memo: "The Secret Downing Street Memo," *The Sunday Times* (London), May 1, 2005.

159 The White House was already using: Michael R. Gordon and Judith Miller, "Threats and Responses: the Iraqis; U.S. Says Hussein Intensifies Quest for A-Bomb Parts", *The New York Times*, September 8, 2002.

159 Condi Rice was warning: David Barstow, William J. Broad, and Jeff Gerth, "How the White House Embraced Disputed Arms Intelligence," *The New York Times*, October 3, 2004.

159 Cheney was using aluminum tubes: Mike Allen, "War Cabinet Argues for Iraq Attack," *The Washington Post*, September 9, 2002.

159 "Pull out?": George Carlin, *Jammin' in New York*, DVD, 2006.

160 "What cut and run": Joseph Williams, "GOP Wants 'Cut and Run' Label to Stick," *The Boston Globe*, June 21, 2006.

160 As early as December of 2003: Ivo H. Daalder and James Lindsay, "Whatever

We Do, We Can't Cut and Run," Brookings Institution, December 15, 2003 (www.brookings.edu/opinions/2003/1215iraq_daalder.aspx).

160 "A few minutes ago": Charles Babington, "House Rejects Iraq Pullout After GOP Forces a Vote," *The Washington Post*, November 19, 2005

160 "Cutting and running is bad": "Iraq: Capitol Hill's War of Words," *CBS News*, June 20, 2006 (www.cbsnews.com/stories/2006/06/20/politics/main1731579 .shtml).

160 "So what about Iraq?": Press Conference, "President Bush Participates in Joint Press Availability with President Sarkozy of France," Mount Vernon Estate, Mount Vernon, Virginia, November 7, 2007 (www.whitehouse.gov/ news/releases/2007/11/20071107-5.html).

161 the modern White House: The White House website, facts (http://www .whitehouse.gov/history/facts.html).

161 "Oh, indeed there is a tie": Condoleezza Rice, "National Security Advisor Condoleezza Rice discusses President Bush's suprise visit to troops in Bagh- dad," CBS News Transcripts, November 28, 2003.

161 "You see, this war came to us": Condoleezza Rice, "Remarks at American Embassy, Baghdad," (http://www.state.gov/secretary/rm/2005/46280.htm), accessed March 3, 2008.

162 a Program on International Policy Attitudes: Steven Kull, "US Public Beliefs on Iraq and the Presidential Election," The Program on International Policy Attitudes, April 22, 2004.

162 Part of the problem comes from stories: "Hundreds of WMDs, Found in Iraq," *Fox News* (www.foxnews.com/story/0,2933,200499,00.html).

162 After the Santorum report: (http://mediamatters.org/items/200606230005).

163 "The duly elected people's bodies": *Meet the Press*, NBC, May 13, 2007.

163 Indeed, in January 2005: Elisabeth Bumiller, David E. Sanger, and Richard W. Stevenson, "Bush Says Iraqi Leaders Will Want U.S Forces to Stay to Help," *The New York Times*, January 28, 2005.

164 it was "no coincidence": Major General William Caldwell, President's Radio Address, October 21, 2006 (http://www.whitehouse.gov/news/releases/2006/ 10/20061021.html).

164 "There's certainly a stepped-up": Dan Froomkin, 'Where's the Cowboy Talk Now?," washingtonpost.com, October 19, 2006.

165 "This war in Iraq is a grotesque mistake": Nancy Pelosi, Speaker's website (http://speaker.gov/issues?id=0001).

165 "owes our military and their families": Kevin Baker, "Stabbed in the Back! The Past and Future of a Right-Wing Myth," *Harper's*, June 2006.

166 "GOP ceded the center": "GOP Ceded the Center and Paid the Price," *Los Angeles Times*, November 8, 2006.

167 "emboldened . . . the enemy": Ibid.

167 "I think that our military is the finest": *Meet the Press*, NBC, June 26, 2005.

168 "This question on the draft is": Town Hall Meeting, Alex Menzek Field House, Minnesota State University, Moorhead, Minnesota, October 25, 2004 (www.whitehouse.gov/news/releases/2004/10/20041025-10.html).

168 About 40 percent: Will Dunham, "Strained U.S. National Guard has hurri- cane relief role," Reuters, August 30, 2005.

169 "Missing the personnel is the big thing": Ann Scott Tyson, "Strain of Iraq War Means the Relief Burden Will Have to Be Shared," *The Washington Post*, August 31, 2005.

169   To see it boiled down even more: Nico Pitney, "Hurricane Protection a Low Priority for Bush," September 1, 2005 (http://thinkprogress.org/2005/09/01/hurricane-low/).

169   "the country's premier agency for dealing": Eric Holdeman, "Destroying FEMA," *The Washington Post*, August 30, 2005.

170   the insurgency is "in the last throes": *Larry King Live*, CNN, May 30, 2005.

170   "America will be safer": Ibid.

170   "We haven't set a deadline": Ibid.

171   According to Defense Secretary Robert Gates: Ken Fireman and Tony Capaccio, "Walter Reed Care Spawns Probes, Political Attacks," Bloomberg, March 3, 2007 (www.bloomberg.com/apps/news?pid=20601087&sid=ahUoNToRujEs&refer=home).

172   "They can get desert training elsewhere": Tony Snow Press Briefing, Office of the Press Secretary, The White House, February 28, 2007 (http://www.whitehouse.gov/news/releases/2007/02/20070228-5.html).

173   "The situation seems far more stable": "Iraqi Death Toll Rises Above 100 Per Day, U.N. Says," *The New York Times*, July 19, 2006.

173   "God knows what comes next": Kirk Semple, "Over 3,000 Iraqi Civilians Killed in June, U.N. Reports," *The New York Times*, July 18, 2006.

174   "We've never been defeated": "Vice President Dick Cheney Says Iraq Handover Still 'Has A Long Way to Go," *Morning Edition*, NPR, October 25, 2006.

174   "refining our training strategy": "In Opening Remarks, President Urges Steadfastness in a Difficult Fight," *The New York Times*, October 26, 2006.

174   In October 2007: Henry Waxman, *Letter from Henry Waxman to Condoleezza Rice*, October 5, 2007 (http://oversight.house.gov/documents/20071005153354.pdf).

175   The events of September 16, 2007: Peter Walker, "Blackwater Guards Shot Iraqis Without Provocation, Report Says," *The Guardian*, October 8 2007.

176   "We cannot win a fight for hearts and minds": Kathryn Fiegen, "Obama Outlines Policy on Private Security in Iraq," *Iowa City Press Citizen*, October 4, 2007.

Chapter 8: Iraq: Petraeus Ex Machina

180   The president's numbers were: "Bush Job Approval Hits 41%," Zogby International, September 8, 2005 (www.zogby.com/news/ReadNews.dbm?ID=1020).

181   "James Baker says that he's looking": *This Week with George Stephanopoulos*, ABC News, October 22, 2006.

181   "Iraq is the central front": "President Bush's Remarks at Utah Air National Guard," Salt Lake City, Utah, August 30, 2006 (www.whitehouse.gov/news/releases/2006/08/20060830-10.html).

181   "We will *stay the course*": "President Bush, President Uribe of Colombia Discuss Terrorism and Security," Bush Ranch, Crawford, Texas, August 4, 2005 (www.whitehouse.gov/news/releases/2005/08/20050804-2.html).

181   "It's a wonderful feeling": "Bush, Blair Discuss Sharon Plan; Future of Iraq in Press Conference," in the Rose Garden, April 16, 2004 (www.whitehouse.gov/news/releases/2004/04/20040416-4.html).

182   But having spat the words: Michael A. Fletcher, "Bush Attacks 'Party of Cut and Run,' " *The Washington Post*, September 29, 2006.

182   The president had repeatedly insisted: press conference in the Rose Garden,

September 15, 2006 (www.whitehouse.gov/news/releases/2006/09/20060915-2 .html).

182 "trust our commanders on the ground": press conference in the East Room, October 25, 2006 (www.whitehouse.gov/news/releases/2006/10/20061025 .html).

182 "I believe that you empower": press conference in the Rose Garden, October 11, 2006 (www.whitehouse.gov/news/releases/2006/10/2006011-5.html).

182 arguing that it would increase Iraqi: Michael R. Gordon and David E. Sanger, "Commander Said to Be Open to More Troops," *The New York Times*, December 24, 2006.

182 increase the appearance: Ibid.

182 "be like throwing kerosene": *NBC Nightly News*, December 20, 2006.

183 General Abizaid said: "General Abizaid Speaks Against Setting Firm Timetable for Iraq Withdrawal," *The NewsHour with Jim Lehrer*, PBS, November 15, 2006.

183 "I'm not necessarily opposed": Michael R. Gordon and David E. Sanger, "Commander Said to Be Open to More Troops," *The New York Times*, December 24, 2006.

183 "What I want to hear": David E. Sanger, Michael R. Gordon, and John F. Burns, "Chaos Overran Iraq Plan in '06, Bush Team Says," *The New York Times*, January 2, 2007.

183 on the cusp of rewarding: "Senate Confirms Shift of Gen. Casey from Iraq to Army Chief of Staff," Associated Press, February 8, 2007.

183 "the possible modest augmentation": Gordon and Sanger, "Commander Said to Be Open."

183 Not exactly a ringing endorsement: Robin Wright and Peter Baker, "White House, Joint Chiefs at Odds on Adding Troops," *The Washington Post*, December 19, 2006.

183 "The Bush administration is split": Ibid.

184 "You can't fight a war": press conference in the Rose Garden, October 11, 2006 (www.whitehouse.gov/news/releases/2006/10/20061011-5.html).

184 General Shinseki's fate: Matthew Engel, "Scorned General's Tactics Proved Right," *The Guardian*, March 29, 2003.

184 Petraeus, as his many fans: Rachel Dry, "Petraeus on Vietnam's Legacy," *The Washington Post*, January 14, 2007.

184 Petraeus' stellar military career: Melissa Block, "General Assays Iraqi Security Force," *All Things Considered*, National Public Radio, May 20, 2004.

184 de facto military governor: Guy Raz, "General Petraeus Profile," *Morning Edition*, National Public Radio, May 13, 2003.

184 Mosul, Iraq's third largest city: Bradley J. Brooks and Steven R. Hurst, "Commanders See Long Operation in Mosul," Associated Press, January 29, 2008.

184 "no force worked harder": Rod Nordland, "Iraq's Repairman," *Newsweek*, October 17, 2007.

184 his efforts in Mosul: Ibid.

185 The president publicly mentioned: Thomas E. Ricks, "Bush Leans on Petraeus as War Dissent Deepens," *The Washington Post*, July 15, 2007.

185 Rich laid it out: Frank Rich, "Who Really Took Over During That Colonoscopy," *The New York Times*, July 29, 2007.

185 the case that the civil war: Linda Robinson, "Petraeus Tries to Make Headway in Iraq," *U.S. News & World Report*, May 20, 2007.

185 "The New Jesus is the guy": James Fallows, "David Petraeus and the 'New Jesus' Problem," *The Atlantic*, July 17, 2007.

186 The surge was: Remarks as delivered by Senator John McCain, Virginia Military Institute, Lexington, Virginia, April 11, 2007.

186 co-written by: Anna Badkhen, "Can Petraeus Lead U.S. to Victory?" *San Francisco Chronicle*, April 15, 2007.

186 from 132,000: Michael Abramowitz, Robin Wright, and Thomas E. Ricks, "With Iraq Speech, Bush to Pull Away from His Generals," *The Washington Post*, January 10, 2007.

186 Having been thoroughly infiltrated: Marc Santora, "Sectarian Ties Weaken Duty's Call for Iraq Forces," *The New York Times*, December 28, 2006.

186 he'd use the sacrifice: "Text of Bush's Final State of the Union," Associated Press, January 29, 2008.

186 he has avoided the funerals: Jeff Schogol, "President Bush Answers Questions from Downrange," *Stars and Stripes*, July 5, 2006.

186 he refused to allow: Dana Bash, "White House: Bush Moved by Casket Photos," CNN.com, April 24, 2004.

187 what CIA veteran John McLaughlin called: *The McLaughlin Group*, PBS, July 20, 2007 (taped) (www.mclaughlin.com/library/transcript.asp?id=607).

187 David Brooks recounted: David Brooks, "Heroes and History," *The New York Times*, July 17, 2007.

187 That's the kind of logical question: Michael Abramowitz and Jonathan Weisman, "Bush's Iraq Plan Meets Skepticism on Capitol Hill," *The Washington Post*, January 12, 2007.

187 "This is an existential conflict": *Fox News Sunday*, Fox News, January 14, 2007.

187 In actuality, he skipped: Katherine Q. Seelye, "The 2004 Campaign: Military Service; Cheney's Five Draft Deferments During the Vietnam Era Emerge as a Campaign Issue," *The New York Times*, May 1, 2004.

188 "I had other priorities": Ibid.

188 Richard Perle offered: *Meet the Press*, NBC, March 18, 2007.

188 "I vowed that day": "President Bush Discusses Iraq War Supplemental, War on Terror," American Legion Post 177, Fairfax, Virginia, April 10, 2007 (www .whitehouse.gov/news/releases/2007/04/20070410-1.html).

189 "This U.S.-led plan": Glenn Beck, "Should Mexico Compensate U.S. for Cost of Illegals?" CNN, February 28, 2007.

189 The first reports: Ann Scott Tyson, "No Drop in Iraq Violence Seen Since Troop Buildup," *The Washington Post*, June 14, 2007.

189 "Iraq's Political": Damien Cave, "Iraqis Are Failing to Meet U.S. Benchmarks," *The New York Times*, June 13, 2007.

190 And the Pentagon admitted: "Measuring Stability and Security in Iraq," U.S. Department of Defense, June 2007.

190 "There are two mentalities": Michael R. Gordon, "U.S. Warns Iraq that Progress Is Needed Soon," *The New York Times*, June 12, 2007.

190 "civil war that took": Nouri Al-Maliki, "Our Common Struggle," *The Wall Street Journal*, June 13, 2007.

190 "professional soccer leagues": Cesar G. Soriano, "Petraeus Says Security Crackdown Working," *USA Today*, June 13, 2007.

190 "There is even some hope": ABC News, June 13, 2007.

190 "America could not ask for a finer": "U.S. Ambassador to Iraq Ryan Crocker Discusses the War and Progress," *Meet the Press*, NBC, June 17, 2007.

192   I caught Ware: *Anderson Cooper 360°*, CNN, May 1, 2007.

193   in July 2007, an interim report: "Benchmark Assessment Report," September 14, 2007 (www.whitehouse.gov/news/releases/2007/09/20070914.html).

194   He stuck his fingers in his ears: *The Situation Room*, CNN, January 24, 2007.

194   "bottom line": Peter Baker, "Defending Iraq War, Defiant Cheney Cites 'Enormous Successes,' " *The Washington Post*, January 25, 2007.

194   "there is a convergence": press conference July 12, 2007 (www.whitehouse .gov/news/releases/2007/07/20070712-5.html).

194   The same administration: "The Conflict in Iraq: Green Zone Deaths; Strategy Doubts; Familiar Bush Theme," *Los Angeles Times*, July 11, 2007.

195   A *New York Times* piece: Gary Langer, "What They're Saying in Anbar Province," *The New York Times*, September 16, 2007.

195   At the time of Petraeus's triumphant: Karen DeYoung and Shailagh Murray, "GOP Skepticism on Iraq Growing," *The Washington Post*, June 27, 2007.

195   "And Anbar province, cited by both": "Address by the President to the Nation on the Way Forward in Iraq," Oval Office, September 13, 2007. (www.white house.gov/news/releases/2007/09/20070913-2.html).

196   "General Petraeus or General Betray Us": Moveon.org (http://po.moveon .org/petraeus.html).

196   "character assassination on an American": Associated Press, "Rudy Blasts Hillary Again Over Move On Ad," September 17, 2007.

196   "Moveon.org ought to": "McCain to Move On: Get Out," *CBS News*, CBS, September 14, 2007.

196   Even Don Rumsfeld popped: Bradley Graham, "Rumsfeld Foundation to Encourage Public Service," *The Washington Post*, September 17, 2007.

197   "How do you ask a man to be": "Vietnam War Veteran John Kerry's Testimony Before the Senate Foreign Relations Committee," April 22, 1971 (http:// facultystaff.richmond.edu/~ebolt/history398/JohnKerryTestimony.html).

198   The first is that radical: Michael Howard, "Iraqi Cleric Threatens to End Militia Freeze Unless Attacks Stop," *The Guardian*, February 1, 2008.

198   The second is that influential: Richard A. Oppel, "Suicide Bomber Kills Key Sunni Leader," *The New York Times*, January 8, 2008.

198   Ambassador Crocker: Steven Lee Meyers and Alissa J. Rubin, "U.S. Scales Back Political Goals for Iraqi Unity," *The New York Times*, November 25, 2007.

198   "Its goal was to create": Matthew Yglesias, "Victory in Iraq," *The Atlantic*, November 25, 2007.

199   "Instead, administration officials say": Steven Lee Meyers and Alissa J. Rubin, "U.S. Scales Back Political Goals for Iraqi Unity," *The New York Times*, November 25, 2007.

Chapter 9: Casualties of War: Neglecting Afghanistan, Empowering Iraq

202   *The New York Times* leaked: "Key Judgments from a National Intelligence Estimate on Iran's Nuclear Activity," *The New York Times*, December 4, 2007.

203   "The War on Terror": Michael Ledeen, "The War on Terror Won't End in Baghdad," *The Wall Street Journal*, September 4, 2002.

203   "Everything we know": Michael Ledeen, "Murder's Row Rules the Mullahs and Us," *National Review Online*, July 15, 2005.

203 Ledeen speculated in 2003: Michael Ledeen, "A Theory," *National Review Online*, March 10, 2003 (www.nationalreview.com/ledeen/ledeen031003.asp).

203 While serving as a consultant: Stephen Engelberg, "A Consultant's Role in the Iran Affair," *The New York Times*, February 2, 1987.

203 "Axis of Evil": State of the Union Address, January 29, 2002 (www.white house.gov/news/releases/2002/01/20020129-11.html).

204 "Iran aggressively pursues": Ibid.

204 "It is the beginning": Sandy Tolan and Jason Felch, "Beyond Regime Change," *Los Angeles Times*, December 1, 2002.

204 When President Clinton: "The Iran Embargo," *The New York Times*, May 2, 1995.

205 "The problem is that the good Lord": Ann Wright, "An 'Enduring' Relationship for Security and Enduring an Occupation for Oil," *Truthout*, December 5, 2007 (www.truthout.org/docs_2006/120507K.shtml).

205 Khatami's 2003 diplomatic overture: Michael Hirsh and Maziar Bahari, "America's Hidden War with Iran," *Newsweek*, February 19, 2007.

206 "The idea that an American attack": Seymour M. Hersh, "The Coming Wars," *The New Yorker*, January 24, 2005.

207 On November 14, 2006: "Iran: Nuclear Program Will Be Operating by February," CNN.com, November 14, 2006 (www.cnn.com/2006/WORLD/meast/11/14/iran.nuclear/index.html).

208 "what no Democrat"; "saving Iran": Seymour M. Hersh, "The Iran Plans," *The New Yorker*, April 17, 2006.

209 "There's only one thing": "Senators: Military Last Option on Iran," CNN.com, January 16, 2006 (http://edition.cnn.com/2006/US/01/15/iran .congress/index.html).

209 In an interview with *Newsweek:* John Barry and Dan Ephron, "War-Gaming the Mullahs," *Newsweek*, September 27, 2004.

210 Bush warned that Iran's: Press conference, October 17, 2007 (www.white house.gov/news/releases/2007/10/20071017.html).

210 Less than two months after: "Key Judgments from a National Intelligence Estimate on Iran's Nuclear Activity," *The New York Times*, December 4, 2007.

210 "I think it is very important": Sgt. Sara Moore, "Bush Says Iran Still Poses Threat," American Forces Press Service, December 4, 2007 (www.defenselink .mil/news/newsarticle.aspx?id=48312).

210 "Iran was dangerous": Ibid.

211 "I must confess": Norman Podhoretz, "Dark Suspicions About the NIE," Commentarymagazine.com, December 3, 2007.

211 the editorial page of *The Wall Street Journal:* "High Confidence Games: The CIA's Flip-Flop on Iran Is Hardly Reassuring," *The Wall Street Journal*, December 5, 2007.

212 "The estimates guys": Mark Falcoff, "A Word from Mark Falcoff on the NIE," Power Line, December 5, 2007 (http://www.powerlineblog.com/archives2/2007/12/019197.php).

212 the "amazing" progress: Donna Miles, "Bush: New Year to Build on 2005 Progress in Terror War," American Forces Press Service, January 4, 2006 (www.defenselink.mil/news/newsarticle.aspx?id=14698).

212 Bush described a "liberated Afghanistan": Commencement Address at the United States Military Academy in West Point, New York, June 5, 2006.

213   In the spring of 2006: Carlotta Gall, "Afghans Riot over U.S.-Caused Crash," *The New York Times*, May 30, 2006.

213   "Afghans often complain": Wesal Zaman and Paul Watson, "Afghan Death Toll Hits 8 Amid Unrest," *Los Angeles Times*, May 30, 2006.

213   "You can't carry": Matthew Hansen, "Iraq, Corruption Hamper Afghan Rebuilding Efforts," *Lincoln Journal Star*, November 27, 2005.

213   There are a few 2007 stats: Jason Straziuso, "U.S. Casualties in Afghanistan Hit Record," Associated Press, January 2, 2008.

214   The executive director of the U.N. agency: Colin Brown, "Bid to Wipe Out Afghan Opium Failed, Says UN," *The Independent*, November 17, 2007.

214   "diplomats and well-informed Afghans": Ron Moreau and Sami Yousafzai, "A Harvest of Treachery," *Newsweek*, January 9, 2006.

214   Canadian Prime Minister: "Canada PM Tells Bush He's Ready to Quit Afghanistan," Reuters UK, January 31, 2008.

214   The BBC reported: "Pressures 'Driving UK Troops Out,' " *BBC News*, January 28, 2008.

214   And an important study: Peter Spiegel, "Afghanistan Report Warns of 'Failed State'," *Los Angeles Times*, January 31, 2008.

215   Efforts to reconstruct: David Rohde and Carlotta Gall, "Delays Hurting U.S. Rebuilding in Afghanistan," *The New York Times*, November 7, 2005.

215   even Kabul gets only: Jason Straziuso, "Kabul Gets 3 Hours of Electricity a Day," *The Boston Globe*, January 27, 2008.

215   from $1 billion in 2005: Griff Witte, "U.S. Cedes Duties in Rebuilding Afghanistan," *The Washington Post*, January 3, 2006.

215   Neumann . . . told Congress in early 2006: Jackson Diehl, "Reselling the Wars," *The Washington Post*, November 7, 2005.

215   "This is too critical": Griff Witte, "U.S. Cedes Duties in Rebuilding Afghanistan," *The Washington Post*, January 3, 2006.

215   "There's going to be other wars": "On Campaign Trail," *CNN Newsroom*, CNN, January 27, 2008.

215   "We're going to have a lot of PTSD": Ibid.

216   It appeared as if: State of the Union Address, January 28, 2008 (www.whitehouse.gov/news/releases/2008/01/20080128-13.html).

216   "A failed Iraq would embolden extremists": Ibid.

216   "Al Qaeda is on the run in Iraq": Ibid.

216   "wanted to set a date for withdrawal": Michael Luo, "What Romney Said About Troop Pullout," *The New York Times*, January 31, 2008.

216   "I was there," said McCain: Michael Luo and John M. Broder, "McCain Goes on Offensive in Tight Race in Florida," *The New York Times*, January 27, 2008.

217   "If we surrender": Ibid.

Chapter 10: Torture: America Loses the Moral High Ground

218   In 2004, when the hideous abuses: *60 Minutes II*, CBS, April 28, 2004.

218   Bush called Abu Ghraib a "terrible mistake": "Press Conference of the President," in the Rose Garden, June 14, 2006 (www.whitehouse.gov/news/releases/2006/06/20060614.html).

218   "no different than what": Susan Sontag, "Regarding the Torture of Others," *The New York Times*, May 23, 2004.

218 "outraged by the outrage": Associated Press, "GOP Sen.: 'Outraged' at Outrage," May 11, 2004 (www.cbsnews.com/stories/2004/05/11/politics/main 616896.shtml).

218 OxyContin-addled Rush: "Limbaugh Admits Addiction to Pain Medication," CNN.com, October 10, 2003 (www.cnn.com/2003/SHOWBIZ/10/10/rush.limbaugh/).

218 the administration has taken a position: Josh White and Carol D. Leonning, "U.S. Cites Exception in Torture Ban," *The Washington Post*, March 3, 2006.

219 "enhanced interrogation techniques": Dana Priest, "CIA Holds Terror Suspects in Secret Prisons," *The Washington Post*, November 2, 2005.

219 "case against torture": ACLU Press Release, "In Torture Case Against Rumsfeld, Lawyers Cite 'Widespread Pattern' of Abuse, Need for Accountability," June 30, 2006 (www.aclu.org/safefree/torture/27643prs20061208.html).

219 the meaning of "is": "Clinton's Grand Jury Testimony," *The NewsHour with Jim Lehrer*, PBS, September 21, 1998.

219 "enhanced interrogation techniques": Scott Shane, David Johnson, and James Risen, "Secret U.S. Endorsement of Severe Interrogations," *The New York Times*, October 3, 2007.

219 **Bush:** Yes?": "Press Conference by the President," in the James S. Brady Briefing Room, October 17, 2007 (www.whitehouse.gov/news/releases/2007/10/print/20071017.html).

220 did not have to comply with the Geneva Conventions: Neil A. Lewis, "The Reach of War: Geneva Conventions," *The New York Times*, May 21, 2004.

220 "illegal enemy combatants": Scott Reid, Memo to the Naval War College, "Terrorists as Illegal Combatants," February 9, 2004 (www.fas.org/man/eprint/reid.pdf).

220 "the worldwide": Jerry Seper, "Mukasey Still Mum on Waterboarding," *The Washington Times*, January 31, 2008.

220 Attorney General Mike Mukasey, who: Scott Shane, "Mukasey Calls Harsh Interrogation 'Repugnant,' " *The New York Times*, January 31, 2008.

220 "whether it's torture": Associated Press, "Intelligence Chief Couches Reference to Waterboarding as 'Torture,' " *The Washington Post*, January 13, 2008.

220 "I'm a water-safety instructor": Lawrence Wright, "Can Mike McConnell Fix America's Intelligence Community?" *The New Yorker*, January 21, 2008.

221 CIA Director Michael Hayden: Greg Miller, "Waterboarding Is Legal," *Los Angeles Times*, February 7, 2008.

221 "We don't maim": Greg Miller, "Waterboarding Is Legal, White House Says," *Los Angeles Times*, February 7, 2008.

222 "A lot has been made": Senator Christopher Dodd, "The Questions I Wish We Were Asked," *The Huffington Post*, November 1, 2007.

222 "Waterboarding," he wrote: Dianne Feinstein, "Sen. Feinstein: Judge Mukasey Has My Vote," *Los Angeles Times*, November 3, 2007.

222 shipped off to the stockade: Sig Christenson, "Pfc. England to Face Judge Today," *San Antonio Express News*, September 20, 2005.

222 It's the CIA and our rendition partners: Stephen Grey, "US Accused of 'Torture Flights,' " *The Times* (London), November 14, 2004 (www.timesonline.co.uk/article/0,,2089-1357699_1,00.html).

223 "The executive branch shall construe": "President's Statement on Signing of

H.R. 2863, the Department of Defense, Emergency Supplemental Appropriations to Address Hurricanes in the Gulf of Mexico, and Pandemic Influenza Act, 2006," December 30, 2005 (http://63.161.169.137/news/releases/2005/12/20051230-8.html).

223 "Wearied to death, his legs are unsteady": "Descriptions of Techniques Allegedly Authorized by the CIA," Human Rights Watch, November 25, 2005 (http://hrw.org/english/docs/2005/11/21/usdom12071_txt.htm).

223 "Still more feared": Translation by Scott Horton, Columbia University Law Professor, "Concentration Camp Document F321 in the proceedings of the International Military Tribunal in Nuremberg," 1949.

224 "abhorrent to American law and values": Dan Eggen and Michael Abramowitz, "Congress Seeks Secret Memos on Interrogation," *The Washington Post*, October 5, 2007.

224 opinion from 2002: "Memorandum from the U.S. Department of Justice Office of Legal Counsel for Alberto R. Gonzales, Counsel to the President," August 1, 2002. Text of memo via *The Washington Post* (www.washingtonpost.com/wp-dyn/articles/A38894-2004Jun13.html).

224 "a White House–dictated footnote": Scott Shane, David Johnston, and James Risen, "Secret U.S. Endorsement of Severe Interrogations," *The New York Times*, October 4, 2007.

224 Four-star General Kevin Byrnes: Josh White, "4-Star General Relieved of Duty," *The Washington Post*, August 10, 2005.

225 "Bin Ladin Determined to Strike": White House, "Text of President's Daily Brief for August 6, 2001," *The New York Times*, April 11, 2004.

225 "132 American soldiers": icasualties.org, "Iraq Coalition Casualty Count," February 16, 2008.

225 "It is the photographs": Jon Frandsen, "Rumsfeld Testimony Leaves Little Resolved," *USA Today*, May 8, 2004.

226 two senior officers who oversaw: Eric Schmitt, "Four Top Officers Cleared by Army in Prison Abuses," *The New York Times*, April 23, 2005.

226 Meanwhile Major General Geoffrey Miller: "The Truth About Abu Ghraib," *The Washington Post*, July 19, 2005.

226 At least 112 detainees have died: Scott Allen and Stephen Xenakis, "Our Duty to War Detainees," *The Boston Globe*, January 22, 2007.

227 "make sure that Egyptian security": Andrew Sullivan, "The Daily Dish," *The Atlantic*, October 24, 2007.

227 "I knew that I couldn't prove": Ibid.

227 "the only thing that went through my head": Ibid.

227 "that is until the airplane pilot": Alan Feuer, "Lawsuit Is Reinstated for Man Wrongly Suspected in 9/11," *The New York Times*, October 20, 2007.

229 "Germans who professed ignorance": Frank Rich, "The 'Good Germans' Among Us," *The New York Times*, October 14, 2007.

229 "The Gestapo in general": Andrew Sullivan, "How the Nazis Defended 'Enhanced Interrogation,' " "The Daily Dish," *The Atlantic*, June 14, 2007.

229 "It is not enough": Gordon Marino, "Separating the Moral from the Practical Argument Against Torture," *The Huffington Post*, October 22, 2007.

230 In fact, an intelligence advisory group: Scott Shane and Mark Mazzetti, "Interrogation Methods Are Criticized," *The New York Times*, May 30, 2007.

230 "There's nothing like the mobilization": Ibid.

231 And in March of 2007: Ibid.

231 However, the men and women of the CIA: Congressional Record, September 28, 2006 (www.fas.org/irp/congress/2006_cr/s092806.html).

232 The CIA's men and women: Milt Beardon, "Torture Is Back!," October 9, 2007 (www.huffingtonpost.com/milt-bearden/torture-is-back_b_67804.html).

232 "There are some things worse than avoiding": Andrew Sullivan, "Live Free or Die," "The Daily Dish," *The Atlantic*, October 10, 2007.

233 At the South Carolina GOP primary debate: "Republican Presidential Debate in South Carolina," University of South Carolina, May 15, 2007, *The New York Times* (www.nytimes.com/2007/05/15/us/politics/16repubs-text.html?pagewanted=print).

233 conditions at Guantánamo Bay: Michael Finnegan and Scott Martelle, "Romney Comes Out Swinging," *Los Angeles Times*, January 7, 2008.

233 "It depends on how it's done": Michael Cooper, "Giuliani Questioned on Torture," *The New York Times*, October 25, 2007.

234 In 2002, George W. Bush: Jeffrey Smith and Dan Eggan, "Gonzales Helped Set the Course for Detainees," *The Washington Post*, January 5, 2005.

234 "Well, it's a no-brainer": Dan Eggan, "Cheney Defends 'Dunk in Water' Remark," *The Washington Post*, October 28, 2006.

234 Sleep deprivation? Torture?: Richard Cohen, "Rudy's Torture Talk," *The Washington Post*, November 6, 2007.

234 "I stand for eight": Alessandra Stanley, "The Slow Rise of Abuse That Shocked the Nation," *The New York Times*, October 18, 2005.

235 songs played at top volume: Suzanne G. Cusiel, "Music as Torture, Music as Weapon," *Transcultural Music Review*, 2008.

Chapter 11: Xenophobia 2.0: The Immigration Fixation

236 "no amnesty for lawbreakers": Press release, "No Amnesty for Lawbreakers," Office of Congressman Patrick McHenry, May 18, 2006.

236 "shamnesty": Joe Consaon, "Why McCain Provokes Paranoia On the Right," *Salon*, February 7, 2008.

236 twelve million undocumented: "The Immigration Debate: Its Impact on Workers, Wages and Employees," The Wharton School of the University of Pennsylvania, June 14, 2006 (http://knowledge.wharton.edu/articlepdf/1482.pdf).

236 President Bush was labeled: Peter Hamby, "Conservative Bloggers in Full Revolt over Immigration," CNN.com, June 15, 2007.

236 "jobs Americans don't want to do": Dana Blanton, "FOX Poll: Views on Illegal Immigration, Bush Job Rating Down," *Fox News*, April 6, 2006.

236 contributions from undocumented: Shikha Dalmia, "Immigrants Contribute More to the Economy Than They Take," *Los Angeles Business Journal*, May 22, 2006.

236 National Research Council estimates: Press release, "Overall U.S. Economy Gains from Immigration, But It's Costly to Some States and Localities," The National Academies, May 17, 1997.

238 militarization of the entire: *CNN Live Today*, CNN, May 16, 2006.

238 moratorium on even legal: Billy House and Susan Carroll, "Hayworth Targets Migrants with Immigration Bill," *The Arizona Republic*, September 29, 2005.

238 "Please don't let the deportations begin": Personal conversation with Marc Cooper.

239 During a 2007 profile: Lesley Stahl, "Lou Dobbs, 'Advocacy' Journalist?" *60 Minutes*, May 6, 2007.

239 April 14, 2005, edition of his show: *Lou Dobbs Tonight*, CNN, April 14, 2005.

239 Stahl questioned the stat: Lesley Stahl, "Lou Dobbs, 'Advocacy' Journalist?" *60 Minutes*, May 6, 2007.

240 The day after: *Lou Dobbs Tonight*, CNN, May 7, 2007.

240 According to the National Hansen's Disease Program: "Number of U.S. Hansen Disease Cases by Year," U. S. Department of Health and Human Services, National Hansen's Disease Program Data and Statistics (www.hrsa.gov/hansens/data/uscases1824.htm).

240 An honest reporter might: Leslie Zganjar, "Leprosy Patients May 'Return to Society' as Hospital Changes Hands," Associated Press, January 1, 1998.

240 When the Southern Poverty Law Center: "GOP Senators Threaten to Force Change in Iraq Policy; Deadlock on Amnesty Deal," *Lou Dobbs Tonight*, CNN, May 16, 2007.

240 "For one thing": David Leonhardt, "Truth, Fiction and Lou Dobbs," *The New York Times*, May 30, 2007.

242 According to a study by Americas Majority: Richard Nadler, "Border Wars: The Impact of Immigration on the Latino Vote," Americas Majority, October 2007 (www.amermaj.com/).

242 After former Governor Pete Wilson: "The Indispensable State," *The New York Times*, August 14, 2007.

242 Governor Eliot Spitzer: Governor Eliot Spitzer Press Release, "Department of Motor Vehicles Changes License Policy to Include More New Yorkers and Implements New Regime of Anti-Fraud Measures to Strengthen the Security of the System," September 21, 2007 (www.ny.gov/governor/press/0921071.html).

242 Unlicensed illegal immigrant: Nina Bernstein, "Spitzer Grants Illegal Immigrants Easier Access to Driver's Licenses," *The New York Times*, September 22, 2007.

242 Bowing to political reality: Nicholas Confessore, "Spitzer Drops Bid to Offer Licenses More Widely," *The New York Times*, November 15, 2007.

242 George Pataki, have put up road blocks: Nina Bernstein, "Immigrant Group to Sue State Over License Crackdown," *The New York Times*, August 27, 2004.

242 Only five states: Emily Bazar, "More States to Deny Illegal Migrants Driver's Licenses," *USA Today*, January 29, 2007.

243 More than a dozen county clerks: Danny Hakim, "Spitzer Tries New Tack on Immigrant Licenses," *The New York Times*, October 28, 2007.

243 Peter Gadiel, the father of: Nina Bernstein, "Spitzer Grants Illegal Immigrants Easier Access to Driver's Licenses," *The New York Times*, September 22, 2007.

243 Lou Dobbs, naturally: *Lou Dobbs Tonight*, CNN, October 23, 2007.

244 all twelve million undocumented: Stephen Ohlemacher, "Illegal Immigrants Rise to 12 Million," Associated Press, March 7, 2006.

244 the cost of rounding them up: Edwin S. Rubenstein, "The Economics of Immigration Enforcement," The National Policy Institute, December 2005.

245 their effect on border safety is negligible: "Minuteman Project; Bridge to Nowhere; Where's Eloise?" *American Morning*, CNN, April 26, 2005.

245 super-fence from San Diego: Ralph Blumenthal, "Some Texans Fear Border

Fence Will Sever Routine of Daily Life," *The New York Times*, June 20, 2007.

245 You show me: "Governor Critical of Border Fence Proposal," Associated Press, December 21, 2005.

246 Even some powerful unions: Byron York, "At Immigration Rallies, Look for the Union Label," *The Hill*, May 4, 2006.

246 some Berlin-like wall: Rachel L. Swarns, "House Votes for 698 Miles of Fences on Mexico Border," *The New York Times*, December 16, 2005.

Chapter 12: The Right's Recession

248 "Senator Kerry says he sees two Americas": Liza Porteus, "Cheney, Miller Attack Kerry's Record," *Fox News*, September 2, 2004.

248 "two Americas—one where John Kerry can vote": "Monday RNC Convention Wire Archive," *ABC News*, September 1, 2004.

248 over 12 percent of the American people: U.S. Census Bureau news release, "Income Stable, Poverty Up, Numbers of Americans With and Without Health Insurance Rise, Census Bureau Reports," *U.S. Census Bureau News*, August 26, 2004.

248 the number of Americans with no health insurance: Ibid., and "Numbers of Americans Without Health Insurance Rise, Census Bureau Reports," U.S. Census Bureau News, September 30, 2002.

248 another report released in 2004 by the Economic Policy Institute: Bob Herbert, "An Economy That Turns American Values Upside Down," *The New York Times*, September 6, 2004.

248 "The economic pie is growing gangbusters": Ibid.

249 The downturn was triggered by a collapse: Edmund Andrews, "Fed Shrugged as Subprime Crisis Spread," *The New York Times*, December 18, 2007.

249 2.2 million: Mike Harris, "Foreclosure Filings Surged 75% in '07 as Subprime Mess Grew," *The Wall Street Journal*, January 29, 2008.

249 Blue chip investment banks: Karen Brettell, "Citi and Goldman Most Exposed to Loan Writedowns," *Reuters*, February 11, 2008.

250 The war in Iraq: Joseph Stiglitz and Linda Bilmes, *The Three Trillion Dollar War* (New York: W. W. Norton, 2008), p. 24.

250 Then there's the little problem of $100-a-barrel oil: John Wilen, "Oil Prices up on Factory Orders, Weather," Associated Press, February 4, 2008.

250 "The soaring price of oil is clearly related": Joseph Stiglitz, "The Economic Consequences of Mr. Bush," *Vanity Fair*, December 2007.

250 "The Bush administration": Andrew Gumbel, "Warning That Iraq War Could Plunge World into Deep Recession," *The Independent*, November 16, 2002.

250 "If the conflict wears on or, worse, spreads": Robert Shapiro, "The Cost of Toppling Saddam," *Slate*, October 2, 2002.

251 Countrywide Financial Group: "Bank of America Buys Countrywide Financial," ConsumerAffairs.com, January 11, 2008.

251 In the year before: Andrew Leonard, "Countrywide's Angelo Mozilo: Busted?" *Salon*, October 17, 2007.

251 Along with the $161 million: Mike Barris, "Former Merrill CEO O'Neal Joining Alcoa as Director," Dow Jones Newswires, January 18, 2008.

251 CEO Charles Prince: "Citigroup's Day of Reckoning," CNN Money, CNN.com, November 4, 2007.

251   "chief executives are": Ellen Simon, "Sex, Lies and CEO Meltdowns," Associated Press, December 21, 2007.

252   David Sirota spotlighted: David Sirota, "GOP Using Katrina to Justify Right-Wing Agenda," *Sirotablog*, September 12, 2005 (http://www.davidsirota.com/2005/09/gop-using-katrina-to-justify-right.html).

252   Pete Domenici, the senior senator: H. Josef Herbert, "Katrina Spurs New Debate on Energy Policy," Associated Press, September 12, 2005.

252   George "Macaca" Allen: Ibid.

253   "The car broke": Ezra Klein, "Privatizing FEMA," americanprospect.org, September 12, 2005.

253   David Brooks wasted an entire post-Katrina column: David Brooks, "The Best-Laid Plan: Too Bad It Flopped," *The New York Times*, September 11, 2005.

253   "Making the [Bush] tax cuts": James Kuhnhenn, "Budget Deficit Seen Rising," *Miami Herald*, September 5, 2005.

253   Halliburton, Bechtel: Tom Englehardt and Nick Turse, "Tomgram: The Reconstruction of New Iraq," TomDispatch.com, September 13, 2005.

254   "the Bush administration is importing": Yochi J. Dreazen, "No-Bid Contracts Win Katrina Work," *The Wall Street Journal*, September 12, 2005.

254   " 'Where has all the money gone?' ": Naomi Klein, "Disaster Capitalism," *The Guardian*, August 30, 2006.

256   there was Mike Huckabee: "Common Sense," television advertisement, January 26, 2008 (www.mikehuckabee.com).

257   "The reality is that the core measures of both the 2001 and 2003 tax cuts": Paul Krugman, "The Tax-Cut Con," *The New York Times*, September 14, 2003.

258   Norquist has popularized the idea: pat208, "Harvard B-School Alums Tear into Grover Norquist," *Daily Kos*, October 12, 2005.

258   "Separation of the spheres of democracy and capitalism": Michael Kinsley, "The Return of Class War," *Slate*, June 5, 2003.

259   look no further than Nancy Nord: Annys Shin, "Product Safety Chief Sees Setbacks in Senate Bill," *The Washington Post*, October 26, 2007.

260   Even where regulations do apply: Robert L. Borosage, "A Cost of Doing Business," *The Huffington Post*, December 4, 2007.

260   Bob's primary method: Dick Durbin, "Toy Safety: What's Wrong and How to Fix It," National Press Club address, Washington D.C., December 5, 2007.

260   the recent suicide: David Barboza, "Scandal and Suicide in China: A Dark Side of Toys," *The New York Times*, August 23, 2007.

261   The best known of them: David Leonhardt, "Lessons Even Thomas Could Learn," *The New York Times*, October 24, 2007.

261   Simplicity Crib: "1 million Graco, Simplicity cribs recalled in U.S.," MSNBC, September 25, 2007 (http://www.msnbc.msn.com/id/20907633/).

261   reducing its staff: OMB Watch, "Congress Hears Pleas for Expanded Authority and Resources at CPSC," September 25, 2007 (http://www.ombwatch.org/article/articleview/3990).

261   55,000 skull pails: *News from CPSC*, U.S. Consumer Product Safety Commission Press Release, "Albert's Recalls Halloween Skull Pails Due to Violation of Lead Paint Standard," October 17, 2007 (http://www.cpsc.gov/cpscpub/prerel/prhtml08/08033.html).

261   350,000 bookmarks: Louise Story and David Barber, "The Recalls' Aftershocks," *The New York Times*, December 22, 2007.

261 5,400 tabletop: *News from CPSC*, U.S. Consumer Product Safety Commission Press Release," Guidecraft Inc. Recalls Children's Puppet Theaters Due to Violation of Lead Paint Standard," October 17, 2007 (http://www.cpsc.gov/cpscpub/prerel/prhtml08/08031.html).

261 2,400 Breyer: *News from CPSC*, U.S. Consumer Product Safety Commission Press Release, "J.C. Penney Recalls Breyer Stirrup Ornaments Due to Violation of Lead Paint Standard," October 11, 2007 (http://www.cpsc.gov/cpscpub/prerel/prhtml08/08024.html).

261 19,000 Deluxe: *News from CPSC*, U.S. Consumer Product Safety Commission Press Release, "J.C. Penney Recalls Deluxe Art Sets Due to Violation of Lead Paint Standard," October 11, 2007 (http://www.cpsc.gov/cpscpub/prerel/prhtml08/08023.html).

261 49,000 Disney: *News from CPSC*, U.S. Consumer Product Safety Commission Press Release, "J.C. Penney Recalls Disney™ Winnie-the-Pooh Play Sets Due to Violation of Lead Paint Standard," October 11, 2007 (http://www.cpsc.gov/cpscpub/prerel/prhtml08/08022.html).

261 7,800 Princess: *News from CPSC*, U.S. Consumer Product Safety Commission Press Release, "Cracker Barrel Old Country Store® Recalls Travel Art Sets Due to Violation of Lead Paint Standard," October 11, 2007 (http://www.cpsc.gov/cpscpub/prerel/prhtml08/08021.html).

261 10,000 bendable: *News from CPSC*, U.S. Consumer Product Safety Commission Press Release, "Bendable Dinosaur Toys Recalled by Kipp Brothers for Excessive Lead," October 11, 2007 (http://www.cpsc.gov/cpscpub/prerel/prhtml08/08020.html).

261 2,500 collectible: *News from CPSC*, U.S. Consumer Product Safety Commission Press Release, "Riddell Recalls Collectible Mini Racing Helmets Due to Violation of Lead Paint Standard," October 11, 2007 (http://www.cpsc.gov/cpscpub/prerel/prhtml08/08019.html).

261 2,400 Kidnastics: *News from CPSC*, U.S. Consumer Product Safety Commission Press Release, "Flaghouse Inc. Recalls Kidnastics Balance Beams Due to Violation of Lead Paint Standard," October 11, 2007 (http://www.cpsc.gov/cpscpub/prerel/prhtml08/08501.html).

261 1.6 million Cub Scouts: *News from CPSC*, U.S. Consumer Product Safety Commission Press Release, Kahoot Products Inc. Recalls Cub Scouts Totem Badges Due to Violation of Lead Paint Standard," October 9, 2007 (http://www.cpsc.gov/cpscpub/prerel/prhtml08/08018.html).

262 11,200 Alpine: *News from CPSC*, U.S. Consumer Product Safety Commission Press Release, "Sports Authority Recalls Aluminum Water Bottles Due to Violation of Lead Paint Standard," October 4, 2007 (http://www.cpsc.gov/cpscpub/prerel/prhtml08/08011.html).

262 192,000 key chains: *News from CPSC*, U.S. Consumer Product Safety Commission Press Release, "Key Chains Recalled by Dollar General Due to Risk of Lead Exposure," October 4, 2007 (http://www.cpsc.gov/cpscpub/prerel/prhtml08/08009.html).

262 15,000 children's toy: *News from CPSC*, U.S. Consumer Product Safety Commission Press Release, "CKI Recalls Children's Decorating Sets Due to Violation of Lead Paint Standard; Sold Exclusively at Toys 'R' Us," October 4, 2007 (http://www.cpsc.gov/cpscpub/prerel/prhtml08/08008.html).

262 63,000 Frankenstein: *News from CPSC*, U.S. Consumer Product Safety Com-

mission Press Release, "Dollar General Recalls Tumblers Due to Violation of Lead Paint Standard," October 4, 2007 (http://www.cpsc.gov/cpscpub/prerel/prhtml08/08007.html).

262 79,000 *Pirates of the Caribbean*: *News from CPSC*, U.S. Consumer Product Safety Commission Press Release, "Eveready Battery Co. Recalls Toy Flashlights Due to Violation of Lead Paint Standard," October 4, 2007 (http://www.cpsc.gov/cpscpub/prerel/prhtml08/08006.html).

262 35,000 Baby Einstein: *News from CPSC*, U.S. Consumer Product Safety Commission Press Release, "Kids II Recalls Baby Einstein Color Blocks Due to Violation of Lead Paint Standard," October 4, 2007 (http://www.cpsc.gov/cpscpub/prerel/prhtml08/08005.html).

262 10,000 wooden: *News from CPSC*, U.S. Consumer Product Safety Commission Press Release, "KB Toys Recalls Wooden Toys Due to Violation of Lead Paint Standard," October 4, 2007 (http://www.cpsc.gov/cpscpub/prerel/prhtml08/08004.html).

262 Agencies are regulating: Laurie Gindin Beacham and Amy Widman, "Regulating Consumers, Aiding Industry," TomPaine.com, March 8, 2006 (http://www.centerjd.org/press/opinions/060308.htm).

263 Big Pharma: Center for Responsive Politics, Lobbying database, 2006 (http://www.opensecrets.org/lobbyists/index/asp).

263 over $66 million: Center for Responsive Politics, Pharmaceuticals/Health Products: Long-Term Contribution Trends, 2008 (http://www.opensecrets.org/industries/indus.asp?ind=H04).

263 over $46 million: Ibid.

263 The FDA is also: Karen Roebuck, "Humans at Risk from Tainted Pet Food?" *Pittsburg Tribune-Review*, April 20, 2007.

263 After assuring the public: David Goldstein, "Poison for Profit," *The Nation*, July 30, 2007.

264 Under the current administration, OSHA: OMB Watch, "Workers Threatened by Decline in OSHA Budget, Enforcement Activity," January 23, 2008 (http://www.ombwatch.org/article/articleview/4143/1/308).

264 "Since George W. Bush became president": Stephen Labaton, "OSHA Leaves Worker Safety in Hands of Industry," *The New York Times*, April 25, 2007.

264 "They've simply gotten": Ibid.

264 Even with those lowered standards: Ibid.

264 "voluntary compliance strategy": Ibid.

264 "true Ronald Reagan Republican"; "firmly believes": Ibid.

264 "Early in his tenure": Ibid.

264 Microwave popcorn: Ibid.

265 A little-known agency: Stephen Labaton, "As Trucking Rules Are Eased, a Debate on Safety Intensifies," *The New York Times*, December 3, 2006.

265 one of the heads: Ibid.

266 "It was a total commitment": John Solomon, Alec MacGillis, and Sarah Cohen, "How Rove Directed Federal Assets for GOP Gains," *The Washington Post*, August 19, 2007.

266 "enlisting political appointees": Ibid.

267 "collaborate more": Ken Ward Jr., "Shafted," *Washington Monthly*, March 2007.

268 "filled [MSHA's] top jobs: Ibid.

268 The Federal Communications Commission: "Lawsuits over Cell Phone Radiation to Continue," Reuters, October 31, 2005.

268 Forest Service has allowed: Terence Chea, "Appeals Court Blocks Bush Logging Rule," Associated Press, December 5, 2007.

268 The administration has: Bruce Barcott, "Changing All the Rules," *The New York Times Magazine*, April 4, 2004.

268 Well, it seems that: Elizabeth Williamson and Annys Shin, "Theme Park Regulation Effort Crippled," *The Washington Post*, December 6, 2007.

268 "Amusement parks need": Elizabeth Williamson, "On Thrill Rides, Safety Is Optional," *The Washington Post*, December 4, 2007.

Chapter 13: Sick, Sick, Sick:
The Right's Unhealthy Approach to Health Care

270 In his final budget: Kevin Freking, "U.S. Official: Bush's 2009 Budget Lean for Domestic, Health Programs," Associated Press, January 31, 2008.

270 What's more, this red-ink budget: John Bresnahan, "Senate Approves $70 billion for Iraq-Afghanistan," *Politico*, December 18, 2007 (www.politico.com/blogs/thecrypt/1207/Senate_approves_70_billion_for_Iraq.html).

270 The president claims that his plans: Freking, "U.S. Official: Bush's 2009 Budget," Associated Press, January 31, 2008.

270 the 2008 budget includes a number: "Bush Budget Coming Monday Cuts Medicare, Medicaid but Not Advantage Plan Subsidy," *Senior Journal*, January 31, 2008.

271 "Under the proposal": Robert Pear, "Bush Seeks Surplus via Medicare Cuts," *The New York Times*, January 31, 2008.

271 "$15 billion from an across-the-board": Ibid.

272 "I mean, people have access to health care": Paul Krugman, "Health Care Excuses," *The New York Times*, November 9, 2007.

272 As if 47 million Americans: Ibid.

272 Ever since the passage: Department of Health and Human Services, Office of Inspector General, "The Emergency Medical Treatment and Labor Act Survey of Hospital Emergency Departments," January 2001 (http://oig.hhs.gov/oei/reports/oei-09-98-00220.pdf).

272 Even if you arrive at the emergency room: Kevin Drum, "Emergency Room," *Washington Monthly*, July 11, 2007.

273 89.6 million: Families USA, "Wrong Direction: One out of Three Million Americans Are Uninsured," September 2007.

273 France, Germany, Great Britain, and: Press release, "World Health Organization Assesses the World's Health Systems," World Health Organization, June 21, 2000 (http://www.who.int/whr/2000/media_centre/press_release/en/index.html).

273 We pay more: Paul Krugman, *The Conscience of a Liberal* (New York: W. W. Norton, 2007), p. 218.

274 As governor of Massachusetts: Scott Horsley, "For Romney, Health Care Fix Nothing to Brag About," National Public Radio, November 13, 2007 (www.npr.org/templates/story/story.php?storyId=16232052).

275 "You don't want": *Hannity & Colmes*, August 15, 2007.

275 Since Bush 43 came into office: Carmen DeNavas-Walt, Bernadette D. Proc-

tor, and Jessica Smith, "Income, Poverty and Health Insurance Coverage in the United States: 2006," U.S. Census Bureau, August 2007; Robert J. Mills, "Health Insurance Coverage: 2000," U.S. Census Bureau, September 2001.

275 The Equal Employment Opportunity Commission: Press Release, "EEOC Moves to Protect Retiree Health Benefits," U.S. Equal Employment Opportunity Commission, December 26, 2007 (www.eeoc.gov/press/12-26-07 .html); Robert Pear, "U.S. Ruling Backs Benefit Cut at 65 in Retiree Plans," *The New York Times*, December 27, 2007.

276 Even the traditionally conservative: Proposal, Valerie Carpenter, editor, Robert D. Otten, director, "Expanding Health Insurance: The AMA Proposal for Reform," American Medical Association Health Policy Group, Division of Socioeconomic Policy Development, 2007 (www.ama-assn.org/ama1/pub/ upload/mm/363/ehi1012.pdf).

276 As of January 2008: Data sheet, *Pharmaceuticals/Health Products: Long Term Contribution Trends*, The Center for Responsive Politics, January 7, 2008.

277 "Passage of the Clinton plan": William Kristol, *The Wall Street Journal*, January 11, 1994, as cited in Mark E. Rushefsky and Kant Patel, *Politics, Power & Policy Making: The Case of Health Care Reform in the 1990s* (1998), p. 110.

277 It was Kristol who mobilized Republicans: "A Detailed Timeline of the Healthcare Debate Portrayed in 'The System,'" *NewsHour with Jim Lehrer*, PBS (www.pbs.org/newshour/forum/may96/background/health_debate _page2.html).

277 Enter, stage right: Elizabeth Kolbert, "The Ad Campaign: Playing on Uncertainties About the Health Plan," *The New York Times*, October 21, 1993.

277 As it happens, Harry and Louise: Laurie McGinley, "Harry and Louise Return, Opposing the Ban on Cloning," *The Wall Street Journal*, April 24, 2002.

278 Some small shred: James Thalman and Elaine Jarvik, "CHIP Veto Riles Advocates," *Deseret Morning News*, October 4, 2007.

279 Because the proposal Bush vetoed: Ibid.

279 Centers for Disease Control statistics: Centers for Disease Control and Prevention, "Fact Sheet: Cigarette Smoking—Related Mortality," updated September 2006 (www.cdc.gov/tobacco/data_statistics/Factsheets/cig_smoking _mort.htm).

279 According to the Annenberg: "Bush's False Claims About Children's Health Insurance," The Annenberg Political Fact Check, September 21, 2007.

280 The Right also took a swipe: Ibid.

280 raise their four children: Matthew Hay Brown, "Boy to Give Radio Address," *Baltimore Sun*, September 29, 2007.

280 "We got the help we needed": Graeme Frost, "12-year-old asks Bush to Sign Children's Health Bill," Democratic Radio Address, (www.democrats.org/ a/2007/09/twelve-year-old.php).

281 Graeme and the Frosts were blogged: "The 'Not So Poor' 12 Year Old Who Rebutted Bush on SCHIP Veto," *Free Republic*, October 6, 2007 (www.free republic.com/focus/f-news/1907687/posts).

281 Here are the supposedly damning facts: Ibid.

281 "It is well known and documented": "SCHIP—Democrats Use Terrorist Tactics: Hiding Behind Children," *Wake Up, America*, October 9, 2007 (www

.wakeupamericans-spree.blogspot.com/2007/10/schip-democrats-use-terrorist-tactics.html).

282 While never entirely free: "Then & Now: Joycelyn Elders," CNN, July 20, 2005 (www.cnn.com/2005/US/07/18/cnn25.tan.elders/index.html).

282 Dr. Richard Carmona, who served: Gardiner Harris, "Surgeon General Sees 4-Year Term as Compromised," *The New York Times*, July 11, 2007.

283 "During my first year as Surgeon General": Testimony Before the Committee on Oversight and Government Reform, Congress of the United States, House of Representatives, "The Surgeon General's Vital Mission: Challenges for the Future," Statement for the Congressional Record, July 10, 2007 (http://over sight.house.gov/documents/20070710111054.pdf).

283 astonishing exchange: Frank James, "White House and Former Surgeon General Still at Odds," The Swamp, *Chicago Tribune*, July 11, 2007 (http://weblogs .chicagotribune.com/news/politics/blog/health/).

284 Carmona was instructed: Gardiner Harris, "Surgeon General Sees 4-Year Term as Compromised," *The New York Times*, July 11, 2007.

284 *The New York Times*, reporting on: Ibid.

285 Wading into the waters: Ibid.

285 "However there was already a policy": Ibid.

285 "one of the most powerful": Ibid.

285 Among his other qualifications: Ibid.

285 "Condoms are a way to prevent": "Be Heard: An MTV Global Discussion with Colin Powell," Washington, D.C., February 14, 2002 (www.state.gov/ secretary/former/powell/remarks/2002/8038.htm).

285 Indeed, Powell and his wife: Lara Riscol, "Sex, Lies and Colin Powell," *Japan Today*, February 5, 2008 (http://www.japantoday.com/JP/comment/153).

286 Their attacks were as spurious: "White House Backs Powell's Safe-Sex Stance," CNN, February 15, 2002 (http://archives.cnn.com/2002/US/02/15/ powell.controversy/).

286 Dobson tried to pretend his problem: "Powell's Condoms Comments Draw Ire," BBC News, February 16, 2002 (http://news.bbc.co.uk/2/hi/americas/ 1823739.stm).

286 Picking up the science baton: Family Research Council, "History/Mission," (www.frc.org/get.cfm?c=HISTORY_ABOUT).

286 His tactic was twisting: Family Research Council, Press Release, "Powell Strays from Bush Policy on Sex Education," February 14, 2002 (http://fathers forlife.org/health/sex-ed.htm).

286 Connor's claims: "Workshop Summary: Scientific Evidence on Condom Effectiveness for Sexually Transmitted Disease (STD) Prevention," National Institute of Allergy and Infectious Diseases, National Institute of Health, Department of Health and Human Services, July 20, 2001.

287 With AIDS claiming 2.1 million: UN/AIDS Report, "2007 AIDS Epidemic Update," UN/AIDS and WHO, November 19, 2007 (www.unaids.org/en/ KnowledgeCentre/HIVData/EpiUpdate/EpiUpdArchive/2007/).

287 thanks to the Bush administration's reform: Donald L. Barlett and James B. Steele, "Why We Pay So Much for Drugs," *Time*, January 27, 2004.

287 On average, the prices: Christopher Lee, "Experts Fault House Bill on Medicare Drug Prices," *The Washington Post*, January 11, 2007.

287 The artificially high prices: Ibid.

287) "Opponents of Medicare bargaining make": Families USA, Press Release, "New Report Shows Medicare Drug Plan Prices 58 Percent Higher Than VA Prices," January 9, 2007 (http://www.familiesusa.org/resources/newsroom/press-releases/2007-press-releases/new-report-shows-medicare.html).

287   Actually, the top drug: Patricia Barry, "The Dope on Drugmakers," AARP Bulletin, September 2004 (http://www.aarp.org/bulletin/prescription/a2004-09-13-drugmakersdope.html).

288   In late 2007, Bush used: Families USA, Press Release, "President Denies Funding for Medical Research," November 13, 2007 (www.familiesusa.org/resources/newsroom/statements/2007-statements/president-denies-funding-for.html).

288   For the last three months of 2005: Kaiser Family Foundation, "Medicare," June 2006 (www.kff.org/medicare/upload/7453.pdf).

289   To add to the cost: Ibid.

289   (about $2,400): "What Is Medicare Drug Coverage?" AARP (http://www.aarp.org/health/medicare/drug_coverage/what_is_medicare_drug_coverage.html).

289   Representative Billy Tauzin, a Republican: William M. Welch, "Tauzin Switches Sides from Drug Industry Overseer to Lobbyist," *USA Today*, December 15, 2004.

289   Tom Scully, head of Medicare: Anne C. Mulkern, "When Advocates Become Regulators," *The Denver Post*, May 23, 2005.

289   Foster, who describes his job: Robert Pear, "Democrats Demand Inquiry into Charge by Medicare," *The New York Times*, March 14, 2004.

289   "The administration seems": Ibid.

289   Notwithstanding the fact that: "Focus on Veterans' Chief as Inquiries on Care Begin," *The New York Times*, March 5, 2007.

289   Department of Veterans Affairs: "V.A. Shift to Outpatient Care Is Efficient and Sound, Study Finds," *The New York Times*, October 23, 2003.

290   "At a time when the rest": Ibid.

290   The VA has also pioneered: Christopher Lee, "VA Honored as Innovator for Medical Records," *The Washington Post*, July 11, 2006.

290   For these reasons (and 292 others): United States Department of Veterans Affairs, "VA Receives 2006 Innovations in Government Award," July 10, 2006 (www1.va.gov/opa/pressrel/pressrelease.cfm?id=1152).

290   According to Families USA: Families USA, Report, "No Bargain: Medicare Drug Plans Deliver High Prices," January 9, 2007.

291   Health Savings Accounts: Families USA, "HSAS: Missing the Target," November 2006 (www.familiesusa.org/assets/pdfs/bad-ideas-hsas-update-nov.pdf).

291   But a third of the uninsured: Ibid.

292   Another touted benefit: Ibid.

292   Also many are uninsured: Ibid.

292   According to a Harvard study: Robert Wood Johnson Foundation, "Illness and Injury Can Lead to Personal Bankruptcy," October 2005 (www.rwjf.org/programareas/resources/grantsreport.jsp?filename=042425.htm&pid=1132).

294   "Universal health care could": Paul Krugman, *The Conscience of a Liberal* (New York: W. W. Norton, 2007), p. 243.

Chapter 14: God, Guns, and the Right's New Democracy

296 "president got off a couple": Elisabeth Bumiller, "The Ventriloquist Jokes Don't Bug the White House," *The New York Times*, May 2, 2004.

296 "bit of a tease": Hope Yen, "Sept. 11 Commission Hears Bush, Cheney Describe Anti-Terror Efforts," Associated Press, April 30, 2004.

296 "I think it was important": Jules Witcover, "An Unusual Duet," *Baltimore Sun*, May 3, 2004.

297 "there are no longer": Press conference in the Rose Garden, April 30, 2004, (White House Office of the Press Secretary).

298 *The Boston Globe:* Charlie Savage, "Candidates on Executive Power: A Full Spectrum," *The Boston Globe*, December 22, 2007.

298 "Bush has bypassed": Ibid.

299 "Legal specialists": Ibid.

299 "our most basic": Charlie Savage, "Mitt Romney Q&A," *The Boston Globe*, December 20, 2007.

299 "A President": Ibid.

299 "an astonishing assertion": Glenn Greenwald, "Mitt Romney's Pursuit of Tyrannical Power, Literally," Salon.com, December 23, 2007.

299 "All US citizens": Ibid.

299 "We live in a country of laws": "Mayor Bloomberg Updates New Yorkers on Illegal Strike by Transit Workers," *News from the Blue Room*, December 20, 2005.

300 Scooter Libby: "Democrats to Bush: Don't Pardon Libby," CNN.com, March 7, 2007 (www.cnn.com/specials/2005/cia.leak).

300 sickening testimony: Michael Luo, "Soldiers Testify to Lawmakers Over Poor Care at Walter Reed," *The New York Times*, March 6, 2007.

300 investigating the firing of eight U.S. Attorneys: Ari Shapiro, "Timeline: Behind the Firing of Eight U.S. Attorneys," National Public Radio, April 15, 2007.

300 study reported by: Paul Kiel, "Study: Feds Chase Dems More Than GOPers," TPMmuckracker.com, February 7, 2007 (http://tpmmuckraker.talkingpoints memo.com/archives/002420.php).

301 "Proverbs 19:25, it caught my attention": Tim Russert, *Meet the Press*, NBC, March 25, 2007.

301 "I am very sorry": Ibid.

301 was physically sickened: David Johnston, "Prosecutors Describe Contacts from Higher Up," *The New York Times*, March 7, 2007.

302 Rep. Doc Hastings: Testimony as delivered by John McKay, "Preserving Prosecutorial Independence: Is the Department of Justice Politicizing the Hiring and Firing of U.S. Attorneys?—Part II," U.S. Senate Judiciary Committee, March 6, 2007 (http://judiciary.gov/hearing.cfm?id=2588).

302 White House counsel Harriet Miers: R. Jeffrey Smith, "Ex-Prosecutor Says He Faced Partisan Questions Before Firing," *The Washington Post*, March 26, 2007.

302 Hastings was the ranking: Dan Eggen and Paul Kane, "Prosecutors Say They Felt Pressured, Threatened," *The Washington Post*, March 7, 2007.

302 four of the fired prosecutors: Ibid.

302 Bush felt Harriet Miers: "President Nominates Harriet Miers as Supreme Court Justice," Oval Office, October 3, 2005 (http://whitehouse.gov/news/releases/2005/10/20051003.html).

302 "disgruntled employees": Ibid.

302 fired U.S. Attorneys: David Johnston, "House Panel Subpoenas 4 Prosecutors of 8 Ousted," *The New York Times*, March 2, 2007.

302 USA PATRIOT Act: Uniting and Strengthening America by Providing Appropriate Tools Required to Intercept and Obstruct Terrorism (USA PATRIOT ACT) Act of 2001, Public Law No.: 107–56, The Library of Congress, October 26, 2001 (http://thomas.loc.gov/cgi-bin/bdquery/z?d107:HR 03162:@@@L&summ2=m&).

303 "By the way, any time you hear": President Bush, "Information Sharing, Patriot Act Vital to Homeland Security," Kleinshans Music Hall, Buffalo, New York, April 20, 2004 (http://www.whitehouse.gov/news/releases/2004/04/20040420-2.html).

303 "disrupted at least ten," "Thwarted Terrorist Plots Since Sept. 11 Attacks," ABC News, February 9, 2006.

304 "I don't think we ever": Warren Vieth and Josh Meyer, "Bush Likens War on Terror to Cold War," *Los Angeles Times*, October 7, 2005.

304 "they hadn't found any evidence": Ibid.

304 "It was not immediately clear": David E. Sangler, " '10 Plots Foiled Since Sept. 11,' Bush Declares," *The New York Times*, October 7, 2005.

306 thirty-two people were gunned down: Sandhya Somashekhar and Nick Miroff, "Injuries Heal, but Mental Scars May Last Much Longer," *The Washington Post*, April 22, 2007.

306 Glock 19 and a Walther P22: Edward Epstein and Carla Marinucci, "Virginia Tech Massacre Gun Control," *San Francisco Chronicle*, April 18, 2007.

306 hollow point ammunition: Sandhya Somashekhar and Nick Miroff, "Injuries Heal, but Mental Scars May Last Much Longer," *The Washington Post*, April 22, 2007.

306 DeLay's answer: Ralph Reiland, "Cho and the Blame Game," *Pittsburgh Tribune-Review*, April 30, 2007.

306 "From my cold dead hands!": Twila Decker, "He's the NRA," *St. Petersburg Times*, August 1, 2000.

306 After the sniper: Tom Jackman, "Sniper Case Goes Before Va. High Court," *The Washington Post*, November 3, 2004.

307 Charlie Rose and Tom DeLay: *Charlie Rose*, PBS, April 19, 2007.

307 200 million guns: "Firearm Facts 2007," National Rifle Association, Institute for Legislative Action 2007 (http://www.nraila.org/Issues/Factsheets/Read .aspx?ID=83).

308 "In the case of the sniper": Karen Tumulty and Viveca Novak, "Dodging the Bullet," *Time*, October 29, 2002.

308 ban on assault weapons: Jill Lawrence, "Federal Ban on Assault Weapons Expires," *USA Today*, September 12, 2004.

308 Combat-ready: Ibid.

308 "supports reauthorization of the current law": Naomi Seligman, "VPC Welcomes President Bush's Reaffirmation of Campaign Pledge to Support Reauthorization of Federal Assault Weapons Ban," Violence Policy Center Press Release, April 14, 2003 (http://www.vpc.org/press/0304bush.htm).

309 over 70 percent of Americans: Mark Cooper, Susan Peschin, "Consumers Support Renewing and Strengthening the Federal Assault Weapons Ban," Consumer Federation of America (http://www.consumerfed.org/pdfs/assault weaponreport.pdf).

309 Even 64 percent of gun owners: Ibid.

309 Just 1 percent of gun dealers: William J. Krouse, "Gun Control: Statutory Disclosure Limitations on ATF Firearms Trace Data and Multiple Handgun Sales Reports," Congressional Reserve Service, Report for Congress, June 16, 2006 (http://fas.org/sgp/crs/misc/RS22458.pdf).

309 Washington's Bull's Eye Shooter Supply: Mike Carter, Steve Miletich, and Justin Mayo, "Errant Gun Dealer, Wary Agents Paved Way for Beltway Sniper Tragedy," *The Seattle Times*, April 20, 2003.

309 refusal of John Ashcroft: Fox Butterfield, "A Nation Challenged: Background Checks; Justice Dept. Bars Use of Gun Checks in Terror Inquiry," *The New York Times*, December 6, 2001.

310 mass mailing warning: Mark Shields, "Bush Campaign's Contempt for 'People of Faith' ", CNN.com, October 4, 2004.

310 an RNC website: Mike Allen, "The RNC's 'Bear' Will Savor Victory from Afar," *The Washington Post*, December 28, 2004.

312 "Huckenfreude": Ross Douthat, "Huckenfreude," theatlantic.com, December 14, 2007.

312 "Huckacide": Rich Lowry, "Huckacide," The National Review Online, December 14, 2007.

312 "overdose of public piety": Charles Krauthammer, "An Overdose of Public Piety," *The Washington Post*, December 14, 2007.

312 "told a producer": Stephen F. Hayes, "The Perils of Huckaplomacy," *The Weekly Standard*, December 24, 2007.

312 "faith has been": Peggy Noonan, "The Pulpit and the Potemkin Village: Would Reagan Survive in Today's GOP?" *The Wall Street Journal*, December 14, 2007.

312 "It is certainly too late": Andrew Sullivan, "The Right and Religion," theatlantic.com, December 14, 2007.

313 "mainstream conservatives": Kevin Drum, "Political Animal," washingtonmonthly.com, December 15, 2007.

313 "The Republican Party's": Steve Benen, "The 'Huckabee Panic,' " talkingpointsmemo.com, December 15, 2007.

314 Don't forget, it took less than: Jonathan D. Salant, "FCC's 'Wake-Up Alarm,' " Associated Press, February 11, 2004.

314 9/11 Commission: "President Signs 911 Commission Bill," White House Press Release, November 27, 2002 (http://www.whitehouse.gov/news/releases/2002/11/20021127-1.html).

314 "one of the top priorities," Barton Gellman, "Recruits Sought for Porn Squad," *The Washington Post*, September 20, 2005.

315 "a running joke": Ibid.

315 *Daily Business Review:* Julie Kay, "U.S. Attorney's Porn Fight Gets Bad Reviews," *Daily Business Review*, August 30, 2005.

315 "This isn't an isolated": Richard Viguerie, "Viguerie Calls House for Immediate Resignation of GOP Leaders," PR Newswire, October 2, 2006.

316 Missing and Exploited Children Caucus: R. Jeffrey Smith, "Foley Built Career as Protector of Children," *The Washington Post*, October 1, 2006.

316 "If I were one of those sickos," Mark Foley interview on *America's Most Wanted*, Fox, November 8, 2005.

316 "It's putting matches": James Thorner, "Nude Summer Youth Camps Alarm Law Maker," *St. Petersburg Times*, June 19, 2003.

316 "It's vile": Bill Adair, "Congress Sees Through Party-Colored Glasses," *St. Petersburg Times*, September 12, 1998.

316 I was part of a panel: *Paula Zahn Now*, CNN, October 9, 2006.

317 "a sign of how sick": Mark Shields, "Why Newt Gingrich Isn't Missed," CNN.com, November 4, 2002.

318 "the test of our progress": Franklin Roosevelt, Second Inaugural Address, January 20, 1937.

318 Florida and Nevada: Dennis Cauchon, "States Say $5.15 an Hour Too Little," *USA Today*, May 30, 2005.

318 "the father of all moral principle": Abraham Lincoln, speech in Chicago, July 10, 1858, in Hadley Arkes, *Natural Rights and the Right to Choose* (New York: Cambridge University Press, 2002), p. 44.

319 36 million: "Household Income Rises, Poverty Rate Declines, Number of Uninsured Up," *U.S. Census Bureau News*, August 28, 2007 (http://www.census.gov/Press-Release/www/releases/archives/income_wealth/010583.html).

Chapter 15: John McCain: Hijacked by the Right

320 John McCain's decision: Pamela Hess and Laurie Kellman, "Senate Votes to Ban Waterboarding," Associated Press, February 14, 2008.

320 "We've sent a message": John McCain, "President Meets with McCain and Warner, Discusses Position on Interrogation," Office of the White House Press Secretary Press Release, December 15, 2005.

320 "When I was imprisoned": "McCain: No Waterboarding, Period," *The Des Moines Register*, October 25, 2007.

321 "It's not about": Bob Herbert, "Who We Are," *The New York Times*, August 1, 2005.

321 "It was never": John McCain, Senate Debate on Military Commissions Act of 2006, *Congressional Record*, September 28, 2006.

321 "tie the CIA": Ibid.

322 "iron triangle": "Sen. John McCain Addresses Shadow Convention," CNN, July 30, 2000.

322 "a born-again Bushophile": James Pinkerton, "Condi, I Can Hardly Keep Up with Ye," *The Huffington Post*, March 26, 2006.

322 "agents of intolerance": Brian Knowlton, "Republican Says Bush Panders to the 'Agents of Intolerance': McCain Takes Aim at Religious Right," *International Herald Tribune*, February 29, 2000.

322 "in haste": Teddy Davis, "McCain Woos the Right, Makes Peace with Falwell," ABC News, March 28, 2006.

322 "walk freely": Kirk Semple, "McCain Wrong on Iraq Security, Merchants Say," *The New York Times*, April 3, 2007.

322 Subsequent TV news: David Olive, "The Alarming Consequences of Two John McCains," *Toronto Star*, February 3, 2008.

323 "I do believe": *Meet the Press*, NBC, December 4, 2005.

323 "standard procedure in Iraq": Ibid.

323 He endorsed a constitutional: Elvia Diaz, "Gay-Marriage Ban Initiative Wins Support from McCain," *The Arizona Republic*, August 26, 2005.

323 "intelligent design": C. J. Karamargin, "McCain Sounds Like Presidential Hopeful," *Arizona Daily Star*, August 24, 2005.

323 a big supporter of Indian gaming: James P. Sweeney, "New Rules on Indian Gaming Face Longer Odds," *San Diego Union-Tribune*, September 11, 2006.

323 limit the right to habeas corpus: Jeremy Brecher and Brendan Smith, "Right to Trial Imperiled by Senate Vote," *The Nation*, November 14, 2005.

323 and then his staff: Carl Pope, "John McCain Should Be Ashamed," *The Sierra Club*, February 8, 2008.

324 McCain-Kennedy bill: Senate Bill S 1033, 109th Congress (http://thomas.loc .gov/cgi-bin/bdquery/z?d109:s.01033).

324 "And while I": Speech at 2008 Conservative Political Action Conference, Washington, D.C., February 7, 2008.

324 CNN presidential debate: CNN Presidential Debate at the Reagan Library, Simi Valley, California, January 30, 2008.

324 "The political tactics of division": David Barstow, "McCain Denounces Political Tactics of Christian Right," *The New York Times*, February 29, 2000.

325 kissing the rings: Michael Scherer, "McCain's Conservative Courtship," *Time*, February 7, 2008.

325 he was an Episcopalian: James Prichard, "McCain: Bush's Low Rating Hurts GOP Not Presidential Candidates," Associated Press, May 10, 2005.

325 Baptist church: Matt Stearns, "McCain Called Out on Religion," McClatchy Newspapers, June 11, 2007.

325 "It plays a role": Jim Davenport, "McCain: Overall Faith What's Important," Associated Press, September 17, 2007.

325 "The most important thing": Betty Nguyen, *CNN Newsroom*, September 18, 2007.

325 "the Constitution established": Dan Gilgoff, "John McCain: Constitution Established a 'Christian Nation,' " Beliefnet.com (http://www.beliefnet.com/ story/220/story_22001_1.html).

326 appearance at the Virginia Military Institute: Transcript, "Senator John McCain at the Virginia Military Institute," CQ Transcriptions, Inc., April 11, 2007.

326 "one of the smartest": Dana Bash, *CNN Newsroom*, February 9, 2008.

327 "Mr. McCain truly": Nicholas D. Kristof, "The World's Worst Panderer," *The New York Times*, February 17, 2008.

327 "the victory of the moderate wing": Ryan Lizza, "On the Bus," *The New Yorker*, February 25, 2008.

327 capitulating on torture: Michael Cooper, "McCain Draws Criticism on Torture Bill," *The New York Times*, February 17, 2008.

327 "I know his convictions": Jim Angle, "Political Headlines," *Special Report with Brit Hume*, Fox News, February 11, 2008.

328 "compassionate conservatism": Ken Herman, "An Upbeat GOP Unites Behind Bush," *Austin-American Statesman*, August 1, 2000.

328 "My friends, this is going to be": Ibid.

Righting the Wrongs of the Right

329 And nearly a century: Noah Adams, "Timeline: Remembering the Scopes Monkey Trial," National Public Radio, July 5, 2005.

330 Otherwise, why did Jack: Edward Epstein, "Murtha Calls for Immediate Withdrawal of U.S. Troops from Iraq," *San Francisco Chronicle*, November 17, 2005.

330 Joe Lieberman never managed: "Lieberman Praises Iraq Political Progress," Press Release, February 13, 2008.

330   What made the late: Helen Dewar, "For Wellstone, Iraq Vote Is Risk but Not a Choice," *The Washington Post*, October 9, 2002.

330   And what made Chuck: Glenn Kessler, "Hagel Defends Criticisms of Iraq Policy," *The Washington Post*, November 16, 2005.

330   Socrates put it: Plato, *The Dialogues of Plato, Volume 3: Ion, Hippias Minor, Laches, Protagoras* (New Haven: Yale University Press, 1998).

Acknowledgments

Right Is Wrong covers many subjects I've written about over the past three years in my blog on *The Huffington Post*. But connecting the dots for this book and delving deeper into the themes I've been exploring, week after week, left me freshly stunned at what we've allowed to happen in our country.

My thanks go to our *Huffington Post* editor—and my great friend—Roy Sekoff, who shouldered even more of the editorial burden while I was writing the book, and still found the time to read the final galleys and work his magic on them.

Many thanks also to *HuffPost*'s senior editor, Marc Cooper, for all the ways he helped improve the manuscript; to our political editor, Tom Edsall, and national editor, Nico Pitney, for reading the manuscript and offering many helpful suggestions; and to our blog editor, Colin Sterling, for always being able to find the perfect piece of research I'm looking for.

Also many thanks to Max Follmer, Rachel Freed, and Tyler Pontier at our L.A. office—and gratitude beyond words to Adriana Dunn and Michael Francesconi for basically giving their lives over to the book during the final crunch.

I'm also grateful to Billy Kimball, who helped with every stage of the book, from organizing the research to editing the final galleys. And to Jim Norton for putting together the original research. Many thanks also to Angel Gibson, Amina Khan, Chris Kyle, Sadath Garcia, Roey Rosenblith, Nicole Alvarado, Megan Baaske, Matthew Bashwiner, Christian Barby, Katherine Bondurant, Barbara Frank, Edward Olson, and Hanna Ingber Win for their work on the source notes, and to Brookes Nohlgren for her help transferring the final changes to the galleys. And a special thank you to Robert Greenwald, Stephen Sherrill, and Jan Shepherd for all the many ways in which they improved the manuscript.

I'm grateful to Andrew Sullivan for his writings on the subject of torture and for introducing me to Professor Scott Horton of Columbia University, who translated a concentration camp document from the Nuremberg trials for this book.

I can't say enough about my wonderful editor, Carole Baron—an amazing combination of wisdom and experience paired with passion for the subject and relentless attention to detail. Of course, we would never have been able to meet our deadlines without the round-the-clock (at least that's how it felt) commitment of Lydia Buechler, who brought both expertise and serenity to the frantic process of finalizing the book. Also many thanks to the rest of the great Knopf team—Carol Carson, Claire Bradley Ong, Fred Chase, Diana Coglianese, Roméo Enriquez, Maria Massey, Anke Steinecke, Virginia Tan, and Mike Kingcaid and his crew at Creative Graphics. And to Paul Bogaards, Erinn Hartman, Jason Kincade, and Nicholas Latimer for launching the book out into the world.

When my longtime agent and friend, Richard Pine, sent me an e-mail suggesting I write this book, I e-mailed back that he had clearly lost his mind if he thought I could do a book in the middle of the 24/7 news cycle of *The Huffington Post* (and during a presidential campaign season, no less!). But I can't thank Richard enough for persevering and helping guide me through our sixth book together.

Finally, my gratitude to my incredible sister, Agapi, and my daughters, Christina and Isabella, who were such a source of love and inspiration for this book—as they are with every aspect of my life.

Index

A Note About the Author

Arianna Huffington is the cofounder and editor in chief of *The Huffington Post*, a nationally syndicated columnist, and author of eleven books. She is also cohost of "Left, Right & Center," public radio's popular political roundtable program. In 2006, she was named to the Time 100, *Time* magazine's list of the world's one-hundred most influential people. Originally from Greece, Huffington moved to England when she was sixteen and graduated from Cambridge University with an M.A. in economics. She lives in Los Angeles with her two daughters.

A Note on the Type

This book was set in Janson, a typeface long thought to have been made by the Dutchman Anton Janson, who was a practicing type-founder in Leipzig during the years 1668–1687. However, it has been conclusively demonstrated that these types are actually the work of Nicholas Kis (1650–1702), a Hungarian, who most proba-bly learned his trade from the master Dutch typefounder Dirk Voskens. The type is an excellent example of the influential and sturdy Dutch types that prevailed in England up to the time William Caslon (1692–1766) developed his own incomparable designs from them.

Composed by Creative Graphics,
Allentown, Pennsylvania
Printed and bound by Berryville Graphics,
Berryville, Virginia
Designed by Virginia Tan